Lorenzo Da Ponte

Lorenzo Da Ponte

The Life and Times of
Mozart's Librettist

SHEILA HODGES

Foreword by
Professor H. C. Robbins Landon

UNIVERSE BOOKS
New York

Published in the United States of America in 1985
by Universe Books
381 Park Avenue South, New York, N.Y. 10016

85 86 87 88 89/10 9 8 7 6 5 4 3 2 1

Printed in Great Britain
by Mackays of Chatham Ltd

Library of Congress Cataloging-in-Publication Data

Hodges, Sheila.
    Lorenzo da Ponte: the life and times of Mozart's librettist.

    Bibliography: p.
    Includes index.
    1. Da Ponte, Lorenzo, 1749–1838.   2. Librettists—
Biography.   I. Title
ML423.D15H6   1985   782.1′092′4   [B]   85–16818
ISBN 0-87663-489-7

Contents

List of Illustrations   vii

Foreword by Professor H. C. Robbins Landon ix

Introduction   xi

LORENZO DA PONTE   1

Chronological Table of the Main Events of
   Da Ponte's Life   224

Da Ponte's Works   226

Acknowledgements   236

Notes and References   239

Note Regarding the Memoirs   249

Appendix   250

Bibliography   258

Index   267

Illustrations

Lorenzo Da Ponte as a young man

Ceneda piazza around the middle of the eighteenth century

Bishop Lorenzo Da Ponte

The Da Ponte family house, according to local tradition

Joseph II (Mary Evans Picture Library)

The Burgtheater, Vienna (Musée des Beaux-Arts, Budapest)

Anton Salieri (Archiv des Gesellschaft der Musikfreunde in Wien)

Wolfgang Amadeus Mozart (Reproduced by courtesy of the Royal Opera House)

Nancy Storace (Reproduced by courtesy of the Royal Opera House)

Adriana Gabrieli del Bene, 'La Ferrarese' (Bildarchiv des Oesterreichischen Nationalbibliothek)

Leopold II (Mary Evans Picture Library)

Nancy Da Ponte

King's Theatre, Haymarket (Mary Evans Picture Library)

Brigida Banti (Reproduced by courtesy of the Trustees of the British Museum)

Fanny Da Ponte

Park Theatre, New York

Da Ponte's appeal for Italian pupils

Da Ponte in old age

For Clarissa
with my love

Foreword

The collaboration between Wolfgang Amadeus Mozart and Lorenzo Da Ponte has often, and rightly, been compared to that between Richard Strauss and Hugo von Hofmannsthal; but whereas the latter collaboration is admirably documented,[1] about the former we have only the tangible results in three of the greatest operas of all time – *Le nozze di Figaro, Don Giovanni and Così fan tutte*. But apart from this substantial and lamentable lacuna, we know quite a lot about the extraordinary Da Ponte, not least because of his fascinating memoirs, which he wrote in America when an old man. Many have seriously questioned the overall veracity of those memoirs: Da Ponte, it is asserted, has stretched the truth, tried to put himself in the best possible light, and so on. Recent research has, however, tended to show that Da Ponte was much more truthful than has been believed, and to illustrate the point, I would like to take the case of *Le nozze di Figaro*. Da Ponte describes the beginnings as follows:

> I set to work . . ., and as fast as I wrote the words, Mozart set them to music. In six weeks everything was in order . . . [*Memoirs of Lorenzo Da Ponte*, translated from the Italian by Elisabeth Abbott, edited and annotated by Arthur Livingston, New York (Dover, 1967), p. 150.]

Naturally, it was seriously doubted that Mozart could have composed that very long opera – the printed score in the great new collection edition comprises 592 pages – in anything like six weeks. But the editor of that magnificent new edition, Ludwig Finscher,[2] considers that, from information in Mozart's own letters and other authentic data (such as Mozart's own thematic catalogue, which contains many invaluable dates), it is likely that Mozart did indeed compose the 'short score' (i.e., without the instrumentation) within six weeks. The evidence of autograph manuscript – part of which belongs to the treasure trove recently rediscovered in Poland where it had been

---

[1] *The Correspondence between Richard Strauss and Hugo von Hofmannsthal*, translated by Hanns Hammelmann and Ewald Osers, London (Collins) 1961. In the original German: Atlantis Verlag A. G. Zürich.

[2] Wolfgang Amadeus Mozart: *Neue Ausgabe sämtliche Werke*, Werkgruppe 5, Band 16, Bärenreiter Verlag, Kassel etc., 2 vols., 1973, pp. VIIIf.

placed (in the Monastery of Grüssau, Silesia) for safe-keeping by the German authorities in World War II – also confirms this almost incredible burst of enthusiasm and sheer hard work on Mozart's part (which resulted in headaches and stomach cramps, sure symptoms of nervous stress; see his letter of 14 January 1786).

We stress this rather pedantic affirmation of a small statement in Da Ponte's *Memoirs* simply to show that such a statement, even though unlikely when first considered, can be, and in this case has been, proved to be entirely accurate.

Da Ponte himself led a very unlikely life, moving from one country to another, often in circumstances less than pleasant, and ending his life as a respected and highly respectable Professor of Italian at Columbia University in New York. His life is fascinating, and it was high time that we had a new evaluation of this unbelievable man, whose achievements are considerable even apart from his connection with music's greatest genius. Da Ponte was a man of great subtlety and complexity. In *Figaro*, wrote the perceptive Hofmannsthal, there is 'little to make one laugh and much to smile at' (op. cit., p. 46): yes, indeed, and this wonderfully delicate pastel-like shade of colour is as much the merit of the libretto as the gift of the music that gave it life – a very *settecento* collaboration and result.

Sheila Hodges has undertaken archival research in Italy, Austria and elsewhere: her account is as fascinating as the man it so admirably brings to life, and it is surely the most accurate portrayal of Da Ponte that we shall have in our generation.

H. C. Robbins Landon
The Old Vicarage
Chepstow
Christmas 1984

Introduction

If, a century and a half after his death, Lorenzo Da Ponte could return to earth, it is likely that he would have mixed feelings about his twentieth-century image. First and foremost, though he would be astonished that the operas of Salieri, Martin y Soler and Winter, so famous in their day, are now virtually forgotten, and the libretti which he wrote for them buried in the same grave of neglect, he would be immeasurably happy that, through his collaboration with Mozart, he has won the recognition for which he longed, and which he never found during his lifetime. In his memoirs and elsewhere he had much to say about the importance of the libretto in the success or otherwise of an opera, and he bitterly resented the low esteem in which the skilled librettist, as he knew himself to be, was held. So he would rejoice that today, wherever *Le nozze di Figaro, Don Giovanni* and *Così fan tutte* are performed, the name of Lorenzo Da Ponte is indissolubly linked with that of the genius whom he used to call 'the divine Mozart'.

Nevertheless, it would grieve him that so little is remembered of his immense contribution to American culture during the thirty-three years which he spent in that country – through his dedicated teaching of Italian literature, through the many thousands of Italian books which he imported from Europe, and through his three valiant battles to establish Italian opera in the new world. All were of great and lasting importance in revealing to Americans the glorious literary and musical heritage of Italy, but, though during his lifetime they brought him the respect of a small yet important section of New York society, they have not given him the immortality which he felt to be his due.

Thirdly – and this would have produced thousands of words from his fluent and indignant pen – he would have been enraged at the comparison which is so often made between his life and memoirs and those of Casanova, with the scales of approval generally coming down on the side of the latter. Da Ponte has suffered much from posterity's view of him as a disreputable libertine, with a string of abandoned lady-loves in every town. In fact, apart from a short and extremely colourful period in Venice when he was still a young man, and again at the end of his Vienna period, his life was not that of an adventurer, if the word is taken to mean one who seeks adventures. By temperament and gifts a teacher whose great love for poetry, as he says, 'led him on a sudden to the dramatic field', through certain facets of his character – gullibility, vanity, the desire to be liked, a genuine wish to do everyone he met a good turn and (not least) his propensity to fall in love – for almost the whole of his eighty-nine years he was at the mercy of fate rather than in control of it, often tossed helplessly from adversity to adversity.

His life, like his nature, was full of contrasts and paradoxes, and this can be said too of the view which those who knew him or have written about him have formed of this elusive, gifted, fascinating man. Fausto Nicolini, joint editor of the standard Italian edition of the memoirs, described them as 'a jungle of lies, an apologia, coarse, badly strung together, unctuous, hypocritical, sentimental moralising', and, prejudiced and ill-judged though this comment is, nevertheless it reflects the opinion, less immoderately expressed, of other commentators. It is true that the accuracy of the memoirs cannot always be relied upon; like countless memoirists, Da Ponte prided himself overmuch on his excellent powers of recall, and with his lively mind, his black-and-white judgements of those who were for and those who were against him, and his skill in writing vivid dialogue, reconstructed from memory conversations which had, he claimed, taken place many years before. This is probably also true of some of the letters which he quotes verbatim, and which – if they ever existed – he would almost certainly have lost as he fled from the arms of the law or angry creditors. Later in life he wrote that he kept a scrapbook of notable things, but it is unlikely that he was able to carry many records from the past when he escaped to America. Equally, he is silent or untrustworthy about certain incidents which show him in a bad light. But the same accusation could be levelled at many other writers before and since – Rousseau, Cellini, Goldoni, Michael Kelly and Casanova amongst them – who are not scolded for their deviation from the exact truth. Often, when he is accused of inventing or exaggerating, careful examination of the documents shows that there is a solider basis for his narrative than he has been given credit for, and that, in the main, where it is possible to verify his statements the memoirs reflect the truth.

Karen Blixen wrote of the Africans whom she loved so dearly, 'They were never reliable, but in a grand manner sincere'; and though the word 'never' is much too harsh to apply to Da Ponte's memoirs, to some extent this is a just comment on their author. He was not a cheat or a liar, and was hurt, bewildered and outraged when he came across people who were, and who took advantage of his credulity. Testimonials from his contemporaries and from later writers bear witness to his sincerity, warmth of heart, generosity, and charity to those less fortunate than he was, even when his own fortunes were at a low ebb.

Nor, in general, are his courage and resilience sufficiently recognised. His long life took him successively to Venice in her last glittering years as a republic; to Vienna under the Emperor Joseph II, a brilliant centre of European culture to which many creative artists gravitated, and where the fight for imperial patronage was cut-throat and merciless; to the London of George III, bustling, elegant, yet in mortal terror of invasion by Napoleon; and finally to the new world, a land of scattered pioneers with little time as yet for the finer influences of European civilisation. In all four countries, each of them offering such a contrast to the others, he arrived a penniless fugitive, and everywhere, with optimism and enthusiasm, he built up a new life. Only in extreme old age, when the fame for which he longed began to seem unattainable, did despondence conquer – and even then never for long. Though the memoirs and his letters sometimes reflect a mood of defeat, his inextinguishable joy in life soon broke through; and the descriptions of his later years which have come down to us reflect a man who carried his immense vitality and exuberance to the end of his days.

Everywhere Da Ponte went he left traces of himself, above all in the state archives of Venice and Vienna and in the university libraries of the United States. Much of this material has appeared only in specialist journals in Italy and Austria; much has never been translated into English; and a considerable amount – especially some of his American letters – has never been printed at all. Many of his libretti, too, are unfamiliar to those who have written about him. All this new material gives a very different picture from the one which is normally painted, showing Da Ponte as a man of erudition and talent, who produced some of the most skilful libretti that have ever been written, and who in his late years gained the respect and admiration of his contemporaries.

His memoirs, published between 1823 and 1830, provide the basis for any biography of Da Ponte; in addition, he wrote two short autobiographical forerunners, both published in America: *Storia compendiosa della vita di Lorenzo Da Ponte*, published in 1807 shortly after he reached New York, and *An Extract from the Life of Lorenzo Da Ponte*, which came out in 1819. Both are valuable sources of information.

I owe a particular debt of gratitude to Angelo Marchesan's *Life and Works of Lorenzo Da Ponte* (Treviso, 1900), so particularly vivid because Marchesan taught at the seminary where Da Ponte had himself been a teacher; Jacopo Bernardi's abridged version of the memoirs, which includes correspondence and early poems not available elsewhere; the excellent version of the memoirs edited by G. Gambarin and F. Nicolini (however prejudiced the latter may have been), who performed a valuable service by reproducing material that Da Ponte excised from later editions of the memoirs (Bari, 1918); Gustav Gugitz's German translation, again very fully and scrupulously annotated (Dresden, 1924); Dr Alfred Loewenberg's *Lorenzo Da Ponte in London*, which gives such a carefully researched picture of Da Ponte's work as a librettist during his twelve years in England – and, tantalisingly, it is London where the fewest clues to his life are to be found, many of the relevant documents having been destroyed; and the annotations to Elisabeth Abbott's translation made by Arthur Livingston, whose detective work in pursuing Da Ponte during the American years is beyond praise.

All quoted material which is unattributed comes from the memoirs; in other cases the source is normally given in notes at the end of the book, but occasionally in footnotes. In the quotations from Da Ponte's writings, his somewhat eccentric spelling of proper names is reproduced without alteration, as are other occasional mistakes – such as the two lines of Latin on page 195 – where his usually excellent memory betrayed him. The translations from the Italian and German, including those from the memoirs, are my own, with the exception of the brief quotations from Mozart's letters, which I have taken from Emily Anderson's translation.

Lorenzo Da Ponte

I

On the 24th day of August 1763, St Bartholomew's Day, the small town of Ceneda, lying about 60 kilometres north of Venice, was filled with the sound of rejoicing. First a salvo of cannon thundered from the Monte di S. Paolo, which rises steeply above the houses; the five bells of the cathedral rang out in response; and the bells of all the principal churches chimed in their turn. For the next four days the ceremony was repeated at regular intervals. At two o'clock on the 29th – the feast of the beheading of St John the Baptist – the bishop of Ceneda, Lorenzo Da Ponte, emerged from the Castello di S. Martino and made his stately way along the winding road which leads down to Ceneda. He was preceded by a company of halberdiers in ceremonial dress, drums beating; next came his household in their best clothes, followed by a large number of clerics. The most illustrious and reverend bishop was accompanied by deputies of the city and by members of the noblest families.

In the midst of this grand cortège were the four people whom it most closely concerned: Geremia Conegliano and his three sons, Emanuele, Baruch and Anania, who were this day to be baptised. Flanked by their godparents, all distinguished citizens of Ceneda and the neighbourhood, they entered the cathedral, which was richly adorned for the occasion, and with joyous pomp were received into the Catholic church. Mass was celebrated, and the bishop gave a brief but loving address which brought tears to the eyes of his listeners. Afterwards, still accompanied by the halberdiers, the newly baptised Christians returned to the bishop's castle for private celebrations, while the citizens of Ceneda, and the many visitors who had come from far and near to share in the festivities, crowded into the piazza to watch the splendid firework display which had been devised by the famous Professor Gaetano Sarti of Bologna. The day was rounded off by six salvoes of cannon from the mountain.

In his memoirs Emanuele Conegliano says nothing about baptism or his Jewish origins. He was born in the ghetto of Ceneda on 10 March 1749, the son of a tanner and dealer in leather. Today the confines of the ghetto are not precisely known, though above one gateway there can still be seen a stone plaque bearing an inscription

3

in Hebrew, but in the eighteenth century a considerable Jewish community lived within its walls.

Emanuele was lucky to be living in Ceneda, which was then part of the Venetian Republic. For centuries there had been Jews in Venice itself, traders from the Byzantine Empire. They were allowed to establish themselves on the Island of Sinalunga, which became known as the Giudecca, and here they set up as money-lenders, a calling forbidden to Christians but extremely important to the state. Because of their usefulness they were tolerated by the government, which otherwise was harsh in its treatment of Jews: the ghetto system was strictly enforced, and the inhabitants were gradually reduced to extreme poverty and misery.

Ceneda, however, had escaped the worst of the antisemitism which was so prevalent elsewhere. At the end of the sixteenth century the town had passed through a period of economic crisis, and the bishop, Monsignor Mocenigo, a man of enlightened views, had invited 'missier Israel Ebreo da Conegliano', whose probity was well known, to come to Ceneda to open a bank there. For at least two centuries before this Jews had been living in the town, peacefully engaged in business, and documents still exist testifying to the benefits which their trading brought. Like Jews elsewhere, they were subject to many restrictions: their religious rites were limited; they were not permitted to build a new synagogue; they could not be employed by Christians; they were allowed to follow only certain callings; and when they travelled abroad the men had to wear red berets and the women red head-scarves. Nevertheless, the sanctions against them were much less rigorous than in other cities. The family from the town of Conegliano, which is a few miles south of Ceneda, prospered in the relatively benign atmosphere of their new home, and during the seventeenth century gave Venice some of her most famous doctors.

With all this, the situation of any Jew was still much less favourable than that of his Christian neighbour, and in the eighteenth century many of them became Catholics, their zeal for conversion dictated less by religious conviction than by practical considerations. In the case of Geremia Conegliano there was certainly another reason too. His wife, Rachele Pincherle, had died when Emanuele was about five, after giving birth to two other sons, Baruch (born in 1752) and Anania (born in 1754). Geremia, now forty-one, wanted to marry again, this time a Christian woman, Orsola Pasqua Paietta; but since Jews were not allowed to marry Christians he had to be baptised first. So the ceremony took place, and twelve days later, on

10 September, he married his bride, who was many years younger than he was, and in fact little older than her stepsons.

According to the custom of the day Monsignor Lorenzo Da Ponte, the presiding bishop, gave the neophytes his own surname, while the oldest son took his first name also: Geremia Conegliano and his children thus became Gasparo, Lorenzo, Girolamo and Luigi Da Ponte. But the good and wise bishop did much more for them, for he admitted the boys to the excellent episcopal seminary of Ceneda, 'with rare kindness,' as his protégé writes, 'furnishing our modest needs as inmates.'

Just as Lorenzo and his brothers were fortunate in their birthplace, so they were lucky to have been born when Da Ponte was bishop, for his goodness and piety were expressed in deeds as well as words. A Venetian patrician, he spent little money on himself, and much on three objects dear to his heart: the cathedral, which was rebuilt during his bishopric; the ill, the old and the poor, whom he never failed to help; and his seminary. He himself paid for much of the cost of rebuilding the cathedral. He constantly visited the sick and those in need of material and spiritual comfort, even when he was ill, and every year he provided clothes for several hundred people, and often beds also. As for the seminary, he made sure that the teachers were men of learning and integrity and the pupils worthy of receiving their education there; as a result of his concern, of those who attended the seminary at this time many later became famous throughout Italy. The bishop was beloved because he was truly good, with a goodness which reached out to every heart. Perhaps – who knows? – if he had lived his namesake Lorenzo, who loved and respected him, might have followed a different path, becoming a great scholar and teacher.

The memoirs are virtually silent about the young Lorenzo's childhood and his family, which was soon to be increased, for his young stepmother bore her husband three more sons and six daughters. The only reference to his own mother occurs in a poem which he wrote in 1816. 'Alas,' he said then, 'that death robbed me of my mother in my earliest years!' His father took little interest in his education, and until he was eleven his only skill was reading and writing. Then his father engaged a tutor for him, but the man, a peasant's son, was boorish and uneducated, and Lorenzo made so little progress that the tutor was sent packing and no more was said about lessons.

Da Ponte describes himself, with justice, as having a prodigious memory, a ready tongue and an insatiable desire to learn, and until his baptism at the age of fourteen he was frustrated beyond words at being deprived of the opportunity to do so. The saving grace was that in the attic of his father's house he discovered a collection of books. Most of them were worthless, but a few he read and re-read avidly – above all the works of Metastasio, poet to the imperial court at Vienna and famous throughout Europe for his poetry, which was set to music again and again by the greatest composers of the day – including Mozart – and sung in every opera house. 'It produced in me,' Da Ponte wrote, 'exactly the same impression as music,' and thereafter the Caesarean poet became his hero.

So for Lorenzo conversion to Christianity opened the door to what he must have longed for more than anything in the world – knowledge. How much he understood the deeper significance of his baptism it is impossible to say, though the customary Bar Mitzvah a year earlier would have made him 'responsible before God' for his own actions. A letter which he wrote six weeks before the ceremony to Dom Pietro Bortoluzzi, the priest who was instructing him, was obviously worded with the desire to ingratiate himself. Badly written and in ungrammatical Italian, it expresses his ecstatic joy at being received into the truth of the Christian Church, and laments 'with bitter shame the blindness of the poor Jews. [I] have no words to thank God who has raised me from the clutches of the Pharaohs. How gracious the Lord has been to me!' But if much of this letter may have been written with an eye to the main chance, the extravagant wording certainly owed a great deal to the fact that all his life Da Ponte was extremely impressionable, caught up in the drama of the moment. Probably he did indeed feel that the gates of Paradise were opening before him.

The three brothers entered Ceneda seminary soon after their baptism. They were taught by first-rate masters, and had access to a splendid library. In less than two years, Lorenzo records, he could write a long oration in Latin in half a day, as well as fifty lines of passable Latin verse. But of his own tongue he was still completely ignorant, and incapable of writing a short letter without making a dozen mistakes. Once again he was lucky, for to the seminary came the Abbé Càgliari of Altivòle, fresh from Padua university, then one of the most famous in the world. Before his appointment little had been done to teach the boys any language but Latin, which – since most of them were destined for the priesthood – was regarded as essential: of their own language and literature they were taught nothing. At Padua the young Abbé had been encouraged to study Dante, Petrarch, Virgil and Horace, which was most unusual at the time; and he communicated to his pupils his own joy in the prose and poetry of the great Italian writers. His lessons became legendary.

6

The second person who exercised a profound influence over Lorenzo while he was at the seminary was a fellow-pupil, Michele Colombo. Colombo was two years the older, but the boys entered the seminary at about the same time. Though today his name is forgotten, Colombo later became one of the most respected Italian stylists and philologists of his day. The boys were soon close friends, sharing madcap adventures as well as a profound love of Italian literature. Their friendship lasted for the rest of their lives, ending only with Colombo's death in 1838, a short time before Da Ponte himself died. 'He was as dear to me as my own life,' Colombo wrote when he was an old man. 'We were as one.' They shared some wild adventures, and were once expelled from the seminary, but were reinstated because, as Colombo said, 'however crazy we may have been, we were worth more than some of the more sensible boys.'

Both Colombo and Da Ponte speak with nostalgic pleasure of their schooldays together. Sometimes they quarrelled. Once Colombo poked fun at a 'sonnet' which Lorenzo had written – his first attempt at verse, a naïve little affair begging his father for a small sum of money. In his mortification Lorenzo refused for several days to speak to his friend. On another occasion Colombo, who was quick to rouse to anger but also quick to cool down, fiercely attacked Lorenzo with a knife, but they broke into roars of laughter, embraced tenderly, and became the best of friends again.

In his memoirs Da Ponte pays the most generous and loving tribute not only to Colombo but also to another friend at the seminary, Girolamo Perucchini; to these two, he says, he owed much of his own rapid progress in literature and in writing poetry. Colombo made him read the finest Italian writers with such single-mindedness that he 'gave no thought to eating or sleeping, or to the idle amusements which are usually so dear to young people, and so often cause them to waste their talent. Dante, Petrarch, Ariosto and Tasso were my first masters: in less than six months I knew by heart almost all the *Inferno*, all the best sonnets and many of the songs of Petrarch, and the most beautiful works of Ariosto and Tasso.' He was inspired to write verses of his own – but he did so in secret, afraid of being laughed at.

His first chance to show how much he had learnt came when the rector of the seminary left, and his pupils wrote verses to salute him on his departure. Apart from Colombo, none of his fellow-pupils believed that Lorenzo was capable of stitching two rhymes together, and their scepticism was a challenge, making him resolve to dedicate himself from then on entirely to poetry, which he read and studied, night and day, for two years.

He began to earn a certain reputation in the seminary for his verses, but this did not, he says, give him a swollen head; he realized that his teachers' praise sprang from their desire to spur him on to still greater efforts, so that in time their approval would be truly deserved. He and Colombo enjoyed composing poetry together. Sometimes they would do so during lessons, writing the lines alternately without having previously discussed what they were going to write about, and their thoughts and understanding were so much in harmony that no one could have told their verses were not the work of one person.

So, early on, Lorenzo showed his skill at writing verse with extreme ease. He also acquired the passion for books which was to remain with him for the rest of his days, one of his most endearing and admirable traits. His longing to acquire them led him into trouble, for he came to an agreement with a bookseller in Ceneda – a stupid and ignorant man, who for some reason had a shop full of wonderful books. This man's son was a shoemaker, and he made a bargain to exchange books for leather. Lorenzo stole some skins from his father's warehouse, but he was caught out by his stepmother, who reported the theft to her husband. Gasparo was furious, but when the bishop heard the story he sent for the boy and asked him what it was all about. The bishop, 'mingling tears and laughter', forgave the young thief and gave him money to buy the books. But this was almost the last gleam of light in Lorenzo's life for a long time. He fell ill – this may have been malaria – and for more than six months hovered between life and death. His father suffered various domestic misfortunes, and their good angel the bishop died in the summer of 1768 after a long illness, born with great fortitude. Since he had paid for the education of Lorenzo and his two brothers, as well as helping the family in other ways, they were reduced to a state of extreme poverty from which they seem never to have extricated themselves.

Lorenzo had to sell his treasured books, partly to keep himself decently clothed, partly to help provide for his family. But once again help came to him and his brothers, this time through the good offices of Monsignor Girolamo Ziborghi, a canon of Ceneda cathedral. He arranged for the boys to go to the seminary of Portogruaro, which lies between Ceneda and Venice. Here the three brothers began their studies in 1769, and at about the same time the step was taken which Da Ponte was to regret for the rest of his life, and for which he later blamed his father: it was decided that he and Girolamo should enter the church. He had in fact taken minor orders in 1765, but this was nothing unusual for boys educated in Catholic seminaries. Thereafter they dressed in black and were forbidden to duel or dance, but in the main their position was not very different from that of laymen, and only a percentage of them went on to become priests.

In Da Ponte's memoirs he writes with great bitterness of this turn in his fate, which, he says, led him 'to embrace a way of life entirely opposed to my temperament, character, principles and studies, thus opening the door to a thousand strange happenings and perils, in the course of which the envy, hypocrisy and malice of my enemies made me a pitiable victim for more than twenty years.' This is not the first or the last time that he makes a disingenuous statement which reflects only part of the truth. Given the circumstances of the day and of his family, in no other way could he have obtained the education for which he hungered with such single-minded passion. Nor, so far as the available documents show, did he offer any resistance to the plan; letters to Colombo written about this time imply the opposite.

At Portogruaro Da Ponte studied philosophy and mathematics, but mainly he worked away at the Latin which was considered so important for these embryonic priests. Fifty years later he was still able to write fluent Latin verse, and he explained to one young American, who was amazed at his skill, how it was that he remembered the language so well. Not only did he study it for many years; all the seminary students, when they had reached a certain level, were made to speak nothing but Latin at prescribed times of the day, and anyone who made a mistake, or lapsed into Italian, had to wear a heavy iron collar. On three evenings a week the best of them would meet to discuss the classical poets, whom in this way 'they would absorb into their bones and blood, and whom they have, as it were, at their finger-tips, like the daily prayers. After the third year the cleverest of them are free to study Greek or Hebrew; but as for their native language, and especially our poets, in the college where I was educated they were little studied; and anyone who wished to study them had to do so in private, and hide it from the vigilance of the directors as best he could.' So, as he explained to this young American, his fluency in Latin fifty years later was nothing out of the way – any of his fellow-students, if they were still living, would be able to do the same.

In 1770 he was appointed an instructor, in the following year professor of languages, and in the spring of 1772, at the invitation of the bishop, Monsignor Gabrielli, vice-rector. He accepted this change in his status with some reluctance, as he explains in a typical passage in his memoirs.

9

At that time I intended to perfect my knowledge of Hebrew, which in my youth I had studied assiduously, and also to study Greek, since I believed that without the ability to read this language no one can become a great poet. For this reason I hesitated for some days before giving my answer. I allowed myself to be convinced by the excellent rector, who loved me dearly, and even more by my father's circumstances, since it would help him if I was earning. So I accepted the offer: and at an age when I should have been learning so much, I was faced with the hard task of teaching *belles lettres* to others. Nevertheless, I do not believe that this interruption delayed or hindered my own literary progress.

The seminary of Portogruaro still looks much as it did in the days when Da Ponte was a pupil, with a big open courtyard surrounded by low buildings where the pupils worked and lived and slept. The library, too, has hardly altered since that day, a large, high-ceilinged room lined with books, where – after he became a master – Da Ponte must often have talked to his pupils about the poets whom he loved so dearly.

He wrote with considerable self-importance to Colombo, with whom he kept up a correspondence much concerned with analysis and criticism of the poems they regularly sent to one another. 'My duties,' he explained, 'are to look after discipline, to write the inaugural speech at the beginning of the scholastic year, as well as the final *accademia*, and to teach the Tuscan language [i.e. the purest Italian] to fifty-two of the best students in this seminary. What do you think of that? None of the other vice-rectors has so much to do, but the generosity of Monsignor and the rector, and their good opinion of me, made them decide to give me these duties.'

The *accademia* was an important occasion, bringing to a close each year in the seminaries, when the best pupils had to recite Latin and Italian, and sometimes Greek, poems written specially for the occasion. As Da Ponte explained to Colombo, his work as vice-rector meant that he had little time to write them. In his memoirs he says that his fellow-teachers were jealous of him, and taunted him with not having studied physics and with being 'nothing but a wind-bag, a versifier without science'. So he decided to make the theme of the *accademia* of 1772 *la fisica particolare*. The praises which his verses won, and the regard of the bishop, of Da Ponte's pupils and of the local citizens, further inflamed the envy of his colleagues. For a time he bore with this, but in the autumn of 1773 in a moment of pique he threw up his post and went off to Venice – a step which was to change the whole course of his life.

* * *

Da Ponte at this time was twenty-four, handsome, with dark, penetrating eyes, lively, attractive to women. The letters to Colombo reflect a warm-hearted young man, precocious, not deeply intellectual but nevertheless exceptionally clever, self-centred, rather priggish, taking praise as his due with some complacency and resentful of criticism – all his life he remained extremely sensitive to unfavourable opinions. One of his biographers rightly describes him as having a mind richer in feeling and imagination than in commonsense and judgement, and for most of his eighty-nine years, though he blamed other people for the many misfortunes which overtook him, he was his own worst enemy. Certainly he was so on this occasion.

But to realise the implications of his impulsive decision to leave Portogruaro it is necessary to go back to 1770, when he and his brothers were newly students of the seminary there. In January of that year he wrote to Colombo, still in Ceneda, to say that they had all been sent to Venice to recover from a serious illness – probably this was once again malaria. It is carnival time, but carnivals aren't for clerics, and he is staying at home to converse with the Muses, though they have an unfamiliar appearance in such surroundings.

Ten days later he is apparently back in Portogruaro, for it is from here that he next writes to Colombo, complaining about the philistinism of some of his fellow-seminarists. But early in February another letter comes from Venice, saying that he is fed up with the carnival and hasn't been out of the house for ten days. In the following summer he seems to have spent a considerable time in this most seductive of cities, for on 8 August 1770 he tells Colombo that he is going there 'next Sunday', and a month later he is still there. In November, with the start of a new academic year, he writes that he has passed a delightful holiday on the country estate of the family of his dead benefactor, Monsignor Da Ponte. It is generally agreed that at some time during this period he met the first of the three women with whom he fell successively and passionately in love, and for all of whom he jeopardised his career, his good name, and much else that was precious to him.

In his letters to Colombo – to whom in the past he had opened his heart – he makes no mention of Angiola Tiepolo; he must surely have felt that even this dearest of friends would disapprove deeply of the entanglement. She belonged to an impecunious branch of the Tiepolo family, one of the oldest and noblest of Venice, and when she was about twenty had married a man much older than herself, to whom she had borne two children. After the birth of the second one, in 1773, her husband left her to become a priest. (It was in this same year, it may be remarked, that Da Ponte departed from

Portogruaro to live in Venice.) She was, he writes, small, delicate, charming, with a skin as white as snow, languidly sweet eyes and two exquisite dimples in her cheeks, like a fresh rose, with absolutely regular features, without much education, but with such grace of manner and vivacity that she entranced everyone she met. She was also – as he soon found out – vicious, an inveterate gambler, jealous and hot-tempered. All three of the women to whom Da Ponte was so hopelessly enslaved seem to have been of this temperament, and though he saw only too well what was happening, and hated the chains that bound him, he was unable to break them. So if he did first meet Angiola during his visits to Venice in 1770, as seems likely, and fell in love with her then, this – as well as the jealousy of his colleagues – is probably the real explanation of why he left Portogruaro so hurriedly.

In his memoirs Da Ponte writes at great length of his first Venetian period, and declares that the affair with Angiola lasted for three years. In fact, however, he lived there for only about twelve months. The discrepancy can be explained only if one assumes that they became lovers while he was still at Portogruaro.

His flight shows that he must have been extremely uneasy in his clerical garb, despite his nonchalant letters to Colombo. For on 17 March 1773 he had become a priest – a momentous event which he announced to his friend in the most humdrum fashion imaginable. 'If God pleases,' he wrote from Portogruaro on 6 March, 'on Sunday *sitientes* I shall be ordained, and shall perhaps have the pleasure of coming to see you and embrace you.' Little more than six months later he said goodbye to Portogruaro for ever – so far as we know without either a job or the prospects of one – and was swept into the voluptuous embrace of the most ravishing mistress of all, the great and beautiful city of Venice.

II

Venice, dear beautiful Venice! scene of harmony and love! where all was gaiety and mirth, revelry and pleasure! ... Day and night were the gondoliers singing barcarolles, or the verses of Tasso and Ariosto to Venetian airs; barges full of musicians on the Grand Canale, serenading their inamoratas; the Piazza of St Marc brilliantly lighted up; ten thousand masks and ballad singers; the coffee houses filled with beautiful women, with their *cicisbeos*;[1] or, if alone, unmolested, taking their refreshments and enjoying themselves without restraint. Venice was the paradise of women, and the Venetian women worthy of a paradise at least of Mahomet's. They were perfect Houri; and the Venetian dialect, spoken by a lovely woman, is the softest and most delicious music in the world to him whom she favours.

So wrote the Irish tenor, Michael Kelly, whose path was soon to cross Da Ponte's. A thirteenth-century writer, Boncompagno da Signia, had written of Venice, 'You will not find its match in all the world', and since then countless people have echoed his words. When Da Ponte went there in the autumn of 1773 it was at the zenith of its splendour, *'ce bal masqué en permanence qu'on appelait Venise'*, as the poet Lamartine described it. For part of the year it was the scene of the greatest carnival in the world, to which flocked all the crowned heads of Europe. Among them was the Emperor Joseph II, who twice visited the city incognito. Da Ponte may have seen him on the second occasion, in 1775, when he came to Venice with his brothers and stayed for eight days, for some years later he wrote a poem to the Emperor on the occasion of this visit.

Masks were universally worn, and this gave the wearers a licence that would otherwise have been impossible. It also led to a particularly classless society, which was heightened by the nature of the city itself, with its open, sunny piazzas and the absence of horses and vehicles: it was 'like one vast dwelling-place where the inhabitants could conduct their lives in the open just as if they were at home, and rich and poor were united as it were in the bond of a common existence'. Every occasion that could possibly be used as an excuse for celebration – religious ceremonies, great victories, the conclusion of a peace, the visits of distinguished foreigners, the marriages of nobles – was marked by processions, fêtes and rejoicing. Unlike other towns in Italy, the streets were illuminated; the shops stayed open until midnight or even later; and the many cafés were thronged with revellers who seemed to think that life began only as twelve o'clock struck. Nobleman and beggar, artisan and poet, gondolier and visiting royalty mingled under the clear winter sky, protected by their masks.

[1] The *cicisbeos*, or *cavalieri serventi*, were a curious breed. Their function was to wait on society ladies (with the consent of complacent husbands who no doubt had amorous business elsewhere), escorting them to the opera, the theatre and the cafés, picking up their gloves and handkerchiefs, attending to their lapdogs, and generally making themselves agreeable. Presumably on occasion they also provided more intimate services.

13

From dawn until long after darkness had fallen the streets rang with the sound of music, which for the Venetians was part of their very being. 'In every square, street, and canal,' says the great Venetian playwright Goldoni, 'singing is to be heard. The shop-keepers sing while they sell their wares; the workmen sing on quitting their labours; the gondoliers sing whilst waiting for their masters.' Minstrels thronged the streets, and Charles Burney, who visited the city in 1770, writes that the first music he heard was from an itinerant band of two fiddles and a cello with an excellent woman singer:

> Upon the Piazzi de S. Marco I heard a great number of vagrant musicians ... Indeed it is not to be wondered at, that the street-music here is generally neglected, as people are stunned with it at every corner ... When they do admire, it is something excellent; and then they never 'damn with faint praise', but express rapture in a manner peculiar to themselves; they seem to agonise with pleasure too great for the aching sense ... If two of the common people walk together arm in arm, they are always singing, and seem to converse in song; if there is company on the water, it is the same; a mere melody, unaccompanied with a second part, is not to be heard in this city: most of the ballads in the streets are sung to a duo.

Burney was amazed, too, by the four *conservatori* where orphaned girls found shelter, and where they were given a remarkable musical education. Every visitor to the city went to hear and admire their excellent concerts. Burney particularly mentions one singer for the extraordinary range of her voice: she was Adriana Gabrieli, who later became the third of Da Ponte's great loves.

If music was among the first passions of the Venetians, gambling was their second, as prevalent among the common people as among the nobility. Intermittently the government tried to suppress it, but when they shut the public *ridotti*, or gambling houses, the pastime was carried on just as feverishly in private houses, cafés, taverns, and even in church.

Da Ponte was swept into a life of gambling and dissipation. His infatuation made him the unwilling slave both of Angiola Tiepolo and of her disreputable brother Girolamo, who belonged to the curious group known as the *Barnabotti* – members of noble families who had no private means of any kind, and whom the laws of the state forbade to take up any employment, either political or ecclesiastical. Originally they were lodged at the public expense in the parish of St Barnabas, from which they took their name. By right of birth they were entitled not only to an income from the state but also to a share in the government, and they formed a corrupt, parasitical and disorderly group in the *Maggior Consiglio*, the Great Council. Girolamo was an inveterate gambler, and soon became dependent on Da Ponte for the gold which he needed to satisfy his obsession.

In the midst of this life of debauchery from which he had not the strength of will to free himself, Da Ponte struggled to study at night for a few hours. In the evenings he might visit the *caffe de'letterati*, as it was called, where writers and intellectuals gathered. Here he met many Venetians who were eminent in the world of letters, and in particular the two brothers Gasparo and Carlo Gozzi, the former one of the best critics and purest stylists in Italy, the latter a lively writer two of whose dramas later formed the basis for the libretti of *The Love for Three Oranges* and *Turandot*. (Their mother was also named Angela Tiepolo, so presumably she was related to Da Ponte's inamorata.) He lingered in bookshops, as he was to do all his life, and perhaps, too, he visited the magnificent library, which had been started in 1362 with some volumes presented to the city by Petrarch, and enriched by later generations, until eventually Venice had the finest and largest collection of manuscripts in the world. For side by side with the corruption and the *dolce vita* went a genuine desire on the part of the population, nobles and rich merchants alike, to acquire knowledge.

No doubt through his literary connections, he found employment as tutor to the two young sons of a noble Venetian lady, who paid him generously and treated him with friendliness. But otherwise he was at the beck and call of Angiola and her brother, of whom he seems to have been extremely frightened. He made one attempt to break away, and fled from Venice for a few days, but his passion for Angiola was too strong. His life at this time reads like a succession of tales from *Sheherazade*, filled with colourful adventures which sometimes make it extremely hard to suspend disbelief. The most extraordinary of all he relates at some length.

One evening, as he was sitting in the *caffe de'letterati*, he felt a tug at his sleeve, and, turning, saw that a gondolier was beckoning him. Thinking that Angiola had come to fetch him, as she sometimes did, he followed, and found himself in a gondola with a beautiful unknown – it was a case of mistaken identity on both sides. He learnt that her name was Matilda, that she was a Neapolitan and the daughter of a duke, and that she had a wicked stepmother who wanted her to marry an ugly, diseased old man. When she refused, her stepmother had her shut up in a convent. She managed to escape, and fled to Venice because there she could wear a mask and so run less risk of

15

discovery. A young man had taken her under his protection, but he was an inveterate gambler, and in the end he abandoned her. Now she offered Da Ponte her heart and the large quantity of jewels and golden coins she had brought with her.

Pitying her plight, susceptible as ever to beauty, and tempted by her riches, for a while he hesitated. By the time he had decided to say yes it was too late, for she had been taken away by the dreaded officers of the Inquisition and put in a convent.

Who can say whether this Arabian Nights tale is true or false? It appears that in the Inquisitors' archives there is no mention of their officials having carried off anyone of Matilda's description – but this diabolical tribune, as Da Ponte calls it, worked in such deadly secrecy, and covered up its tracks so well, that the absence of any record is not necessarily proof that the event never happened. Da Ponte supports his account by retailing a conversation in Vienna some ten years later with Sebastiano Foscarini, Venetian Ambassador to the Imperial court. Foscarini, too, had known the lovely Matilda, and he told Da Ponte that after six years in the convent he had managed to secure her freedom. Her stepmother had by then died, so Matilda was able to take her rightful place in her father's household.

Probably, as with so many of Da Ponte's romantic tales, there is at least a substratum of truth, as there may be in the story of the gondolier who lent him money when he had lost every penny gambling. He rushed to the gambling tables with the borrowed zecchini and won back everything he had lost and a goodly sum besides, so that he was able to repay the generous gondolier and give him a present also.

Still more fantastic was the occasion when Girolamo Tiepolo gambled away the last of their money. Penniless, brother and sister went disconsolately home, while Da Ponte retired to the 'Room of Sighs', where rejected lovers and unlucky players betook themselves to talk, to bewail their lot and to sleep. A masked man asked him for some small change, and in an inner pocket Da Ponte found an unexpected store of gold coins. He gave one of them to the masked man, who accepted it on condition that Da Ponte would come to his house in person to be repaid.

Da Ponte thought no more about the matter, until some time later he found the playing card on which the stranger had written his name and address. From idle curiosity he went to the house, and heard the man's story. A native of Livorno, in four years, through inexperience and gullibility, he had lost the flourishing business which his father had left him. So he came to Venice, and since he now had a horror of business, but no training in anything else, made a living by begging, with such success that he had become a rich man.

He had a lovely young stepdaughter for whom he wanted to find a husband; and he now offered this girl to Da Ponte, whom he had often observed and who had many times given him alms. (This last point certainly rings true, for Da Ponte was generous to the point of recklessness.) Once again Da Ponte allowed his passion for Angiola to sway him, and said no, but he repented his decision when, not long afterwards, he heard that the girl had married someone else. The young couple, together with the girl's stepfather, moved to Vienna, where, Da Ponte says, he became very friendly with them when he was himself living there. Tantalisingly, he gives no clue to their identity. Nor does he explain how, as a priest, it would have been possible for him to marry the girl.

Night after night, with Angiola and her brother, he gambled feverishly in the public *ridotto*. At first they were lucky, but then their fortunes turned and they lost everything, pawned whatever they could, and fell heavily into debt. Da Ponte was by now living in Angiola's palace – perhaps he had begun to do so after her husband went off to become a priest – and with feigned sighs and bitter tears she told him that her brother had determined to chase him from the house and instal in his place a rich man who was his avowed enemy.

It happened that this was just about the time when Da Ponte found the hidden store of money in his inner pocket. Since gold was the key to Girolamo Tiepolo's heart – as it was to Angiola's – she and Da Ponte agreed that they would convince him that Da Ponte could 'make' precious metals, and that this was the source of the present store. This was not difficult, for the Venetian nobles firmly believed in alchemy. The government tried to combat this superstition, which among other things led to the forging of money, but in vain. So for a while Da Ponte was able to pull the wool over Girolamo's eyes, and to remain in this tempestuous household.

One evening he came home late, after a visit to the rich beggar and his stepdaughter. Angiola, in a paroxysm of jealousy, hurled at him a heavy inkstand which hurt his hand so badly that he could not use it for a month. Worse still, in order to stop him from going out, she stole into his room that night, while he was still asleep, and like a second Delilah cut off his hair. This cost him dear, for the patrician whose sons he taught came to seek him out, quickly realised what unsavoury people he was living with, and dismissed him on the spot.

So now he had no work and no money. Angiola could not bear

him out of her sight, and the only time he left the house was in her company and at night. They gave themselves up to frivolous amusements, frequenting society suppers and visiting the theatre and the opera, round which the carnival revolved – Venice was famous for her opera houses, having seven at a time when Paris possessed only three. Their store of riches dwindled, and when Girolamo demanded money he was not satisfied with the reply that Da Ponte had none. 'I know perfectly well, Messr Lorenzo,' he said threateningly, 'that you can make gold, and I insist that you should teach me the secret.'

At the time of the hair-cutting episode Da Ponte had appealed to Michele Colombo for money – not as a gift, but as an advance on books which Colombo had asked him to buy in Venice. 'Say nothing of this to my father or to anyone else in the world,' Da Ponte wrote. 'If you have not got the money yourself, find it somehow, but do not leave me without this help. Remember that any delay is the same as denying me help, and that to deny me help is to ruin me . . .'

Desperation springs out of every line of this letter, but it was still some months before he had the strength to extricate himself from a situation which he must by now have regarded with horror. He has been much condemned for the vicious life which, as an ordained priest, he spent in Venice: he himself wrote of this period that he did not believe he learnt anything new or worth learning during the years while the intrigue lasted. But it must be remembered that, in all the brilliance and gaiety of this magical Venetian world, many abbés – as Da Ponte was – were as dissolute as the rest: large numbers of them lived as if they were laymen, acting as *cavalieri serventi* to rich Venetian women, or even working as domestic servants. The monasteries and convents, often to be found beneath the same roof, were notorious for the scandalous behaviour of their inmates. Many of the young girls who took the veil had been shut away, like the unfortunate Matilda, not because they had a sense of vocation but quite brutally to suit the convenience of their families. Imprisoned against their will, these girls received their friends, nobles and gallant abbés, from behind transparent screens, wearing low-necked dresses and with pearls in their hair, more like beautiful courtesans than nuns. So Da Ponte's behaviour, though he was sufficiently ashamed not to want any hint of it to trickle back to his family or to anyone else in Ceneda, was no worse than that of many others, and would not have attracted any particular censure.

His delivery came about partly through his younger brother Girolamo, a priest like Lorenzo (he was ordained in Venice in 1776) but in other ways totally unlike him. A scholar and a man of sober, virtuous life, he was generally regarded as an excellent priest and a gifted writer, with a life of great promise before him. The bond of affection between the brothers was very great, and Girolamo Da Ponte supported Lorenzo through thick and thin. He had for a long time tried to persuade his brother to leave Venice, to no avail. But one day Lorenzo's eyes were opened, through yet another of the fantastic adventures which so often changed the course of his life.

A priest who had been a fellow-student at Portogruaro came to visit him, and on the way out stole his cloak, which he then pawned. Da Ponte's servant, wiser and less gullible than his master, found the cloak in the local pawnshop, and it was redeemed by Girolamo, who brought it back with tears in his eyes, saying only, 'You see, dear Lorenzo, the state to which the passions reduce us!' Left alone, Da Ponte at last thought seriously of the road he was travelling. 'How is it,' he asked himself, 'that principles of religion, of education, of honour, do not stop someone from being a slave to his passions, or save him, if not from a life of profligacy, at least from acts which are an offence against society? A man comes into my house under the mantle of friendship and hospitality, and allows himself to be so blindfolded that he steals a cloak from his friend, his benefactor, his schoolfellow! And what leads him to this? Love and gambling!' Da Ponte writes that as he said these words he trembled from head to foot, and resolved there and then to abandon cards, his mistress, and above all Venice.

His brother, with typical generosity, emptied his purse for Lorenzo, who, despite the prayers and threats of his lady, had enough strength of purpose to return to Ceneda. He arrived in the autumn of 1774, just as two teaching posts became vacant at the seminary in the nearby town of Treviso. One of them was offered to him and the other to Girolamo Da Ponte, who, for the sake of being with his brother, gave up his post as secretary to the noble Venetian family of Giovanni da Lezze.

Almost immediately the offer to Lorenzo was withdrawn, for a priest accused him of having eloped with a woman from Ceneda and of other sins, and declared that this was why he had been dismissed from Portogruaro. As Da Ponte wrote to Colombo:

Everyone in Treviso believes his charges, and as a result I have been dismissed by the Prelate there [this was Monsignor Giustiniani, the bishop, later to get into serious hot water because of Da Ponte], who previously had confirmed my appointment in a letter written in his own hand. Dearest friend, you can imagine how bewildered I am. To see myself ruined at the starting-point of my hopes; to know that my reputation is being torn to shreds for no reason, and by someone whom, though I do not know him, I have always greatly venerated and esteemed; to realise how difficult it is to find some defence against such a powerful attack – these are all things which disturb me as much as anything has ever done. My only hope lies in you, since you love me so much, and are yourself so greatly loved by this priest. You are wise, and will understand my need better than I can explain it. Above all I ask that your help should be speedy. A day, an hour or even less will decide my fate.

It seems that Colombo, as always the best of friends, intervened, for Da Ponte was reinstated and became master of humanities at Treviso seminary, while his brother Girolamo was appointed master of lower grammar. But Da Ponte was still not entirely free of the hateful bonds which had chained him for three years, for Angiola – who had taken a new lover as soon as he left Venice – made one final attempt to exercise her power over him.

It was her custom to write to Da Ponte every day, and on 1 January 1775 she wrote, 'Lorenzo, if you love my honour and my life, come to Venice without delay.' The weather was bitterly cold, but Da Ponte travelled post haste to Mestre, a distance of about 20 kilometres, and though, he writes, the lagoons were frozen over,[1] persuaded four strong young gondoliers to force a passage through to Venice. But when he drew near to the palace where his lady dwelt he was intercepted by a former servant of his, now employed by Angiola, who told him that it was all a trap. Her current lover, out of jealousy, had persuaded her to summon Da Ponte to Venice to beat him up. Luckily Da Ponte, despite his haste, was late, and by the time he arrived the lover had gone.

Boiling with rage, he raced up the stairs, and when Angiola, with false joy, tried to embrace him, he threw her off and cried, 'May the hand of God destroy such an infamous race!' Like a man possessed he ran to the nearest landing, took a gondola and returned to Treviso, freed at last from Angiola's thrall. 'It seems,' he writes, 'as if a ray of light from heaven filled my mind, illuminated my reason, and healed me of everything.'

[1] It seems that his memory was at fault, for, though the lagoons were frozen in 1709, 1755, 1788 and 1789, they were not in 1775.

III

More than most of us, perhaps, Da Ponte had two warring personalities within himself: on the one side was the man who delighted in the life of pleasure and debauchery which characterised Venice in the last years of her existence as a republic; on the other was the scholar whose passion was to read, study and memorise great literature, especially the great Italian poets, and who was a teacher of genius. His joy in intellectual conversation was deep and genuine, and that he himself was a witty and stimulating companion is clear from the friendships which he enjoyed with so many of the brilliant men whom he met during his long life.

So when, after the tempests of Venice, he found himself in calm waters in the charming town of Treviso, his soul rejoiced. Treviso has changed a great deal since his day, for it suffered very badly, and with great gallantry, in two world wars, and many of the ancient buildings were demolished by bombing. But the modern visitor will detect an air of prosperity and liveliness, and, as he walks beside the many shallow, sparkling waterways which flow between the streets, will be reminded of nearby Venice.

In Da Ponte's time it was a summer refuge for the Venetians, the common citizens as well as the nobles, who fled there to escape the foetid and unhealthy air rising from the canals. Michael Kelly, who about this time was singing in Venice, describes the town as 'extremely neat and pretty. I was delighted by the appearance of the elegant villas which surround it, belonging to noble Venetians who, during the theatrical season, pass their *vendemmias* there, and have what they call their *cuganas* (i.e. revelries).' In Treviso was to be found one of the most famous theatres in Italy. Today, rebuilt after the destruction of the last war, it is still as entrancingly pretty as it was when Kelly wrote of it. Owned in the eighteenth century by the noble family of Onigo, but allowed to fall into decay, in 1765 it was restored and reopened. Here were staged serious and comic operas, concerts, charity evenings and balls. Some of the finest singers from the Venetian opera houses performed in it, before an audience which rivalled Venice in brilliance, wit and elegance.

For many years Treviso had been a centre not only of pleasure but also of learning, and here 'my free spirit,' Da Ponte wrote, 'began once more to wander through the sweet and lovely fields of the Muses.' He was very happy in the seminary: the boys whom he taught were clever and ambitious; the bishop, Monsignor Giustiniani, was learned, noble of mind and fond of his school; the people with whom he came into contact were cultured and eager for congenial society; the air was cool and pure and the landscape a delight. Moreover, he was in charge of the library – could anything have delighted him more, with his lifelong passion for books? – and he had authority to add to it any volumes which he felt would increase its usefulness. In his free time he sought out his brother Girolamo and Giulio Trento, a member of one of the aristocratic families of the city and a writer of discernment and learning who was much admired in his day.

Da Ponte says that he and Girolamo were the first to introduce into the seminary a real taste for literature, by which he presumably means Italian literature. This claim is refuted by one of his earliest and most sympathetic biographers, Angelo Marchesan, who one hundred and twenty years later succeeded him in the chair of humanities at Treviso, and who says that the seminary had always been distinguished by a high standard of teaching in this subject.

> However [Marchesan goes on], no one – least of all myself – would want to deny the immense influence exercised over the students by a young master, as Da Ponte was, full of life, of passion, of poetry, extremely clever, with a lively imagination, quick of tongue, and very learned. All their lives his young pupils remembered their teacher, who not only fired them with the joy of studying literature but showed them such genuine affection and influenced them so greatly through his teaching, by this very influence making the tedium of the seminary walls seem less oppressive and the schoolroom benches less hard – so that, even more than would otherwise have been the case, in their childhood they felt the need of laughter, of sunshine, and of the urge to exercise their brains and their limbs without restraint.

It was while he was in Treviso that Da Ponte, who up till now had produced a quantity of undistinguished verse, wrote one of the first poems that can be said to have merit. This was read at a literary gathering which had met to discuss the proposition *Se in core di donna si dia spirito virile*. His poem was received with such enthusiasm, he wrote to Colombo, that within a week it had been copied fifteen or twenty times.

In his second year Da Ponte was promoted to be master of rhetoric and Girolamo took the post he had vacated, as well as being master of the Gregorian chant. One of Lorenzo's duties, as at Portogruaro, was to write verses in Latin and Italian on a subject of his own choice, which at the end of the academic year would be read aloud by the best pupils in the presence of the bishop, the town magistrate, the cathedral dignitaries and other prominent citizens. Da Ponte – as always his own worst enemy – chose the Rousseauesque theme 'Whether the happiness of mankind is increased within the social system, or whether he would be happier in a simple state of nature'. The eleven Italian and four Latin poems, with a prose preface in Italian, by no means gave unqualified support to the revolutionary idea that man is happier in a state of nature: some of them did so, arguing that laws have lessened mankind's chance of attaining happiness; but others maintained that because of man's frailty he needs laws, which are therefore an unavoidable necessity. Equally, while one poem contended that 'happiness is in proportion to wealth', the next claimed that 'the rich are not happier than the poor'; and while one sonnet declared that poverty prevents many gifted people from developing their talents through lack of education, the following poem put forward the thesis that the learned man is no more contented than the ignorant one.

Da Ponte calls the *accademia* poems a *jeu d'esprit*, a poetical whim which he wrote simply to give his students practice in declamation; and certainly he is genuine in protesting that he had no idea they would have such grave repercussions. That they could have been delivered at all reflects the liberal attitude among intellectual circles in Treviso, for no doubt they echoed the kind of conversation which he was having with friends such as Giulio Trento. Well enough in Treviso, as one commentator remarks, but Venice had long ears and keen readers, who smelt out dangerous ideas. And dangerous they were, at a time when rumblings of revolution were already being heard in France, when the war of independence was being fought in America, and everywhere the spirit of liberty was beginning to struggle free from oppressive rulers.

It is significant that nemesis did not strike at once: the bishop, the church dignitaries and all the other worthy citizens went home after the reading, which probably took place on 1 August 1776, and, as was the custom, the poems were published. Trouble began to stir as rumours about them spread through the provinces of the Serenissima. The priest of one diocese read them to another, with shocked questions about whether the teacher was perhaps not a Jew at all but an atheist; the second priest expressed his amazement that permission had been given for them to be published; a third wrote about them to the bishop's chancellor in Venice; and Padre Giuseppe Frassen, an inquisitor, finally denounced them to the magistrate of

23

the *Riformatori dello studio di Padova*, who submitted a report on the affair to the Senate. (The *Riformatori* consisted of three patricians who acted as a kind of ministry of state education. They not only directed the university of Padua but supervised all studies and publications within the Venetian territories of Italy.) One phrase was regarded as particularly subversive – a reference to *corna aurate*, or golden horns, which was interpreted as referring to the Doge's horned cap and as being a direct challenge to his authority – heresy indeed.

Da Ponte, who took the matter lightly, continued to teach in the seminary. But in October, as the ripples of the scandal spread, he was persuaded by his family and friends to go to Venice to defend himself. Once there, he set about enlisting the help of various nobles and members of the intelligentsia. One of the most influential was Bernardo Memmo, a senator, patron of scholars and writers, friend of Goldoni, and later a member of the Council of Ten and Procurator of San Marco. Another was Gasparo Gozzi, who had for many years been censor and overseer of printing in Venice. The most highly respected literary figure in the republic, he was, moreover, 'beloved of the *Riformatori*'. Da Ponte also appealed to Pietro Antonio Zaguri, a member of one of the great aristocratic families, a clever, well-educated man who was at the centre of the gay society of Venice at that time. Though he himself wrote nothing of lasting value, he was a good patron of men like Da Ponte, the most famous of his protégés being Casanova. He was much attached to the latter, and they exchanged many letters which contain interesting – and often spiteful – references to Da Ponte. It was, in fact, in the houses of Zaguri and of another patrician, Giorgio Pisani, that Da Ponte and Casanova now first met, as they were to do intermittently over the years. These men did their best to protect Da Ponte. At Memmo's suggestion he addressed a rhyming appeal to Gozzi asking for support, *Gozzi, se un cor gentil*. And Zaguri, Memmo and Giovanni da Lezze, Girolamo's one-time employer, drew up a petition on his behalf, which Girolamo presented to the Council of Ten, to whom Gozzi also addressed several appeals.

The Senate met on 14 December to consider the matter, and Da Ponte, who was not present, gives a lively account of the proceedings as they were reported to him by Memmo. Some of the *accademia* poems were read aloud, one of them being in Latin so that, as their author comments, the Senate must have 'heard much, understood little and known nothing'. But, interspersed with a good deal of invective and sarcasm on the part of the prosecution, it helped to rouse their ire, as did a second poem, this time in Italian, on the theme that 'Man, by nature free, through laws becomes enslaved'. Not only was this heretical, but it contained the unfortunate reference to the *corna aurate*. There was a cry of outrage among the senators, and Da Ponte's supporters, with ashen faces, fearing for his liberty or even his life, begged him to flee. 'But,' he writes, 'I laughed at them and their fears. I could not believe that the punishment would be so severe when they had tried so hard to achieve an appearance of pomp. Venetian politics never bark hard when they intend to bite . . .' He was quite right. After some days he was summoned before the Senate and forbidden ever again to teach in any school, village, seminary or university of the Serenissima – a relatively light sentence for so heinous an offence.

But this was not all, for the repercussions in the republic itself were very wide. The *vicario pretorio* who had passed the poems was admonished and forbidden ever again to be entrusted with this task; the Senate's grave displeasure was conveyed to Monsignor Giustiniani, the bishop of Treviso; orders went out that the education being given not only at Treviso but in all other schools and places of education in the republic should be investigated and the results reported back to the Senate; and every copy of the poems was confiscated. News of the affair spread even further afield, for a Florentine newspaper reported that a projected discussion in France on this same subject of whether man is happier with or without laws was hastily abandoned when it was heard of the trouble it had caused in another state.

According to Da Ponte, the Venetian authorities wanted to punish not only him but also his patron, Bishop Giustiniani, whose brother had incurred their displeasure some years earlier. However true this may be, the bishop tried hard to absolve himself from blame, writing to the Senate that Da Ponte had originally submitted to him a most excellent and innocuous theme for the *accademia*, but once this had been approved had substituted for it the other one, without informing the bishop or giving him a chance to see it. There is nothing to suggest that this accusation is true; certainly Da Ponte can never have known of the betrayal, or in his memoirs he would hardly have written of Monsignor Giustiniani in such warm terms.

On the day when the Senate pronounced its verdict, Memmo carried Da Ponte back to his house and they spent the evening in feasting and rejoicing. For some time Da Ponte continued to live with Memmo, whose purse, he says, was always open to him. He blossomed in Venetian society, welcomed all the more warmly because of his brush with the Senate. He met alike intellectuals who were renowned for their learning and aristocrats made much of

25

because of their rank; handsome, debonair, witty, flirtatious and courtly in his manners, he became the darling of the lovely ladies of Venice. He also became very friendly with the poet and librettist Caterino Mazzolà, who had been educated at Treviso seminary and who was, Da Ponte writes, the first man to learn how to write a *dramma buffo*, or comedy (meaning, in this context, one intended to be set to music). Later on this friendship was to be very important to him. His popularity can have done him little good in the eyes of the Senate, and it aroused the envy of many people, including (according to one writer) his friend Casanova.

Da Ponte's pleasure in Venetian life was increased because Girolamo was also back in the city, once more employed by Giovanni da Lezze. The two brothers engaged enthusiastically in a new pastime – improvising. Italy at this period was famous for her *improvvisatori*, men and women who had the gift of improvising verses and songs on any theme and in any metre. Tobias Smollett, as he remarked in his *Travels through France and Italy*, was much struck by them:

> One of the greatest curiosities you meet with in Italy is the *Improvisatore*; such is the name given to certain individuals, who have the surprising talent of reciting verses extempore, on any subject you propose. Mr Corvesi, my landlord, has a son, a Franciscan friar, who is a great genius in this way. When the subject is given, his brother tunes his violin to accompany him, and he begins to rehearse in recitative, with wonderful fluency and precision. Thus he will, at a minute's warning, recite two or three hundred verses, well turned, and well adapted, and generally mingled with an elegant compliment to the company. The Italians are so fond of poetry, that many of them have the best part of Ariosto, Tasso, and Petrarch, by heart; and these are the great sources from which the *Improvisatori* draw their rhymes, cadence, and turns of expression.

Perhaps the most famous improviser of all was Maria Maddalena Morelli, known as La Corilla, whose admiring visitors in Florence included Mozart, Casanova and Dr Burney. Almost as renowned was Talassi, who demonstrated his skill before Dr Johnson, much to the latter's astonishment. The Italian language, Da Ponte believed, with its grace, melody and richness, was peculiarly suited to improvisation. Later he came to the conclusion that the practice was harmful to the writing of really fine poetry, and that verses which had sounded so impressive while they were being recited extempore turned out to be mediocre when committed to paper. However, for the time being he and Girolamo enjoyed showing their skill, and were so adept that they became known as 'the improvisers of Ceneda'.

Like many good things in Da Ponte's life, this pleasant interlude soon came to an end. Memmo had a young mistress, Teresa Zerbin. He was infatuated with her, and she lived in his house together with her whole family. There was little love lost between her and Da Ponte, though exactly what happened between them will never be known. It has been suggested that they had an affair, and that for this reason Da Ponte was shown the door. His own story is that the man Teresa hoped to marry – with Memmo's blessing – feared his, Da Ponte's, influence over Memmo, and so Teresa decided to offer him such studied insults that he would be bound to take his leave. Whatever the truth of the matter, he packed up a few clothes and went off to Padua, where his young brother Luigi was studying medicine.

He had virtually no money, and Luigi was as poor as he. But appearances – *la bella figura*, a treasured concept of the Italians – must be kept up at all costs. He was able to appear always decently dressed, and no one, not even Luigi, knew of his secret life of austerity. He had just enough money to pay for his bed, for a cup of coffee every morning, and for bread and olives, which, being salty, increased his appetite for water. In this way, he writes, he lived for forty-two days. He met many of the intelligentsia of the city, including Melchiore Cesarotti, professor of Greek and Hebrew at the famous university and the author of many prose works and translations from Homer – whose style was, however, criticised for its Gallicisms. Da Ponte often apologises, in his memoirs and elsewhere, for expressions which he had picked up from Cesarotti, whom he greatly admired.

His fortunes took a turn for the better when he played dominoes and *ombre* for money with some young men who fancied themselves at the games but were no match for their opponent. But this idle, pointless way of life quickly lost its charm, and he returned to Venice. Here he encountered Mazzolà, who took him back to Memmo's house. The misunderstandings were cleared up and the friendship resumed, though Da Ponte refused Memmo's offer to go back and live with him and Teresa. He became secretary and companion in his studies to Zaguri, who may have taken a special interest because his younger brother, Mario Zaguri, a good and charitable man, was bishop of Ceneda between 1777 and 1785. Da Ponte was also appointed tutor to the sons of Giorgio Pisani, whom he describes as 'the Gracchus of Venice'. 'Unscrupulous, ingenious and vehement,' as Molmenti describes him, he was one of the leaders of the *Barnabotti* and a thorn in the side of the government, whom he continually attacked.

'I wrote few poems at that time,' Da Ponte records, 'for my double employment, and perhaps even more the pleasant distractions of the city, which were only too well suited to my age, my inclinations and my temperament, did not leave me enough time.' In this bland sentence he passes over the most disreputable – and colourful – period of his life, one that he bitterly repented and always covered up. It was to take him for ever from the cultured society of Venice, which he loved so dearly, and from the republic itself; he was only to re-enter it very briefly many years later, after it had fallen to Napoleon. Once more his fate was sealed by a passionate, jealous woman, and one considerably below him in intellect and education. Her name was Angioletta, and she was the wife of one Carlo Bellaudi. Angioletta was a bad hat: at the age of ten she had flirted in an unbecoming manner, and at fifteen she was pregnant by Carlo, whom she then married. But marriage did not stop her from taking lovers, and even in church she was observed to be engaged in mutual fondling of the most intimate kind with any young man who caught her fancy.

The truth – or at any rate the partial truth – of what actually happened between the spring of 1777 and the summer of 1779 remained hidden for a century and a half. It came to light some time before 1915, but was regarded as so shocking that for many years it was either ignored or buried beneath a mist of euphemisms. Not till Fausto Nicolini published an article in 1942 entitled *La vera ragione della fuga di Lorenzo Da Ponte da Venezia (The Real Reason for Lorenzo Da Ponte's Flight from Venice)* was some of the veil drawn aside, and even Nicolini shrank from relating the more sordid details.

The story is contained in a thick bundle of documents kept in the archives of Venice – a verbatim account of the hearings before the *Esecutori contro la bestemmia*. The *Esecutori* had been brought into existence in 1437 to put down the vices of swearing and blasphemy and to keep an eye on public morals, especially with regard to gambling. From a study of the cases with which they dealt it is possible to see the mixed bag of activities that were regarded as criminal: evil living, gambling, secret marriage, exporting grain, rape, violence, irreverence in church, fraud, masquerading as a priest.

The documents implicating Da Ponte testify that on 28 May 1779, when he had been living in Venice for a little over two and a half years, an unsigned denunciation was thrown into the mouth of the stone lion at San Moisè (it was the custom for anonymous accusations to be left in the mouths of these lions, which were scattered round the city). In a badly written and ungrammatical letter he was accused of practising terrible and scandalous crimes; of having been converted to the Christian faith only to bring it into disrepute (his enemies never allowed it to be forgotten that he had been born a Jew); of harming two honourable families who had only their reputation to protect them; of seducing another man's wife and taking her to live with him far from the sacraments; of conceiving with her infamous and illegitimate children; and so on and so on. The three *Esecutori* thereupon instituted legal proceedings against Da Ponte for the rape of an honest woman (how Angioletta must have laughed at this), adultery and public concubinage, all wrapped up in a parcel of *mala vita*. The hearing began on 5 June 1779. There were about sixty witnesses, and it is unlikely that anyone will ever be able to disentangle truth from lies in the accusations they made. Many of them were actuated by malice, and Da Ponte was not present to give his own version. But, true or false, this is what emerged at the trial:

Laura Bellaudi, Carlo's mother, lived in the district of San Luca, where at some point Da Ponte was employed as a priest. He took a room in her house, which she shared with Angioletta and Carlo and also with her daughter Caterina, who was married to one Gabriele Doria. Doria lived with his father, but nevertheless he and Caterina were, it was said, on good terms.

When Da Ponte joined the household some two years earlier, in the spring of 1777, Angioletta was four or five months pregnant, but this did not prevent her from taking a friendly interest in the handsome young lodger. Caterina testified that in July she noticed Da Ponte putting his hand under Angioletta's skirt while she placed her hand in his breeches. Taxed with this, Da Ponte had sworn with such vigour that he was completely innocent ('May God strike me with a thunderbolt while I'm celebrating mass!') that Caterina thought she must have been mistaken.

However, Laura Bellaudi declared that soon afterwards she had seen him standing in the doorway of his room, entirely naked and visible to Angioletta, who was in the room opposite. As a result, he was smartly told that at the end of August, when the period for which he had rented the room came to an end, he must betake himself elsewhere. Carlo Bellaudi, a weak-spirited young man, was meanwhile having an affair with a girl called Francesca Bertati, though whether they were genuinely in love or merely flirting is not known. Da Ponte had been acting as go-between, carrying their letters back and forth (and also, the evidence suggested, receiving his own favours from Francesca). Among these letters was one in which Carlo declared his intention of acting as midwife when Angioletta gave birth. 'The woman whom I hate will soon be a mother,' he wrote. 'I will deliver her myself and our troubles will be over. If this is not enough, I will send her to sleep.' At the trial, though Carlo and Francesca admitted that all the other letters were genuine, they insisted that this particular one was false, and it is quite possible that they were right, and that Da Ponte forged it in order to persuade Angioletta to elope with him, as the prosecution claimed. It is written with considerably more attention to grammar and spelling than the other letters, which are extremely illiterate.

Somehow or other – just how did not emerge at the trial – Da Ponte got hold of these letters, and showed copies of them to Angioletta. She was so frightened that she agreed to go away with him on a certain day. On the evening of the day in question Da Ponte took Carlo to another part of the city on some trumped-up pretext, while Angioletta put together a few clothes and hailed a gondola to carry her to the arranged meeting-place. Unfortunately her birth-pangs started, so she got out of the gondola and lay in an alley-way until Da Ponte found her and took her to the house of his cousin, also a converted Jew. Here, within the hour, she gave birth, and the next day he, his cousin, his cousin's paramour and the midwife (a washerwoman) went in procession to the Bellaudis' house to present Carlo with his baby daughter. Not surprisingly, he refused to have anything to do with it, and the child was sent to the foundling hospital.

After this matters went from bad to worse. Da Ponte took another room in the district of San Luca and his association with Angioletta continued in the most scandalous fashion. She became pregnant again, this time by Da Ponte, and at the end of April 1778, after a tiff with Da Ponte's cousin and his girlfriend, she was told to remove herself, and Da Ponte found new lodgings for her.

It is not possible to sort out the dates, but from the evidence given before the *Esecutori* it is clear that he and Angioletta lived now here, now there, sometimes together, sometimes apart, and that for a while they had rooms in brothels where he organized the entertainments, playing the violin[1] in his priest's garb, by now having no other. Both he and Angioletta became intermittently involved with other lovers. Da Ponte was not sexually jealous, and seems not to have minded

---

[1] This is puzzling, for nowhere else is it suggested that Da Ponte played the violin – or any other musical instrument, for that matter. The only indication that he might have done so comes in the customs declaration when he fled to America, and had to pay duty on 'one fiddle and some fiddle strings'. But at that time he had for some years been involved in a business which sold such merchandise, and he may have taken the violin with him as a means of raising capital. It seems strange that he should never have mentioned learning the violin, and in fact given the impression that he was not a practising musician of any kind; and the likelihood seems to be that this charge was one of many made by hostile or ignorant witnesses.

Angioletta bestowing her favours elsewhere, but she violently objected to his doing the same thing with attractive young women, and one evening such a fracas occurred, and Angioletta was so viciously attacked by three other women, that Da Ponte went to her assistance with a knife and one of the women was wounded.

In January 1779, the evidence revealed, he moved her to yet another dwelling, and here they were joined by his brother Luigi and his stepmother, a shadowy figure whom Da Ponte barely mentions in his memoirs, and who, since she was only two or three years older than Da Ponte himself, was now in her early thirties. History does not say how long she and Luigi stayed at the inn where Da Ponte and Angioletta were living, but in February they all went to Ceneda, where the stepmother remained. Luigi returned to Venice with the other two, and early in Lent went off to complete his studies at Padua university. Angioletta was once more pregnant, and although she gave herself out as Da Ponte's sister no one was fooled, and she was known in the quarter as 'the priest's whore'.

Complaints were made, and Da Ponte was given a dressing-down by the *vicario generale* of the district of San Bartolomeo, where he now seems to have been living. This reprimand made little difference to his way of life. One witness at the trial was the vicar of San Luca, who added fuel to the flames by testifying that he knew Da Ponte by reputation rather than by sight. Asked why, he replied that he had seen him only once, three years or more earlier, when Da Ponte had first celebrated mass in his church, his long hair combed in the latest fashion and with the air of a ladykiller, casting sidelong glances at all the girls. The vicar was so shocked by what he saw that he banned Da Ponte from his church. (However, this conflicts with the evidence of other witnesses, who declared that he would go from an adulterous bed to conduct mass.)

What finally caused the authorities to take action against him had probably little to do with his way of living, but rather with their dislike and fear of his support of Giorgio Pisani, who was such an influential figure among the disaffected and riotous *Barnabotti*. As always, when Da Ponte gave love and loyalty he did so without stint or judgement; and he found qualities in Pisani which no one else recognised – an incorruptible sense of justice, profound knowledge of the law, formidable eloquence and unchallenged integrity. Naturally enough, the government detested Pisani, and were greatly alarmed at his efforts to win political power. Da Ponte, with ill-considered partisanship, wrote a witty, scurrilous poem in support of Pisani, calling on the government for certain reforms and violently attacking by name three influential senators. Worse still, the poem was in the

Venetian dialect, so that anyone, aristocrat and humble citizen alike, could read it and laugh over it; within days it was the main talking-point in every café and at every dinner-table and street corner.

In some ways the Venetian government was extremely tolerant, but if it felt that its authority was being questioned or the state insulted the punishment was terrible. Michael Kelly relates that he was advised 'never to utter one word against the laws and customs . . .: do not suffer yourself to be betrayed even into a jest on this subject, in every corner spies are lurking, numbers of whom are employed at a high price to ensnare the unwary, and report the language of strangers.' After the seditious poems of the Treviso *accademia*, with their heretical reference to the *corna aurate*, and now the poem in defence of Pisani, Da Ponte was a marked man. But they did not arrest him on the strength of the poem – were they afraid of repercussions, or did they want to provide such convincing evidence against him that a sentence of banishment would seem right and just? Whatever the reason, it seems possible that they used the scandalous affair with Angioletta as an excuse for bringing proceedings against him for *mala vita*.

For three and a half months the trial followed its leisurely course, until on 13 September 1779 the order went out for his arrest. By this time, however, he was beyond the reach of the Venetian authorities.

At first he seems to have treated the affair as lightly as the Treviso incident. Early in July he was still living with Angioletta, eight months pregnant, in the district of San Bartolomeo, unperturbed by the trial. At the end of the month he was in Treviso, and soon afterwards in Padua. Here Angioletta joined him, having given birth on 24 August.[1] But by now it was no longer safe for him to remain within reach of the long arm of Venice, and he slipped over the border to Gorizia.

Four days after orders had been issued for his arrest, his absence from Venice was officially established and the command went forth to Padua that he should be clapped into prison. Since he could not be found there either, a second mandate was sent out ordering him to appear before the Tribunal. Finally, on 17 December, sentence was pronounced: it was published in Ceneda on 24 December and in Venice on 5 January 1780. It declared that Padre Lorenzo Da Ponte was banished from Venice and from all other cities, lands and places

[1] Both her children by Da Ponte were sent to the foundling hospital, a common practice at the time with unwanted babies. He has been criticised for allowing this to happen – but Rousseau, with far less reason, got rid of all five of his children in this way.

of the Serene Republic for a term of fifteen years. If he defied this ban and was apprehended, he was to be imprisoned in a room without light for seven years. Meanwhile, it seems that Carlo Bellaudi had come to Padua to collect his wife, with whom he thereafter lived in prosperity and happiness.

Although it is impossible to say how much of the evidence against Da Ponte was true and how much invented by his enemies, some of the accusations, such as that he was expelled from the Treviso seminary because of evil living, are totally false. Nor does anyone seem to have been particularly shocked by his way of life. He continued to be employed by Pisani in the education of his sons; it was nearly two years before Carlo Bellaudi complained of Angioletta's seduction; and the church took no measures against him. Da Ponte was not alone in believing that he had been banished because of his support of Pisani, and many subsequent references by other people give this as the reason.

By the time he came to write his memoirs he was a respected teacher and *savant* in America, friendly with the cream of New York society; the world had changed, and the delights and dissipations of Venice belonged to another era; and he was writing for the chaste eyes and ears of his young lady pupils. It would have required a man of a very different stamp to tell the true story. Da Ponte, who always had such a great need to present himself in a good light, could not do so. So when, in the memoirs, he came to this period of his life, he explained his banishment by means of a vague statement that a certain wicked man had accused him of eating ham on a Friday ('He had eaten it with me!') and of not having gone to church on various Sundays ('This man had never been to mass in his life!'), and declared that this was used as a pretext for getting rid of him.

In 1798 he went back to Venice and by chance met Carlo and Angioletta Bellaudi. At this point in the memoirs he gives a bowdlerised account of their previous association, though without relating it to his banishment. He admits, however, without actually writing the words, that he succumbed to Angioletta's charms, 'forsaking all the rules which I had made, all the salutary principles I had established in the course of my life', and forgetting the truth of the saying that 'only by flight can we conquer love' – '*non si vince amor, se non fuggendo*'.

One other factor must be taken into account, a link which, to the best of my knowledge, has not so far been made. When the Treviso *accademia* scandal came before the Senate, the adviser to the Holy See in Venice was one Pietro Barbarigo, whom Da Ponte insultingly refers to as 'the lame one'. It was Barbarigo who read aloud with sarcastic venom the verses that roused the anger of the senators, and who, by his accusations, bore much of the responsibility for Da Ponte's sentence. He must have been riled beyond measure to see how little the Senate's punishment affected Da Ponte, and how warmly he was courted by Venetian society. It so happens that Barbarigo's cook was also Gabriele Doria's father. So it may well have been that Barbarigo wreaked his vengeance through Doria, who seems to have been a rather sinister figure: Doria, in collusion with Barbarigo, may have persuaded the weak-spirited Bellaudi that the authorities would be by no means displeased if he slipped the denunciation into the lion's mouth. Doria would have been all the readier to do so if, as Da Ponte claims, he was himself enamoured of Angioletta and bitterly jealous of his rival.

Before Da Ponte left Venice, Giovanni da Lezze had offered him hospitality in one of his country houses until the storm should have blown over – yet another indication of the fact that he was in no way an object of scorn amongst people of standing and culture.[1] But by this time there was nowhere in the republic where he was safe. Still covering up the real facts, he writes, 'I could no longer live in a country which behaved so unjustly towards both Pisani and myself, which was so blind to its true interests and so close to its dissolution. So I decided to leave Venice for ever. I went to see my three patrons and a few old friends, who with tears in their eyes heard what I had decided and felt I had chosen the right course. Thus I abandoned my ungrateful country and went to Gorizia.' But he was never to forget his native city or cease to love it, and twelve years later he made a desperate bid to return there.

[1] A letter is often quoted that Zaguri wrote to Casanova in 1792, in which he says that he banished Da Ponte from his house because he was involved in too many mishaps. 'This present one,' Zaguri declares he said to Da Ponte, 'when you had to come to the rescue of a woman who was giving birth in the street, a woman whom you had yourself made pregnant, is the last I intend to hear from your mouth while you're living with me!' This is typical of Zaguri's often malicious remarks about Da Ponte, however amiable their relationship on the surface, and it contains two errors of fact. Da Ponte was not the father of this child of Angioletta's, though he was of the next two. The evidence given before the *Esecutori contro la bestemmia* shows that when he went to live in the Bellaudi household Angioletta was already four or five months pregnant; and none of the witnesses suggested that she was bearing Da Ponte's child. If she had been it is inconceivable that he would not have been charged with this crime also. The accusation was a typical piece of Venetian gossip which has been repeated ever since. Secondly, Angioletta did not give birth in the street with Da Ponte in attendance – an even more discreditable version than the true one.

IV

It cannot have been chance alone that led Da Ponte to seek refuge from the Council of Ten in the little town of Gorizia, about 35 kilometres north of Trieste. True, since it was in the Austrian Empire it provided a safe haven from which Da Ponte could keep in touch with his friends in Venice, for he was hoping to be able to go back sooner or later. But Gorizia had other attractions: its mild climate made it a popular resort among Italian patricians, many of whom owned country houses in and around the town, and, like Treviso, it had become a centre of learning comparable even with Tuscany. Da Ponte describes the town as charming, ancient and noble, and he writes with pleasure of the river Isonzo which, flowing through it and 'descending rapidly from the Northern Alps, waters all the countryside'. Erudition and a love of literature were valued far more highly than money or position, and the nobles, both men and women, abjured the frivolous pursuits which were *de rigueur* elsewhere, spending their time in serious study; anyone of culture, whatever his station, could take part in the vigorous intellectual life.

Gorizia was also a noted centre of printing. Books seem to have been published there since 1754, and they were distinguished by a high artistic level and by the good taste with which they were produced. The quality of the type, the accuracy of the composition, the design and the use of ornaments were alike excellent, and they found a ready market among the nobles, many of whom built splendid libraries to adorn their castles and villas. There was also an admirable theatre, which had been built about forty years before Da Ponte's arrival and which at once became the centre of the intellectual life of the town. Here were put on an almost uninterrupted series of plays, or concerts at which the popular music of Cimarosa, Paisiello, Salieri, Marcello and Anfossi would be performed. So Da Ponte could feel at home, in a milieu where books and plays and music were important and where lack of money was no hindrance to congenial society.

It was probably at some point in September 1779[1] that he reached

[1] There is another discrepancy in chronology here, for Da Ponte himself states that he arrived in Gorizia early in September 1777, yet from the dates of his trial *in absentia* before the *Esecutori contro la bestemmia* we know that this is about two years

35

the town, a fugitive who brought with him nothing but a little bundle containing a few clothes, a Dante that he had annotated, an old Petrarch and a small volume of Horace, which later accompanied him to Vienna and London, where he lost it, finding it again in Philadelphia. He knew no one and had no letters of introduction, so he went to the first inn he came to.

The innkeeper happened to be a lovely girl, either German or Slovene, who was much taken by her handsome guest. He paints a delightful picture of her: 'This lady was very beautiful, young, unspoilt, and amazingly vivacious. She was dressed in the German fashion: on her head she wore a little cap of gold lace; a fine Venetian chain encircled at least thirty times a rounded throat whiter than alabaster and, falling in crescent loops, reached her lovely bosom, which it partially and charmingly hid; a closely fitting jacket adorned her shapely limbs with wanton elegance; and silken stockings, ending in two rosy slippers, revealed to the covetous gaze the admirable shape of a tiny foot.'

Who could have resisted her? Not Da Ponte, a hot-blooded young man of thirty, and he fell in love with her instantly. She knew no Italian, but this hardly mattered. Sending one of her maids for a dictionary, she pointed out the words 'Ich – liebe – Sie', and Da Ponte, turning to the Italian half of the dictionary, soon discovered that they meant 'I love you'. He had no difficulty in translating 'And I love you' into 'Und – ich – liebe – Sie'. In this way the evening passed pleasantly, though Da Ponte, who was ravenously hungry, failed to make his delicious landlady understand that he needed supper – she misinterpreted his signs as amorous compliments. Luckily a tray laden with food for another traveller was carried by. Hurling himself upon it with the speed of a cat, he seized a large piece of chicken and devoured it, which at once enlightened his hostess, who had an excellent supper brought, made all the more palatable by her charming presence.

Under the Empress Maria Theresa the Austrian Empire was notorious for its harsh emphasis on morality, and Da Ponte, who

---

out. It has been suggested that he deliberately 'fudged' the date of his arrival in order to bury those two discreditable years in Venice. It seems more likely that, as in other places in the memoirs, his memory was at fault – hardly surprising after nearly half a century – since the kind of tortuous reasoning which would have been necessary in order to cover up his tracks in this way is not at all characteristic of the man. In any case, he would have given himself away immediately, for a few pages later on he says that soon after his arrival in Gorizia (in fact, a few months before) the Peace of Teschen was signed, and the date of this event was 13 May 1779.

was expecting to find a severe code enforced with the utmost rigour, was astonished at the free and easy ways of the inn. Soon after he had settled down comfortably in his room it was invaded by a procession of women with baskets full of knick-knacks, ornaments, needles, pins, handkerchiefs, necklaces and ribbons. It was a revelation to Da Ponte that, in a country where such a vigilant eye was kept on public morals, 'it should be so easy to sell certain items which are not to be found in baskets'.

Alas, his purse was soon empty, and with much sorrow he and his lovely innkeeper took leave of one another. She, generous soul, had tried to help him by putting beneath his pillow a purse containing gold coins, but he gave it back to her with tears and kisses, for 'I have never followed the trade of emptying the purses of women, even though they have emptied mine'. But they remained good friends, and Da Ponte shed many more tears when she died of a fever not long afterwards, at the age of twenty-two. She was, he writes, one of the best women he ever met, more fitted to be a princess than an innkeeper. Fifty years later – but not until after the death of his wife – he wrote that the few days which he spent with her had perhaps been the most joyful in the whole of his life. One useful result of his stay was that he had learnt from her a German vocabulary 'consisting almost entirely of amorous words and phrases, which served me very well in the course of my youthful flirtations in Gorizia and elsewhere'.

He decided to see if he could make a little money writing verse. The Peace of Teschen, which had been signed between Austria and Prussia and ended the War of the Bavarian Succession, had been negotiated by the son of Count Guidobaldo di Cobenzl, one of the most eminent citizens of Gorizia. So – no doubt with an eye to the main chance – Da Ponte composed a celebratory ode which he called *Le gare degli uccelli (The Contest of the Birds)*, the title alluding to the coats of arms of the Habsburgs and of the reigning family of Prussia. This he dedicated to the Count, who had it printed at his own expense and distributed many copies among his friends. Da Ponte thus gained the patronage he needed so much, and soon he was moving among the leading families. 'I cannot,' he writes, 'remember without a lively feeling of gratitude the names of Strassoldo, Lantieri, Cobenzl, Attems, Thurns, Coronini and Torriani.' He was flattered by the friendliness they showed him – unlike Casanova, who had visited Gorizia a few years earlier and who was considerably more acid in his comments; but he was always less impressed by birth and titles than Da Ponte, and considerably more cynical. After he left the inn Da Ponte took a small, poor room in the house of a grain-merchant, but his humble surroundings made no difference to his new friends, who eagerly sought him out and drew him into their activities.

At this time many men of letters in Italy were taking part in a curious association known as *l'Accademia degli Arcadi*, which had come into being nearly a century earlier. In 1690 fourteen writers had banded together under the name *Ragunanza degli Arcadi*, dedicating themselves to Italian literature, to upholding the purity of the language, and to eschewing anything that was lewd, irreligious, impious or libellous. Arcadian colonies, as they were called, sprang up all over Italy, reflecting the struggle which Italians were having to resist the attempts from Vienna to stifle their language and culture. Their members took pastoral names and met at the country houses of the nobility for gatherings at which they devoted themselves to bucolic amusements, eating and drinking, dancing, listening to music and reading aloud the poems which they had written. It all conjures up a charming picture of idyllic picnics under shady trees, as the elegantly dressed men and women listened to one another's compositions, often, no doubt, stifling yawns. In some ways these gatherings must have been artificial and ridiculous, and the poetry ludicrously bad. Yet they also formed a great service, in that they helped to lower social barriers, to bring together disparate elements which might have seemed irreconcilable, and 'to smooth away many an aristocratic frown', as one writer puts it. They contributed much to Italian culture, education and tolerance, and even to a concept of the unification of the whole country.

Some months after Da Ponte's arrival in Gorizia such a colony was established there, calling itself *l'Accademia letteraria degli Arcadi Romano-Sonziaci*, after the name of the river Isonzo. Da Ponte joined immediately, taking the pastoral name of Lesbonico Pegasio (with which he signed a considerable number of his poems). The president was his patron Count Cobenzl, and the founder and secretary a man called Giuseppe de Coletti.

Beginning life as a soldier, Coletti had come to Gorizia some years before and turned printer. He was a good typographer and historian; he translated from the German and French; and when later he moved to Trieste he initiated an Arcadian colony there, became the founder and director of the first public library in the town and of the first antiquarian collection, and started the much-respected newspaper *L'Osservatore Triestino*.

Da Ponte loathed Coletti, whom he describes as mad, fanatical, licentious, a liar, flatterer, hypocrite, and totally devoid of true poetic taste. He attacked him through a bad and savage little poem called *Il capriccio*, which, he said, was read with amused appreciation by the nobility, one of whom, Count Rodolfo Coronini, asked him to translate into Italian a Latin effusion which the count had written. This described the noble families of Gorizia, and Da Ponte added verses of his own extolling the greatness of his aristocratic friends and the charms of their beautiful houses and gardens. The translation was published in 1780, as were several other poems. One of them was *Il cechino o sia la storia del cane e del gatto*, a pastoral allegory and a charming, graceful piece of writing.

A company of players came to Gorizia and he was asked to write a play for them. Since he had never tried his hand at anything of the kind, and had no desire to risk his reputation by writing a bad one, he translated a German text. This was duly performed, but it was a flop, and lasted for only two nights. A second attempt, also a translation, this time of a play by the popular French dramatist J. F. de La Harpe, on which he and Girolamo had already collaborated in Venice, fared better, and was later put on in Trieste.

Da Ponte was happy in Gorizia, his pleasure no doubt greatly increased when he was welcomed into the household of Count Torriani, whose wife he describes as 'an angel of goodness rather than a woman'. Here he lived for some time, and it was to Count Torriani that he dedicated another of the poems which he wrote in Gorizia, *La gratitudine, o sia la difesa delle donne*. All the same, he longed for Venice – was the elegantly cultured life of Gorizia becoming a trifle cloying and uneventful? He had a passionate desire to see his family and his friends, especially Zaguri, Memmo and Pisani. Pisani had been elected in March 1780 to the important position of Procurator, and his influence might, Da Ponte believed, make it possible for him to return despite the banning order. He was disillusioned. Not long afterwards, probably in the early summer, his friend Caterino Mazzolà passed through Gorizia on his way to Dresden, where he had been appointed poet to the opera at the elector's court. He brought the news that two months after his election Pisani had been arrested and thrown into prison. Da Ponte knew that he now had no chance of returning to his homeland. He asked Mazzolà to try and find him a post in Dresden, and his friend promised to do all he could.

Da Ponte's vendetta against Coletti – to which Coletti seems always to have turned the most Christian of cheeks – had been somewhat abated by their co-membership of the Arcadian colony, and Da Ponte told Coletti of this new turn of affairs. Coletti professed to be surprised and regretful at the possibility that Da Ponte might leave Gorizia and seek his fortunes in Dresden, but 'I saw at once that he was delighted,' writes Da Ponte with implacable hostility.

Two months later a letter arrived, signed but not written by Mazzolà, summoning Da Ponte to Dresden to take up a good post at court. Bidding his friends a sad farewell, and generously supplied with money for the journey and a letter of introduction from Count Cobenzl to his son in Vienna, early in January 1781 he set out with a heavy heart on the next stage of his journeyings.

He spent only three days in Vienna, which was in deep mourning for the Empress Maria Theresa, who had died five weeks earlier. He wrote a sonnet *Per la morte di Sua Maestà l'Imperatrice Maria Teresa* and presented his letter of introduction to Count Philipp von Cobenzl, by now State Vice-Chancellor, who received him graciously and speeded him on his way with the gift of a book to which he had pinned a banknote for a hundred florins.

From Vienna Da Ponte hastened to Dresden, where he went at once to Mazzolà. To his consternation, his friend greeted him with astonishment and asked whether he had been 'called to the theatre at St Petersburg'. Da Ponte managed to hide his confusion and replied only that he had come to Dresden 'to see my friend Mazzolà and to profit, if possible, from his friendship'. Mazzolà replied, 'Bravo! You may have come at just the right moment.' They went to an inn and talked about various matters – but no mention was made of Mazzolà's letter.

Da Ponte returned to his inn and spent the night wondering what on earth had happened. Next day he met Mazzolà again, who told him that as yet there was no opening at court, though he was hopeful of finding one, and that he had written to Da Ponte to this effect. This letter, Da Ponte writes in his memoirs, he had never received; but instead there had come the one telling him that a position was awaiting him. What was the explanation? Without much difficulty, and with no evidence at all, he fixed the guilt on his hated enemy Coletti, who, he decided, had forged the letter as a means of getting rid of his rival. Why he disliked Coletti so much is a mystery, but whatever the reason he devotes tedious pages of the memoirs to a description of their encounters in Gorizia, in which Coletti is always painted in the blackest of terms.

He did not breathe a word about the misunderstanding to Mazzolà; the only person in whom he confided was an ex-Jesuit[1] and a friend of Mazzolà's called Father Michael Hueber, a man of great learning with a perfect knowledge of Italian. Hueber was an admirer of Bernardo Tasso, whom Da Ponte revered all his life as one of Italy's greatest writers. His friend had a particular regard for Bernardo

---

[1] The Jesuit order had been suppressed within the Austrian empire in 1773.

Tasso's *Psalms*, and in compliment to him Da Ponte wrote seven penitential psalms which he dedicated to Hueber. Deeply felt, written with eloquence and a felicitous choice of words, they have a gravity and a sincerity untypical of much of his poetry.

Despite his disappointment with regard to a position at court, Da Ponte lingered in Dresden for a while – he had nowhere else to go. He still hoped to find employment there, and meanwhile not only was Mazzolà full of friendliness and hospitality but Da Ponte was able to help him with his work. 'I passed most of every day and part of every night with him. He was very busy writing, translating or adapting operas for the theatre, which boasted one of the best companies in Europe. So as not to be idle I offered to share his labours, and to some extent he accepted my offer. So I translated, and wrote for his texts now an aria, now a duet or an entire scene which he first outlined to me.' Da Ponte also translated a libretto by the popular French dramatist Philippe Quinault, which had been set to music by Lully and performed a few years earlier. Mazzolà liked it so much that he asked Da Ponte why he did not make a career for himself by writing for Italian opera companies. Da Ponte replied by stating no more than the truth: that librettists were abominably paid in Italy by greedy impresarios, who poured out fortunes on the chief singers, and all the good poets went off to work abroad, where the rewards were greater. So gifted Italian composers were forced to write for wretched libretti provided by indifferent poets who were unable to find more lucrative work. However, the suggestion stayed in his mind; and meanwhile he was getting invaluable practice for his next career.

But eventually it became impossible for him to remain in Dresden. First, he began to feel that, despite Mazzolà's kindness, his friend was far from anxious that he should write or publish poetry in the city. No doubt Mazzolà was worried by the thought of competition, as were all those artists who earned their meagre salaries by working for fickle emperors and electors and kings, their employment always uncertain and their rivals legion. Da Ponte understood his dilemma and felt no resentment, though he had no desire to earn his living by improvisation, now popular in Germany, which Mazzolà had suggested as a possible career.

Secondly, he became entangled in another of the amorous adventures which he describes in such dramatic terms in the memoirs, the romantic tale no doubt containing a substratum of truth even if the details are highly coloured. Through the *Setti salmi* which he had written for Father Hueber, and which had been a great success, winning the approval of many men of letters, he had met an Italian painter with two beautiful daughters and a wife who, 'though nearing forty', was still extremely attractive. Da Ponte fell in love with both daughters, and both lost their hearts to him; simultaneously he flirted with their mother, who by no means spurned his gallantries. The situation began to get out of hand, and the mother told him gently that, if his intentions were serious, he must choose one or other of the girls.

Almost before he could draw breath their father brought them in, weeping bitterly, to say goodbye, and this was the last Da Ponte saw of them. Excusing himself to the readers of his memoirs, he says:

> From the moment when I first fell in love, at the age of eighteen, until the forty-second year of my life, when I took a companion for the remainder of it, I have never said to a woman 'I love you' without knowing that I could love her without any breach of honour. Often my attentions, my glances and even compliments paid out of common civility were taken as declarations of love; but my mouth never sinned, and never without the consent of heart and reason did I try through vanity or a whim to awaken in an innocent or credulous breast a passion which could only end in tears and remorse.

On this occasion Da Ponte went home, weeping and crying distractedly, 'O Rosina! O Camiletta! O Camiletta! O Rosina! What will become of you?' Mazzolà came unexpectedly into his room and burst into fits of laughter as he listened to this lament, and his good sense gradually restored Da Ponte to some degree of calmness. But this tranquillity did not last long, for Mazzolà had brought with him two letters, one with sad, the other with disagreeable, news.

The first letter was from Da Ponte's father, announcing Luigi's death at the age of twenty-seven, when he was on the point of obtaining his medical degree at Padua university. Da Ponte, whose thoughts of his family were nearly always tender, burst into a further access of grief. When he had recovered a little Mazzolà, ostensibly to amuse him and raise his spirits, read aloud an extract from the second letter, which he had received from a friend. 'It is said in Venice,' the letter declared, 'that Da Ponte has gone to Dresden to wrest from you the post of court poet. Dear friend, be careful. These Da Pontes are dangerous, as you well know.'

Rightly or wrongly, this confirmed Da Ponte in his instinct that Mazzolà did truly fear his rivalry. He knew that he must say goodbye to Dresden, and next morning, filled with grief, he decided to seek his fortunes in Vienna. He went early to reserve a place in the diligence which was leaving for Prague. But first he went to Father Hueber to say goodbye. Hueber pressed upon him a basket containing coffee, sugar, chocolate, tarts which were specially made for travellers, two packets of sugared almonds and some bottles of exquisite liqueur. With his own hands he dressed Da Ponte in a fine fur coat and a cap, and insisted that he should take Hueber's own muff, in which he had hidden some gold coins and two devotional books.

> I wept tender tears [Da Ponte writes], and I can assure my readers that never, either in joy or in laughter, have I felt such sweetness and delight as I experienced in those tears of gratitude. When I left him he embraced me warmly and said, 'Go, dear Da Ponte; my heart tells me that all will be well.' As he spoke, his face seemed to glow with a sacred light. And indeed for some years these words seemed prophetic rather than simply wishes for my prosperity. If my happiness did not last for ever, that was because the wheel of fortune does not allow mankind a truce; and as I write these memoirs, approaching my sixtieth year, I can say that, if I have not always been happy, equally I cannot say that I have always been unhappy.
>
> When it struck ten o'clock I bid him goodbye for the last time and went straight to Mazzolà, wrapped in the fur coat. I did not give him a chance to say a word but threw my arms round his neck, embraced him tenderly and said only, 'Dearest friend, thank you for everything. I am leaving Dresden at once and going to Vienna. I beg you to write and tell your friends in Venice.'

Mazzolà was astonished and, Da Ponte felt, also very sorry. He ran after Da Ponte, and when he caught up with him at the diligence took a piece of paper and wrote these words: 'Friend Salieri, my good friend Da Ponte will bring you these few lines. Do for him everything that you would do for me. His heart and his talent merit whatever help you can give him. He is, besides, *pars animae dimidiumque meae*.'

Mazzolà could have given Da Ponte no greater gift. Antonio Salieri was one of the most famous and popular composers of the day, court composer at Vienna and a favourite of the Emperor. There was no one better placed to introduce Da Ponte to the career which was to bring him immortality.

V

When Da Ponte came to seek his fortune in Vienna, Joseph II had occupied the imperial throne for some sixteen years – for the first fifteen of them as co-regent with his mother, the formidable Maria Theresa, and since her death in 1780 as sole ruler. Joseph was a remarkable and complex man, whom one historian has described as having 'a terrible genius. He touched not only the shape of things, but also the spirit within them . . . [He] is perhaps the completest enlightened despot in European history.' Dogmatic, self-opinionated and impatient of opposition, he was 'as unconciliatory in manner as he was in principle. He was capable of generosity, but not of tenderness or consideration; on the contrary, there was in him a streak of sadism which caused him to take real delight in humiliating and wounding those who . . . seemed to stand in the way of the realisation of his objectives, especially the representatives of historic tradition, and the aristocracy as a class.' He longed to emulate Frederick the Great, who said of him *avec le désir d'apprendre, il n'avait pas la patience de s'instruire.'*

His foreign policy was disastrous – over-ambitious, ruthless and unsuccessful – and towards the end of his reign was to lead to overt rebellion in a number of the states which composed the Austrian Empire. But side by side with these less agreeable qualities went a variety of good ones. He was an earnest and enlightened reformer at home, anxious to ameliorate the lot of the poor, to lower social barriers, and to establish intellectual freedom, religious tolerance and equal justice for all. Never did a ruler work harder or spare himself less. Versatile and inventive, he had an intellectual brilliance and charm, when he wanted to display these attributes, which much endeared him to his entourage and his subjects. And, true to his dislike of class distinctions, he had a great dislike of pomp and ceremony; the violinist and composer Karl von Dittersdorf remarks that anyone summoned to his presence knew he must speak 'shortly, clearly, boldly and without cringing', for, as the Emperor told him coldly, 'I hate flattery'.

By many of his subjects Joseph was disliked – by those who distrusted his reforming zeal, his sympathy for the poor, his determination to carry through his reforms too fast and at whatever cost, his intolerance of conservative prejudice. But Da Ponte, so often waspish in his summing up of the people with whom he came into contact, never, so far as is known, uttered a single critical word of the Emperor. 'When I wrote about him,' he remarked later in life, 'my pen seemed to have been dipped in honey'; and from everything one can gather the affection and esteem were mutual. Doubtless Da Ponte, who detested the German language – a barbaric tongue, he thought – enjoyed conversing with the Emperor in Italian, which Joseph spoke fluently, as he did German, French and Latin, as well as a little Hungarian.

Neither in his memoirs nor elsewhere did Da Ponte write about his journey from Dresden to Vienna, and the date of his arrival is not known with certainty. Presumably it was in the latter part of 1781, since in that year he published over a Viennese imprint his elegant, charming pastoral poem *Filemone e Bauci*, based on an Ovidian theme, among his best poetical works.

This poem led to one of the most memorable events of his life, a meeting with Metastasio, who had been court poet for fifty years, never troubling to learn German because the cultural life of the capital was carried on in French or Italian. Now an old man, he had for many years been inactive, since, in a period when opera was changing rapidly, his plays seemed archaic. But his reputation as the greatest poet of his generation, and as a man of exquisite taste and manners who had no enemies, remained as high as ever. As a newcomer to Vienna Da Ponte was doubly lucky to meet him, for he was 'very difficult of access, and equally averse to new persons and new things'. He used to hold a kind of levée each morning, when he received distinguished guests; and every evening poets and writers and other intellectuals gathered in his house. It was on one of these occasions that Metastasio read aloud the opening lines of *Filemone e Bauci*, in Da Ponte's presence, graciously inviting their author to read the rest of the poem to the assembled company. A few weeks later, after a short illness, he died.

Partly because of Metastasio's approbation, partly because Da Ponte was witty and good company, the news got about that he was a poet and an improviser, and people began to seek his company. But this did not help him to earn a living. The money he had brought from Dresden gradually vanished, and he was haunted by memories of the black olives and water which for forty days – 'a second Lent' – had formed his diet in Padua. He moved from expensive lodgings in the centre of Vienna to a small room in the suburbs in the house of a tailor. Luckily, he writes, 'at this time I made the acquaintance of a young man, cultured, learned and passionately fond of Italian literature, who, although he was not rich, was generous enough to look after me in such a way as to satisfy my needs for several months.'

At various stages in his life Da Ponte showed an instinct amounting to genius for being in the right place at the right time, and one of these occasions was his presence in Vienna in 1783. Since 1775 the Emperor had taken a firm hand in the management of the imperial theatre, the Burgtheater. As part of his liberal programme of reform he had introduced German Singspiel – comic opera with spoken dialogue – in place of Italian opera, which had previously been performed in the theatre. But after some years of this he became increasingly dissatisfied, complaining of mistakes, mishaps and squabbles, and in 1783 decided to reinstate the Italian company.

Joseph was devoted to music and a discerning judge of it, as his mother had been also, and indeed many of his ancestors: they had done a great deal to encourage music at the court of Vienna, and several of them had been competent performers and even composers. Joseph himself was an excellent bass singer, and he also played the violoncello, viola and clavier. It was his custom to have a short private concert in his apartments every afternoon immediately after he had dined, when many of the operas which were to be performed in the Burgtheater were gone through, his brother, the Archduke Maximilian, often taking an active part. On his travels through Italy, too, Joseph kept a sharp ear out for promising singers, and by the spring of 1783 he had summoned to Vienna one of the best *opera buffa* companies in Europe: it included the English *diva* Nancy Storace, later to be the first Susanna in *Le nozze di Figaro*; Francesco Benucci, one of the most famous bass baritones of the day; and Michael Kelly, a fine Irish tenor, the first Curzio and Don Basilio, whose lively reminiscences tell us so much about contemporary society and opera. It was Kelly who described the Viennese court as perhaps the most brilliant in Europe. 'All ranks of society,' he wrote, 'were dotingly fond of music, and most of them perfectly understood the science.'

Rumours of this new venture reached Da Ponte, and, heartened by what he had heard about the Emperor, he plucked up courage and asked Salieri whether he might dare to apply for the post of poet to the theatre. Salieri not only encouraged him, but promised to speak to Count (later Prince) Rosenberg, the Grand Chamberlain and director of the court theatre, in whom the Emperor put immense trust. Rosenberg in his turn spoke to Joseph, so that, Da Ponte records,

46

. . . the first time I went to the Emperor it was not to ask a favour but to thank him for one. Before this I had never spoken to a monarch. Although everyone had told me that Joseph was the most humane and affable prince in the world, nevertheless I could not appear before him without feeling great awe and terror. But his smiling countenance, his pleasant voice, and above all the extreme simplicity of his manner and clothes, which in no way reflected what I had imagined of a king, not only raised my spirits but scarcely gave me time to realise that I was standing in front of an emperor.

I had heard it said that he often judged people by their physiognomy; it seemed as if mine did not displease him, so graciously did he welcome me and in so kindly a fashion did he grant me my first audience. Always eager to learn, he asked me many questions about my country, my work, and why I had come to Vienna. I replied quite briefly, which seemed to please him. At last he asked me how many plays I had written, and when I said frankly, 'None, Sire', replied with a smile, 'Good, good! We shall have a virgin muse.'

Da Ponte was thus appointed not court poet, as has often been claimed (though not by Da Ponte himself), but poet to the Italian theatre, with an annual salary, the right to print and sell the libretti of the operas which were performed at the theatre, and extra payment for libretti which he himself wrote. His main duty was to make any adaptations that were needed to the libretti of other poets. This was no sinecure. The company opened with their first opera, *La scuola de' gelosi*, with music by Salieri to a text by Mazzolà, on 22 April 1783, and by the end of the year nine others had been put on. Quite certainly Da Ponte would have been involved in all of them. We know this not least from a letter which Mozart – who met him early this year in the house of Baron Wetzlar – wrote to his father in May, in which he said that 'the new poet to the theatre, a certain Abbé Da Ponte, has an enormous amount to do in revising pieces for the theatre.'

There is one particularly interesting aspect of Da Ponte's appointment – that a baptised Jew should have been given this coveted post in a country where heretofore, under Maria Theresa, the Jews had been treated with great harshness. While his mother was alive Joseph could do little to ameliorate the persecution and humiliation to which they were subjected, but after her death he removed many of the restrictions governing their lives – to such an extent, in fact, that in 1778 the Archbishop of Vienna made a formal complaint about the ever-increasing contact between Christians and Jews. He was horrified, amongst other things, that Jews should be allowed to dress like Christians of rank. (The Pope even came to Vienna early in

47

1782 to try to halt the social and ecclesiastical reforms that Joseph was introducing. The visit was a fiasco, but it gave Da Ponte the chance to write a poem *Alla Santità di Pio VI*.)

The Emperor said, 'To me, toleration means only that in purely secular matters . . . I am prepared to employ anyone, let anyone practise agriculture or a trade, or establish himself in a city, who has the required qualifications and would bring advantage or industry into my states.' It is possible, therefore, that he took a special pleasure in choosing Da Ponte – whose Jewish origins were well known – to be the new poet in his Italian theatre. In doing so he won Da Ponte's eternal gratitude, love and loyalty. It was, he writes, 'the sweetest and most delightful moment of my life', and the Emperor's support, friendship and approval gave him courage to endure the intrigues and misfortunes which he encountered in Vienna.

> This was the fount of my inspiration, this was what guided my pen in many of the plays which I wrote for his theatre; this, finally, enabled me to emerge victorious from a fierce conflict in which I was involved from the beginning of my appointment, from an implacable gang of critics, of stupid pedants, of novices, semi-literates, poetasters, and, finally, at the hands of one of the most famous and celebrated poets of our century, who did me the great honour not only of envying me, but of intriguing for my post in a thousand shameful ways. [This last allusion was to the Abbé Giovanni Battista Casti, with whom Da Ponte had an extremely ambivalent relationship.]

Anxiously aware of his inexperience, Da Ponte went to see a certain Varese, self-styled poet, who had a collection of about three hundred texts. Varese – whom Kelly describes as a miser – laughed when Da Ponte asked whether he might borrow some of them. 'This collection, sir, is worth a fortune,' he replied. 'I am the only person in the entire world who can boast of having them. You would never believe how much money and trouble they have cost me. No, no, do not imagine that I will allow a single volume to leave these rooms. They are jewels, sir, they are treasure! Everything I have in the world is not worth even one of these volumes. I would rather have an ear cut off, or all my teeth taken out' – and, Da Ponte comments, although he was old he had a lot of them – 'than lose a single one.' The most he would allow was that Da Ponte should read a small number in his presence. Varese kept a sharp eye on him as he did so, very suspicious that he might put a couple in his pocket.

The exercise did Da Ponte little good, for without exception the texts were wretched, lacking plot, characterisation, interest, any proper division into scenes, or grace either of language or of style. He went away determined that he would do better, but it was some time before he was given the chance, though he did make a translation of the French libretto of Gluck's *Iphigénie en Tauride*, which was performed in December in the Kärtnerthortheater.

His financial anxieties were compounded at this time by the death in August of his brother Girolamo, which was a bitter grief to him. Girolamo had shown considerable gifts as a poet, and from everything we know about him seems to have been a talented, good and generous man, and a steadying influence on his restless elder brother. He died in Ceneda after a long illness, probably tuberculosis. He had contributed the greater part of his salary to the family income, and after his death this burden fell heavily on Lorenzo.

There is much documentation of the miseries endured at this time by most of those who had anything to do with Europe's opera houses, which were hotbeds of intrigue and rivalry; the only people who seemed to do well were the principal singers, who commanded enormous salaries and terrorised everyone else. One of the most amusing accounts is contained in a little book published anonymously in about 1720, *Il teatro alla moda*. The author was in fact one Benedetto Marcello, a Venetian and a popular composer, as well as a lawyer, violinist and singer. His book is a mocking satire which has never been bettered as a description of eighteenth-century opera.

Listing in turn all those involved, he begins with advice to the poet, who, he says, will never ask any questions about the ability of the singers, but rather whether the theatre has a good bear, a good lion, a good nightingale, and good thunder, lightning and earthquakes. The poet who wants to keep in the swim must always claim that he wrote the libretto in his youth, or that it took only a few days, even if it took years. There is no need for him to know anything about music. The composer, too, may feel perfectly safe if he is totally ignorant of musical theory, since all that is required is a little experience; nor need he feel any qualms if he knows nothing about poetry or the instruments of the orchestra. His salary will be low, and he will show great respect to even the humblest of the actors, since on the stage they may be metamorphosed into important personages such as generals or captains of the guard.

It is not really necessary for the singers to be able to read or write, pronounce the words properly or understand what they mean, so long as they can make shakes, sing cadenzas and perform other vocal gymnastics. If two people sing of their love, exchange vows or accuse one another of unfaithfulness, they must always do so in the presence of pages, extras, etc. Gardeners must always be introduced into ball-scenes and courtiers into woodland ones. It is essential that many of the arias should be long, so that by the middle of them the audience will have forgotten the beginning. The part of the father, or of the tyrant, must always be given to a *castrato*, while tenors and basses should be kept for captains of the guard, confidants of the king, shepherds, messengers, etc. The role of a son should always be given to a virtuoso twenty years older than his mother.

If two *virtuose* contend for the chief part, the impresario must instruct the poet to write parts for them which are equal in the number of arias, lines, recitatives and everything else, taking care, also, to see that the names of the characters whom they portray contain the same number of letters. As for the wretched pages, they will make a point of eating on the set, and on the first evening must take care to lose their gloves, handkerchiefs and caps.

However mocking Marcello may have been, his satire was not far from the truth, as many first-hand accounts bear witness. In one of his plays Goldoni, that most popular of eighteenth-century dramatists, bemoans the lot of the writer, who after endless sweat and toil sees his script thrown on the ground, criticised, torn to pieces and generally castigated. Da Ponte, too, both in his memoirs and else-where, has a good deal to say of his own torment. The chief singers demanded – and got – arias which suited their voices, interpolating songs from completely different operas if they felt that these showed their virtuosity to advantage; they turned up at rehearsals or not as the whim took them, and bullied alike composer and poet. It was taken for granted that the audience would talk animatedly through the recitatives, only paying attention when one of their favourites began to sing an aria. Or else, as Da Ponte remarked, they all composed themselves comfortably for sleep. Metastasio, in one of his plays, has a sardonic comment about a typical opera audience: 'In the recitative you can sing in whatever language you like, for then, as you know, the audience generally has a good gossip.' Even Mozart once talked all through one of Paisiello's operas.

There was no producer in the modern sense: the staging of an opera was a co-operative enterprise with everyone working and consulting together. 'All in their own way,' as Michael Robinson remarks, 'were considered creators in the scheme, so had some claim to be treated as equal partners . . . While the composer sat down to write his music, the carpenters were engaged on the woodwork and the furnishers on the upholstery.' As he points out, Marcello mentions poets, composers, singers, impresarios, instrumentalists, stage engin-eers and painters, dancers, comedians, tailors, extras, prompters, music copyists, attendants and custodians and other minor officials – as well as the 'protectors' of the *virtuose* and their mothers and chaperones (the mothers, guarding like dragons their daughters' interests and modesty, were a particularly fiendish breed) – but, 'No mention is there of any opera producer. The person in Marcello's list whose role comes closest to the modern producer is the *suggeritore*, or prompter, who acted as the impresario's liaison, arranged rehearsal times, ordered props, lit the stage before the performance and gave the starting signal to the music maestro when all was ready.'

Somewhere near the bottom of the pile was the poet, and of his unenviable position Da Ponte often writes, notably in a rhyming letter to Casti. First the *maestro di capella*, or musical director, has to be satisfied, and he is full of whims: he wants to change the metre or the rhyme, to have an A instead of a U, to switch the verses round and then switch them back again, and (especially in the final ensemble) to put in the singing of birds, the trickling of streams, the banging of hammers and the chiming of bells, the rumble of wheels, the sound of tambourines, millstones and mills, frogs and cicadas and a thousand other incompatible elements.

Next the singers get to work: everyone squabbles with everyone else, one wants a better part, another a bravura aria, this one different words, until the poet feels inclined to knock their heads together. At last the opening night comes. Good heavens! What a din! One of the singers sings badly, another speaks badly, a third has a cough and a fourth a cold – and the poet gets all the blame.

Then there is the finale which brings down the curtain on the first act: it must be closely connected with the rest of the opera but also provide a little comedy or drama in its own right, with some new plot or focus of interest. Everyone sings in it, even if there are three hundred of them, by ones, by twos, by threes, even by sixties; and if the plot does not permit of this then the poor poet must find some way of making it do so, despite his critical faculties, the voice of reason, and all the Aristotles on earth. And if it goes badly, so much the worse for him.

It was natural that the first composer for whom Da Ponte was eventually asked to write an opera was Salieri, the court composer and conductor of the Italian opera, whose pupils included Beethoven, Schubert, Hummel and Liszt. Salieri was an extremely influential figure at court, well liked not only by the Emperor but also by Count Rosenberg; his influence was felt in every corner of musical life in the city. Kelly describes him as 'a little man, with an expressive countenance, and his eyes were full of genius . . . [He] would make a joke of anything, for he was a very pleasant man and much esteemed at Vienna.' He was clever, witty and versatile – and a born intriguer: where his rivals were concerned he was jealous and spiteful, capable of the most oblique and subtle arts in his battles against them, and totally unscrupulous about any harm he might do them.

All this Da Ponte was to find out later; for the moment, at some point in 1783, he sat down to write his first libretto. He offered Salieri a choice of themes, and was disconcerted when the *maestro* chose the least attractive of them, *Il ricco d'un giorno*, based on a text by Giovanni Bertati. This Da Ponte now set himself to adapt. He tackled the job with a sinking heart, for he soon realised that 'in every undertaking the execution is much more difficult than one has imagined. The difficulties I encountered were infinite. The theme did not provide enough characters or variety of plot to give interest to a work that lasted for two hours or so; the dialogue seemed to me dry, the scenes cold: in a word, I felt that I had never known how to write or compose verse or how to give interest and colour, and that I had undertaken the labours of Hercules with the strength of a child.'

At last he finished, for good or ill, the first act – except for the dreaded finale. This it was an agony for him to write, and when he had finished – and at last, indeed, the whole opera – he locked it away and did not look at it for a fortnight. Alas, when he dared to take it out it seemed to him worse than ever. But he had to give it to Salieri, who had already written part of the music. So, as he says, 'with his ears flattened back' he took it to the *maestro*, and was greatly relieved when Salieri expressed approval 'subject to some small changes'. But what did these changes consist of? In ruthlessly cutting not just with scissors but with shears, 'shortening or lengthening most of the scenes; introducing new duets, trios, quartets; changing the metre of half the arias; introducing choruses (which had to be sung by Germans!); taking out most of the recitatives and consequently all the plot and the interest, such as it was; so that, when at last it was performed, I do not believe that even a hundred lines remained of my original libretto.'

Some time elapsed before the opera was put on. Salieri, having written the music, went off to Paris. Before he returned, two dangerous rivals arrived in Vienna in the spring of 1784, the famous and popular composer Paisiello and the Abbé Casti, a well-known poet. Casti was very friendly with Rosenberg, whom he had met in Florence at the court of the Emperor's younger brother Leopold, grand duke of Tuscany. Casanova detested him, describing him as 'an impudent, worthless fellow whose only merit was a knack of versification, a fool and a pimp', who was, however, useful to

Rosenberg *'comme bouffon et comme pourvoyeur de filles'*. Da Ponte claims that he was no favourite of the Emperor, who heartily disliked his unchaste ways,[1] which were so much at variance with his name, but other writers say that Joseph enjoyed his wit and good humour. Certainly he was entertaining, affable and extremely well read, and Burney remarked that he had 'energy, humour, fire, and invention'.

The Emperor asked him and Paisiello to collaborate in an opera, and this they did: *Il rè Teodoro in Venezia* was put on in August 1784, and was such a success that more than ever Da Ponte dreaded the reaction to *Il ricco d'un giorno* – though when he read Casti's libretto he realized that 'it is not enough to be a great poet (for this Casti was without any doubt) to write a good play'. But he did not dare to pass this opinion on to anyone, 'for fear of being stoned or sent to a lunatic asylum. Casti was more infallible in Vienna than the Pope in Rome . . .'

Il ricco d'un giorno, when at long last it was performed in December 1784, was an unmitigated disaster. Rightly so, says Da Ponte, who is unusually frank about the fiasco of his first effort, for 'the libretto was positively awful and the music not much better' – though he does lay much of the blame on the cabals organised by his enemies. Another critic of the music was Count Zinzendorf, one-time governor of Trieste, who had lived in Vienna since 1761 and was a devoted follower of the opera. He left behind a treasure-trove of 57 volumes of diary, written in French and providing a vivid glimpse of the hundreds of performances which he watched. His verdict on Salieri's music was that it had been 'stolen from all over the place'.

Though the laughter and the scoffing drowned the singers on the first night, and almost brought the performance to a halt, the opera was repeated on six other occasions (though it was never given

---

[1] Da Ponte says that the Emperor disliked Casanova for the same reason, and he vividly describes one occasion when Casanova asked Joseph for an audience, as he had a proposition to make for a Chinese entertainment which (to fill his ever-empty purse) he hoped the Emperor would support. Da Ponte was present when he entered, bowed, and explained his project. Joseph asked him his name. '"Giacomo Casanova," he replied, "is the humble person who asks for Your Majesty's favour." Joseph was silent for a few moments, then, saying with his usual affability that Vienna did not like such spectacles, turned his back and began to write. The supplicant said not a word but departed, completely abashed. I made to follow him, but Joseph called me back, and after exclaiming three more times, "Giacomo Casanova!" began to talk again about the theatre.'
Casanova himself describes in his autobiography another interview which he had with Joseph, and how greatly in awe he felt. 'I found the reason for my timidity in the holy Bible, where I remembered reading that God, when he spoke with Moses, turned his back, and I understood the excellence of this testimony.'

53

outside Vienna). The libretto is in fact considerably better than its detractors made it out to be, and, since it is set in Venice, portrays a society which Da Ponte knew well. One of the visual splendours that must have evoked loud hurrahs – for opera audiences of the day demanded immensely costly and elaborate scenery and effects – was an illuminated gondola which appeared on the stage.

The two and a half years following his appointment as poet to the opera house were a period of misery for the luckless librettist. He wrote a little verse: a translation from the Latin of prayers said at mass in Italian churches, a tribute to the Emperor, and a sonnet, *Al bel sesso*. Possibly he was also part-author of a second sonnet, *I bei capelli di Silvia*, written in conjunction with Casanova, who was now in Vienna as secretary to the Venetian ambassador, Sebastiano Foscarini.

Of his life at this time, and of the attempts which were made to depose him as poet, he gives a vivid description in a rhymed letter to Zaguri, relating how the favours which were showered on him when he first came to Vienna changed to neglect and scorn. He accuses Casti (probably with justice) of being involved in a plot to replace him by a stripling poet, still with soap around his ears, and with not the faintest idea of one end of a line of verse from the other. And he describes how, after *Il ricco*, Salieri swore that he would rather have his fingers chopped off than set to music another libretto by Da Ponte – and it was four years before he broke his vow. But Da Ponte had the firm support of the Emperor, and in the memoirs he repeats a conversation between Joseph and Foscarini after the catastrophic first night, which the ambassador repeated to Da Ponte. It seems that Rosenberg had remarked to the Emperor, 'We need a new poet,' hoping perhaps that Joseph would reply, 'Let us take Casti.' But instead he answered, 'Let us first see another opera by Da Ponte.'

Writing philosophically in his letter to Zaguri, Da Ponte says that he is leading the life of a good Venetian. 'I eat and drink and write and think.' Cooped up in his small dwelling, worthy of a modern Diogenes, he reads, studies the habits of the Viennese, and searches in their chronicles for material to use as the basis of some comic or serious scene. 'And the hours which Minerva, my goddess, allows me for leisure I spend with Casanova, feeding now the mind, now the heart . . . and talking of you, gentle signore, as of something precious and good.'

This poem contains one point of great interest. In it Da Ponte writes that his enemies cried, 'Crucifier! Go back to the ghetto whence your race came!' This, so far as we know, is the only written reference he ever made to his Jewish origins. When he mentions

54

Jews, which he very rarely does, it is always from a distance, without reference to himself or his background, and sometimes in a faintly derogatory way which strikes a rather disagreeable note. Describing the Venetian *ridotti*, for instance, he remarks that while the rich nobles were allowed to play with their own money, the less wealthy gamblers could only play, 'at a certain price, with that of others, and mainly with that of the fat-pursed descendants of Abraham'.

In Venice Casanova and Da Ponte had had a period of estrangement, arising from a trivial argument about Latin metres. 'This strange man,' Da Ponte writes, 'always disliked being in the wrong' (though according to Zaguri it was Da Ponte who was wrong on that particular occasion). 'For more than three years after I left Venice I heard nothing of him. At the end of this time I dreamt that I met him on the Graben [one of the main streets of Vienna] . . . Next morning, when I went to the Graben, I spied some distance away an old man who stared at me and seemed to know me. Suddenly he began hurrying towards me with cries of joy: "Da Ponte, my dear Da Ponte," he cried, "how glad I am to see you!" (These were the exact words he had used in my dream.)' The two men renewed their friendship (which didn't stop them from making malicious remarks behind one another's backs), and Da Ponte, always eager to help his friends, lent Casanova money, and when he needed it gave him a roof also. Memmo and Zaguri, he said, 'loved all that was good in Casanova and forgave the bad. They taught me to do the same.'

Da Ponte's misfortunes at this time were compounded by a cruel accident, the result of a sinister plot by an Italian who lodged in the same house. This man, Doriguti, was hopelessly in love with a pretty girl who also lived there. She, on the other hand, was enamoured of Da Ponte, though he, his affections engaged elsewhere, had no particular interest in her and no idea that she had fallen for him. (A plot worthy of one of his own libretti.) Violently jealous, Doriguti took revenge one day when Da Ponte complained of an abscess in his mouth. With the promise of an infallible cure, Doriguti gave him a bottle which turned out to contain aquafortis, or nitric acid, a powerful solvent used in engraving. It did indeed cure the abscess – but at what a cost! One by one Da Ponte's teeth fell out, while the poison which he had swallowed deprived him of any appetite for two years, so that his friends marvelled that he managed to keep alive. For a fortnight he ran about Vienna like a madman trying to find Doriguti, but the Italian fled from the city to escape his fury.

For once Da Ponte understated his case, for the acid must have done the most appalling damage to the whole of his digestive system, and it is a marvel that he survived the experience. The pain and discomfort would have been excruciating – and, still a young man, he was faced with the prospect of toothless gums for the rest of his life.

Da Ponte had been so abashed by the failure of *Il ricco d'un giorno* that he had no courage to wait on the Emperor as he usually did. One day, however, they met by chance, and Joseph said kindly, 'You know, Da Ponte, your opera isn't so bad as they're trying to make you believe. You must take your courage in your hands and give us another.' Though he had to wait patiently, and with dwindling hope, before the opportunity came, at last the wheel of fortune turned, and carried him into what was to be truly an *annus mirabilis*.

VI

Encouraged by the Emperor's favour, Da Ponte at last set to work on a new opera. At Joseph's suggestion he collaborated with a young Spanish composer, Vicente Martin y Soler, who had come to Vienna in the hope that he would be asked to write an opera for the Burgtheater. He was a protégé of the Spanish ambassador's wife, who was reputed to be on terms 'of the most intimate friendship' with the Emperor, so no doubt she used her influence to good effect. Da Ponte wrote of him in 1819:

> This young composer, though a Spaniard by birth, had an exquisite taste for the Italian music, but though highly esteemed for his ballets, he was quite unknown as a composer for the voice [1] . . . In spite of the unhappy fate of my first essay, he was advised by his friends to have recourse to me for the words. I took time to reflect, not knowing much of him, and asked the advice of the emperor, who was glad of the opportunity, and urged me to embrace it. I called immediately on Martini, and after various reflections we determined to choose some subject that was already known, to avoid the criticism which might have been made upon the plot, conduct, and characters of the drama. I made use accordingly of the excellent play of Goldoni, entitled *Il burbero di buon cuore*. Many persons thought it would be impossible to form a comic piece from this comedy. Among these was the *vigilant Casti*, who hoped that the weight of his

[1] In point of fact Martin y Soler was already a popular composer of operas in Italy.

authority alone would be sufficient to occasion me another failure. He was however disappointed . . .

Goldoni, one of the most popular and prolific dramatists of the eighteenth century, and the real founder of modern Italian comedy, had done much to reform the Italian theatre. Wishing to portray the realities of social life, he made his actors play without masks, and introduced a more natural form of drama, without the usual cast of stock characters and with lively, witty, colloquial dialogue. He was a Venetian, but he was nearly forty years older than Da Ponte and the two men never met, since by the time Da Ponte arrived in Venice Goldoni had already left for Paris, where he spent the rest of his life. The Venetian *letterati* loved to discuss him (often disparagingly, for the purists among them felt that the everyday speech of his characters debased the Italian language). Da Ponte was greatly influenced by him, and adapted many of his texts.

Goldoni had originally written *Il burbero di buon cuore* in French, under the title *Le bourru bienfaisant*, to celebrate the marriage of the Dauphin (later Louis XVI) to Marie Antoinette; it is an entertaining play, full of misunderstanding in the best traditions of comic opera, about a gruff old man with a heart of gold. In the year which had passed since *Il ricco d'un giorno* Da Ponte had learnt a great deal about the art of writing libretti: he realised now, he says, that the poet must study the actors and try to understand them individually, in order to make their parts fit them (for at this period every composer wrote his operas to suit the vocal resources of the singers who were to sing them). He must also observe on the stage the faults of other librettists, as well as his own, and learn how to correct them.

In no way is Da Ponte's adaptation of Goldoni's text – the first libretto which he wrote after he had really begun to appreciate the complexities of his craft – simply a translation, as Casti claimed (Goldoni himself made a translation into Italian, but was dissatisfied with the result); it is a brisk, very skilful adaptation and reduction, with interesting and by no means conventional character development, and with the lilt which the best of Da Ponte's libretti always possess. Interestingly, it foreshadows *Le nozze di Figaro*, not least because the servants have sharply defined personalities and take a lively but sardonic, unobsequious interest in the goings-on of their employers.

It has often been said of Da Ponte's libretti that they were not original but were generally 'stolen' from existing texts. But this is true of every librettist of the day, all of whom raided the output of earlier poets – it was accepted that they should do so. Like other

European opera houses, the Burgtheater worked on the repertory system, and during the course of the year an enormous number of productions were staged there. Some of these were already in the repertoire, and here it was a question of minor adaptations – fresh arias to suit the voice of a new singer, for instance. The remaining productions were fresh to the Burgtheater, either specially composed and written or else imported from other opera houses, and these would need far more preparation, particularly, of course, in the case of those which were specially commissioned. But the importations also required a good deal of work to meet the demands of composer, director, audience, and all those intransigent singers. Da Ponte was expected to have a hand everywhere, and to make all the necessary alterations, additions and cuts to the text, as well as playing a large part in the actual production.

His libretti can be divided into four categories: translations, of which there are very few, and which are faithfully made; adaptations from 'straight' plays, especially those of Goldoni; adaptations from existing opera libretti; and original texts, which again constitute only a small part of his work. So by far the largest part of his output falls into the second and third classes, the adaptations. But nowhere does he slavishly copy, and often there is virtually no textual resemblance between the model and his libretto. His particular genius lies in his vast knowledge of classical and contemporary literature to which to go for his sources, his sense of stagecraft, his skill in turning prose into 'singable' verse, and his understanding of the relationship between words and music and of the music of words.

Da Ponte himself had strong views on this question of recourse to the work of earlier writers. In 1819 he wrote, 'If a writer of a theatrical piece does not deserve to be praised, or even noticed, when the subject of his composition is known, what praise is due to Shakespeare for all the pieces taken by him from Boccaccio, and Bandello's novels; what praise to Voltaire for his Merope; to Alfieri for his Antigone; to Metastasio for his Semiramide; to Monti for his Aristodemo, and to all those poets who, in common with them, not only wrote tragedies and dramas on well known subjects, but wrote them after having seen the performances of pieces on the same subjects?'

Also of crucial importance – and this is another reason why he is one of the greatest librettists who have ever lived – was his versatility. Opera at this time was sharply divided between *opera seria*, the older form, and *opera buffa*, which had developed as a reaction against *opera seria*. The composers and poets who worked within the earlier genre chose classical and mythological subjects, almost always with a

Greek or Roman theme; emotions were formalised, ensembles were rare, and arias and *recitativo secco* (accompanied only by harpsichord or piano) predominated. *Opera buffa*, on the other hand, developed into a kind of social comedy, reflecting everyday life and characters whom the audience would recognise from their own experience. Aria and recitative were much more closely related, one leading naturally into the other, and the arias were more varied than was possible in *opera seria*. Da Ponte, with his quick wit, his ability to adapt to his ambience, the need to be liked which was always so strong a part of his nature, possessed a chameleon quality that enabled him to turn – as few other librettists were able to do – from the high tragedy and drama of *opera seria*, where gods and men lived within a close relationship and men were required to show themselves at their most heroic, to the domesticity of everyday life, and to plots concerned with intrigue, star-crossed lovers, stern fathers, jealous husbands and pretty chambermaids.

He probably finished the libretto of *Il burbero di buon cuore* during the autumn of 1785, for Zinzendorf describes how he went to visit Rosenberg and found there 'an Italian poet' reading the text aloud to the Count and Casti. Casti, according to Da Ponte, was exceedingly jealous, and declared that the subject was not suitable for an opera and would fail to make people laugh. The Emperor repeated this remark to Da Ponte, who replied, 'Your Majesty, we can't do anything about that: it would be better for me if it made him cry.' The Emperor understood his meaning, and said, 'I hope it will.'

The opera had its *première* on 4 January 1786 and was a huge success. It was applauded from beginning to end – the audience even clapped the recitatives. Da Ponte relates that the Emperor, meeting him on his way out of the theatre, said in a half-whisper, '*Abbiamo vinto!*', 'We have won!' (shades of *Figaro* and Susanna's triumphant aside to her betrothed, '*Hai già vinto la causa!*'); and these two words, the librettist says, 'were worth more than three hundred books full of praise'. The opera stayed in the Burgtheater repertoire for some years, and was performed in a great many opera houses in Europe, bringing both composer and librettist much fame. When it was revived in Vienna in 1789, Mozart wrote two new arias for Louise Villeneuve, who in the following year was to be the first Dorabella.

> The success of this my second attempt [Da Ponte writes], and still more the favour shown me by the emperor, seemed to create a new spirit within me; redoubled my strength for the labour I had undertaken, and not only gave me courage to encounter the violent persecution of my enemies, but enabled me to look with contempt upon their criticisms,

lampoons, and satires, that, under Casti's secret protection, came out every day against my works, and myself, and to baffle all the efforts of their hatred and envy. I soon received numberless applications from various composers, to furnish them with pieces; but among all, there were but two whom I esteemed and loved: Martini, the emperor's favourite composer, and the first engine of my theatrical victory; and W. Mozart, with whom, at that time, I became acquainted.

Da Ponte forgets that he and Mozart had first met over two years earlier. Mozart's *Die Entführung aus dem Serail* had been a great success when it was put on in Vienna in 1782 (though the cabals did their best to ruin it), despite the apparent lack of enthusiasm of the Emperor, who after the *première* is said to have made his celebrated remark, 'Too fine for our ears, and an immense number of notes, my dear Mozart!', to which Mozart shot back, 'Just as many notes, Your Majesty, as are necessary.' Joseph preferred the simpler melodies of Salieri, Paisiello and Martin y Soler, and a couple of years later wrote to Rosenberg, '*La Musique de Mozard est bien trop difficile pour le chant.*' On another occasion, according to Karl von Dittersdorf, he commented, '[Mozart] has only one fault in his pieces for the stage, and his singers have very often complained of it – he deafens them with his full accompaniment.'

But although *Die Entführung* had been well received, Mozart knew that he would be really successful in Vienna only if he wrote an Italian opera, even though he much preferred writing to German libretti, and did not believe the Italian company would last for long. In 1783 he had struggled through a mass of the latest *opera buffa* texts, but liked none of them. In the spring of that year, while Da Ponte was battling with *Il ricco d'un giorno*, Mozart had told his father that when this was finished the poet – who 'has an enormous amount to do in revising pieces for the theatre' – had promised to write a text for him. 'But who knows whether he will be able to keep his word – or will want to? For, as you are aware, these Italian gentlemen are very civil to your face . . . If he is in league with Salieri, I shall never get anything out of him. But indeed I should dearly love to show them what I can do in an Italian opera!'

Two months later he wrote again: 'An Italian poet here has now brought me a libretto which I shall perhaps adopt, if he agrees to trim and adjust it in accordance with my wishes.' This was probably *Lo sposo deluso*, for which he wrote the overture, two arias, a trio and a quartet before abandoning the project. The suggestion has sometimes been made that the libretto was by Da Ponte, mainly on the grounds that he was the only Italian poet in Vienna of any stature at that time. But there were any number of poets prowling hungrily around, scribbling libretti of one kind or another; Da Ponte himself alludes to all the 'pygmies of Parnassus who aspired to be poet to the court theatre', and in any case by then his standing was at a low ebb. He himself makes no allusion, in the memoirs or elsewhere, to *Lo sposo deluso* – but then, neither does he to one undisputed collaboration with Mozart in 1785. This was a song of joy *Per la ricuperata salute di Ophelia*, celebrating the return to health of Nancy Storace, the darling of the Vienna theatre audiences. By all accounts she was a ravishing and highly intelligent singer, and in her teens was singing leading roles in Florence, Parma and Milan. Jahn describes her as possessing 'in a degree unique at that time, and rare at any time, all the gifts, the cultivation, and the skill which could be desired for Italian comic opera'. Zinzendorf says she had 'a pretty figure, voluptuous, beautiful eyes, white neck, fresh mouth, beautiful skin, the naïveté and the petulance of a child, sings like an angel.'

Nancy had come to Vienna not long before, followed soon afterwards by her brother Stephen, a talented composer. They were half-Italian – their father was a Neapolitan double-bass player – but had been born in England. Legend has it that the Emperor wanted to win Nancy as his mistress, and in order to smooth the way commissioned Stephen to write an *opera buffa*, although he had no experience in the theatre. He wrote *Gli sposi malcontenti*, but in the middle of the first performance Nancy suddenly lost her voice, and for some months, much to the Emperor's chagrin, was totally unable to sing. It was to celebrate her recovery that Da Ponte wrote his verses, which were set to music 'to be sung at the piano by the three famous Kapellmeister Mozart, Salieri, and Cornetti' – the last untraceable, and probably a pseudonym.

'Although he was gifted with talents greater, perhaps, than those of any other composer in the world, past, present or future,' Da Ponte wrote of Mozart (but with hindsight, for at the time he preferred the music of other composers, especially Martin y Soler, for whose 'sweetest melodies' he had a particular love), 'he had never been able, thanks to the cabals of his enemies, to exercise his divine genius in Vienna, and remained unknown and obscure, like a precious stone which, buried in the bowels of the earth, hides the brilliant prize of its splendour. I can never remember without a sense of exultation and satisfaction that Europe and the whole world owe in great part the exquisite vocal compositions of this wonderful genius solely to my perseverance and firmness.'

Wildly exaggerated though the claim is, it does contain an element of truth, so strong was the cabal working against Mozart. If the fascinating account of the genesis of *Le nozze di Figaro* which Da Ponte gives in the memoirs has even a substratum of truth – and there is no reason why it should not – the librettist played a considerable part in making possible its performance on the stage of the Burgtheater. But, above all, in Da Ponte Mozart had for the first time found an ideal partner.

In letters to his father Mozart expressed in uncompromising terms his criteria for the kind of librettist he was seeking, and for the role which such a poet should play. 'I should say that in an opera the poetry must be altogether the obedient daughter of the music. Why do Italian comic operas please everywhere – in spite of their miserable libretti? . . . Just because there the music reigns supreme and when one listens to it all else is forgotten.' 'The best thing of all,' he wrote in the same letter, 'is when a good composer, who understands the stage and is talented enough to make sound suggestions, meets an able poet, that true phoenix . . .' As Jahn, one of Mozart's earliest biographers, writes, 'The words of an opera have a definite object; they provide foundation and support for the musical expression, and are therefore not absolutely independent, as in the drama, but are obliged to recognize and respect the laws of music, as well as those of poetry . . . The poet must be "intelligent", clever, and cultivated enough to fall in with the intentions of the musician, and poet enough to retain his poetical powers in spite of these limitations.'

It was, presumably, just because Da Ponte was able to meet these requirements that his collaboration with Mozart resulted in three of the most sublime operas which have ever been written. He was not a great poet, or even a very original one; but he had a genius for grasping the needs of the particular composer with whom he was working, and was able, through very great intelligence allied to an extraordinary degree of understanding, to divine what each of them was seeking from his librettist. It is no accident that several of the best-known composers of the day – Martin y Soler, Winter, Salieri, and Mozart himself – wrote their greatest operas to texts by Da Ponte, and that it was for these composers that he himself wrote his best work; good composers inspired him to write good libretti, while for *maestri* of whose work he had a low opinion, or with whom he found collaboration unrewarding, he sometimes wrote extremely bad ones.

Da Ponte has much of great interest to say about the qualities needed to write a satisfactory libretto – qualities which, as he rightly says, few theatre poets of the day possessed, so that excellent composers were forced to marry their music to wretched texts.

If the words of a dramatic poet [he wrote in 1819] are nothing *but a vehicle to the notes, and an opportunity to the action*, what is the reason that a composer of music does not take at once a doctor's recipes, a bookseller's catalogue, or even a spelling book, instead of the verses of a poet, and make them a vehicle to his notes, just as an ass is that of a bag of corn? . . . Mozart knew very well that the success of an opera depends, FIRST OF ALL, ON THE POET: that without a good poem an *entertainment cannot be perfectly dramatic*, just as a picture cannot be good without possessing the merit of invention, design, and a just proportion of the parts: that a composer, who is, in regard to a drama, what a painter is in regard to the colours, can never do that with effect, unless excited and animated by the words of a poet, whose province is to choose a subject susceptible of variety, incident, movement, and action; to prepare, to suspend, to bring about the catastrophe; to exhibit characters interesting, comic, well supported, and calculated for stage effect; to write his recitativo short, but substantial, his airs various, new, and well situated; in fine, his verses easy, harmonious, and almost singing of themselves, without all which requisites, the notes of the most sublime and scientific composer will not be felt by the heart, the passions remaining tranquil, and unmoved, their effect will be transient, and the best of his airs, after a short time, will be heard with no more attention or pleasure, than a trio or a sonata . . .

I think that poetry is the door to music, which can be very handsome, and much admired for its exterior, but no body can see its internal beauties, if the door is wanting.

Some years later, writing in defence of Rossini (of whose music he had a very high opinion), he laid down other criteria for libretti: feeling and heart, liveliness of affection, truth of characterisation, merit of situation, grace of language, poetic imagery, and understanding of how to alternate 'the gentle and the fierce', 'the light-hearted and the pathetic', 'the pastoral and the heroic'. Salieri, Soler and Mozart, he went on, had the great merit of being able to read, 'a merit of which, in truth, not all our composers can boast, some of them not knowing the great difference between the poetry of Metastasio and that of Bertati or Nunziato Porta. I should almost be bold enough to believe that in the twelve operas which I wrote for these three great *maestri* there are not two arias or two so-called concertati which are alike.'

From the days when he was a schoolboy in Ceneda, Da Ponte had studied the poetry and the dramatic texts of the finest writers in the Italian language, for whom he had a respect amounting to adoration; and this fount of knowledge, an integral part of his very being, was accompanied by an ear attuned to verbal and musical beauty and harmony. It has sometimes been said that he was not musical. True, so far as we know he did not play a musical instrument, but at the various seminaries where he had been a pupil or teacher (and at one of which his brother Girolamo was master of the Gregorian chant) he would have taken part in the singing and, with his quickness of learning, have acquired valuable musical experience. As in other aspects of his life, he is exasperatingly reticent about his understanding and love of music, but now and then he lets fall a clue which shows that he had a profound insight into the relationship between words and music in opera. For instance, he wrote, 'In order to translate an opera from one language into another, it is necessary to know more than just how to write verse. One must do it in such a way that the accents of the poetry respond to those of the music, which few can do well, and especially necessary is a musical ear and long experience.' No one who studies his libretti will believe that he was a musical babe in the wood, or that music did not stir him just as deeply as other manifestations of beauty.

Both Mozart and Da Ponte are tantalisingly silent about how they worked together, and virtually nothing is known of their collaboration. Since Mozart was so exacting in what he required from his librettists, it is revealing that the libretti of *Le nozze di Figaro*, *Don Giovanni* and *Così fan tutte* all, in important respects, contradict views which he expressed very forcibly. For instance, as he wrote to his father in 1783, he believed that 'the more comic an Italian opera is the better', whereas Da Ponte was convinced that changes of mood were essential if the listener's sympathies were to be engaged. Such changes of mood occur in all three operas, and it is partly this which makes them immortal, and gives us the feeling that we are watching human beings struggle with real emotions, rather than stock characters. Had Mozart changed his opinion between 1783 and 1785, or was he convinced by Da Ponte's skill and persuasion?

Secondly, Mozart detested rhymes in opera libretti. 'An opera is sure of success,' he wrote to his father, 'when the plot is well worked out, the words written solely for the music and not shoved in here and there to suit some miserable rhyme (which, God knows, never enhances the value of any theatrical performance, be it what it may, but rather detracts from it) – I mean, words or even entire verses which ruin the composer's whole idea. Verses are indeed the most indispensable element for music – but rhymes – solely for the sake of rhyming – the most detrimental.' Yet rhymes – which Da Ponte wrote as easily as he breathed – abound in all three operas, both in the recitatives and in the arias, and give the listener just the same feeling of 'rightness' and completion as when he reads or listens to poetry. Was this again Da Ponte's influence, in showing Mozart that rhyme, as he used it, was functional and had a unique contribution to make?

Then again, as Daniela Goldin points out in an interesting article which throws much light on Da Ponte's work as a librettist (*Da Ponte Librettista fra Goldoni e Casti*), all three texts 'presuppose a detailed knowledge of literary – and theatrical – Italian tradition, which cannot be explained as being within the competence of Mozart'. They show, too, a close acquaintance with colloquial speech, with the modes of expression used by different classes and with other subtleties of language which someone whose native tongue was not Italian, or who had not lived in Italy for a long period of time, would be unlikely to possess. Daniela Goldin also remarks that

> ... according to his dramatic outlines, for Mozart comicality must be expressive, violent, often absurd, *alla* Schikaneder. Da Ponte, on the other hand, is never aggressive or excessively comic, and all his libretti are full of literary, cultured elements, not least because Da Ponte was a convinced Arcadian, as was Goldoni ... But his literary education never allowed Da Ponte to abandon his ideals of metre, of stylistic control or of cultural commitment, even in the texts which apparently are least committed, such as *Il finto cieco*, which in the memoirs Da Ponte describes as a *pasticcio* ... Juvenal, Ovid, Horace, Sannazaro, Dante, Ariosto, etc – poets ancient and modern are used by Da Ponte even in this minor form of literature.

Il finto cieco – a tiresome commission which Da Ponte had to undertake, on Rosenberg's instructions, before embarking on *Le nozze di Figaro* – was by Giuseppe Gazzaniga, whom the librettist calls 'a composer of some merit, but of a style no longer in vogue. In order to get it out of the way as quickly as possible I chose a French comedy entitled *L'aveugle clairvoyant* and dashed out the libretto in a few days. No one liked it, as much because of the words as the music. A passionate attachment to a woman of fifty, which was troubling this brave fellow, prevented him from finishing the opera at the appointed time. So I had to insert in the second act various pieces which he had written twenty years earlier; to take various scenes from other operas, both by him and by other composers; in short, to make a hotchpotch which had neither head nor feet. It was put on three times and then laid to rest.'

The libretto is indeed wretched – one of the worst Da Ponte ever wrote – and quite unlike his other work in that it has a cruel and heartless story with characters who display a total lack of feeling for one another. A second remarkable aspect is the complete freedom

65

between employers and servants, who are rude and overbearing to their social 'betters' – no wonder the aristocracy felt that the whole fabric of society was crumbling.

This disagreeable task out of the way, Da Ponte could fulfil his promise to write an opera for Mozart. It was the composer who suggested *Le mariage de Figaro* as a possible text. It was a risky proposition: Beaumarchais' comedy, which uncompromisingly attacked the *ancien régime*, had been banned for three years in Paris, where it was not performed until 1784. Early in the following year a German company had brought it to Vienna, but the Emperor had given instructions that the censor should either ban it or admit it to the stage only after various licentious elements had been suppressed or altered. How, then, to put it forward to him as the subject of an opera? According to Da Ponte his solution was to write it secretly and present it as a *fait accompli*. His claim in the memoirs that the whole thing, words and music, was completed in six weeks – elsewhere he writes two months – has been instanced as an example of his unreliability; but, as Professor Robbins Landon points out, recent research appears to vindicate his statement and confound his critics.

Mozzart's good luck [Da Ponte writes] was that the theatre lacked a score at this time. Seizing the chance, without a word to anyone I went to the Emperor and showed him *Figaro*. 'What!' he said. 'You know that Mozzart, who is a marvellous composer of instrumental music, has written only one opera, and that wasn't much!' I replied softly, 'Without the clemency of Your Majesty, I too would have written only one opera in Vienna.' 'That is true,' he answered, 'but I forbade the German company to act this *Nozze di Figaro*.' 'Yes,' I said, 'but since I have written an opera and not a play, I have had to omit many scenes and shorten others, and I have omitted or shortened anything which might offend the delicacy and decency of a spectacle at which Your Majesty would be present. As for the music, so far as I can judge it seems to me marvellously beautiful.' 'Very well; if that is the case, I will trust to your taste with regard to the music and to your prudence with regard to the morality. Give it to the copyist.'

I hurried to Mozzart, but before I had finished telling him the good news an imperial page arrived with a letter commanding him to go immediately to the King with the score. He obeyed the command, and played to him various pieces which pleased him immensely and even – it is no exaggeration – filled him with amazement. He had exquisite musical taste, as indeed he had for all the *belle arti*.

So far so good; but Mozart and Da Ponte still had to reckon with the powerful cabal which had no wish that the opera should succeed –

Salieri, Casti, and the whole fry of hangers-on at the court, who loved neither composer nor librettist. According to Da Ponte they saw their opportunity when Francesco Bussani, one of the chief singers (he played both Dr Bartolo and Antonio in the first production of *Figaro*), who was also in charge of the wardrobe and scenery, discovered that a ballet had been introduced at the end of the third act, when Susanna gives the Count a note arranging a rendezvous while a chorus of village maidens presents the Countess with posies of flowers. It so happened that Joseph had recently forbidden ballets in the theatre, and Bussani went with the glad news to Rosenberg. The Count at once sent for Da Ponte:

'So the Signor Poet has introduced a ballet into Figaro?'
'Yes, Your Excellency.'
'The Signor Poet does not know that the Emperor does not wish to have ballets in his theatre?'
'No, Your Excellency.'
'Very well, Signor Poet, I am telling you now.'
'Yes, Your Excellency.'
'And I am further telling you that you must take it out, Signor Poet.'
This 'Signor Poet' was repeated in an expressive tone of voice which seemed to imply 'Signor Donkey' or some such phrase. But my 'Your Excellency' had its own innuendo.
'No, Your Excellency.'
'Have you the libretto with you?'
'Yes, Your Excellency.'
'Where is the ballet scene?'
'Here, Your Excellency.'
'This is how we shall do it.' As he spoke, he tore two sheets out of the play, threw them gently on the fire, gave the libretto back to me and said, 'You see, Signor Poet, that I can do anything,' and honoured me with a second 'Vade'.

Mozart was in despair, but Da Ponte, confident of the Emperor's favour and resourceful as ever, bided his time until the dress rehearsal two days later, at which, according to his custom, Joseph was present, accompanied by Casti and the Viennese nobility.

The opera proceeded to universal applause; but when the third act came to an end

. . . all that could be seen was the Count and Susanna gesticulating, and since the orchestra was silent it looked like a puppet-show. 'What does this mean?' the Emperor asked Casti, who was sitting beside him. 'You must ask the Poet,' the abbé replied with a malicious smile. I was summoned, but instead of replying I gave him my manuscript, to which

I had restored the scene. The Sovereign read it and asked why there was no dancing. My silence told him that there had been some trouble. He turned to Count Rosenberg and asked him to explain, and he muttered that there was no dancing because the opera lacked ballerinas. 'Are there none in the other theatres?' the Emperor asked. 'Yes,' said Rosenberg. 'Very well, then, let Da Ponte have as many as he needs.' In less than half-an-hour twenty-four ballerinas and extras had arrived and the end of the third act, which had been omitted, was repeated. 'That's better!' cried the Emperor. The opera had its *première* on 1 May 1786, and in spite of the 'perhapses' and 'we shall see's' of all the other *maestri* and their partisans, in spite of the Count, of Casti and of a hundred other devils, it met with general approval, and in the opinion of the Sovereign and of the real connoisseurs was regarded as sublime, almost divine.

Even Casti remarked that the libretto contained a few good lines here and there and a few good arias, for after all, he remarked, it was only a translation of Beaumarchais' play. According to Da Ponte, Beaumarchais himself had a different opinion, which he expressed to Salieri. 'I gave a copy of your Figaro to Monsieur De Beaumarchais,' Salieri wrote to Da Ponte from Paris, 'who desired me to thank you kindly for your attention. I met him a few days afterwards, and demanded his opinion. *I admired,* said he, *the art of the Italian poet, in contracting so many Colpi di Scena in so short a time, without the one destroying the other. Had I altered thus a comedy of another author, I would not hesitate a moment to call it my own work.*'

Da Ponte quoted this letter many years later, presumably from memory. Or it is possible that he imagined it had been written, as he may have done in the case of other letters which he reproduces. But to say that *Le nozze di Figaro* is a mere translation of Beaumarchais' play is a travesty of the truth, as Da Ponte himself justly writes: 'A comedy of 230 pages 8vo. in prose, I have reduced to 51 12mo. in verse, and sixteen dramatis personae to eleven: this is calculated by my *friend Observer* a few retrenchments!!!' Though he keeps more closely to the original than in some of his other adaptations, the modifications called for in turning a play into an opera libretto necessitated not only many cuts but also the introduction of new material – arias, ensembles, choruses and recitatives. These not only provide poetry worthy of Mozart's ravishing music but also do much to heighten the character-drawing. Consider, for instance, Cherubino's two lovely arias: the first is an inspired verse adaptation of the cool and elegant French prose, while the second owes nothing at all to Beaumarchais but is pure Da Ponte, as are the Countess's aria *Dove sono i bei momenti*, which gives her such added depth and pathos, Marcellina's aria in defence of women, and Figaro's stirring song as he paints for a horrified Cherubino the glories which await him on the field of battle.

Also, as Da Ponte points out, he omitted or softened passages that might have offended the imperial ears, especially Figaro's verbal duels with the Count. In Beaumarchais the valet is blunt to the point of insolence; in Da Ponte this egalitarian approach is far less marked, which would be in tune with the librettist's own dislike and fear of offending the great. Probably, too, it was to avoid any objection from Joseph that he subtly altered the relationship between the Countess and Cherubino. In Beaumarchais it is plain to see that the page's adoration of his beautiful young godmother, so cruelly neglected by her husband, finds an echo in the Countess, who is more than a little moved by the attentions of this radiantly beautiful boy, suddenly, it would seem, turned into a man capable of rousing the Count to a fury of jealousy. In Da Ponte's text the Countess still treats him as a child – clever, charming, precocious, but a child none the less.

Da Ponte's mastery of his craft is everywhere remarkable in *Figaro*, for, with a text the length of which is a mere fraction of Beaumarchais', nothing of importance is lost from the plot. And there are innumerable Da Pontean touches, such as Figaro's famous aria *Se vuol ballare, Signor Contino*, with the contemptuous diminutive of the title, which was surely inspired by Figaro's remark in the Beaumarchais text, '*Puis dansez, Monseigneur*'. (Twice elsewhere Da Ponte's Figaro ironically remarks that he is making the unconscious Count dance to his tune.) The characters of Susanna and Figaro are sharpened through their racy, colloquial, sometimes vulgar dialogue, and through small but significant linguistic touches such as the change from Suzanne's affectionate '*mon fils*' to her betrothed to Susanna's '*caro il mio Figaretto*', the diminutive, as Daniela Goldin points out, wholly typical of Venice and Goldoni.

The only place, perhaps, where Da Ponte's touch falters is in the last act. In Beaumarchais the Count, making love to the woman whom he believes to be Suzanne, but who is really the Countess in Suzanne's clothes, remarks that he loves his wife dearly but that after three years of marriage their relationship has grown humdrum – you can have a surfeit of being offered love without spice, and women should remember that their duty is not only to catch their husbands but to hold them. 'What a lesson!' the Countess says to herself, not in the least pleased that all the onus of keeping the marriage off the rocks is placed squarely on the wife's shoulders. For some reason Da Ponte omitted this short but telling exchange.

Significantly, though he retained Beaumarchais' names (with the exception of Fanchette, who becomes Barbarina), Italianising them where necessary, he did make one important alteration. When Marcelline and Bartolo discover that Figaro is their long-lost son, Marcelline cries, '*C'est Emmanuel!*' Did Da Ponte feel ghosts walking over his grave? Perhaps he did, for he departed as far from the original as he very well could, making Marcellina exclaim instead, 'Raffaello!'

Since much of the plot hangs on whether or not Count Almaviva shall exercise his *droit de seigneur* and claim the right to deflower Susanna on her wedding night, it is interesting to read a passage from a letter – written in jest or with serious intent? – from the Emperor to Rosenberg five months after the first night of *Figaro*: 'The marriage between Mombelli and Laschi [both principal singers at the Burgtheater – Louisa Laschi was the first Countess Almaviva] may take place without awaiting my return, and on this occasion I cede to you the *droit de Seigneur*.'

Figaro was an undoubted success, though Zinzendorf wrote that it bored him, and (when he saw it again two months later) that the music was 'singular, hands without head'. There were nine performances in 1786, but thereafter it was not revived until 1789.

It was about this time that Da Ponte took up his pen to write another of his rhyming letters, this time to Casti. His contract entitled him to certain monies which the directors of the theatre had withheld from him, and he felt that an appeal to Rosenberg's protégé would be most likely to achieve results. As he writes frankly in the memoirs, it seemed tactful to lace his request with some heavy flattery. The tone of the letter is light-hearted and intimate, such as one would adopt in writing to a friend: 'This is the situation, good Casti; pay attention, because the argument is serious; we are talking about money, which in our day is a rarity, and apparently it is heretical to pay it out for poetry.'

After many flowery phrases in praise of Casti, Da Ponte begs him to intercede with Rosenberg. To his fellow-poet, he continues, he is not ashamed to reveal that his purse is empty, that he has a number of debts, 'an old father who cannot exist on poetry, and nine sisters as well, who are not goddesses living on Parnassus but have limbs, bones, skin, stomachs, mouths, teeth and noses, and who from time to time send me terrible bills which I must pay on the spot in order to avoid disgrace and ruin, so that these good girls, who may become mothers, shall not have to choose the fathers from poetical families.' Casti found the verses 'most beautiful' and recited them to Rosenberg and his friends, and the money owing to Da Ponte was duly paid.

Though doubt has been cast on Da Ponte's assertion that Casti and Rosenberg were in league against him, it seems indisputable that this was the case. While Casti was in Vienna he stayed in the Count's house, and Rosenberg certainly hoped to secure for his friend the post of court poet which had fallen vacant at Metastasio's death, and which Joseph was determined not to fill again. Least of all, according to Da Ponte, did the Emperor want Casti, for 'he loved the poetry but not the man'. Casti, now over sixty, was riddled with syphilis, which had destroyed his palate so that he spoke through his nose. A contemporary who saw him shortly before his death at the age of eighty-three described him as 'a perfect model for the satyrs of old', and his voice that of a satyr too, loud, 'barely human, barely comprehensible'. As Da Ponte wrote on various occasions, Casti would play the part of devil's advocate, praising Da Ponte's libretti yet adding so many 'buts' that the praise was worse than any amount of criticism. 'Da Ponte doesn't know how to write a libretto, but what does that matter? Is it impossible to be a man of worth without knowing how to write libretti?'

Da Ponte's remarks about Casti are always interesting, showing a characteristic readiness – with which his detractors are reluctant to credit him – to give honour to literary excellence. He often refers to Casti's infinite merits as a poet, though he writes disparagingly of his lack of true culture. 'He had,' Da Ponte writes, 'a dictionary-cum-encyclopedia which he referred to when he wanted to know something, when it occurred to him to consult it.' Once, in his capacity as printer of libretti for the opera house, Da Ponte corrected a grammatical mistake in one of Casti's plays, and told Casti why he had done so. Casti 'ran at once to his encyclopedia, found his mistake, gave himself a great slap on the forehead, reddened, thanked me, and insisted that I should accept the encyclopedia as a gift. I kept it for more than twenty-five years, until some greedy hand robbed me of it.'

In other circumstances the two men, both so devoted to literature, such good company, and with such an unquenchable zest for life, might have become good friends. But their rivalry was too bitter, and Da Ponte was certainly right in believing that Casti regarded him as the main obstacle in the race for advancement at the Viennese court. He relates with some resentment the way in which Casti made fun of him in a one-act opera that was performed at the splendid Schoenbrunn palace early in February 1786. The entertainment, given by the Emperor in tribute to the ladies of Vienna, consisted of two one-act pieces, Mozart's *Der Schauspieldirektor* and Salieri's *Prima la musica e poi le parole*. It seems that Casti was commanded by the

Emperor to write the words of the latter to music already composed by Salieri (hence the title), and was highly annoyed at the assignment. 'It was,' writes Da Ponte, 'a real pastiche, without salt, without plan, without characters.' This is sour grapes, for the libretto is witty and skilfully written, taking off with some unkindness temperamental leading ladies but giving a sympathetic portrait of the beleaguered poet who is supposed to provide them with arias which will show off their voices to the best advantage. 'But,' Da Ponte goes on, 'if they imitated my clothes and the way I wore my hair, the rest of the portrait was more of Casti than of me. Among other things he spoke of my amours with the theatrical ladies, but the joke was that he was the protector and the gallant of the two ladies who sang in this farce' – the ladies in question being Nancy Storace, who gave a brilliant take-off of Luigi Marchesi, the most famous counter-tenor of the day, and Celestina Coltellini, another of the Emperor's favourites.

Da Ponte was soon to be delivered from his rival. A year and a half earlier Casti had written a poem entitled *Poema tartaro*, a satire on the court of the Empress Catherine of Russia. At the time it appears that Joseph had been amused, but by 1786 the poem seemed to him politically inexpedient, since he wished to enter into an alliance with Russia and was shortly to visit the court of St Petersburg. Deciding that Casti was now an embarrassment, he 'summoned the Abbé to his box at the opera and gave him six hundred zecchini, saying, "This will meet the expenses of your journey." What a gracious way to give someone his congé! Casti understood what he meant, and some days later left Vienna.' The poet had a passion for travelling, and promptly went off on a long journey: he was never to see the Emperor again.

What must be taken with great reserve in Da Ponte's memoirs are the passages in which he implies that Rosenberg was not totally in the Emperor's confidence. Chaser of *filles* the Count may have been, but he was also a wise statesman, a perfect courtier, and above all a true and devoted servant. Joseph trusted him implicitly, and on his deathbed wrote him a deeply moving letter of gratitude for his constant friendship and loyalty.

VII

Da Ponte tackled his next commission with extreme reluctance. So many influential *maestri* were pressing him to write libretti for them, or else the leading gentlemen of Vienna were putting forward the claims of their particular protégés, that he was not free to choose those whose music he preferred and with whom he could work most harmoniously and fruitfully. One of the most insistent was Salieri, who, his vows forgotten, now wanted Da Ponte to write a text for him, but who meanwhile asked him to prepare an opera for Vincenzo Righini, a successful teacher of professional singers as well as a composer. He played an important role in Vienna, for he and Da Ponte were together responsible for the opera house when Salieri was in Paris. So, though Da Ponte writes with a certain smugness that he agreed to Salieri's request because, 'in view of his good offices in recommending me as poet, it seemed the honourable thing to please him', no doubt he also had an eye to expediency.

The opera was *Il demogorgone ovvero Il filosofo confuso*. It was just as big a failure as the librettist had foreseen, and after four performances disappeared from the repertoire. A more accurate title, Da Ponte writes, would have been 'The composer and the poet punished in turn . . . Righini's friends put the blame on the words; I blamed the music and the composer's worthless ideas, which suffocated my poetic soul.'

Kelly, who sang the chief role, writes in his *Reminiscences*,

In his opera, there was a character of an amorous eccentric poet, [1] which was allotted to *me*; at the time I was esteemed a good mimic, and particularly happy in imitating the walk, countenance, and attitudes of those whom I wished to resemble. My friend, the poet, had a remarkably awkward gait, a habit of throwing himself (as he thought) into a graceful attitude, by putting his stick behind his back, and leaning on it; he had also a very peculiar, rather dandyish way of dressing; for in sooth the Abbé stood mighty well with himself, and had the character of a consummate coxcomb; he had also a strong lisp and broad Venetian accent.

The first night of the performance, he was seated in the boxes, more

[1] Not a poet but a philosopher, who is made to look singularly ridiculous.

conspicuously than was absolutely necessary, considering he was the author of the piece to be performed. As usual, on the first night of a new opera, the Emperor was present, and a numerous auditory. When I made my *entrée* as the amorous poet, dressed exactly like the Abbé in the boxes, imitating his walk, leaning on my stick, and aping his gestures and his lisp, there was a universal roar of laughter and applause; and after a buzz round the house, the eyes of the whole audience were turned to the place where he was seated. The Emperor enjoyed the joke, laughed heartily, and applauded frequently during the performance; the Abbé was not at all affronted, but took my imitation of him in good part, and ever after we were on the best of terms.

Kelly died in 1826, and it is unlikely that he ever came across a small book which Da Ponte published in New York in that same year, containing the text of four of his libretti. In this he speaks with great rancour of the Irishman, whose reminiscences he describes as a farrago of nonsense. Apostrophising Kelly in the brief introduction to *Le nozze di Figaro*, he writes,

> The jests and the romantic nonsense which you wrote, or *had written for you* [Kelly's book was 'ghosted'], in your ridiculous book, are so worthless that it is a waste of time for a man of any sense to give himself the trouble of denying them; I know that a man of your *mimicking* nature believes he can say anything and everything, however false, because what he says will make people laugh: I shall take care, however, to make it clear to others, and above all to those who do not know you, even if not to you yourself, that everything you have said about me in your crazy book contains not one syllable of truth, and that if it had been the truth you would have been the last to publish it.

Whatever the front which Da Ponte managed to put on at the first performance of *Il demogorgone*, he of all people, to whom appearances were so important, would have disliked being made to look a fool. But his bitterness forty years later had a special edge because when he fled from Vienna to England, penniless and without work, Kelly, who then occupied an influential position in the operatic world in London, apparently did nothing to help him.

So after this it was an especial pleasure to turn to the composer with whom he had had his first great success, and who had become a close friend, Martin y Soler. To revenge himself on his enemies he decided, with Soler's connivance, to play a trick on them. Stephen Storace, Nancy's brother, had also obtained permission from the Emperor that Da Ponte should write a text for him. So Da Ponte embarked simultaneously on two libretti, one for Storace and the other for Soler. However, he did not tell anyone about the latter, and

Soler kept mum about it too. Entering into the fun, he pretended that he was angry with Da Ponte for being so slow about producing the text, and gave out that he was meanwhile setting to music a libretto which another poet had sent him from Venice.

To please him and also the Spanish Ambassador's wife, who was his patron [Da Ponte wrote], I decided to choose a Spanish subject, which greatly pleased both Martini and the Emperor, to whom I confided my secret, of which he warmly approved. After reading a number of Spanish comedies, in order to learn a little about the drama of that country, I found one which I liked very much, a comedy by Calderon[1] entitled *La luna de la Sierra*; and, taking from it the historical background and some of the character-drawing, I painted my canvas, in which I was able to give the best singers in the company a chance to shine . . . I called the opera *Una cosa rara ossia Bellezza ed onestà*, following this title with the famous line of the satirist, *Rara est concordia formae atque pudicitiae*.

Armed with Guevara's text, he set swiftly to work. 'Never in my life have I written poetry so quickly and with such pleasure. Whether it was my affection for the composer, who had brought into my life the first gleams of encouragement and of glory in the theatre, or the desire to strike my unjust persecutors a mortal blow, or the nature of the theme, so poetical and delightful – whatever the reason, I finished the opera in thirty days, and the excellent composer finished the music at the same time.' The singers who were to take part 'had their usual battles with the composer even before they were given their parts', but Da Ponte they could not trouble as they did not know who the librettist was.

As soon as the parts were distributed, all hell was let loose. Some of the singers had too many recitatives, some not enough; one had an aria which was too low, another one which was too high; some of them did not sing in the ensembles, others sang in them too much; one singer was sacrificed to the *prima donna*, another took second fiddle to the first, second, third and fourth *buffi*; there were endless fireworks. However, everyone said (in the belief that they were dealing a death-blow to Martini and me, since they had no idea that I had written the words) that the poetry was lovely, the characters interesting, the subject quite new; that the play, in short, was a masterpiece but the music unutterably feeble and trivial. 'Take a lesson, Da Ponte,' one singer said to me in all seriousness, 'in how to write a comic opera.' You can imagine how I laughed. At last matters came to a head. Nearly all of them handed their

[1] Here Da Ponte's memory is at fault. The play is by Luis Vélez de Guevara, a popular poet and dramatist. *La luna de la Sierra* was one of his best works.

75

parts back to the copyist and told Martini that this wasn't their kind of music and they didn't want to sing it . . .

The news of this theatrical insurrection reached the ears of the Emperor, who sent for Martini and me and asked us to tell him all about it. I ventured to assure him that the singers had never been presented in an opera which showed them to better advantage than did my libretto, and that Vienna had never before heard music so charming, so pleasing, so new and so popular. He asked to see the libretto, which luckily [!] I had with me. By chance it opened at the first finale, which ended with these lines:

> But what is done, is done,
> And cannot be undone. [1]

'Nothing could be more appropriate,' Joseph exclaimed with a smile. He took a pencil and wrote:

'Dear Count, Tell my singers that I have heard their complaints about Martini's opera, which I greatly regret, but that "What is done, is done, and cannot be undone." Joseph.'

I immediately sent this note to Count Rosenberg, who had it read that same day to the singers at the rehearsal. When they heard the royal decree they were frightened, but it didn't make them any less angry. They took back their parts, but went on complaining, criticising and fulminating against the Spaniard and his music. The evening of the *première* arrived. The theatre was full, most of the audience being composed of enemies ready to hiss. However, right from the beginning of the performance they found such grace, sweetness and melody in the music, and such novelty and interest in the words, that they seemed to be overcome by an ecstasy of pleasure. A silence, a degree of attention never before accorded to an Italian opera, was followed by a storm of applause and exclamations of delight and pleasure. Everyone understood the intrigues of the cabal, and with one accord clapped and praised.

After the first act the ladies in the boxes asked who the poet was. Since they had heard Casti and his satellites speak so slightingly of my dramatic skill, it did not occur to anyone that I could be the author, and although the style of *Una cosa rara* was not unlike that of *Burbero*, *Figaro* and my other early plays, in the whole of Vienna it was only Kelly, though he was neither educated nor well-read, who realised the similarity, and one day, without beating about the bush, he said to me, 'Admit that you wrote the libretto, Da Ponte.' I begged him not to arouse the suspicions of the others by talking about it. He said nothing: and I, to colour my joke the better, kept my name off most of the libretti which, for the benefit of the audience, are usually sold in the theatre.

However, I had confided the secret to Signor Lerchenheim, the

[1] '*Ma quel ch'è fatto, è fatto,*
E non si può cangiar.'

secretary to the Emperor's cabinet and a particular friend of mine. He walked among the beauties in the parterre and listened to what they were saying. He told them that the poet was a Venetian who was then in Vienna, and that at the end of the performance they would be able to see him. 'This is the poet,' they exclaimed, 'whom we should like to have for our theatre, and we'll ask the Emperor himself to engage him, if necessary.' 'It won't be necessary,' said my friend, 'because the Emperor has already engaged him.' The lovely ladies were delighted to hear this, and the second act began, which had as great a success as the first, or perhaps even greater. In particular one of the duets seemed to electrify the audience and fill them with a kind of heavenly fire. Joseph was the first to demand an encore, breaking a rule which he had made a few days earlier forbidding ensembles to be encored. [This was after the first two or three performances of *Le nozze di Figaro*, when encore after encore was demanded.]

When the performance was over Signor Lerchenheim presented me to the ladies who wanted a new poet for their theatre, and told them that I was the author of the libretto. Impossible to say which was the greater, my amusement or their confusion and surprise. They asked why I had kept my name such a jealous secret. 'To make the cabal blush,' Signor Lerchenheim replied graciously. Then I went to see my theatrical colleagues, and presented each of them with a libretto which bore my name in capital letters. No words can describe their confusion . . .

But all this amusement was nothing in comparison with the real pleasure which I felt at the happy outcome of this opera. The Germans, naturally kind and hospitable, who until now had taken little notice of me, thanks to the censure of my enemies and the praises, seasoned with 'buts', lavished on me by Casti, vied with one another to make amends for the wrong they had done me with marks of courtesy, embraces and kindly welcomes. The ladies in particular, who wanted to see only *Cosa rara* and to dress in the fashion of *Cosa rara*, really did believe that there were two *cose rare* – Martini and myself. We could have had more amorous adventures than all the Knights of the Round Table could have had in twenty years. No one talked of anything but us or praised anyone except us; this opera had performed the conjuring trick of disclosing graces, beauties, rarities which had never been seen in us before and which were not to be found in other men. We were invited for drives, lunches, suppers, trips into the country and fishing expeditions, and regaled with sugary love letters, enigmatic verses, and so on and so on.

The Spaniard, who was delighted by it all, took advantage of everything. As for me, I laughed, reflected on the human heart, and decided if possible to write another *Cosa rara*, all the more so because Caesar, after giving me conspicuous marks of his approval, advised me to write another opera without delay 'for this brave Spaniard'. Count Rosenberg also (perhaps because Casti had already left Vienna) became more amenable and, meeting me a few days later, stopped me, gave me his hand, with a friendly air which seemed to be sincere, and said, 'Bravo, Signor Da Ponte! You have excelled our expectations.' I inclined my head, but said frankly, 'Your Excellency, not much was needed to do that.'

Da Ponte did not exaggerate the success of *Una cosa rara*, which caused a sensation. The melodic ease and charm of the music conquered both the Emperor and the Viennese audience, who preferred its simpler line to the complexities of *Le nozze di Figaro*, which it immediately overshadowed. (Mozart said of Soler's music that in many ways it was really very pretty, 'but in ten years nobody will take any notice of it'.) And the libretto, though it lacks the depths of character-drawing, refinement and poetry which Da Ponte achieved in his operas for Mozart, is both gay and touching, with some charming arias.

As so often with Da Ponte's libretti, the accusation is made by some of his critics that he copied his text almost word for word from the Spanish. In fact, with his customary skill in compressing and adapting, and in providing new material to draw the whole libretto together, he has created a completely different play. He has reduced the original thirteen characters to seven, and has eliminated the political aspect – the conquest of the Moors; and though he retains the broad outlines of the plot (which relates how a lovely Spanish maiden of the sierra keeps her purity and her troth to her affianced despite the fierce assault on her virtue by the Infante), his libretto otherwise bears little relation to Guevara's, which is full of enormously long and stately speeches that would be impossible for an opera.

Una cosa rara was repeated many times at the Burgtheater and in every musical capital in Europe until about 1825. It brought Vienna almost to a state of frenzy when it was performed there in 1786, and at each performance three to four hundred people who crowded to buy tickets had to go home disappointed.

Five weeks later saw the first night of *Gli equivoci*, the opera by Stephen Storace on which Da Ponte had also been working. For this the composer and poet, in compliment to Storace's English origins, chose an adaptation of Shakespeare's *Comedy of Errors*, basing their text on a French translation entitled *Les Méprises*. Storace – a pupil and a great friend of Mozart, by whom his music was much influenced – seemed to have a brilliant career before him, but he died while he was still quite young. Kelly describes him as 'the most gifted creature I ever met with . . . a genius. But in music and painting he was positively occult. His was a soul of melody, and melody is the rarest gift a composer can possess, and one which few attain to.'

Nancy Storace and Kelly both sang leading parts. Kelly praised the libretto, declaring that the poet had made the play 'operational', and adapted it with great ingenuity. 'He retained all the main incidents and characters of our immortal bard; it became the rage ... the music of Storace was beyond description beautiful.' The opera has a particular interest in that it is believed to be one of the very earliest operatic adaptations of Shakespeare; and anyone who compares the two texts must admire the immensely skilful manner in which Da Ponte has shortened and adapted the complicated plot.

In 1936 Alfred Einstein wrote of it,

> Da Ponte's effort was modest,[1] but one must give him the credit for having made a delicious *opera buffa* out of Shakespeare's comedy. He knew his trade ... To follow step by step the methods by which [he] converts Shakespeare's five acts into two would be tantamount to writing a short study of the dramatic technique of the opera libretto – a technique from which many a librettist of the twentieth century could learn much. The principal thing is that Da Ponte has seized the opportunity to introduce arias and build up ensembles. He is at his best in the finales ... Da Ponte has a peculiar appreciation of all that is most beautiful, most Shakespearean in Shakespeare's comedy ...

The opera seems to have had a mild success, though Joseph disliked one aria so much that he had it removed. It was, however, performed only four times, though it was revived for another seven performances in 1790.

The year 1786 was indeed an astonishing one for Da Ponte. Between January and December – the Burgtheater was open the whole year, except for the six weeks of Lent, and there were eleven to fifteen performances each month – twenty-two Italian operas were staged, ten of them entirely new. Of these ten, Da Ponte wrote the libretti for no fewer than six, including one of the greatest operas ever written and one of the most spectacular operatic successes of the last quarter of the eighteenth century. He must have been closely concerned also in the adaptation and staging of the others, since that was part of the poet's task. It was a staggering achievement, and marked the apex of his Vienna period.

His next assignment he disliked as much as he had done the ill-fated *Il demogorgone*. The composer was Francesco Piticchio, whose six operas have disappeared into limbo, and the libretto, entitled *Il*

---

[1] The choice of this adjective is puzzling, as Einstein himself makes clear in the rest of the quoted passage; Da Ponte's adaptation achieves far more than the word 'modest' implies.

Bertoldo, was based on a text by Gaetano Brunati, a very minor poet indeed, and 'it went to rack and ruin, as was to be expected. Apart from the difficulty of writing poetry for a wretched composer, infinitely worse was the difficulty of having to write new words for music already written for wretched words by Brunati. That was enough to know what its destiny would be. Two or three days afterwards I saw the Emperor. "Da Ponte," he said, "write texts for Mozzart, for Martini, for Salieri! But never again write for this Potacci, Petecchi, Pitocchi, Peticchi, or whatever he calls himself! Casti was craftier than you; he only wrote plays for a Paisiello or a Salieri."'

Il Bertoldo was performed eight times within two months, and despite its inordinate length, ridiculous plot and indifferent libretto – which, however, was cleverly adapted from Brunati's original text – was reasonably popular. It seems that Piticchio's music suited the taste of his audience. What is quite remarkable about the libretto – and perhaps helps to explain why it found favour with Viennese audiences – is the uncompromisingly egalitarian note which it strikes in regard to the relationship between the king and one of his subjects, the eponymous protagonist: a humble shepherd, he nevertheless believes that all men are created equal, and fearlessly expresses this conviction to the king.

Da Ponte gives a lively account of the venture (or rather, three simultaneous ventures) which followed – an account that should perhaps be taken with a large pinch of salt:

> I felt it was high time to revive the poetic inspiration which seemed to dry up entirely when I wrote for Reghini and Peticchio.[1] I had my opportunity when all three of the much-praised *maestri*, Martini, Mozzart and Salieri, came to me and asked for a libretto. I liked and respected all three of them, and with all three hoped to repair the recent failure and add to my theatrical reputation. Would it be possible, I wondered, to please all three of them and write three operas at once? Salieri did not want an original text. In Paris he had written the music for the opera *Tarare*, and he wished to turn it into a play with Italian words and music, so he wanted me to do a free translation. Mozzart and Martini left it entirely to me what to choose. For Mozzart I chose *Don Giovanni*, which pleased him enormously, and for Martini *L'arbore di Diana*, for I wanted to give him a charming theme, suited to his beautiful melodies, which linger in the mind, but which few can imitate.

[1] Da Ponte's spelling of Righini and Piticchio. To the day of his death he always wrote Mozzart.

Having decided on the three themes I went to the Emperor, told him of my plan and said that I intended to write the three operas simultaneously. 'You won't succeed!' he replied. 'Perhaps not,' I answered, 'but I shall try. At night I shall write for Mozzart and imagine I'm reading Dante's *Inferno*. In the morning I shall write for Martini, and feel as if I'm studying Petrarch. In the evening it will be Salieri's turn, and that shall be my Tasso.' He liked my parallel; and as soon as I was at home again I began to write. I went to my desk and stayed there for twelve hours without a break. A bottle of Tokay on my right, the ink-well in the middle and a box of Seville snuff on my left. A beautiful young girl of sixteen (whom I would have liked to love simply as a daughter, but . . .) lived in the house with her mother, who looked after the family, and she came into the room whenever I rang the bell, which in fact I did pretty often, and especially when it seemed to me that my inspiration was beginning to cool: she would bring me a sweet biscuit, a cup of coffee, or only her beautiful face, always gay, always laughing, and created especially to awaken poetic inspiration and witty ideas. I went on working for twelve hours every day, with brief intervals, for two months without a pause, and all this time she stayed in the next room, with a book or some sewing or embroidery, ready to come to me at the first sound of the bell. Sometimes she sat close to me, absolutely still, without opening her mouth or blinking an eyelid, looking steadily at me, smiling cajolingly, sighing, and now and then seemingly on the verge of tears: in short, this girl was my Calliope for the three operas, as she was for all the poetry which I wrote for the whole of the next six years.

At first I permitted these visits quite often; later I had to make them less frequent, so as not to lose too much time in amorous dallying, of which she was a perfect mistress. On the first day, meanwhile, between the Tokay, the snuff, the coffee, the bell and my young muse, I wrote the first two scenes of *Don Giovanni*, two of *L'arbore di Diana*, and more than half the first act of *Tarar*, the title of which I changed to *Azzur*. Next morning I took these scenes to the three composers, who could hardly believe the evidence of their eyes, and in sixty-three days the first two operas were finished and almost two-thirds of the last.

A few pages later in the memoirs there is a slightly different account of the genesis of *L'arbore di Diana*, the first of the three operas to be performed; this suggests that its inspiration was somewhat more haphazard than the passage quoted above suggests. Two or three days before Da Ponte gave the first part of the script to Martin y Soler, he writes, Signor Lerchenheim, who had been so helpful at the *première* of *Cosa rara*, and who was a great friend and admirer of Soler's, visited him with the composer and asked when Soler would be able to see some of the libretto. 'The day after tomorrow,' Da Ponte answered. 'Then the subject has been chosen?' 'Of course,' Da Ponte replied – though in fact he hadn't the slightest idea what it was going to be about. 'The title?' *'L'arbore di Diana.'* 'Have you written the synopsis yet?' 'Don't worry about that,' Da Ponte answered, playing for time.

By a lucky chance supper was served at that moment, and he invited his two visitors to stay, assuring them that after supper he would show them the synopsis. Telling them that he had something to see to, he left them with his beautiful young muse and his brother – it seems that his half-brothers Agostino and Paolo were living with him at this time, and that Paolo was studying music – and went into the adjoining room. In less than half-an-hour he had written out the whole synopsis, much to the delight of his guests.

It was, he says, on a theme which, besides 'having some merit of novelty', admirably fitted certain policies of Joseph, who during his reign gradually closed the monasteries. It tells of Diana, goddess of chastity, who has in her garden a miraculous apple tree hung with enormous golden apples. If any of her nymphs pass under this tree who are not absolutely pure, the apples turn black and fall on the offending lady. Love, regarding this as an intolerable outrage, so arranges things that not only all the nymphs fall in love with various shepherds who invade the garden, but even Diana herself succumbs to the wooing of Endymion. So, in order to avoid discovery, she orders that the tree shall be uprooted.

The opera had its first performance on 1 October 1787, as part of the festivities to celebrate the arrival in Vienna of the Archduchess Maria Theresa, the daughter of Joseph's brother Leopold and the bride of Prince Anton of Saxony. It was almost as great a success as *Una cosa rara*, and was performed not only in Vienna but in opera houses the length and breadth of Europe; before the end of the century it had been heard in Leipzig, Milan, Trieste, Passau, Madrid, Warsaw, Barcelona, Rotterdam and London.

So far as is known, the libretto is not based on an earlier text but is original – though both in the words and in the music it has echoes of *Una cosa rara*. Da Ponte writes in his memoirs that he thought it the best of all his libretti, both for the invention and for the poetry, 'voluptuous without being lascivious, and holding the interest'. There was, however, some criticism of its licentiousness – one contemporary pamphlet describes it as 'a miserable botched-up piece of *double entendre*, smut and abomination' – and certainly it is full of equivocal remarks which the audience would have understood and enjoyed. It is light-hearted, with a nonsense of a plot, little attempt at characterisation and few of the changes of mood on which Da Ponte laid such stress. (At one point the nymphs exclaim, *'Che scompiglio! che disordine!'* – 'What a muddle! what confusion!' – and they are absolutely right.) However, it is written with great skill, with a charming lilt, and with a gaiety which clearly appealed to contemporary audiences. Visually it must have been splendid, with many opportunities for spectacular stage effects and machinery, including, it would seem, one of the first attempts to produce a revolving stage. Certainly the Emperor liked it, for the theatre accounts show that on 'instructions from the highest quarter' Da Ponte was given an extra payment for the libretto.

One small but interesting point is the recurrence of a phrase of which Da Ponte was particularly fond, and which epitomises so neatly his own life – '*Quanto è possente amor!*', 'How powerful is love!'. The phrase first occurred in the sonnet which he and his friend Michele Colombo had written together for their rector at Ceneda, and it was to appear yet again in one of his London texts, *Il trionfo dell'amor fraterno*, as well as in the second edition of the memoirs.

L'arbore di Diana is also noteworthy because, when it was revived in the following year, it brought to Vienna the woman who became Da Ponte's third passionate love and the source of many of his later misfortunes. This was Adriana Gabrieli, known as La Ferrarese because she was born in Ferrara. In about 1770, at the age of fifteen or so, she had been admitted to the *Conservatorio dei mendicanti* in Venice, where, like the other inmates, she was given a thorough education in singing. When he visited the *conservatorio* in that same year Burney wrote, 'One of [the girls], la Ferrarese, sung very well, and had a very extraordinary compass of voice, as she was able to reach the highest E of our harpsichords, upon which she could dwell a considerable time in a fair, natural voice.' We next hear of her ten years later, in a letter from Casanova to Count von Smecchia, the Venetian consul in Trieste: 'The son of the Roman consul in Venice,' he writes, 'has fled with two young women from the *ospitale dei mendicanti*, Adriana la Ferrarese and Bianchi Sacchetti. The father has had them followed. That is all I know.' Presumably the runaways were not caught, for fifteen months later Zaguri wrote to Casanova, 'I don't know where the Ferrarese is, but I believe in Pesaro, and well, with the consul's son, her husband.' [1]

She soon made a European reputation, singing in London in 1785 and 1786, where she was much applauded (though Earl Mount Edgcumbe, an opera enthusiast who was closely connected with the King's Theatre, the home of Italian opera in England, was lukewarm about her talents). She was in Milan for the 1787 season, and came on to Vienna in 1788; here she sang the roles of Nancy Storace, who

---

[1] His name was Luigi del Bene.

had recently left for England. Joseph, who never liked her, wrote, *'Elle a une voie assez foible de Contrealt; sait tres bien la musique mais est d'une laide figure'*, but in Zinzendorf's opinion she sang ravishingly and was an adequate actress. Contemporary newspaper articles remarked on her extraordinary range, as Burney had done, from an incredible top note to an astonishingly low one, and on her ability to sing *prima buffa* parts as well as dramatic coloratura ones. Her appearance in *L'arbore di Diana* must have created a sensation; the *Rapport von Wien* commented, 'Connoisseurs of music claim that not within living memory has such a voice been heard within the walls of Vienna'.

In his memoirs Da Ponte makes no reference to her until some time later, but from what he writes then it seems as if they became lovers soon after her arrival in Vienna. This is what he says: 'Unhappily for me, a singer came to Vienna who, without being particularly beautiful, entranced me with her singing; so, since she showed a great liking for me, I ended by falling in love with her. She did in point of fact have great merits. Her voice was a delight, her method new and marvellously affecting; her figure was not especially pleasing and she was not a particularly good actress, but with two ravishing eyes and a charming mouth, there were few operas in which she did not please immensely.' There seems no doubt that in the early days La Ferrarese was popular with the Viennese audiences; but, like Angiola and Angioletta before her, she had an impulsive, violent, jealous disposition, and these traits, added to Da Ponte's exaggerated and ill-advised partisanship, aroused the envy and dislike of the other singers and the hostility of the directors of the opera house.

However, for the moment all went well, as Da Ponte embarked on the next of his three 'simultaneous' operas. This was the second of his Mozart libretti, in the writing of which, as he had told the Emperor, he would imagine that he was reading Dante's *Inferno*. The Don Juan theme which, according to the memoirs, he suggested to the composer (although, writing in 1819, he says that it was Domenico Guardasoni, the impresario of the Prague theatre, who proposed this subject to Mozart) had been treated by innumerable dramatists and librettists in the past. For his own version Da Ponte drew heavily on the one-act opera by Giovanni Bertati, with music by Giuseppe Gazzaniga, a minor but popular composer, which had first been performed in Venice earlier in the year. Bertati, who had been educated at Treviso seminary, but many years before Da Ponte taught there, worked mainly for the Venice theatres. He was a mediocre poet (Zaguri spoke disparagingly of his 'wretched libretti'), but he possessed an excellent sense of stagecraft and plot construction.

Mozart's opera was to have its *première* in Prague, where the composer's music was cherished infinitely more than in Vienna – according to the press, *Figaro* had a greater success there than any previous opera. So, says Da Ponte, when Guardasoni asked Mozart to write an opera, the composer had no hesitation in coming to him for the libretto. The first performance was scheduled for mid-October 1787, and Mozart, having written most of the music, went off to Prague with Da Ponte following immediately after the Vienna *première* of *L'arbore di Diana*.

Tantalisingly, he tells us nothing about the rehearsals, only that, 'I stayed there eight days to direct the actors who were playing in it, but before it was performed I had to return to Vienna'; but from other sources two fascinating sidelights are thrown on the opera. The first relates to Casanova. Sebastiano Foscarini having died in 1785, he was now librarian to Count Waldstein, whose castle was at Dux, near Prague. Through the years since the opera was written he and the Don Juan prototype have become synonymous, while the rascally Leporello is an echo of Casanova's equally rascally servant Costa. It is known that Casanova was at the first performance of *Don Giovanni*, so what must have been his thoughts as he watched this portrait created by the friend who knew him so well? It is even possible that Casanova was with Mozart and Da Ponte when they were putting the finishing touches to score and text, for among his papers at Dux there is a sketch, in his handwriting, of what appears to be an alternative version of the escape scene. No one knows how or why it came into being.

Nor will anyone know to what extent Da Ponte was reminded of Casanova as he painted his picture of Don Giovanni, but there are many striking parallels. In the opera Giovanni exclaims to Leporello, 'Women are more necessary to me than the bread I eat or the air I breathe!' Perhaps, during their long conversations in Vienna, Casanova had expressed exactly these sentiments to Da Ponte, for in his autobiography he wrote, 'The chief business of my life has always been to indulge my senses; I never knew anything of greater importance. I felt myself born for the fair sex, and I have been loved by it as often and as much as I could.' In this sentence he sums up one of the great differences between himself and Da Ponte, who have often been compared – generally to Da Ponte's disadvantage – but who were, in fact, so little alike in many respects; for Casanova, in the midst of his delight in women and his desire to give and to receive sexual pleasure, had a cold, almost brutal attitude towards them, regarding them simply as essential and delectable objects with which he could indulge himself at will, constantly promising marriage (as Don Giovanni promises Donna Elvira and Zerlina), but, once he had effected his conquest, leaving them without a backward glance. So far as we know, Da Ponte never did this in his life.

Also of great interest are two passages from a little book called *Rococo-Bilder*, published in 1870. It is by Alfred Meissner, whose grandfather, August Gottlieb Meissner, was appointed Professor of Classical Literature and Aesthetics at Prague University in 1783, and it records many conversations between grandfather and grandson. Two of these concern encounters which Alfred Meissner claims that his grandfather had with the composer and librettist of *Don Giovanni*. It is inconceivable that these meetings can have taken place exactly as Alfred Meissner relates them, for, although Mozart is known to have been in Prague at the time when both are supposed to have occurred, everything we know of Da Ponte's movements indicates that he was not. In the first conversation some of the comments which Professor Meissner apparently repeated to his grandson echo passages in Da Ponte's memoirs, which had appeared in German in an abridged form in 1861, so the younger Meissner may in part have been repeating what he had read. Nevertheless, partially spurious or not, these narratives have their own fascination; for it is perfectly plausible that on the second occasion the professor did indeed meet Da Ponte in Prague, or talked to other people who had done so, for his lively portrait both reinforces what is known about the librettist and convinces enough to suggest new facets of his complex personality.

In the first passage Professor Meissner describes how he attended a magnificent ball given in Prague in the house of Baron Bretfeld von Kronenberg, who was also a professor at Prague University. There were two people present whom the company seemed to regard with particular interest. One of them was very vivacious and appeared to be unaware of the attention he aroused:

> He was thickset, inclined to corpulence, rather short, barely over thirty, wearing his unusually thick hair in a big knot; it was Mozart, whose *Marriage of Figaro* had not long since been performed in Prague and caused a furore . . . [1]
>
> The second stranger – a man in his forties – who seemed to be paying court collectively to the singers who were there, was small, slender, with quicksilver movements and dark, fiery, southern eyes. Unlike Mozart, he seemed always to be watching to see what impression he was making.

[1] Mozart is known to have been at this ball.

His broken German showed that he was Italian, people called him Abbé, but that didn't necessarily mean he was a priest. In France and Italy the term Abbé or Abbate is used for people who were originally destined for a priestly profession, or who had studied at a theological college, in the hope that the ruler would give them a real share, that is a specific share, in the income of some monastery. They constituted a special class of society; some of them were rich, some poor, some distinguished, others humble; they were family friends of the household. Curls wound round in a knot, a short brown, purple or black habit, and the Abbé was ready . . .

[The Baron] took the arm of the stranger with the southern eyes. 'I like your friend Mozart very much,' he said. 'He is a true Viennese, always in good spirits, *bon enfant*, and, incidentally, wonderful at dancing the minuet, which is no mean thing!'

'Oh, my dear Amadeo is always happy when he comes to Prague!' the stranger answered. 'Prague is close to his heart. *Prende cuore, piglia animo.* He knows that here he will be among friends who – how do you say it? – understand how to appreciate him, value him, prize him . . .'

'Indeed, I believe that Prague esteems him more than Vienna,' the Baron suggested.

'Oh, in Vienna he is a buried jewel. I do everything in my power to advance him, to bring his genius *al lume del giorno* – but this great talent, beautiful as the day, *bello come il sole, splendide come l'astro del giorno*, has to battle with thick air, *colla nebbia dei giudizzi*, with lack of understanding and malice. Oh, and that often puts him in a bad mood . . .'

'Indeed, you are a true friend to him,' answered the Baron. 'I have heard that without your energy and persistence *Figaro*, which we all love so much, would never have been performed.'

'No, never. Beaumarchais' play, on which I based the opera, was regarded as immoral, indecent, dreadful. And then there were the cabals to be reckoned with. It took all my determination and strength to surmount the *impedimenti*. I had an audience with His Majesty, who made his personal *decisione* – '

The second passage in *Rococo-Bilder* relates to the composition of the overture to *Don Giovanni*. This, as all the world knows, was not written until just before the first performance, which in the event was delayed for a fortnight until 29 October 1787. Da Ponte himself says that he spent only a week in Prague – that is, until about the middle of the month, when he had to hurry back to Vienna; is it conceivable that, if he was still there on the day before the *première*, he would not have stayed on for another thirty-six hours or so, in order to be present? Yet from his memoirs it is clear that he did not do so. Nevertheless, the passage is worth quoting in part for the interesting and, one feels, convincing picture which it draws of both Da Ponte and Casanova.

On a balmy autumn day, Professor Meissner told his grandson, Mozart and Da Ponte went together to the country house on the outskirts of Prague belonging to the Duscheks, both musicians and close friends of Mozart: when he was in Prague he always spent much time with them. Although winter was coming on, it was still warm and beautiful. 'The trees had lost nearly all their leaves, but the sky shone clear and blue on the earth below and people lingered happily in the open air with the feeling that days like this were a rare blessing . . .'

> A couple of days before the *première* a great party of people had come by carriage to the Duscheks' house, which was not far from Koschirsch – the impresarios Bondini and Guardasoni, the singer Luigi Bassi and the three women singers, Saporiti, Bondini [the impresario's wife] and Micelli [who at the Prague performance took the roles, respectively, of Don Giovanni, Donna Anna, Zerlina and Donna Elvira], the last-named with her mother. Da Ponte was there too, and he had brought with him a certain Signor Casanova.
>
> Afternoon coffee had been drunk in a big room on the ground floor, and everyone was getting gayer and gayer. Mozart, in the knowledge that he had written an immortal work, sure of its success, moved about with a godlike freedom and ease, the pure horizons of his soul unshadowed by even the smallest cloud. An optimist in the best sense of the word, full of a naïve joy in the world and all that is beautiful in it, without envy because he was without rivals, with an almost childlike candour, he anticipated the day of the *première* as though it were a carnival. He paid extravagant court to the ladies, played all kinds of tricks, talked in rhyme, which gave him especial pleasure, and everyone let him do anything he wanted as if he were a child or a very young man.

Meissner goes on to say that the only people who were not in a good humour were the young baritone Bassi,

> . . . very handsome but stupid beyond words, who was annoyed because he didn't have a single good, big aria, and the two impresarios Bondini and Guardasoni, who were only too mindful of the fact that the overture had not yet been written, and that Mozart, like a light-hearted child with a holiday task to finish, had put off writing it down from day to day. They had already made many attempts to persuade him to write it, which he shrugged off half-laughing, half-annoyed. So they said no more, but behind the ladies' backs made signs to Mozart to go away and put it down on paper. However, Meister Amadeo behaved as if he didn't see these signs, and apparently was listening with great attention to the conversation between Signor Casanova and Abbé Da Ponte on the one hand and Duschek and the women singers on the other.
>
> Signor Casanova had been introduced as librarian to Count Waldstein

of Dux and Oberleutensdorf; he was in his sixties, of herculean build and a vigorous stance . . . [He] and Da Ponte had much in common. Both of them had lived in Venice when they were young, both had travelled the world restlessly, in both there was an unmistakable vein of vanity. They both boasted of the honours that had been heaped upon them, and took pleasure in talking about the potentates with whom they had had dealings. If Casanova brought out Frederick of Prussia and Catherine the Great, Da Ponte countered with Joseph II. However, Da Ponte had the edge. He could talk about present favours, while in the case of Casanova it must have been apparent that the monarchs who had liked him so much and had showered so many distinctions upon him had not retained him. The ladies, every one of whom had ambitions to leave Prague for the first theatre of the German empire, lavished their especial favours on Da Ponte, as the 'poet of the theatre' in Vienna . . .

'The Abbé seems to be a man of distinguished birth,' Micelli remarked to Casanova. 'He spoke of "my good uncle, the Bishop" – '

'Don't be deceived by that!' the Chevalier replied. 'Anyone can see that he belongs to the Jewish race! His parents died when he was quite young, and he was put in the seminary which was presided over by the Bishop of Ceneda. Since then he has taken to calling the bishop his uncle.'

'Do you really mean that? He's a baptised Jew! But he's a priest . . .'

'As to that, I wouldn't advise anyone to be married by him,' Casanova remarked with an admonishing finger. 'I'm afraid the marriage would be no more valid than if I had performed it.'

'Signor Casanova seems to be a really worthy old man,' Saporiti was meanwhile remarking to Da Ponte. 'And he must have held distinguished posts at a number of courts – '

'There you're making a terrible mistake!' replied Da Ponte. 'He's an adventurer who has spent his days playing cards, brewing elixirs and fortune-telling. To be sure, he's shrewd enough, and a cunning fox. Since I last met him he has been raised to the aristocracy, but I'm absolutely certain he performed the elevation himself.' [1]

'You Italians certainly say bad enough things about one another!' put in Duschek, who had been listening to the conversation.

'There are Italians and Italians!' replied Da Ponte. 'Can I say of Casti: he is a man of honour? Can I say of Salieri: he can be trusted? Casanova says he is fascinated by the Cabbala. Can I, for love of him, accept the Cabbala as a serious science? My dear friend, in this country you can say what you think, but among my compatriots you have to be careful. I haven't always been so, and my lack of caution is the main reason for my misfortunes. The Italians, my dear Duschek, are much too clever, and that is why they are masters in the art of deception. I trust no one, I yield my heart to no one.

'So far as Salieri is concerned, I am poet to the theatre. I give him my

[1] Da Ponte was quite right.

libretti just as I do Mozart; but it is only Mozart who is close to my heart, and I have the feeling that the only operas I have written which will survive are the ones he has put to music. I give him the operas which are dearest to me.'

To the horror of the two impresarios, Mozart now declares his intention of returning to Prague to meet some friends. Bondini, lowering his voice, says that something drastic must be done – 'The bird must be caged.' But how can they get him indoors?

'Child's play!' cried Signora Bondini. 'Dear *maestro*, I've left my gloves on the harpsichord. Would you be so kind as to get them for me?'

'With pleasure!' Mozart replied, and disappeared into the house. After a few minutes he appeared at the window and cried, 'I can't find them!'

'Then I must look for them myself,' Bondini replied, and the whole company trooped upstairs.

'There they are!' the singer cried, pretending to rummage under the music. She opened the harpsichord and pleaded: 'Mozart! Just a few chords from the overture, only one or two!'

Mozart sat down and played a loud, reverberating chord. He had no idea that a conspiracy was in train. Everyone tiptoed silently backwards, opened the door without a sound, and one after another crept out of the room.

When the key turned in the lock Mozart realised what was happening. He sprang up. 'What are you doing? What on earth does this mean?'

'It means that you're caught, and instead of spending the evening in the Tempelgässchen you'll spend it here in your room.'

'But what have I done?'

'Hear the sentence of the court!' cried Saporiti, laughing. 'Wolfgang Amadeus Mozart, who has been criminally in debt for such a long time for the overture to his opera, thereby jeopardising both his own interests and ours, is condemned to several hours' imprisonment, during which time he will be obliged to redeem his debt.'

'But, ladies,' said Mozart, appearing at the window as everyone gathered below, 'you won't deprive me of your company? How can I write without light or anything to eat or drink?'

'There's nothing you can do about it – you're a prisoner! If you want to be set free quickly, then get to work straight away. You shall have light, and wine, and a big cake – you shan't lack for anything.'

'You're a lot of traitors!' Mozart cried. 'I can't bear being alone. Supposing I was so miserable that I decided to end my life, and jumped out of the window?'

'No need to worry about that! You enjoy life far too much, little Amadeo!' Micelli cried.

'And what about you, Duschek, are you going to allow this?' Mozart said to his friend, who was almost invisible at the back of the group.

'We mean well, we really do!' Duschek said,

'It seems that good intentions excuse anything, even treachery,' Mozart cried, now really concerned that they would leave him locked up, but his face, which had grown serious, broke into laughter, despite himself, as he saw the three women singers march up in line. They had shared out the long poles from the vines, which lay in a corner of the courtyard, and to each of them had tied the various requisites that the prisoner would need for the night.

'Here are two lamps – and a couple of bottles of wine – and cakes and sweets!' they called out as the various objects were balanced on the edge of the window-sill. But Da Ponte, more down-to-earth than the others, appeared with a rake to which an article was attached which was as necessary as it was unaesthetic, and cried, 'You'll need this too. Take it, divine *maestro*.'

'A pity it's empty,' Mozart retorted, 'otherwise it would be the worse for you,' and he stood there half-annoyed, half-amused, among the objects which had been hoisted up to him . . .

'The end justifies the means,' called Guardasoni. 'Goodnight, Mozart. Tomorrow morning early we'll come and see if the overture is ready.'

'Yes, yes, all of us!' the ladies echoed. 'Goodnight, dearest Mozart, goodnight! Set to work!'

And so a light-hearted group of people played a joke on an immortal genius; for on earth a genius is cloaked by a human body, generally more modest than other men, and only occasionally is it possible to see the crown on his head shining like a flame . . .

The first night of *Don Giovanni* was a triumph, and in the next hundred years the opera was performed in Prague 532 times. In 1819 Da Ponte claimed that Mozart wrote to tell him of its success, but there is no other trace of this letter and it is almost certainly apocryphal.

'Our opera of *Don Giovanni*,' Mozart wrote – according to Da Ponte – 'was represented last night to a most brilliant audience. The princess of Tuscany, with all her company, was present. The success of our piece was as complete as we could desire. Guardasoni came this morning almost enraptured with joy into my room. Long live Mozart, long live Da Ponte, said he: as long as they shall exist, no manager shall know distress. Adieu! my dear friend. Prepare another opera for your friend Mozart.' Mozart returned to Vienna in the middle of November, so probably he told Da Ponte then of the splendid reception which *Don Giovanni* had had. But apart from any other factors which throw doubt on the authenticity of the letter, the Princess of Tuscany, the Archduchess Maria Theresa, who was to have seen the opera as part of her wedding celebrations, had already left Prague before the first night.

As with Da Ponte's other libretti, there has always been much discussion of the extent of his dependence on earlier versions of this archetypal story, and in particular on Bertati's *Don Giovanni o sia Il convitato di pietra* (which itself owed much to previous texts). Certainly he went to Bertati for the plot and for a great deal of the actual text of the first act; but, since he was writing an opera which was twice the length of Bertati's, he had to rely on his own invention for the second act, which, if it doesn't take us much further so far as the action is concerned, is nevertheless full of life and humour. Da Ponte's skill lay in depicting situations and relationships and human interaction rather than in devising well-constructed plots; at this Bertati was much the cleverer.

But Da Ponte's reliance on Bertati by no means led him slavishly to copy, for he has brought his own particular genius to the task. One of the women has been eliminated, thus allowing more weight to be given to the other three. Most of the characters have greater subtlety and are more sharply defined, and all have far more refinement, especially Don Giovanni and Zerlina, whose part gains in importance and who becomes less of a country hoyden and considerably more interesting and complex. Don Giovanni is more credible as the all-conquering gallant, more graceful and elegant – perhaps owing something to Casanova? Bertati can be ungrammatical, which Da Ponte never is. And, as in his other operas, his acute ear enables him to differentiate between the social classes through the dialogue, and so add to the depth and conviction of his characterisation.

There are two scenes where this is especially striking. In the first Leporello, disguised as Don Giovanni, is making love to Donna Elvira, warming to his task as he progresses. While Donna Elvira talks in the elevated tones of Metastasio – 'She's just like a printed book!' Leporello exclaims admiringly elsewhere – his own speech is full of plebeian slang. The second occasion comes right at the end of the opera. Donna Anna and Don Ottavio lament in tones of high tragedy that they must sacrifice their love to a year of waiting, so that Donna Anna can give vent to her anguish at her father's murder, while Donna Elvira declares that she will spend the rest of her life in a convent. Zerlina and Musetto bring us back to earth by announcing that they are going to have a cosy supper at home, and Leporello declares his intention of repairing to the inn to find a better master. The three of them join in a jolly, heartless little trio consigning Don Giovanni to the nether regions –

> *Resti dunque quel birbon*
> *Con Proserpina e Pluton!*

This counterpoint in the dialogue is a typical Da Pontean device, which helps to explain his extreme skill as a librettist (and also has its own share in revealing him as a man). It is used a good deal in *Figaro*, and is particularly noticeable in the last act when Susanna is masquerading as the Countess. In her recitative and aria here she sings in a manner which is quite foreign to her normal brisk mode of speech, in verse full of airy fancies and in exaggeratedly romantic language such as her aristocratic employer might indulge in but which would be quite alien to a *donna triviale*, a common woman, as she describes herself to the Count in one deliciously ironic passage. (See Appendix, p.250.) And surely no one would deny Da Ponte his share in the creation of the many beautiful arias and of all the poetry in *Don Giovanni*. '*Là ci darem la mano*' must have been one of his favourites, for he often refers to it in his writings.

He now set his hand to the adaptation of Salieri's *Tarare* – his 'Tasso', as he had described it to the Emperor. Set by Salieri to a libretto of Beaumarchais, this opera had been performed in Paris a few months earlier. According to Salieri's friend and biographer, I. F. von Mosel, Joseph commanded Salieri to arrange for a production in Vienna, with an Italian translation by Da Ponte. For three or four days this was precisely what composer and librettist tried to do, meeting every morning for the purpose but becoming more and more discouraged. Salieri felt that his music, which had been written for French singers, was too thin for their Italian counterparts. When Da Ponte was satisfied with the words, to Salieri's ears the music seemed to suggest a translation; and when the translation fitted the existing music Da Ponte was unhappy with his poetry.

> 'So,' Salieri decided, 'since we didn't want our work to be in vain . . . I asked the poet to write a new opera, based on the French original, which would be suitable for the Italian opera company, the arias to be apportioned in agreement with me but otherwise leaving him to write the poetry in accordance with what seemed to him best; I would look after the rest . . .'
>
> So that is how it was done. Poet and composer began afresh, walking hand in hand along the path they had chosen. Where the composer could glean a musical idea from the French version he did so; where he could not, he composed entirely new music.

Salieri had an attack of rheumatism which kept him at home for three weeks, so he got on with the music very quickly, writing it scene by scene as Da Ponte brought him the libretto.

Axur, rè d'Ormus, as Da Ponte called his libretto, had its *première* on 8 January 1788, on the occasion of the marriage of Joseph's nephew

Francis – the future Emperor – and Princess Elizabeth of Württemberg, of whom Joseph became extremely fond (too fond, Mozart thought), but whose life was to be very short. It was much praised, and is rated as the finest of Salieri's operas; Mosel, writing forty years later, describes it as the best of all serious Italian operas, comparable even with Mozart's *Clemenza di Tito*.

Unlike the great majority of operas which Da Ponte wrote for Vienna, it is not an *opera buffa* but an *opera seria* – in eighteenth-century terms, that is to say, a heroic drama with a historical or mythological theme. Da Ponte was always most at ease with *opera buffa*, and the best scenes in *Axur* are those involving intrigue, disguise and misunderstanding. Nevertheless, his adaptation is typically skilful and dexterous, and the opera as a whole is stirring stuff, full of drama and action, with splendid opportunities for the visual effects of which contemporary audiences were so fond. For this libretto too Da Ponte received a handsome *ex gratia* payment over and above the sum laid down in his contract.

Don Giovanni was not seen in Vienna until May of that year, and it was considerably less popular than *Axur*. Da Ponte writes that when the news of its Prague success reached the Emperor he

> ... sent for me, heaped on me the most gracious expressions of praise, made me a present of another hundred zecchini, and said how much he wanted to see it. Mozzart came back and immediately gave the score to the copyist, who hastened to copy out the parts, as Joseph had to leave Vienna. It was put on the stage and ... must I say it? No one liked *Don Giovanni!* Everyone except Mozzart thought it lacked something. We added to it, changed some of the arias, and put it on again; and no one liked *Don Giovanni*. And what did the Emperor say? 'The opera is divine, perhaps even better than *Figaro*, but it isn't the right food for the teeth of my Viennese.' I repeated this to Mozzart, who answered calmly, 'Give them time to chew it.' He was not mistaken. On his advice I so arranged it that the opera was repeated quite often; each time the applause grew, and little by little even the Viennese with their bad teeth enjoyed the flavour and understood its beauty, rating *Don Giovanni* as one of the loveliest operas that had ever been put on in any theatre.

A charming anecdote, but in fact, though Joseph may very well have expressed his great desire to see *Don Giovanni*, he could not have done so until its last performance of the year, in December, for he was not in Vienna; he left in February to fight the Turks, and did not return for ten months.

One other opera with a libretto by Da Ponte was performed in 1788 – *Il talismano*, taken from a play by Goldoni and set to music by

Salieri. This was received indifferently – the words, apparently, were more to blame than the music – but thanks to Salieri's influence it nevertheless had a considerable number of performances during the next three years. Da Ponte also, during this year, published two small volumes of poetry, which he called *Saggi poetici*. They included *Filemone e Bauci*, the psalms he had written in Dresden for Father Hueber, and the rhyming letter to Zaguri. In the years to come he was to publish various editions of *Saggi poetici*, each containing a slightly different selection of his poetry. A number of these poems give fascinating glimpses into his life which can be gleaned from nowhere else, and which are sometimes more reliable than his formal writings such as the memoirs. In particular these slender volumes of poetry, both those written in Vienna and the later collections published in America, contain precious nuggets of information about his family, and show how passionately devoted he was to them, and how closely he involved them in his own life, even when he was living on the far side of the Atlantic.

VIII

Some time before *Il talismano* was performed, Joseph had decided that the opera house was too costly, and in July 1788 he wrote from the battlefield to instruct Rosenberg to dismiss the company after the end of the next season. Da Ponte told an old school-friend, Antonio Michelini, that he had reason to believe the notice of dismissal would not affect him, since the sovereign was so just and because of 'a certain special kindness which he has always deigned to show me'; but the Emperor's letter to Rosenberg gives no indication that these hopes might be fulfilled: the only exceptions were four German singers who performed with the Italian company.

The unwelcome news reached the company through one of the librettist's particular enemies, Count Johann von Thorwart. He was Rosenberg's secretary and, as deputy and financial director of the opera, a power behind the scenes. Four years earlier the Emperor had been annoyed to find that he was occupying no fewer than three positions at court, and had ordered that he should cease to have any connection with the theatre, but his friends stood in high places and he was soon back again. Da Ponte declares that he was a mortal foe of the Italian company, and now he 'came with a light heart to one of the rehearsals' and read out the Emperor's letter.

Typically, Da Ponte took immediate and vigorous action. Appealing 'to all the ladies who love our theatre more than anything in the world' and to the foreign ambassadors in Vienna, he devised a plan whereby private sponsors would guarantee enough money to keep the opera going. In less than eight days, he writes, he had collected a subscription of a hundred thousand florins, and planned that this should be entrusted to Baron von Gontard, a well-known banker who had taken an interest in the Viennese opera house for many years.

As soon as the Emperor returned to Vienna in the middle of December 1788 Da Ponte hurried for an audience. Joseph invited him into his study and asked how the opera was going.

'Sire, it could not go worse.'

'How? Why?'

'Because we are all overwhelmed with despair and grief at having to leave our adored patron in September.' As I said this my eyes filled with tears, which he noticed; and with a goodness impossible to describe in words said, 'No, you will not lose him.'

'But if the theatre no longer exists, how many people and families will perish!'

'But I can't go on spending such immense sums to amuse myself and others when I need the money so badly for more important things. Do you realise that the Italian opera costs me over eighty thousand florins a year? I can't take money from some to give it to others. And then . . . and then . . . dear Coltellini . . .' [1]

While he was speaking I cautiously drew out an enormous piece of paper, folded several times in such a way that he would notice it and ask me what it was. When he did so I replied that it was a short petition.

'Short?'

'Very short.'

'On such a huge piece of paper?' I unfolded it with a solemn face, but in all this great space there were just two lines:

Anyone can make suggestions;
The point is whether they are accepted or not. [2]

[1] Celestina Coltellini was a noted singer whom the Emperor had engaged for the Burgtheater. He was much taken with her, and presumably she became his mistress. By now his ardour had cooled, for he had instructed Rosenberg to get rid of her. She wrote him two furious letters of complaint, and Da Ponte believed that it was these letters which made him decide to dismiss the Italian company. The Vienna State archives, however, do not contain any evidence to support this theory.

[2]   *'Proposizioni ognuno far le può;*
Il punto sta nell'accettarle o no',
which Da Ponte took from Casti's libretto, *Prima la musica e poi le parole.*

96

He couldn't help laughing, and asked me what suggestions I had to make. 'Sire,' I answered, 'I ask only for the use of your theatre, and I will give Your Majesty and Vienna the same company and the same spectacles three times a week.'

'You! Are you so rich?'

'No, Sire. But this is what I have done, since we heard the sad news of our dismissal.' I took out of my pocket two other pieces of paper, on one of which I had listed the names of various ladies and gentlemen each of whom undertook to pay five hundred florins for a box in the first, second or third tier, or a certain sum for so many tickets, as was the custom in London; on the other was an exact calculation of the box office receipts and expenses, taken from the theatre account books. He glanced over them.

'Very well,' he said. 'Go to Rosenberg and tell him that I give you permission to use the theatre.'

Rosenberg, Da Ponte writes, was delighted, for he was a keen supporter of the Italian opera, but Thorwart poured cold water on the scheme. When Rosenberg changed his tune and began to echo him, saying 'It can't be done, it can't be done,' Da Ponte ran back to the palace, found the Emperor alone, and panted breathlessly, 'Sire, Thorwart says, and the Count echoes him, that it cannot be done.'

'Give me your plan,' he said. He took it and wrote at the bottom, 'Count, tell Thorwart that it can, and that I am keeping on the theatre, on the basis of the project drawn up by Da Ponte, whose salary is to be doubled. Joseph.'

I went back to the Count, who received me with great joy and couldn't help exclaiming, 'Bravo, bravo, Da Ponte!'

Soon the news spread all through the city, and more than eighty people came to my house to thank me and express their gratitude, esteem and friendship.

The Viennese press showed a lively interest in the issue, and on 24 January 1789 the *Rapport von Wien* wrote, 'At last the business with the *opera buffa* is decided! We have pleasure in giving all the friends of the Italian theatre the delightful news that this temple of comedy – will not be profaned!'

The theatre records do not show what happened next, but, though it is clear from the account books that Da Ponte's salary was not doubled, the Italian company continued to perform at the Burgtheater. And confirmation that he went some way in inaugurating a subscription scheme comes from Count Zinzendorf, who on 15 January wrote in his diary that he visited Rosenberg, where he found Da Ponte; the poet was discussing his project, and declared that all the foreign ambassadors wanted to contribute. 'The Ferrarese came there in a pelisse,' Zinzendorf went on. 'You couldn't see her figure and she didn't look too bad.'

For the moment the German faction was silenced. Nevertheless, Da Ponte's days in Vienna were numbered, and one reason was his partisanship of the Ferrarese, for whom he now proceeded to write a series of libretti. The first was *Il pastor fido*, which had its *première* early in February 1789, during the carnival. The music was by Salieri and the libretto was based on the play by Giovanni Battista Guarini which Da Ponte had read and re-read so often while he was at Portogruaro that he knew it almost by heart.

The audience did not take to it, for which the composer blamed the librettist. But the real trouble may have been its unsuitability as a carnival opera, when everyone was in a gay mood and ready for something charming and frivolous. This charge could not be levelled against Da Ponte's next production, a fortnight later, which he called *L'ape musicale*, or *The Musical Bee*. It was a pastiche based on a text by Goldoni, linked by arias which Da Ponte had himself chosen from the operas of some of the favourite contemporary composers, Salieri, Martin y Soler, Cimarosa and Gazzaniga among them. (Mozart was represented only by a parody of '*Là ci darem la mano*', sung by Benucci, the first Figaro and the first Vienna Leporello, and Louisa Mombelli, the first Vienna Zerlina.) Da Ponte described it in a preface to the libretto as 'a kind of little comedy that – now parodying, now changing, now retaining the original words – introduces the finest arias which we have so far heard in our operas.' It is cast in the well-tried, ever-popular framework depicting singers, composer, poet and impresario gathered together to discuss and rehearse a new opera, at one moment fighting like cats, at the next applauding one another's songs. In his introduction Da Ponte says that the programme would be changed from night to night, and unpopular items dropped. The dialogue which links the arias is pointed, witty and very funny, and the whole project bears witness to Da Ponte's understanding of the singers, his profound knowledge of the operatic repertoire and his lively sense of humour.

L'ape musicale was extraordinarily successful and – quite exceptionally – played for eight consecutive nights, broken in the middle for a performance of *Una cosa rara*. 'The Ferrarese sang marvellously,' Zinzendorf wrote on the opening night. But all the singers who were left out were furious, as were the composers, who resented the fact that Da Ponte had put together the musical pieces without benefit of any of them.

In the summer there was a revival of *Le nozze di Figaro* in which the Ferrarese sang the part of Susanna. Mozart wrote for her an additional rondo, *Al desio di chi t'adora*, and an aria, *Un moto di gioa mi sento*, for which Da Ponte no doubt supplied the words. The opera had thirteen performances during the next five months, alternating with five other Da Ponte operas – *Una cosa rara*, *L'arbore di Diana*, *Axur*, *Il pastor fido* and a revival of *Il burbero di buon cuore*. In fact, during this period only two of the works performed did not have libretti by Da Ponte – and even in one of the exceptions he had a hand.

The last opera to be put on in 1789 for which he wrote the libretto was *La cifra*, also with music by Salieri. The text, an adaptation, is not one of Da Ponte's better efforts: the verse is indifferent and the characterisation minimal. The music is not exciting either, for by now Salieri was no longer the composer he had been. But it was well received – perhaps because of Salieri's influence – and was repeated several times in the next few months.

Interestingly, *La cifra* contains an echo of Cherubino's second aria from *Le nozze di Figaro*, sung in Salieri's opera by the Ferrarese, for whose voice he had composed the music, since, as he wrote on the score, she knew how to sing it, and was acclaimed for her performance. The aria, which is sung by the heroine, runs:

> *Chi mi sà dir cos'è,*
> *Quello che in seno io sento,*
> *Speme, desio, spavento,*
> *Inganno, affanno, amor?*
> *Cerco non sò che cosa,*
> *Fuggo, nè sò perchè,*
> *Chi mi sà, dir cos'è*
> *Quello ch'io sento in cor!*

Early in 1790 came the last of the operas which Da Ponte wrote with Mozart; this was *Così fan tutte*, which had its *première* on 26 January. (Perhaps Da Ponte took the title from a comment of Basilio's in *Figaro* – '*Così fan tutte le belle! Non c'è alcun novità.*'[1]) The part of Fiordiligi was once again written for the Ferrarese, with her immense range and flexibility. Tantalisingly the librettist – who always refers to the opera by its sub-title, *La scola degli amanti* – has nothing to say about it except that it 'held third place among the sisters born of this celebrated father of harmony'.

Countless pages have been filled with learned discourse about the provenance of the libretto, for the basic plot, in one form or another,

---

[1] 'This is what all beautiful women do – there's nothing new about it.'

99

had for centuries been a favourite among story-tellers; but so far as anyone knows the actual text is Da Ponte's own, with, no doubt, many suggestions from Mozart. For many years the libretto, with its tale of how an elderly cynic makes a bet with two confident young army officers that they shall put to the test the constancy of their respective beloveds by wooing them disguised as sexy Albanians, and of how, with the connivance of the girls' maid, Despina, they quickly succumb to the strangers' suit, was roundly condemned for its frivolity and immorality. Mozart, too, was taken to task for lending his genius to such a trivial and improper libretto, which 'was universally pronounced to be one of the worst of its kind', as Otto Jahn wrote dismissively. Throughout the nineteenth century earnest attempts were made to produce alternative texts which in the eyes of the critics would be worthy of the music. Luckily no one succeeded, and from these two masters of their craft posterity has inherited a work which comes straight from heaven, and which many people nowadays regard as the most perfect of all Mozart's operas.

Designed for the carnival, it is a charming, witty work which pokes delightful fun at some of the conventions of *opera seria*, and shows much insight into the human heart. (How strange that Da Ponte, who in his opera texts displays such understanding of human behaviour, was so endlessly taken in by people in real life, and so little able to differentiate between rogues and honest men.) What brilliant parody, for instance, in the scene when Don Alfonso, with crocodile tears, tells Fiordiligi and Dorabella that Ferrando and Guglielmo have been summoned to the field of battle, the ludicrous (yet touching) despair of the lovers heightened, for the audience, by the knowledge that it is all a spoof. 'Swear that you will write to me every day!' Fiordiligi cries, while Dorabella, not to be outdone, demands no fewer than two letters daily. Or consider Fiordiligi, tortured lest she should betray her lover by succumbing to her 'Albanian' suitor, as her heart commands her to do, impulsively ordering a mystified and resentful Despina ('*Donna Arroganza!*' she mutters angrily under her breath) to hurry and bring her two of the many uniforms which their departed lovers, inexplicably enough, have left in the girls' house. These, Fiordiligi decides, she and Dorabella will don, and thrust temptation aside by joining Ferrando and Guglielmo on the battlefield. This scene, too, explicitly serious, yet with an irresistible underlying comedy, marvellously takes off *opera seria*.

The accusation is often made that *Così fan tutte* is sexist because the women capitulate so quickly to their new suitors. But if they are to be condemned for fickleness, what about the behaviour of the two men, who for a wager of a hundred zecchini are perfectly happy to enter into a cold-blooded plot to deceive their sweethearts? Da Ponte, in his libretti as in his life, was always on the side of women, whose charms – since he loved beauty in all its forms – he could never resist. Though it is perilous to read his own predilections into his libretti, too many show sympathy for women for the signs to be ignored. 'Oh,' exclaims Marcellina in *Figaro*, 'when our hearts are not moved by self-interest, every woman takes up arms in defence of her poor sex, so greatly oppressed by ungrateful men.' And Don Alfonso himself says, 'Everyone accuses women, but I excuse them if they change their affections a thousand times a day. Some call it a vice, others a habit: but to me it seems a need of the heart.'

One noteworthy aspect of the opera is that when it was being written both composer and librettist were travelling through a period of bleakness in their personal lives. Mozart, with only two more years to live, was beset by money troubles; Da Ponte was fighting to keep his position at court in the knowledge that his protector, the Emperor, was gravely ill, and that he himself was surrounded by unscrupulous rivals anxious to get rid of him. Yet nothing of this is revealed in the radiance of *Così fan tutte*, which, in the music and the words, covers such a range of moods and emotions. As in the two earlier Mozart operas, the personalities of the participants in the comedy are sharply differentiated through their speech; but the most interesting aspect of the exploration of character is the change which is revealed by the two pairs of lovers once real emotions – jealousy and disillusionment on the part of the men, self-doubt and abandonment to passion on that of the women – take the place of conventional lovers' sighs.

A fascinating question mark hangs over the mystery of who pairs off with whom at the end of the opera. In stage productions it is assumed that they return to their original partners, Fiordiligi to Guglielmo and Dorabella to Ferrando; but, though this is probably the men's preference, the women, in switching lovers, seem to have found their true partners, and to have experienced a sexual arousal they have never known before. Da Ponte, whether deliberately or not, gives no indication of what happens after the reconciliation, but merely makes Alfonso remark '*Siete sposi*' – 'You're married'. The two couples have just been through a bogus marriage ceremony, each with the 'wrong' partner, though only the women have signed the marriage contract. So what are we meant to understand? The ambiguity gives an unexpected and intriguing twist to the end of the story.

Also of great interest is the portrait of Despina, the pert, bossy, self-confident, cynical maid who runs rings round her mistresses. 'I've led a thousand men by the nose,' she tells Don Alfonso. 'I can certainly lead two women.' More self-assured and much tougher than Susanna in *Le nozze di Figaro*, sharp as a pin, and obviously clever (she knows at any rate a smattering of Latin, whereas her mistresses haven't the faintest idea even what language she is talking when, disguised as the doctor, she airily tosses out two lines in that tongue; and she is familiar with the work of Dr Mesmer, the fashionable Vienna-trained physician who not long before had thrown Paris into a state of shock with his theories of animal magnetism), she is nevertheless bamboozled by the Albanians' disguise, and greatly vexed when she discovers that in this at least she has been taken for a ride.

In *Così*, too, Da Ponte's skill in the use of rhyme reaches a new peak of subtlety and invention, especially in the recitatives. Individual scenes, incidents and moods are encapsulated and emphasised, the drama is heightened and the comedy increased, by the repetition of the final rhyme. Presumably Mozart, despite his expressed dislike of rhyme, recognised how much it added to this opera, and accepted it as he would not have done from a less skilled librettist. For his next opera, *Die Zauberflöte*, Schikaneder provided him with a perfectly conventional pattern of rhyme, mainly confined to rhyming couplets. In *Così* Da Ponte seems, with total mastery, to be toying with rhymes, tossing them hither and thither, underlining the impression which the whole opera gives of seeming to play with consummate skill, both in the music and in the libretto, with the operatic conventions of the day. (See Appendix, p.250.)

As R. B. Moberly writes, the libretto is 'many-sided, lyrical, swift, witty, perceptive, classical, casual, polished, elegant'; it is 'comic yet serious, obvious yet subtle, derivative yet original, artificial yet realistic, trivial yet a parable, immoral yet profoundly moral, mocking yet compassionate.' With what conviction and poetry, yet with the lightest of touches, always ready to break into laughter, does it express the deepest human emotions of jealousy, anger, love, passion, remorse. It is a marvellous libretto to read, each time revealing some new subtlety of characterisation or felicity of language. What a pity that, in order to chop a little off its length, it is so often cut nowadays; and how much is lost in the process. And how vastly mistaken, too, the current tendency – in this as in other Mozart operas – to play for laughs by turning the subtle and delicious comedy into farce.

* * *

For a considerable time now the Emperor had been gravely ill, and some months earlier his nephew Francis had come to Vienna to transact the imperial business. Joseph's life had been despaired of, yet for a while his health improved, and the opera house, which had been stagnating, took on a new lease of life. But this was a temporary respite, for on 20 February 1790 – when *Così fan tutte* had been seen five times – Joseph died, and the Burgtheater was shut for nearly two months.

Never did sovereign have truer servant than Joseph had in Da Ponte. He uttered not one single word of disparagement of the man who had been, as he says, his protector, supporter, benefactor, lord and sovereign, and even more his counsellor and father. Many years later, in America, he wrote a poem describing how the Emperor had defended him against his enemies in Vienna – not least Casti and his powerful allies – and published it with an excellent translation by his daughter:

> Twas then my life's accumulated pains
>   Yielded my broken spirit, to despair,
>   And misery bound me with her iron chains:
> Till one arose, of godlike form and air,
>   With smiles the gloom of adverse fate represt,
>   And bade me in his own bright glory share.
> Then burnt with native fires my glowing breast,
>   Then swelled my lyre to notes of joy again.
>   And Envy's pallid cheek my fame confest,
> Ister and Elbe approving heard my strain,
>   And he too smiled, my gracious Prince, whose praise
>   Was ne're withheld, nor e're bestowed in vain.
> But ah! in darkness set these brilliant days;
>   Relentless Death my blooming chaplet tore,
>   And sunk in tones of deepest woe my lays.
> All Austria then the garb of sadness wore,
>   A Tyrant fill'd his throne, and nought for me,
>   Save life, remained of all that charmed before . . .

He could not but feel apprehensive at the prospect of a new régime. However, in the hope that all would nevertheless go well, he composed an ode *Per la morte dell'imperatore e avvenimento al trono di Leopoldo II*, written in imitation of Petrarch's ode on the death of Laura, which he signed with his Arcadian pseudonym Lesbonico Pegasio. It was reissued in Venice with a glowing tribute by his friend Giulio Trento, and was also published in many Italian cities.

Leopold, who reached Vienna three weeks after Joseph's death, inherited a sprawling empire two of whose members, the Austrian Netherlands and Hungary, were in open rebellion. There was also much unrest at home. During the latter part of his reign Joseph, once so open-minded, had become increasingly intolerant and censorship had grown much stricter. He had appointed the first Habsburg Minister of Police, Count von Pergen, who was given authority to recruit spies from amongst every section of the population, to use *agents provocateurs*, to persecute anyone regarded as politically dangerous, and to detain without trial, for an indefinite period, any potential suspect. Vienna, which had once rejoiced in freedom of speech, became a city where everyone was fearful to discuss politics or to talk openly. As in Da Ponte's earlier days in Venice, there was the feeling that spies lurked everywhere.

For twenty years Leopold had ruled Tuscany with wisdom and moderation. Cold and remote he may have been, and the simplicity of his manner of living sometimes offended his subjects (as that of Joseph had done the Austrians), but his reforms had been far-reaching, and had been rewarded by the gratitude of many of his people: an article in an influential journal in Florence thirty-five years later described him as 'one of the greatest men of the past age'. Perhaps he would have instituted the same reforms in his new empire if he had had the chance; but he lived for only two years after donning the imperial crown, and for the whole of that time was engaged in a desperate attempt to maintain the empire in the face of threats from Russia and Prussia and the upheaval caused by the French Revolution.

Vienna was buzzing with rumours about the doubtful future of the opera. Casanova, buried in Count Waldstein's library and always agog for the latest news, wrote to a Viennese friend not long after Leopold's accession, 'I'm dying to know whether it's true that the new Emperor intends to dismiss the Italian *opera buffa* company. I should be sorry for the Abbate Da Ponte, although he has forgotten me.'

However, for the moment no drastic changes were made, and during the first year of Leopold's reign Da Ponte wrote three operas, two of them taken from existing sources. The first was Paisiello's *Nina o sia La pazza per amore*, which had been written for the Naples opera house the year before. This he shortened and turned into verse, and eight new arias were written for it by Joseph Weigl, a young pupil and protégé of Salieri's who was just beginning to make his way in Vienna. Although popular in Naples, in Vienna the opera had only three performances. The next one was seen only twice. This was *La quacquera spirituosa*, a wretched affair, much too long and with music consisting of bits and pieces from here, there and everywhere.

The third caused Da Ponte nothing but trouble. It was given as part of the festivities to welcome the King and Queen of Naples, who came to Vienna in the autumn of 1790 for the marriage of their two daughters to two of Leopold's many sons (he had sixteen children). They were entertained with a splendid series of balls, fêtes and dinners, lasting over several months. *La caffettiera bizzarra*, one of the first spectacles staged for the delight of the royal visitors, was a strange choice, a mediocre libretto with a trivial subject, and again much too long. Da Ponte adapted the text – though very freely, so that there is little resemblance between play and opera – from Goldoni's *La locandiera*, and the music was composed by Weigl, who himself remarked that he could not understand why a 'nothing' (as the opera was) by a beginner should have been chosen for such a grand occasion. Da Ponte writes bitterly that he was blamed as usual, but that he had no say in the matter; that he had written the libretto some months earlier, and begged the directors of the theatre not to select it, or at any rate to allow him to remove the equivocations which might be unsuitable for such an occasion; but that on the advice of Salieri they had insisted on going ahead with it.

The festivities also included two musical evenings, given respectively by the Neapolitan ambassador to Vienna, the Marquis of Gallo, and the Prince von Auersperg, a former governor of Trieste. For both of these Da Ponte was asked to write the libretti. He much disliked the Marquis – young, good-looking, witty and a favourite at court, but also, it seems, arrogant and mean – but did not dare refuse the commission, for, as he says, he was always wary of tangling with the great. His reward was miserly, consisting in part of a gold watch of little value which he promptly passed on to his 'verse-inspiring muse' – no doubt the Calliope who had been such a delight during the writing of *Don Giovanni*. His contemptuous gesture filtered back to the Marquis, and from this moment the ambassador became his bitter enemy.

The cantata for the Prince von Auersperg, who seems to have been very well disposed to him, was luckily a great success. Da Ponte was entrusted with the choice of composer, the place where the entertainment was to be staged, the singers, dresses and scenery, and he decided that the performance should take place in a beautiful rotonda in the Prince's magnificent garden. In the middle of the rotonda there stood a statue of Flora, so Da Ponte called the cantata *Flora e Minerva*. He asked Weigl to write the music, and they worked together at top speed and in complete harmony.

Da Ponte – who describes the music as exquisitely beautiful – gives an enchanting account of the performance; it seems that the production caused a sensation:

> The rotonda held about three hundred people, in addition to a small space reserved for the actors. The statue of Flora had been removed, and her place on the pedestal had been taken by a singer who, since she was quite motionless, seemed to the spectators to be made of marble. A kind of drop-cloth behind the statue hid a large orchestra of wind players, and the rotonda was pitch-black. At my signal the royal party entered with their following, lit by a small lantern. When they first appeared everything was quite silent and dark; but suddenly the rotonda was lit by an infinite number of small lights concealed in the cornices, and the hidden orchestra, at first softly, then more and more loudly, filled the rotonda with music from paradise.
>
> To their surprise, the spectators found that they were sitting on thrones of flowers, and after Flora's first aria and recitative little cupids leapt down from the stage to present roses and myrtle to the brides and bridegrooms; but as they presented the flowers Minerva appeared, forbade the offerings, and declared that a more suitable gift to the spouses and their fathers would be the olive trees of Minerva and the laurels of Apollo. The dispute became so fierce that Flora descended from her pedestal, lifted the garland from her brow, knelt before the queen, the mother of the brides, and, singing a charming aria, presented it to her. But the queen, kissing her on the forehead, gave it back to her, not as a goddess but as a singer.

The Prince was delighted, and distributed rich presents among the singers. To Da Ponte he gave a beautiful little gold-leaf hind, a box of the same metal, and a purse containing fifty sequins. The cantata was later performed in the Burgtheater.

The Ferrarese had been in Vienna for nearly two and a half years, and her contract was soon to come to an end. Two other singers had already been engaged to take her place: Irene Tomeoni-Dutillieu, a prima donna from Naples, and Cecilia Giuliani, who had been appointed at the request of the Empress. Tomeoni was a beautiful singer, and when she made her debut she enraptured the audience; but Giuliani, whatever her other merits, sang only in *opera seria* and could not take *buffa* roles, so, as hardly any *opera seria* was being sung in the Burgtheater, there would be little for her to do.

In his anxiety to ensure that his mistress's contract should be renewed, Da Ponte impulsively set in train the events which were to lead to his downfall. In a long memorandum addressed to Rosenberg in December 1790, he urged that in view of the Ferrarese's versatility, and her ability to play both *buffa* and serious roles, the extra cost of her salary, if she were retained, would be more than offset by her value to the opera house. He begged Rosenberg to treat the memorandum as strictly confidential, but it seems that the Count told several people, especially those who loathed the Ferrarese, and the squabble reached the ears of Leopold and his Empress, increasing the dislike which they already felt for this troublesome poet.

Not long afterwards Martin y Soler, now director of the Italian opera at the court of St Petersburg, wrote to ask Da Ponte whether he would like to go to Russia as court poet. Da Ponte by this time realized how insecure his position was becoming, and since Rosenberg was not in Vienna he went to Thorwart to ask for permission to accept the offer. The answer came back from Leopold that he must wait until his contract had come to an end – a period which Da Ponte gives variously as six months and a year – and the librettist wrote to Martin y Soler accordingly. As a second string to his bow, he tried to persuade Mozart to go to London with him, presumably in the hope that they would find employment through Kelly and Stephen Storace. But Mozart, busy with *The Magic Flute*, asked for six months in which to make up his mind; and long before this period had expired Da Ponte had turned his sights in other directions.

For a full account of what happened next we must refer not only to the memoirs but also to a series of memoranda which Da Ponte wrote a few months later, when he had been forced to leave Vienna and was desperately trying to win his way back into the Emperor's favour. They give a revealing picture of the intrigues and jostling for position at the Burgtheater, and of the machinations of Da Ponte's foes.

He identified four deadly enemies. First and foremost Salieri, who wanted to have entire control of the theatre and to ensure that operas by other composers should fail, including Mozart's. (Salieri's dislike and jealousy of Mozart are well known; after the composer's death he is said to have remarked, 'What a shame so great a genius has died – but what a good thing for us! If he had lived, any music the rest of us composed wouldn't have earned us even a crust.') He was hostile to Da Ponte not only because of the librettist's active involvement in the running of the opera but also because of the rival claims of the Ferrarese and of his own protégée and pupil, Catarina Cavalieri, who had been the first Constanze in *Die Entführung aus dem Serail* and the first Vienna Donna Elvira. She is reputed to have had an excellent voice if a colourless personality, but recently she had rarely appeared on the stage of the Burgtheater, so Da Ponte was probably quite justified in proposing that she should be pensioned off. His partisanship of the Ferrarese and Salieri's of Cavalieri was one reason for the cooling of a friendship and partnership that had brought pleasure and profit to both composer and librettist, and later in life Da Ponte deeply regretted the estrangement from a man 'who had been like a brother to me', and with whom he had passed many delightful hours of learned conversation.

Enemy Number Two was Thorwart, the deputy director of the opera, whose dislike of Da Ponte sprang partly from the fact that the librettist had kept the Italian opera going two years earlier, since Thorwart had hoped then that the German company would be reinstated at the Burgtheater. But mainly he hated Da Ponte because, as controller of finances, he was making nice sums of money on the side, and was well aware that Da Ponte knew of his peculations.

The third enemy Da Ponte identified as Francesco Bussani (who had been so officious in the matter of the ballet in *Le nozze di Figaro*). The first Alfonso in *Così fan tutte*, he was a gifted singer, as was his wife Dorotea, who had sung Cherubino in 1786. But they had always worked under the shadow of better singers in Vienna, and were ready to enter into any intrigue in order to further their prospects. They had a bitter grudge against Da Ponte, who they felt bore much of the responsibility for not giving them the parts which they regarded as their due.

Then there was Giuseppe Lattanzi, who was employed by Leopold as a spy and was a very dubious character indeed. In 1785 he had been convicted in Rome of forging banknotes and sentenced to ten years in prison, and to another seven years for a different crime. He soon escaped, and in 1787 came to Vienna to ask for permission to live there. His plea was refused, and he was ordered to leave the city. Through the intercession of the Bishop of Pistoia he was taken on as secretary to Leopold, then still Grand Duke of Tuscany. When Leopold came to Vienna as Emperor, Lattanzi followed him, and was appointed a member of his secret cabinet. He also worked as a journalist. The police files describe him as a *littérateur* of a kind, but willing to do anything for money. All the evidence points to the fact that he actively intrigued to bring about Da Ponte's ruin.

Da Ponte also has bitter words to say about Sgrilli, the prompter and an important figure in the opera house. On many occasions, the librettist says, he had given Sgrilli clothes and money, and had also got him out of prison (he had letters to prove this); but in return Sgrilli did nothing but spread slanders about him. Finally he accuses Piticchio of double dealing, and of working in concert with Sgrilli to bring about his downfall.

When Da Ponte wrote the memoranda setting out these charges, he had learnt from bitter experience just who, and how powerful, his enemies were. And he had conceived a bitter and lasting hatred for Leopold. There are discrepancies in the different versions which he gives of the events of the next few months; and about some of the more discreditable methods which he used to try to buy back his pardon he is silent. But enough evidence exists to show that in all important respects he was speaking the truth in his account of how his enemies tried to get rid of him – and succeeded.

But this was in the future. At the beginning of 1791 he knew only that he was in disfavour with the Emperor, and also that he was becoming less and less *persona grata* in the opera house, where everyone was in a state of uncertainty and insecurity, anxious not to lose ground under the new ruler. He decided to ask for a private interview with the Emperor, and at the suggestion of Piticchio went to see Lattanzi at his house in the hope that he would act as intermediary (the police records show that he went there on 24 January). Two days later Lattanzi told him that a private audience was impossible, but that he would give Leopold anything Da Ponte cared to write. Soon afterwards Da Ponte heard of a slanderous rumour which Bussani was spreading about him,[1] and tried once more to see the Emperor. This time it was Thorwart who dissuaded him, giving amongst other reasons that Rosenberg was soon to be removed as director of the opera and that the new director, Count Ugarte, was well-disposed towards him. (Ugarte did in fact take up his new post early in March.)

Hearing of more slanders, Da Ponte now committed what was perhaps the most foolhardy act of his life. Boiling with fury and anxiety, he wrote the Emperor a letter in blank verse which Leopold could only regard as the acme of impertinence and *lèse majesté* – not least because of its echoes of egalitarianism at a time when all Europe was terrified by the excesses of the French revolution, and Leopold in particular was distressed by frantic appeals for help from his sister Marie Antoinette, appeals to which, as ruler of the Austrian empire, he had to turn a deaf ear.

Leopold, you are king, Da Ponte wrote. I implore justice, I do not ask for mercy. I know that justice is the first of your virtues; but good intentions are often not enough for a man, and you are a man, subject like other men to fraud, surrounded by flatterers and false

---

[1] This may tie up with the remark in the memoirs: 'One day I was told that Rosenberg wanted to clap me into prison, because Bussani had informed him that it was my fault that a certain opera could not be performed.'

counsellors. Skilled as you are in the art of reigning, there are too many tempters – more, I think, than you realise. Listen to a sincere voice, the most sincere which your kingdom can claim to have. My destiny does not depend on you; with all your power you have no rights over my soul. If I feel no guilt, if my conscience is clear, I can adore you, I can love your name and your virtues, but I cannot fear you . . .

There is much more in the same tone, protesting that Da Ponte is being persecuted by his enemies, who have the Emperor's ear, and imploring him to see that justice is done. Da Ponte could have done nothing to harm his cause more deeply. But 'when I wrote [the verses],' he says in a passage which appeared in the first edition of the memoirs but which he later took out, as he did the verses themselves, 'I did not know Leopold.'

Reading the poem next day he doubted the wisdom of sending it to the Emperor. However, he read it to Lattanzi, who he still thought had no reason to betray him, and who had given him many proofs of his closeness to Leopold. 'As soon as I read the letter to him, he threw his arms round my neck with the utmost joy and approval. This, he cried, is the right letter for our lord. I said I was afraid it would seem too ardent, since I had written it in a dangerous mood. This he brushed aside. He told me to copy it out again, and assured me that it would be given to the Emperor and that the results would be to my advantage. After thinking about it for a little, I tried to persuade him to present the letter in such a way that it would not have an adverse effect, and to observe how His Majesty reacted as he read it. This he promised to do.'

Well may Lattanzi have rejoiced, for Da Ponte had delivered himself into the hands of his enemies. It seems that the spy presented the poem to the Emperor together with a note saying, 'Here is a letter which a wise king should censor. It is said to have been written by Da Ponte.' Soon afterwards he told the poet that the Emperor approved of the poem, and that Da Ponte should have it printed and present it to Leopold in this form.

Before he could do so, the verses were already being circulated in the city, and there is no doubt that it was Lattanzi who arranged for this to be done. Among his papers in the Vienna police archives a note was found declaring, 'Everyone in the city is reading with absolute amazement the letter which, so it is said, Da Ponte circulated. It is written in such vehement terms that one can't imagine how anybody could be so foolhardy as to address the Sovereign in this way unless he were involved in some very dangerous intrigue.'

(Zaguri describes the verses as 'Sans Servolici', equating them with the madhouse of this name in Venice.)

Da Ponte still had no idea that Lattanzi was intent on bringing about his downfall, for a few days later he once again visited the spy at his house. Almost immediately there appeared on the streets of Vienna a sixty-eight page anonymous pamphlet entitled *Anti-Da Ponte* and written in German. It was a vicious attack on the poet, reproducing the letter to Leopold line by line with sneering comments and damning innuendoes which the reader would have no means of knowing were often false.

Soon this document was being read and laughed over in every café in Vienna. Leopold could not ignore it, and on 9 March Da Ponte was informed that his contract would be terminated at once, and that he would be given compensation.[1] Negotiations as to exactly how much this should be dragged on: Da Ponte gives two different versions, one written four months and the other thirty-five years later, and neither agrees with the Vienna archives. He himself states in the memoirs that he was given his salary for five months, the profits on the opera libretti and payment for an opera that he was at this time writing with Salieri, *Il filarmonico*, which was never completed. According to the theatre account books he seems to have received two years' salary and compensation for the money he had paid out for printing the libretti.

He decided to stay in Vienna until he had planned what to do next, for he had committed no crime and no one could force him to leave the city. What is astonishing is that during this period, when his affairs were in such disarray, he was as active as ever at the Burgtheater. Early in March 1791 he wrote for the Ferrarese a sacred oratorio – that is to say, an opera with a biblical theme – entitled *Il Davide*. The Ferrarese financed this and pocketed the receipts, and of course she sang in it, as well as Bussani and the leading tenor at the theatre, Vincenzo Calvesi. The score, and the identity of the composer, have both disappeared into the mists of time.

Da Ponte also devised for the Ferrarese's benefit another 'musical bee', *L'ape musicale rinnuovata*, thus reaping not nectar but a dose of poison from all the composers whom he failed to consult in putting the entertainment together, and all the singers who were aggrieved at not being included.

---

[1] It has often been claimed that Da Ponte wrote a libel on the Emperor, which mysteriously has never been found, and that it was this which brought about his downfall. From the documents, however, it is quite clear that it was the rhymed letter to Leopold which caused his dismissal.

What role Da Ponte was playing at this time in his mistress's household is a matter of speculation. He was simultaneously the Ferrarese's acknowledged lover and on good terms with her husband, Luigi del Bene, as a letter which Luigi wrote to him early in February 1791 clearly shows. Del Bene *père* had died a month earlier, and his son was anxious to step into his post as papal consul to Venice – which, since in those days diplomatic appointments often descended from father to son, would have been by no means unusual. Leaving his wife in Vienna, Luigi set out for Rome to apply to the Pope in person, travelling by way of Venice. It is from this city that he writes to his 'dearest friend' Da Ponte, telling him that he has found the financial affairs of his late father in a great tangle. The estate is owed a considerable amount of money by many Venetian nobles to whom his father lent large sums, but he hasn't been able to find any documents which will help him to sort out these debts. Since his father died intestate, according to Venetian law the estate has to be divided equally between his sister and himself, and in a few days they are both going to Rome, where he hopes to be appointed consul, in spite of many competitors. 'Meanwhile,' he goes on, 'please persuade my wife to exercise the greatest possible economy, because if possible I don't want our embarrassment to leak out to the family. Meanwhile, I hope that with the Oratorio, the Pasticcio and the *accademie*[1] everything will go well with a little good management; meanwhile please tell my wife to be sure to take up at once with Prince Galitzin the matter of my pictures, which, together with the two large oils, I leave it to her to dispose of, even if she only gets two hundred zecchini, if this will help her.'

How fascinating that Luigi sent these messages of caution and advice through his wife's lover . . . Perhaps it was the proceeds from the sale of the pictures which she used to finance *Il Davide*.

In mid-March Leopold left Vienna for Italy, having resolved before he departed that Da Ponte could no longer stay in the city. Soon afterwards the handwritten newspaper *Heimliche Botschafter* announced, 'The Italian court poet Abbé Da Ponte has had his dismissal and in a few days will leave for Italy in the company of Madame Ferrarese'; and a little later the *Gazetta urbana Veneta* declared – prematurely – that Bertati had been appointed as his successor. But still he lingered, and not until 9 April did the last performance of *L'ape musicale rinnuovata* take place. Meanwhile he was also writing

---

[1] Del Bene is probably referring to subscription concerts which Da Ponte and the Ferrarese may have been planning.

or rewriting arias and recitatives for Benucci, Calvesi and Tomeoni for the operas in which they were singing.

It is probable that one reason why he lingered in Vienna was that he was hoping to find a haven in Venice. Some time in April his family presented a petition to the Council of Ten begging that his three remaining years of banishment might be remitted, and, always sanguine, he was no doubt playing for time until the answer came. It cannot have helped his cause that the appeal was presented by his oldest stepbrother Agostino, who was now living in Venice, for a year earlier Agostino had been in serious trouble with the authorities both in Venice and in Vienna. There is no doubt that Agostino was a shady character. Da Ponte's earliest reference to him occurs in a rhyming letter which he wrote to his father in 1788: 'When Agostino renounces lies, love and cards, and begins to think about providing for his three children . . .' The register of births in Ceneda cathedral shows that by 1788 he was married and did in fact have three children, and from the evidence it seems likely that it was his own father and mother who were landed with the care of them. Then in the spring of 1790, while he was living in Vienna, he seduced a young Viennese woman, Giovanna Müller, and persuaded her to flee with him to Venice. Here, in order to escape detection, he moved her from lodging to lodging, until she became seriously ill and he was forced to call in a priest to administer the last sacraments. The priest, with great courage, managed to smuggle her into the house of a German watchmaker, whence she was restored to her distressed husband and family. Agostino, meeting the watchmaker in the street one day, threatened his life, and was sentenced to a month's imprisonment.

Whatever part this sordid affair may have played in the decision of the Council of Ten, their verdict was a rejection of Da Ponte's petition to be allowed to return to his homeland. But already, pressed by the theatre directors, he had left Vienna. In mid-April he informed the theatre cashier that he would be departing on the 20th. But then, it seems, his father was told that he had committed a grave crime and had been commanded to leave the city within twenty-four hours. In order to prove that the accusation was false, and thus allay the old man's anxiety, he decided to stay a little longer; so it was not until some time between 26 and 30 April that he did at last depart, taking refuge in Brühl-bei-Mödling, a pretty village in the hills not far from Vienna.

IX

'How great was my torment when I found myself in that solitude!' wrote Da Ponte – disgraced, dismissed from his post, his purse nearly empty, unable to foresee the future, at his wits' end to know how to support himself and continue to help his family in Ceneda:

> The first day was one of the most terrible of my whole life. The victim of hatred, of envy, of the interests of scoundrels, driven from a city where, honoured for my talent, I had lived for eleven years; abandoned by my friends, towards whom I had often acted with great generosity; scorned, slandered, humiliated by idle men, by hypocrites, by my triumphant enemies; finally driven from a theatre which only existed through my efforts – often I was on the verge of taking my life. The knowledge that I was innocent, instead of being a comfort, only redoubled my desperation. *I* knew that I was innocent, but how to prove it to a judge who had condemned me without hearing me, and who – to make things even worse – was then far distant from his dominion?

Two people only, he writes, came to see him. He does not say who they were, only that before he left Vienna he told them where he would be, though from everyone else he kept this a secret. These friends advised him to stay where he was until the Emperor returned to Vienna from Italy, so that he could then call his accusers to judgement and defend his honour.

It was a third man who proved a real friend. This was Major Thaddäus Stieber, a professional soldier who had been in the employ of Joseph II and who was now one of Leopold's many private agents. It is clear from the correspondence that he and Da Ponte had got to know one another in Vienna, that Stieber was well aware of what was happening in the Burgtheater, and that he went to extraordinary lengths to help the exile.

Da Ponte wrote to him on 8 May 1791, soon after he reached Brühl, having already sent him two letters without getting a reply:

> I am in the extreme of desolation . . . and have decided to appeal to your humanity since everyone is deaf to my tears, and this is the only protection and help left to me. Although my enemies have tried to burden me with many crimes, I swear by all that is most sacred, I swear by

omnipotent God that I am innocent of them all. You have means of discovering the truth. My story is known to all Vienna, but all Vienna knows too that I am honest, a friend of humanity, that I deprive myself of necessities for the poor and the wretched, that I do not cheat or commit base deeds, and that for many years I have supported the large family of my old father and educated his children.

Major Stieber, Da Ponte goes on, also knows only too well – as he showed on all the occasions when Da Ponte had the honour of talking to him – who the scoundrels are who have made him the victim of their cabals. No matter that he is reduced to the extreme of misfortune: that can't be helped. He no longer asks to have his job back; he asks only for the opportunity to justify himself, to save his reputation, to be shown the compassion if not the favour of the Emperor. 'I am aware of having committed no other error than of having written him a letter which perhaps I should not have written.' In this too he was betrayed, and he must either reveal the identity of the traitor (he means Lattanzi) or die, since this man's ambitions are likely to betray the Emperor also.

With his letter Da Ponte enclosed a memorandum for the Emperor. This Stieber must have agreed to send on to Leopold in Italy, for a week later Da Ponte writes full of gratitude for his help. In fact the archives contain two documents: one is a fulsome letter from Da Ponte to the Emperor repeating more or less what he had written to Stieber; the other is a detailed account of the events leading up to his dismissal. As has already been made clear, Da Ponte gave conflicting versions of these events, which have been related in the last chapter, but there is no reason to doubt that what he set down on paper for the Emperor's eyes is basically the truth, since he was writing immediately afterwards, while his memory was still fresh, and he knew that Stieber could investigate and report on the accuracy of everything he said. Above all, in his own report to the Emperor Stieber confirmed in essence all Da Ponte's accusations.

In the latter half of May Stieber arranged a meeting with Da Ponte outside Brühl. Meanwhile he had been carrying out the most exhaustive research into Da Ponte's claims and general circumstances, and, as he reported to the Emperor, had uncovered a great number of feuds and squabbles in the Burgtheater. He had spoken to people who knew Da Ponte – in particular two extremely respectable citizens and two canons of 'the cathedral' (presumably Ceneda) – and without prompting they had given excellent reports of Da Ponte, confirming that he honoured his parents to an extraordinary degree and regularly and generously helped to support them financially. He also helped his eleven siblings, several of whom were still under-age, and he gave what relief he could afford to the poor. [1]

> But, most gracious lord [Stieber's report goes on], when we reached the wood where Da Ponte was and he came to meet us, I swear that Your Majesty could not have seen and heard him without being greatly moved. He looked like a madman, and repeated a hundred times that no grief could be greater than to know himself for ever rejected by Your Majesty, that his earthly well-being would thereby vanish for the rest of his life, and that he would drag his father and brothers and sisters into misfortune with him. Da Ponte may be guilty in this or that respect, but after the most thorough investigation I have discovered that he is the victim of many cabals, and is abused by evil men for his good deeds, misled, and made the object of suspicion, in which a certain Poussani [Bussani] is much involved – a man who, to my knowledge, has been mixed up in many criminal activities . . .
>
> Da Ponte's enemies therefore hastened his banishment from Vienna, and barred all doors which might give him the opportunity to throw himself at Your Majesty's feet and reveal to your great insight and future judgement a large number of malpractices in public affairs. When this was forbidden him, he wrote them down. His earthly fate and well-being, and that of his old father and eleven brothers and sisters, hang on Your Majesty's clemency.

For the time being Da Ponte wrote no further memoranda to Stieber (there were to be more later on). Towards the end of May, without warning, he was visited by two policemen who 'dragged me out of bed and without uttering a word took me to Vienna, where, after leaving me in suspense for two hours without knowing if I was going to be taken to prison or the scaffold, they ordered me *pro tribunali*, "in the name of the all-powerful", to betake myself, within the space of twenty-four hours, away from the capital and from all the neighbouring cities. I was used to heavy blows. Calmly, I asked who this order came from. One of them replied drily, "From him who commands."'

Da Ponte was fortunate in that he was allowed to have an interview with Count Saurau, Count von Pergen's deputy, who was a Privy Councillor and captain of the civil guard. To Saurau, whom he

---

[1] How Stieber arrived at 'eleven siblings' is not quite clear. The register of births, deaths and marriages in Ceneda (now Vittorio Veneto) cathedral records the birth of six stepsisters and three stepbrothers, two of whom (Paolo and Enrico) were still young enough to need Da Ponte's help – a total of eight. Stieber's figure can only be explained if one adds Agostino's three children. Since their father was such an unsatisfactory breadwinner, it seems more than likely that their care fell on Gasparo Da Ponte. Lorenzo Da Ponte himself is inconsistent in the number of stepsisters he claims to have.

describes as 'one of the wisest, justest and most respected citizens of his country', Da Ponte gave a full account of everything that had happened. 'He told me that he was only the executor of the will of others; that he did not know what my crimes might be; that no accusation had ever been brought against me in the police courts, of which he was a director; but that I had powerful enemies in the theatre, who had painted me in black colours to the court, and particularly to the Empress.'

On 3 June he was given permission to extend his stay in Vienna for eight days by Francis, who was acting as regent during the absence in Italy of his father, in order that he might present his defence. He was still there on the 18th, when he wrote to Casanova:

> I could not follow your advice to go to Rome or Madrid, because on the day your letter arrived I was ordered to return to Vienna and put my defence in writing. My return to the city terrified my enemies, all the more because everyone was saying that I had been formally sent away by order of the most high. We shall see how things turn out. In any case, my sights have turned to Venice at the moment: a thousand reasons summon me, and particularly the longing to raise my family out of misery, which I can achieve if I can win the famous lawsuit, which we talked about so often. With this end in view I wrote to Zaguri, Memmo and Da Lezze, who supported a petition that my brother presented to the Council of Ten, but with no success, since it was defeated by two votes. I have been advised to make a second attempt: the Ferrarese, who has already left for Venice with her husband, will act for me with more judgement and interest.

Da Ponte says that Francis – who seems to have treated him with kindness both now and in the following year – pitied him but could do nothing to help him, since he was only the executor of his father's wishes. Francis advised him to go to Trieste and lay his case before Leopold, who was expected there shortly on his way back from Italy, and accordingly towards the end of June Da Ponte said goodbye to Vienna. With him went Paolo and 'a [female] friend of ten years' standing'. It has generally been assumed that he was referring to the Ferrarese, but this is certainly not the case, for she had already left for Venice. He can only mean his Calliope – whom, alas, he appears to have ditched in Trieste.

'Trieste, the usual refuge of those in disgrace' – such was Zaguri's description of this prosperous freeport on the Adriatic. Though belonging to the Austrian empire, it was close to the Venetian frontier, and its population and culture were considerably more

Italian than Austrian. As soon as Da Ponte – who could now truly be put among the disgraced – arrived, he went to see the governor, Count Pompeo Brigido, who, he says, already knew his story. Brigido received him kindly, and throughout his stay of just over a year seems to have been uniformly helpful. In his memoirs Da Ponte expresses profound gratitude, and nearly thirty years later he wrote from America to say that for the rest of his life he would bless both him and the lucky city where he had had the good fortune to get to know Brigido. A second important figure was the commissioner of police, Baron Pittoni. The commissioner was on good terms with many of Da Ponte's friends, including Casanova, with whom he kept up a lively correspondence.

On 5 July, soon after Da Ponte's arrival, four imperial carriages clattered into Trieste bearing a secretary, two couriers, and a cook with full kitchen equipment. A few days later the Emperor himself arrived, accompanied by two of his sons and his principal chamberlain, Prince Liechtenstein. The next morning he held audience, and that same evening, after inspecting a majolica factory, went to the Teatro San Pietro for a performance of *Lo studente bizzarro*. Da Ponte had been trying desperately to obtain an interview with him, so perhaps it was partly in the hope of catching the Emperor's attention that he too attended the opera. Leopold was highly displeased to find him there. 'He was astonished and grieved to see him at the theatre,' Pittoni wrote to Casanova. 'He spoke to me, and said that it couldn't be tolerated, that he was a rogue, and had been banished from Vienna on his orders.'

> The Governor Count de Brigido explained to H.M. that he had come to Trieste on purpose to have an audience with H.M., to answer the various complaints which had been made against him. H.M. absolutely refused to see him, and confirmed his first instructions.
> The next morning H.M. gave orders that the Abbé Da Ponte should come to see him at 11 A.M., he came, and was there for an hour and a half. I was not informed of the matters which they discussed, but the result was a suspension of the police orders against him.

All of which completely tallies with Da Ponte's own account. He himself writes that he was in a passion of despair, when suddenly he heard a voice outside his door crying, 'Da Ponte! Da Ponte! The Emperor wants to see you!' He thought it must be a dream, but in fact it was Prince Liechtenstein, who had come to summon him for an audience. Da Ponte entered the imperial presence with words of self-justification bursting from his lips, but the Emperor, his back turned, was looking out of the window, and Da Ponte waited, ill at ease and not daring to speak, until Leopold turned round.

For a first-hand account of the interview we have only Da Ponte's words, on which a good deal of scepticism has been cast. No doubt Da Ponte, relying on his excellent memory, and with his strong imagination and gift for writing lively dialogue, embroidered his account of the interview when he described it thirty years later. That the gist of the narrative is true is borne out by subsequent events and by the Vienna archives. One impartial testimony to his basic veracity is provided by the first review in Italy of the memoirs when they appeared in America: 'Everything I have ever heard recounted of different conversations held by Leopold,' the critic wrote, 'gives [Da Ponte's] narration in my eyes the strictest air of truth.'

During the interview Da Ponte related in detail the sequence of events leading up to his dismissal, bitterly accusing the men whom he now realised were his enemies – Thorwart, Rosenberg, Salieri, and the new director, Ugarte. Leopold at first listened coldly, but gradually he became less hostile, and in his turn spoke with some anger not only of these four, but also of Francesco and Dorotea Bussani and Lattanzi. All of them, he agreed, hated Da Ponte, and had every reason to want to get rid of him. 'From everything you tell me,' he went on, 'I realise that you aren't the man they want me to believe you are.'

'I am not, Sire! As God be my witness, I am not!' Da Ponte replied passionately.

The Emperor then asked him where he intended to go next. When the librettist replied, 'Vienna', Leopold told him that this would not be possible so soon, that the impression he had left behind was still too unfavourable, and that it would be his, Leopold's, job to put the record straight before there could be any thought of Da Ponte's returning to the city. Da Ponte burst out that he could not wait so long, that he had an old father and many brothers and unmarried sisters who depended on him for help.

'I know how good you are to your family,' the Emperor replied. 'I know that you are educating two brothers, that you are their benefactor; and I am glad of it. But why not bring your sisters to Vienna? Are they talented? They could find employment in the theatre.' [1]

'My sisters would die if they had to abandon their old father even for three days. Their only talent and their only beauty lie in their honesty. If Your Majesty wishes to make twelve people happy at a stroke, allow me

[1] Leopold is known to have had a large number of mistresses. Perhaps he wanted to add Da Ponte's sisters to their number!

to return to Vienna alone: I will work for all of them, as I have worked for eleven years: all the time I can give succour to this honest family, twelve mouths will bless and thank Your Majesty's justice. If I am not worthy to be poet to the theatre, give me some other employment, set me to serve with the least of your servants, but without delay, and above all in Vienna.'

'My theatre might be able to use two poets. I know that you are a good poet, and for serious drama as well; but for the moment it cannot be.'

'Your Majesty must do it, so that justice may triumph, for the honour of the throne, for the vindication of my honour which has been impugned. I kneel at Your Majesty's feet, and will not rise until my prayers have been fully granted. Allow yourself to yield to these tears, which are tears of innocence. Yes, Sire, I can say to you, I can swear to you – they are tears of innocence, if it is not a sin to be a man and to have the passions of a man . . .'

'It is not; but they told me . . .'

'And for a "they told me" the moderate, the wise Leopold will deprive me of bread? For a "they told me" he will make me leave a city which for eleven years honoured me, which during all this time saw me follow the path of true religion – charity towards my family, towards my enemies, a city which gives me the right of citizenship, or at least of public protection?'

'Rise!'

'For a "they told me" my name is stained with the eternal infamy of a double banishment, I am put on a level with the greatest scoundrels on earth, I am denied an asylum of a few feet of earth in any of the imperial states, I am to become the laughing stock of idlers, the butt of hypocrites and traitors?'

'Rise!'

'Sire, I must not, I cannot. Give me the strength to do so by yielding to my plea. Do not leave me to the horrors of a sentence which my enemies have won by deceiving Your Majesty's sense of justice, and which is not authorised by any laws save those of force. This is not the code of Leopold.'

'Rise! I command you. A sovereign is master in his own house, he can do what he wishes, and has no obligation to account to anyone for what he wants to do.'

'I prostrate myself, oh Sire, even more humbly to implore your clemency and pardon. I swear at all costs to tell you the truth. This sentiment cannot displease the magnanimous Leopold. A sovereign should do only what is just.'

'He is also master of keeping in his service those who please him and of dismissing those who do not.'

'I dare not doubt this. But this dismissal is punishment enough for a man who has had the misfortune not to please his sovereign, punishment enough without dishonouring him with a double banishment and accusing him, simply on conjecture, of every conceivable crime.'

'I have not accused you of anything.'

'Would to heaven that Your Majesty, before condemning me, had accused me of something! Then they would have said, "The Emperor has punished him for a crime." Now they will say it is for a million crimes. The priests, because my behaviour was scandalous; the singers because of my cabals and favouritism; the weak because my libretti were dangerous; the slanderers, because of satires against the sovereign; the lazy, the ill-informed, the café gossips, for anything that comes into their heads, or simply out of caprice, to advance themselves or because they enjoy saying evil things: so that there won't be a single person in Vienna who will not invent some crime or other on my part, or believe it, and who, at the expense of my reputation, will not find justification for the severity of Your Majesty's punishment.'

He was thoughtful for a moment, walked up and down the room a couple of times without speaking, and suddenly coming to a halt in front of me – I was still kneeling – said calmly, holding out his hand to help me up, 'Rise! I believe you have been persecuted, and I promise you shall have recompense. Do you ask for more?'

'No, Sire. It is enough that my name should be remembered by a monarch who is preoccupied with so many matters of much greater importance, and that Your Majesty should deign to believe that the fire, perhaps too great, which I have shown today springs only from a conscience outraged by the wrongs inflicted by my unjust enemies.'

'I believe you and forget everything. Where are you planning to stay?'

'I shall stay in Trieste, Sire.'

'Good. Stay here, and let me hear from you from time to time. Meanwhile, listen. Today I received letters from Vienna telling me that affairs at the opera house are going very badly, and that my singers are being persecuted and intrigued against. That is why I sent for you, and I should like to have your suggestions as to how this can be stopped.'

'Your Majesty sees now whether Da Ponte is the source of the cabals, or whether the people who want to make you believe that he is are responsible.'

'Oh, I see it clearly enough.'

'First of all, Sire, one must destroy the causes.'

'Very well, tell me the principal ones.' He sat down, took up a pen and prepared to write. I repeated all the things I had already suggested to the directors, and he wrote it all down word for word, from time to time approving what I said . . . For a whole hour he wrote at my dictation.

Once more the Emperor reassured Da Ponte that he would remember his former theatre poet, and asked whether he was in need of money. Da Ponte, from pride or vanity, told Leopold that he was not. His purse was, in fact, soon empty, and his wardrobe too, not least because he was supporting his 'muse', Paolo and a second brother, presumably Agostino. He complains bitterly because his friends refused to help him, and instead reproached him for his imprudent conduct. A sense of pride forbade him to appeal to the governor, Pompeo Brigido, who would, he says, certainly have helped him. Only one compatriot responded to his appeals, but he was not rich. Sometimes Da Ponte would dine with him, but he did so with bitter regret at the thought of his brothers and his Calliope who could not share this bounty.

However tempting it is to read the account of his interview with Leopold as if it were one of his more melodramatic libretti, the proof of the pudding is in the eating. The Emperor returned to Vienna on 20 July, and on the 27th he gave orders that Thorwart was to have nothing more to do with the opera house. Lattanzi was dismissed some time during the summer, led a wandering career and died in 1820 after having been accused of trying to poison his wife. Ugarte also left in 1791, recompensed with a year's salary and the warning that the Emperor would be happier if he removed himself from Vienna. The Bussanis, still unable to secure the coveted top roles, departed in 1794. Salieri, too, fared less well under Leopold than under Joseph. He had already taken his one-time pupil, Weigl, as his assistant, and in 1792 relinquished to the younger man his post as composer to the opera.

At first Da Ponte was full of hope that he would soon be summoned back to Vienna. A fortnight after his interview with Leopold he wrote to Stieber enclosing further memoranda: a list of his principal enemies and a note of the events leading up to his dismissal (presumably repeating what he had already told the Emperor); a plan for running the Burgtheater which, he said, he had long since presented to the management; and thoughts on how best to direct an opera house. The last two are full of good, practical sense, and show how much Da Ponte must have contributed to the success and reputation of the opera.

It seems that Leopold had asked him to suggest a replacement for Thorwart, and he now put forward the name of Giuseppe Lucchesi, a highly respected Trieste lawyer and a good friend – it was in Lucchesi's house that Da Ponte occasionally ate the meals that kept body and soul together. Even with the Atlantic between them they remained faithful to one another, and thirty-five years later Da Ponte described Michele Colombo and Lucchesi as 'two friends who are dearer to me than life itself'. He was full of confidence in the Emperor – no longer, in his eyes, an unjust man, but one who had been deceived; 'it was a pity that he had by his side evil counsellors, and that a horde of flatterers obeyed and at the same time betrayed him'.

But time went by and no summons came. Stieber wrote back vague and unsatisfactory replies to his anxious enquiries, though they always held out the promise that Leopold would recall him. But Stieber himself was ceasing to be *persona grata* with the Emperor, for he lost his post early in 1792. According to an unreliable source, he was committed to trial on suspicion of democratic tendencies, and although he was allowed to keep his pension he was detained in the fortress of Kufstein until his death in 1795.

Da Ponte's hopes were dealt another blow by Casti, who passed through Trieste in July en route for Vienna. Da Ponte, differences forgotten and eager, as always, to talk to a man whose wit and literary merit he revered, asked Casti's advice. '"Seek your living in Russia, in England or in France," this eminent politician said drily. "But the Emperor has promised to recall me." "The Emperor will not keep his word." "But his secretary has written that I should wait." "The secretary is a buffoon." "But my honour, my enemies . . ." "From Russia, England or France you can revenge yourself on your enemies, and you will soon find places where you will be loaded with honour."'

Da Ponte found this counsel difficult to understand, until Casti explained that Leopold had promised to appoint him Caesarean poet as soon as he arrived in Vienna: this the Emperor did in the spring of 1792. As for the poet to the theatre, after a short interim period, during which Mazzolà filled this post, in July 1791 Da Ponte's rival Giovanni Bertati was chosen to take his place.

So his thoughts turned once again to Venice. He writes in his memoirs, as he had written to Casanova, that he was relying on the Ferrarese to do what she could for him, and is full of reproach that she failed to do so. One of the reasons, he says, is that she had yielded to 'the seductions of a vile man who does not deserve to be named by me'. The only bonus that resulted from her perfidy, he writes, is that it liberated him from 'the shameful passion which for three years had bound me as the unhappy slave of this woman'.

For what happened next we must turn, not to the memoirs, but to the Archivio di Stato in Venice. From the records there it is possible to form a clearer picture of Luigi del Bene, the Ferrarese's shadowy husband. It seems that his father, the papal consul in Venice, had never approved of his marriage and had treated him abominably ever since, preventing him from coming to that city – and it is certain that the Ferrarese did not sing there until after her father-in-law's death. The threat to Luigi's safety was so great that when he did pay a visit to Venice in 1790 the Emperor and Rosenberg ordered the Austrian ambassador to take him under the imperial protection, as otherwise he was liable to suffer the most brutal violence at the hands of his father.

As we have seen, when the consul died early in 1791 Luigi travelled to Rome, over exceedingly bad roads, to ask the Pope to appoint him to his father's post. Before leaving Vienna he wrote to the Pope, undertaking, in addition to his ordinary duties, to keep the Vatican supplied with information about the innermost secrets of the Venetian government, which he would be able to do because of his familiarity with the whole system and with the personalities of the rulers, as well as through bribes – not least of splendid meals – as his father had done.

Somehow or other a copy of this letter came into Da Ponte's hands, together with one which Luigi wrote to his wife from Rome early in March. Addressing her in affectionate terms, Luigi begged her, until the question of the consulacy had been decided, to behave with discretion, 'for in these circumstances everything is taken into account'. Also in Da Ponte's possession were two letters from one Corradini, a secretary, one to Luigi and the other to the Ferrarese.

In what was indisputably the most shameful act he ever committed, Da Ponte now offered to deliver these documents into the hands of the Venetian authorities, in the hope that he would thereby be pardoned. He did so through a man called Carlo Maffei, who lived in Trieste and had some connection with the theatre; it seems that Da Ponte had been recommended to him by a person of authority in Vienna. To Maffei he wrote saying simply that he had matters to communicate which were of the first importance to the Venetian government. Maffei passed this information on to one Zan Francesco Manolesso, the Mayor of Capodistria, a small seaside town about 15 km south of Trieste, just within the borders of the Venetian republic. Manolesso in his turn forwarded the message to the Inquisitors of State, and like lightning the answer came back that he was to meet Da Ponte, but with the utmost secrecy. The two men met by night – so that no one would know of Manolesso's absence – and Da Ponte gave the mayor the various letters to read, including Luigi's letter to him which has already been referred to, so that the handwriting could be compared and verified. He refused actually to hand the letters over to Manolesso, but promised to send him copies.

Time passed, and the copies did not arrive. Then, on 20 August, Da Ponte wrote to Manolesso to say that he had been ordered by his protectors in Venice to go no further in the matter (who were these protectors, one wonders?), and that Leopold had meanwhile banished his chief enemy from Vienna and his second enemy from the theatre. By this he must have meant Lattanzi and Thorwart.

There the matter rested for a couple of weeks. But on 8 September Da Ponte himself wrote to the Inquisitors, in an abject letter full of protestations of loyalty and love for his mother country, enclosing all the documents which he had shown to Manolesso. No doubt he did so because his hopes of being allowed to return to Vienna, which had become warmer with Lattanzi's and Thorwart's dismissal, had once more grown cold as no summons came from Leopold. The letter was forwarded through Manolesso, to whom the Inquisitors sent a laconic acknowledgement.

And here the correspondence seems to have ended. Luigi del Bene was not appointed consul, and rumours of Da Ponte's willingness to betray his mistress's husband trickled out, for in October Zaguri wrote from Venice to Casanova, 'If it is true that [Da] Ponte has been banished, and that he is capable of acting as an informer, God knows what country he will go and disturb next. He was passionately in love with the Ferrarese; he said he had lost everything for her sake; she dropped him and doesn't write to him any more.' (According to an earlier letter, the Ferrarese had now lost any looks she had once possessed.) And again, in January, 'Da Ponte doesn't write to me any more. The Ferrarese, whom I spoke to, says he is mad.'

Significantly, one of the three Inquisitors who signed the various letters to Manolesso was Agostino Barbarigo. If, as seems likely, he was related to the Pietro Barbarigo who had become entangled with Da Ponte over the Treviso *accademia*, perhaps revenge once again stretched out its long arm and played some part in the rejection of Da Ponte's plea to be allowed to return to Venice.

Da Ponte himself is totally silent about his unsuccessful attempt to 'shop' Luigi as a quid pro quo for the forgiveness of the Serenissima. Nor is there any indication of how the letters came into his hands, of whether the Ferrarese gave them to him or whether he stole them. Whatever the answer to this mystery, the Ferrarese and her husband had nothing more to do with him.

While Da Ponte was debating what to do next, four of his influential Trieste friends persuaded him to finish a tragedy, *Il Mezenzio*, which his brother Girolamo had begun but never completed. This was put on in December 1791 for five evenings, and was watched by about three thousand people. In January an opera company came to Trieste for the carnival, and Da Ponte helped to produce a new version of

L'ape musicale, in which Paolo sang the part of the second *mezzo carattere*. This too was much liked. Da Ponte's name was familiar to the citizens of Trieste, for three of the operas for which he had written the libretti – *Una cosa rara, L'arbore di Diana* and *Il burbero di buon cuore* – had been performed at earlier carnivals, and had been very popular indeed.

But this success brought only temporary relief, and no solution to the problem of where he was to go next. Paris was a possibility, for he had, he writes, a letter of recommendation to Marie Antoinette from her brother Joseph, which the late Emperor had given him at the time when the opera company was dismissed, saying 'Marie Antoinette loves your *Cosa rara*'. 'So I wrote to Casti,' Da Ponte says in the memoirs, 'and asked him to tell the Emperor, or see that he was told, that in view of my changed circumstances all I was now asking for was some help to enable me to leave Trieste and go to Paris.' There was no reply, and in desperation he appealed to Leopold himself. When still no answer came he resolved to go to Vienna to put his case in person to the Emperor.

By the time he arrived Leopold was dead. He was succeeded by his oldest son Francis, whom Da Ponte had often seen while Joseph was still alive, for he spent much time at the Viennese court. Da Ponte must have hoped for great things from the new ruler, and he hastened to Casti, who promised to help him.

> To the glory of truth [writes Da Ponte], let it be said that there was nothing he did not do to my advantage, and, whatever his reasons may have been, I was none the less grateful, and the gratitude which I expressed then, and express now, after his death, is completely sincere. He was my persecutor, and my feelings as a man, and even more my duty as a historian, have forced me to paint him as such in my memoirs. He was my benefactor, and, as such, it is my duty to acknowledge the obligation which I am under in this respect . . .
>
> The Abbé Casti advised me to go to Count Saurau, his great friend, whose goodness, integrity, and kindly disposition towards me he could vouch for; besides, he was extremely powerful by virtue of his position as head of the police. Casti offered to come with me, and he became my defender, apologist and most zealous eulogist.

It seems that Saurau interceded with Francis, who, though he did not retract Da Ponte's dismissal, sent him money for his journey and to settle his debts in the city, which had been a source of great concern to him. He also, he writes, received permission to stay in Vienna at his own discretion, and to publish in every Austrian journal a statement that his innocence had been recognised. Whether or not this claim is true, no such announcement appeared. But the consideration which Da Ponte received from Francis was great enough for him to write later of 'the clemency with which the reigning Emperor consoled and sweetened my misery in Vienna', and to remember Francis all his life with the deepest gratitude.

'I stayed in the city for three weeks,' the memoirs go on. 'More than a hundred Italians came to see me, but I received very few of them. In their faces I could see consternation, vexation, and above all a devouring curiosity to know how such a metamorphosis had come about. Behind their backs I laughed a lot. To some I said one thing, to others something different, and to none of them the truth.'

One person who was particularly anxious to see the last of Da Ponte was Giovanni Bertati. Da Ponte describes how he visited the poet in residence, ostensibly to make his acquaintance and ask for copies of his own libretti. He writes with amusement and scorn of how he found Bertati's desk littered with books: a volume of French comedies, a dictionary, a rhyming dictionary and a grammar. When he went to the Burgtheater he found to his delight that all his libretti had been sold, and that 'his' operas were much performed, 'especially those with music by Mozzart, Martin and Salieri' (but in this his memory plays him false, for since his departure from Vienna there had been an almost complete change of repertoire). As for Bertati, his reign was short, for after three years he was deposed in favour of Giovanni de Gamerra.

On 28 March 1792 Count Collalto, one of Casanova's Viennese patrons, wrote to Dux, 'Madame Ferrarese passed through here a little while ago and stayed for a few days on her way to Warsaw, where she is engaged for the theatre. The Abbé Da Ponte has also been seen here, but according to rumour her husband would not allow him in the house' – hardly surprising, if Da Ponte's attempt to betray del Bene to the Venetian authorities had become known, as Zaguri's letter to Casanova suggested was the case.

It was either shortly before or after the visit to Vienna that Da Ponte met the woman who was to become his wife, in fact if not in law. After parting from the Ferrarese, he writes:

I did not think it was possible for me ever to fall in love again. I was wrong. My heart was not, and perhaps still is not, made to exist without love; and however much women may have deceived and tricked me in the course of my life, in all honesty I cannot remember ever having passed six months in the whole of it without loving someone, and loving (may I make the boast?) with a perfect love.

It happened that at this time I was introduced to a young English girl, the daughter of a rich merchant who had lately arrived in Trieste. She was said by everyone to be extremely beautiful, and to unite gentle manners with all the graces of a cultivated mind. Her face was covered with a black veil, which prevented me from seeing her, so, wanting to find out if the reality matched her reputation, I approached her and, with a certain boldness given to me by the intimate relationship which I had already formed with her family, said as if in jest, 'Mademoiselle, the style in which you are wearing your veil is not *à la mode*.' Not realising what was in my mind, she enquired, 'What is the present fashion?' 'This, signorina,' and taking her veil by the edge I drew it over her head.

The girl, understandably enough, was displeased and left the room, to Da Ponte's regret and remorse, and for a few days he did not have the chance to see her, for she was staying with an English lady nearby. Meanwhile he continued to visit the house of her parents and brother. The name of the family was Grahl; the father had been born in Dresden and his wife was French, but they had spent many years in England, where their daughter, Ann Celestine Ernestine Grahl, had passed the first sixteen years of her life. Like Da Ponte, she is said to have been a converted Jew, but she had become a member of the Anglican church. She had travelled with her parents in France and Germany, and had for a time been tutor to the family of General van den Boetzelaer in Holland. She was an accomplished linguist, and Da Ponte's comment about her beauty is confirmed by the fact that in Trieste she was known as *la bella inglesina*.

John Grahl and his son Peter were expert chemists: they traded in drugs, spices, liquors and medicines, as well as distilling. They were also usurers and speculators in bad debts, discount, mortgages, real estate, and similar ventures. They seem to have arrived in Trieste in December 1790, for an advertisement in the *Osservatore Triestino* announces that they have for sale English and French jewellery, gold watches and chains, knives, scissors, buckles, artificial flowers and ostrich feathers. In 1793 they went bankrupt – probably not for the first and certainly not for the last time: alas for Da Ponte's hopes that he was marrying into a rich family. But there is no foundation at all for the claim that he married Nancy (as she was known) because he believed that she would bring him a comfortable dowry. His own account, in any case, contradicts this.

To begin with, he writes, he had agreed to act as a kind of marriage broker between Nancy and a rich Italian friend of his, living in Vienna, who was seeking a bride. While negotiations were proceeding, he and Nancy spent many hours together exchanging French and Italian lessons, and soon fell in love. By the time the letter which was to have finalised matters came from Vienna Da

Ponte was in an agony of apprehension. Luckily for him, John Grahl was incensed by the potential bridegroom's enquiries about a substantial dowry, and asked Da Ponte whether he would like to have Nancy for his bride, and Nancy whether she would like him for her husband. Their looks gave the answer. 'My joy,' Da Ponte goes on, 'was so great, and I believe hers was also, that neither of us could say a word for the whole of the rest of the evening. I left the house filled with emotions which I cannot easily describe. At that moment my entire fortune consisted of 5 piastres; I had no employment and no hope of any; and the letter which her father had torn up because of the suitor's demands gave me neither encouragement nor wish to have a fortune from him. But I loved, and was loved in return; and this was enough to give me courage for anything, and to enable me to overcome any obstacle.'

So on 12 August 1792 *la bella inglesina* was given into the care of Lorenzo Da Ponte, now in his forties and twenty years older than his bride, but still attractive to women. No evidence has been discovered that, as a Roman Catholic priest, he ever actually married his 'beautiful, fresh and loving companion', simply that she became his 'after social ceremonies and formalities'. Nor is there any evidence that from this day forward he was consistently faithful to her. But neither is there anything, in the memoirs or elsewhere, to suggest the opposite. Though he may sometimes have found a pretty face and figure a temporary distraction – it is hard to imagine that he did not – so far as we know he was a loving husband until the day of Nancy's death. This is not to deny that he was often a dreadful trial to her, and she can rarely have known a moment's calm with her weathercock, impulsive husband. But from the glimpses, tantalisingly small, that we catch of her, and above all from the verses which Da Ponte wrote after her death, everything seems to show that she loved him dearly in return, and that for most of their married life they faced its tempests together.

In Venice and Trieste there was endless gossip about their marriage, one of the most curious observers being Zaguri, who passed on to Casanova any titbits which he heard. A century later, according to oral tradition, the story ran that 'Lorenzo Da Ponte threw away his priestly collar in Trieste, married a cook and fled to America'.

X

On the same day that Nancy gave herself into Da Ponte's keeping they set out on their journey to Paris. That night they reached the town of Laibach, 'where Love and Hymen taught me to dry the tears of a tender daughter who had abandoned family and friends, perhaps for ever, for my sake.'

For some days they travelled happily, until one evening they had a mishap. Crossing a mountain, they alighted from their carriage to ease their horses in the steep descent, Da Ponte supporting his wife with one hand while with the other he held an umbrella as protection against a thin drizzle of rain. Nancy thought she could see two armed men coming towards them, and, frightened by the approaching darkness and the solitude of the place, she slipped between her husband's clothes a purse which her mother had given her, containing much of their slender capital. 'Meanwhile the two men approached us, greeted us courteously and went on their way. We saw then that what we had thought to be guns were two long sticks with metal ends, designed to help them on their path, and the thieves themselves two aged labourers on their way home; and we laughed heartily at our fears.' However, when they reached the monastery where they were to shelter for the night they laughed no longer, for they found that the purse was missing, and a long search of their route over the mountain failed to reveal it. They told the abbot of their loss, and he promised to send the purse on to them if it was found. They lingered for some days in Prague, their next port of call, hoping for news, but in vain. (If they had stayed a little longer, they would have seen the Prague *première* of *Die Zauberflöte* – and Da Ponte would no doubt have detested the barbaric language of the libretto.)

He had intended to journey on to Dresden, but remembering that Casanova owed him some money, decided to make a small detour and travel via Oberleutensdorf. He realised at once, however, that Casanova's purse was as empty as his own, so, without putting him to shame by mentioning money, stayed only three or four days before going on to Dresden.

As the two friends said goodbye Casanova gave Da Ponte three pieces of advice: to go to London rather than Paris; and, in London, never to enter the caffe degl'Italiani, and never to sign his name. Da

Ponte followed the first of these counsels – by necessity rather than choice – but not the other two, and he writes that almost all his subsequent disasters sprang from his disregard of Casanova's golden precepts, for, though he liked neither Casanova's principles nor his way of life, he valued his counsel, which was almost always sound.

After they parted, Da Ponte whiled away many hours of their journey by relating some of his friend's colourful escapades to Nancy, who was fascinated by the old adventurer. The two friends kept in touch, and Da Ponte's letters, which often bore a postscript from Nancy, tell us much about the next stage of his life.

In Dresden, he wrote, they were received with great friendliness by Mazzolà and Father Hueber. Nevertheless he decided not to try to make a living there, sensing that Mazzolà would not welcome a potential rival. He felt, he told Casanova, lost and without direction, a swimmer struggling against a strong current to find a friendly shore. He was still contemplating France as his destination, but when he and Nancy were a few miles from Spires they heard of Marie Antoinette's imprisonment, and knew that their hopes of finding patronage in Paris were dashed. So they journeyed on to London, which pleased Nancy, for her sister Louisa and brother-in-law Charles Niccolini were living there. The two families were much bound up in London and America. Da Ponte conceived a violent hatred for Louisa, believing until his death that she was responsible for many of his and Nancy's misfortunes.

For the time being, however, they stayed with the Niccolinis in Silver Street (now Beak Street), off Golden Square, which, once a fashionable quarter, had gone down in the world. Not long afterwards they moved to a small room at No. 16 Sherrard Street, today Sherwood Street, which seventy years earlier had been 'a handsome, broad, well-built and inhabited place'. By now Da Ponte's meagre purse was virtually empty, and the Niccolinis, 'being neither rich nor generous', could not help them.

Many years later, writing of his London life, Da Ponte said, 'So strange, so varied, so new are the things which happened to me in that city, that to give an idea in a brief compendium would be like trying to enclose the ocean in a walnut.' But for the moment little enough happened. Prospects seemed good, since his name was known to London opera-goers: *Una cosa rara* had been performed in 1789; his old friends Michael Kelly and Stephen Storace were acting managers at the King's Theatre, the home of Italian opera; and the post of poet to the opera was vacant. His rival was one Badini, who, Da Ponte says, knew as much about the job as Bertati's shoes (and we know what contempt he had for Bertati), but who was well established in London. To avoid unpleasantness he suggested that Badini should be made poet, but that he himself should be engaged to write two libretti a year. After some delay, and much to his annoyance, this proposal was rejected.

Only one person showed signs of humanity and friendship, a minor composer called Carlo Pozzi, who occasionally wrote songs for insertion in other men's operas. He opened his purse to Da Ponte and introduced him to his friends, among them Madame Mara, one of the greatest singers of her day and still, although she was now over forty, a favourite with London audiences. She asked Da Ponte to write an opera for her, and he adapted his play *Mezenzio*. For this she paid him thirty guineas, though there seems no evidence that it was ever performed. According to Badini it was put to music by Giacomo Ferrari, an Italian composer who was then staying with Pozzi in Great Pulteney Street.

Da Ponte no doubt met many of the foreign – and especially the Italian – musicians living in London at this time, with two of whom he was later to be involved in a disastrous business enterprise: Domenico Corri, a singing and music teacher, and Jan Ladislav Dussek, a composer and virtuoso pianist of great talent and some fame, who married Corri's daughter Sophia. He was, says Ferrari, known as *le beau Dussek*, 'the wittiest and most amiable man in the world, always jolly and in a good humour, never worried by business matters. He played magnificently, and had a natural and ingratiating talent for composing.' His compositions were mainly for the piano, and he often performed them at concerts in London. He also played with Haydn, who described him as 'one of the most upright, moral, and, in music, the most eminent of men'. Da Ponte, with his love of witty conversation, must have rejoiced in his company until their business dealings began to go sour.

He writes to Casanova of the various noble patrons who tried to help him, among them the Marquess of Salisbury, Prince Lichtenstein, various foreign diplomats and the Duke of Bedford, who was much involved with trying to establish the opera house on an even keel (a herculean task). More than once he warns his friend not to call him Abbé when addressing his letters – hardly a proper title for one who now had a wife – and he writes tenderly of his Nancy, who loves him as dearly as he loves her, and with whom he could be happy if it were not for the wretched state of his purse. He thanks Casanova for his good advice, which he will scrupulously follow so far as he can – except for the suggestion that he should set himself up as a teacher of Italian, 'a profession which at the present time is followed by waiters, cobblers, exiles, cops, etc., etc., who by way of payment have flung in their faces a few ha'pence, or a shilling, or a glass of beer.' He did, however, contemplate hiring a room where he could hold Italian readings.

'If you asked me how I've managed to live for six and a half months, I shouldn't know what to answer. I know I've already spent ninety guineas, but whether they sprang out of the earth or fell from heaven only an angel could tell you. The best thing is that I haven't many debts, and those which I have got don't bother me because I can pay them when I want to, and because everyone thinks I'm pretty well off, since I'm careful not to tell anyone what the situation really is.' (Da Ponte never lost his belief in the importance of keeping up appearances.) He also confided that he was writing to the Emperor that very day to beg for permission to return to Vienna, though there is no evidence that he ever did so. And in every letter he implored Casanova to ask Count Waldstein to send him money. He had met the Count in London, where Waldstein, who had escaped from Paris at the height of the French revolution, lived for some months, but in a state of penury almost as wretched as Da Ponte's own. The hapless poet, who was continually trying to touch him for money, in five months had managed to extract only four guineas. And appeals now through Casanova elicited equally dusty answers.

Casanova, busily writing to his various correspondents, passed on the gossip about Da Ponte. 'I enjoyed Da Ponte's letter,' Zaguri had written the previous summer. 'He is fulfilling your prophecy. If he really does write his memoirs, they will be interesting only because of that fact. [How tantalising that we do not know what Casanova's prophecy was.] He is a scoundrel, but since scoundrels greet one another, greet him from me.' 'Da Ponte is completely mad,' he wrote a couple of months later – but he never ceased to be eager for the latest news.

Da Ponte contemplated starting up a review, *La bilancia teatrale*, which would appear on the morning after each operatic performance, and (since no doubt he intended that it should tear every opera to bits) would show the management what a bad mistake they had made in not appointing him poet to the Italian opera – he had, indeed, even aspired to become manager. Nothing came of the plan, owing to the high cost of printing in London, and probably also to a dearth of subscribers. And he wrote an ode on the death of Louis XVI, which produced a violent and obscene lampoon from Badini. Da Ponte, needless to say, replied in kind.

When he realised that his hopes were likely to be stillborn, he decided to take most of the money which Madame Mara had paid for *Il Mezenzio* and see if he could find better fortune in the Low Countries. Early in July 1793, leaving Nancy in London, he set out for Brussels. Here he sought rich patrons to support his project of establishing Italian opera there, and from Belgium he went to Rotterdam and The Hague with the same aim. He found, he writes to Casanova, a considerable amount of enthusiasm among influential noblemen, including Baron Boetzelaer, whose family Nancy had at one time taught. But the overwhelming victory of the French army over the Anglo-Hanoverian forces at Hondschoote early in September, and the wounding of the youngest Prince of Orange, turned all thoughts of enjoyment to desolation and weeping. The only good news came from Nancy. Da Ponte already knew that the purse which they had lost on their journey to England had been found, and he had been impatiently awaiting its arrival in England. Now Nancy wrote that it had reached her, and some days later she joined him.

But 'eighty florins did not last long in the hands of a man who had never learnt to economise'. The autumn was bitterly cold, Nancy was pregnant (his letters to Casanova show his great concern for her), and soon, even after selling his clothes and linen, they had money neither for the rent nor for food.

'We had bread for breakfast, bread for lunch, and sometimes not even bread for supper but only tears. However, it was not my companion who shed those tears. She bore everything with angelic patience: she managed to laugh and joke; she made me play chess with her and insisted on playing for huge sums of money, the loser paying with caresses and kisses. These tender devices, which at other times would have made me so happy, only increased my wretchedness and despair.'

He wrote to Nancy Storace to offer her a contract for his shaky operatic venture, to Guardasoni in Prague, even to the Ferrarese, but no one took him up – and who can blame them? 'Holland yielded nothing and cost me almost 120 louis,' he wrote to Casanova. 'I should have gained a small fortune if I hadn't been betrayed first by the Storace, and then by Rovedino and Ferrari,[1] the first a singer, the other a competent composer whose music the Count knows well.'

One good friend helped them when he could, and their German landlord was kind, but prospects were bleak when, out of the blue, a letter arrived from Nancy's sister Louisa, telling them that Badini had been sacked and that William Taylor, the impresario of the opera house, wanted to appoint Da Ponte in his place. Come quickly,

[1] Ferrari and Rovedino were both in Brussels in the autumn of 1793.

Louisa wrote, for your friends are anxiously awaiting you, and I'm dying to embrace my Nancy. Da Ponte, overwhelmed with gratitude, knelt by the bedside to say a prayer of thanksgiving.

The offer, he wrote to Casanova, 'arriving at a moment when I seemed to be on the edge of a precipice, and in a state of desperation, made me truly believe that there is a hand in heaven which rules all things below.' It would seem that Casanova, to whom he had once more made a desperate appeal for money, had sent the usual negative reply, combined with a suggestion that his friend should use Nancy's charms to raise funds, for Da Ponte replied. 'So far as I'm concerned, I can say: *Anything in the world, but not horns*. I believe that God has given me a heart and a brain: this will enable me to suffer all the ill turns of fortune; to open one way or another of living honourably, without having to reproach myself for any base or dishonest deed. *Aude aliquid*: but not at the expense of virtue.' As Nancy's own surprisingly restrained postscript suggests, she was more than a little upset by Casanova's brutal proposal.

They set off for London a fortnight after Louisa's letter arrived, waiting until Da Ponte could settle his debts and arriving in the latter half of November. William Taylor, known as 'Opera Taylor', was manager and part-owner of the King's Theatre. Born in Aberdeen, the son of a tenant farmer – he always kept his 'harsh Scottish dialect' – he had started his London career as a bank-clerk. He was an extraordinary character, and is described in vivid colours in a book by John Ebers, who, to his cost, became manager thirty years later: 'One of the most singular of mankind . . . His whole life was a continued hoax . . . He quarrelled with everybody, ridiculed everybody, and hoaxed everybody.' But, says Ebers, he was also a fellow of infinite merriment, and it was impossible to refuse his requests for money.

Da Ponte has his own viewpoint:

I do not believe that anyone in the world could give a fair and exact idea [of Taylor], but for me it is even less possible than for anyone else. Plucked casually by him from the terrible situation in which I found myself in Holland, I had, and have always kept, all the feelings for him which gratitude, pity and friendship inspire in a sympathetic and well-intentioned mind . . . I never wanted to examine too closely or severely his defects and his weaknesses, which I tried to defend or excuse as a father does those of his son; and when they wounded me I was silent, or took no revenge except tears . . . This singular man was a perfect mixture of two contrary natures. Left to himself, he was humane, noble, generous; led by others he entirely assumed the colour of those who led him, and

135

particularly of the woman whom he loved and of her favourites, who immediately became his own.

Certainly he was totally unscrupulous in money affairs, and for much of his life lived within King's Bench Rules for debt, escaping, however, for days on end to go fishing; he even travelled to Hull to stand for Parliament. In the King's Bench, wrote Ebers, he continued his gay life, meeting 'with many persons there of habits congenial to his own; and the enjoyment of the rules rendered confinement there in some measure only nominal . . . I have often met, when visiting Taylor, Sir John Ladd and his lady, as well as Lady Hamilton,[1] a coterie being thus formed which, in point of vivacity and zest of enjoyment, could not be excelled by the freest of the free . . . One evening he so broke through all restraint, that Lady Ladd found it expedient to empty the boiling contents of the kettle on him.' (Debtors under the King's Bench Rules were permitted, on giving security to the marshal, to live within prescribed limits outside the walls of the prison. Conditions in the debtors' prisons were not necessarily at all unpleasant: some people preferred to remain there, and even kept winter and summer residences in different prisons.) Da Ponte, always fascinated by dashing, debonair figures, was immensely attracted by Taylor, even though, after he had become embroiled in the manager's dubious financial dealings, he came to feel that Taylor was responsible for his own ruin.

The finances of the King's Theatre were a never-ending headache, and since the beginning of Taylor's association in 1781 enormous debts had piled up. Unlike continental opera houses, the theatre – which between 1792 and 1843 was the only one licensed to perform Italian opera in London – was privately owned, under the patronage of aristocratic lovers of music and with no state subsidy, and it was impossible to run it except at a huge loss. The unfortunates in charge of it were perpetually running hither and thither to try to raise funds. Ebers relates that one day, when a group of friends were discussing capital punishment in Taylor's presence, one of them said that he would abolish it entirely. 'What would you inflict, then, on a criminal of the worst kind?' asked another. 'By . . .,' said Taylor, starting up, 'make him manager of the Opera House. If he deserved a worse punishment, he must be the devil incarnate.' Nevertheless he clung like a limpet to his job as manager, despite many efforts to get rid of him.

[1] The beautiful Emma, Nelson's mistress, who in 1813 spent a year in prison for debt.

The Italian Opera, 'the rendezvous of all that is gay and pleasurable in the metropolis', was patronised by the whole of the aristocracy, including the Prince of Wales. Unfortunately – and this was one great difference between audiences in Vienna and London – they came not for the music but for the social occasion. Ladies of fashion took their boxes for the season, and here they entertained their friends. Lord Mount Edgcumbe, a noted opera lover whose observations provide a priceless record of the musical life of the day, wrote, 'Every lady possessing an opera box considered it as much her *home* as her house, and was as sure to be found there, few missing any of the performances.' The ladies and their friends, perhaps snugly concealed behind the rich curtains which could be drawn across the front of the boxes, would chat happily away, stopping only to applaud a favourite singer, for musical taste was the last thing many of these elegant spectators possessed. 'Whatever we may pretend,' the *Morning Chronicle* wrote in 1795, 'we are too ignorant of musical science as a nation, to find pleasure in what produces rapture on an Italian stage'; and one traveller who spent two years in England wrote in 1821, 'There has never been a dearth of excellent virtuosi in London. Here their talents have always found ample reward, and this has ever attracted them from every quarter of the globe.[1] But they seldom endure its atmosphere for long. Upon acquiring a handsome competency they generally forsake a country, where the art indeed is sure to meet with patronage, but where the patrons are destitute of all sympathy and enthusiasm. This is chiefly conspicuous at the Italian opera.' Da Ponte had a low opinion of the English as a musical people.

Performances were noisy occasions, what with the chatter, the cabals, the partisanship for this or that singer, the booing, and the battles which were fought out on the stage between 'the Pinks of Fashion and the Bucks of Distinction' on the one hand and 'Lamplighters, Scene-Shifters, Carpenters, etc.' on the other. Sometimes blows were exchanged, and on one occasion at least the Bow Street officers and the Guards had to be called in to restore order. The audience claimed the right to crowd on to the stage, which became so packed that the singers had difficulty in moving and it was impossible to work the heavy machinery which provided the spectacular scenery the audience expected. Not until 1813 did a decree by the Lord Chamberlain forbid this custom, though there were endless complaints about it.

[1] The fees paid in London to singers and composers in the late eighteenth and early nineteenth centuries were much higher than they could have found anywhere in Italy.

Contemporary newspaper cuttings vividly reflect the scene, with the occasional advertisement inserted by gentlemen imploring that the ladies 'will not deprive them of the pleasure of seeing the performance by crowning their heads with an *ostrich's tail*'; the warning that 'neither Ladies in Undress Hats or Bonnets nor Gentlemen in Boots' will be admitted into the pit; and the intimation of what was perhaps London's first one-way traffic system, with the plea to the nobility 'to give directions to their servants to set down and take up at the Theatre with the horses' heads turned towards Pall Mall'.

The management was much at the mercy of the chief singers, and particularly of the *prima donna*, who at the least whim would refuse to sing or plead illness. On such occasions the performance might be cancelled with little or no warning – as it might be, too, if the weather was bad. Occasionally a medical certificate testifying to the singer's illness would be displayed in the opera house to soften the wrath of the audience. Operas were far less popular than ballet and were rarely given in their entirety, but were ruthlessly cut and shortened, with ballets between each act which might be longer than the acts themselves. And, just as in Vienna, the impresario had to deal with ego-blown, temperamental virtuosi. 'Let a new opera be intended to be brought forward,' John Ebers wrote. 'Signor This will not sing his part, because it is not prominent enough; so, to enrich it, a gathering must be made of airs from other operas, no matter whether by the same composer or not, nor whether there be any incongruity between the style of the original piece and the adventitious passages introduced' – just the same absurd situation about which Da Ponte had complained so bitterly in Vienna.

English audiences – often with reason – had the lowest possible opinion of the words of Italian operas (and anyway could not understand them), and the hapless librettist was regarded with equal contempt. Frequently his name was not mentioned on the printed libretto or the theatre announcements, and his main duty was to adapt existing libretti rather than write original ones. This, in the main, is what Da Ponte did at the King's Theatre, his first assignment being an adaptation of Cimarosa's *Il matrimonio segreto*, which two years earlier had had a brilliant *première* in Vienna. Leopold was so taken with it that after listening to it he first gave the cast supper and then commanded them to sing it all over again. For the King's Theatre Da Ponte adapted and shortened the text, and strengthened the comic element. The libretto, in Italian and English, was sold in the opera house, according to the usual custom. The poet had a right to 50% of the proceeds, a useful addition to his modest income, which was not much higher than that of considerably more menial employees. The translations at the King's Theatre were generally made by John Mazzinghi, who, working at great speed, sometimes produced surprisingly skilful results, though Da Ponte thought little of them.

Il matrimonio segreto opened the opera season with great splendour early in 1794, before a large and fashionable audience, the social standing and stylishness of the company unequalled by that of any other audience in Europe. It was followed by *I contadini bizzarri*, with music by Sarti and Paisiello and additions by Da Ponte's benefactor Carlo Pozzi. Da Ponte altered and added, and for his pains the opera was criticised as being too long, more suited to Italian tastes than to English ones.

The next offering in which he had a hand was a double bill, consisting of *Il capriccio drammatico* (based on a one-act work by Cimarosa with the well-worn theme of the trials and tribulations involved in trying to put on an opera) and *Don Giovanni*. This was not Mozart's opera but the text by Bertati which had been performed in Venice in 1787 with music by Gazzaniga, and which was now set to music by a mish-mash of composers. Da Ponte begged Taylor and Michael Kelly to put on Mozart's opera, but the answer came back that 'the music was not fit for the English taste'. The version given at the King's Theatre did, however, include the 'Catalogue song', so perhaps a snatch of Mozart's music was heard then. According to Da Ponte, the first performance nearly caused a riot among the audience, while *The Times* remarked that it 'was throughout disapproved. So determined an opposition to this kind of entertainment we have never witnessed.'

After two performances it was withdrawn and the second part of the evening was devoted to an adaptation of an opera by Guglielmi, a popular and respected composer of the day. *La bella pescatrice* had been much enjoyed by continental audiences; Da Ponte now cut down the text to one act, and additional music was written by Joseph Mazzinghi, the brother of John and one of the musical directors. He wrote several mediocre operas which were performed at the theatre. On a couple of occasions *Il capriccio drammatico* was followed by *La prova dell'opera*, which seems to have been written by Da Ponte as a kind of second act and fitted to existing music by Cimarosa.

No opera house could function without the *virtuose* who both drained the coffers with their enormous salaries and attracted the audiences, and the King's Theatre was no exception. The stars for Da Ponte's first season were Brigida Banti, whose forte was *opera seria*, and Anna Morichelli, an excellent *buffa* player. They arrived in

April on the same packet boat from Spain, and as they were ferocious rivals, and the terror of managers, composers, singers and poets alike, the journey must have been a stormy one. [1]

Banti, then in her mid-thirties, was remarkable for her ravishing voice and total lack of musicianship. When she was a girl she had earned her living as a street singer, and had been discovered in Paris by a theatre impresario. Lazy and reluctant to study (on her first visit to London in 1779 she was taught by Signor Piozzi, Mrs Thrale's husband, but 'she exhausted his patience because of her obstinacy and laziness'), she made up for these deficiencies by the extraordinary beauty of her voice, and by her true ear, excellent intonation and clever acting. For many years she was the darling of London audiences, though one paper criticised her regrettable habit of conversing *mezza voce* with the orchestra instead of 'attending to the business of the scene'.

This is how the painter Vigée-Le Brun, who saw her in Naples, describes her:

> She is tiny, and very ugly, with such a lot of hair that her chignon looks like a horse's mane. But what a voice! There has never been one like it for power and compass; the room, big as it was, could not contain it. Her style of singing, I remember, was exactly like that of the great Pacchierotti [a famous castrato], who was Madame Grassini's [2] teacher.
>
> This superb singer had a very extraordinary figure: her breast was high and shaped exactly like a pair of bellows; we saw this after the concert, when some other ladies and I went with her into a small room; and I think that this strange build may have explained the strength and agility of her voice.

Morichelli, who had sung in Vienna for a couple of seasons while Da Ponte was there, was, said Mount Edgcumbe, beyond her prime when she came to London (though she was three years younger than Banti), but nevertheless she had her influential patrons. Da Ponte loathed them both in equal measure, though, with his usual fairness where artistic merit was in question, he paid tribute to the strength, sweetness and sublimity of Banti's singing and to Morichelli's splendid acting.

---

[1] Singers and instrumentalists were accustomed to travelling immense distances, from London to St Petersburg to Warsaw to Naples, or wherever their engagements called them. As John Rosselli puts it, 'Since the late seventeenth century most of the opera world had been perpetually on the move.'

[2] An Italian contralto who later sang at the King's Theatre.

Alike in their vices, in their passions, in iniquity and badness of heart, they were totally unlike in character, and pursued entirely different paths in the furthering of their designs. Morichelli, who was very clever and cultured, was an old wolf who concealed all her schemes in a veil of mystery and cunning. She always took her measure from a distance, trusted no one, never lost her temper, and, though she greatly loved voluptuous pleasures, nevertheless managed to behave with the modesty and reserve of a virgin of fifteen; and the more bitter the gall in her soul, the smoother and more honied her smile. Of the nature of her passions it is not necessary to speak. She was a lady of the theatre, so her principal gods were those of all her kind, but to an excessive degree: pride, envy, self-interest. Banti, on the other hand, was an ignorant, silly, insolent woman who, accustomed in her early youth to sing in cafés and on the street, brought into the theatre, where only her voice led her, all the habits and manners and customs of a shameless Corisca. Free in her speech, still freer in her actions, given to debauchery, to dissoluteness and the bottle, she always appeared to be just what she in fact was, knew no moderation and had no self-restraint; and when one of her passions was aroused through meeting difficulties or opposition, she became an asp, a fury, a demon of hell, who could have overturned an empire, let alone a theatre.

Da Ponte's opinion is supported by Ferrari, who speaks of her greed and lack of sensitivity.

Unfortunately for Morichelli, a liaison quickly grew up between Taylor and Banti. 'How did the world smile at this attachment,' a contemporary satirist wrote, 'a doting Cisebeo [sic] with an Harraden, who had children in every town in Italy. A loving stage-treading pair, whose joint ages might be nearer 120 than 100 ...[1] The money this dotard spent upon this Signora is incredible.'

Da Ponte was faced with the daunting task of producing a libretto for the debut of each. According to custom, the leading singers were entitled to choose the opera in which they first appeared, and Banti and Morichelli were each determined that hers should be performed first and that it should be a greater success than her rival's. Inevitably, Banti won, and chose *Semiramide*, with a text by Moretti which Da Ponte added to and altered. She made a triumphant debut, even though she had such an atrocious cold that she was unable even to attempt the principal song. (Many of the leading singers immediately caught ghastly colds the moment their feet touched England's inhospitable shores.) The music was by Francesco Bianchi, who also came to London at this time and remained there for many years (he committed suicide in 1810). He was a competent

---

[1] In fact their joint ages were 78.

141

if unexciting composer who, however, showed great skill in writing the kind of music which English audiences enjoyed. Certainly he did so on this occasion. 'No opera ever had greater success or a longer run,' Mount Edgcumbe wrote. 'Indeed, it was one of those of which it is impossible to tire.'

Morichelli's debut, three weeks later, was also well received, but her reviews did not approach those of her rival. She chose *Il burbero di buon cuore*, in which she had already appeared in Vienna. Since the composer, Martin y Soler, was safely in St Petersburg, the singers took their usual liberties with the music, introducing songs by other composers (including Ferrari and Pozzi) to show off their voices. A popular duet which Haydn wrote in 1782 for his opera *Orlando Paladino* was resuscitated and provided with new words by Da Ponte ('*Quel cor umano e tenero*'), but curiously when Haydn gave the duet at his benefit concert in the King's Theatre in May 1795 he did not use Da Ponte's words but the old ones from *Orlando Paladino*. Nowhere in the memoirs does the poet mention Haydn, though he must have met the composer both in Vienna and in England.

Again according to custom, the two stars were each entitled to a benefit performance. Banti chose *La serva padrona*, with music by Cimarosa, and Morichelli *La frascatana*, by the popular composer Paisiello. For each occasion Da Ponte, under his Arcadian pseudonym Lesbonico Pegasio, printed at the beginning of the libretto a fulsome tribute to the prima donna, enquiring whether her voice was mortal or divine. To *La frascatana* he made many alterations and additions, including one new aria which was set to music and published by Domenico Corri.

Just before the close of the season, at the end of June 1794, he adapted for Banti a grand cantata, *La vittoria*, with music by Paisiello, which she had first sung in Naples on quite another occasion, and which was now performed to celebrate Lord Howe's glorious victory over the French fleet in the English Channel. Banti ended the performance by singing *Rule Britannia* to wild applause. (This singing of patriotic songs by the prima donna was no novelty: Banti had already sung 'the popular air of "God Save the King"' more than once, though she had to be prompted when she forgot her words. Some years later the press was still imploring her to learn it properly, since 'a British audience will never be satisfied with but one verse'. The chorus were also deficient in their knowledge of the text.)

From the libretti and the theatre announcements it is clear that Da Ponte had been involved in most of these operas (and perhaps in others as well), cutting, expanding, adapting, translating. During the next season (1794–95) his chief work was to write two libretti for

Martin y Soler, whom, at Kelly's behest, he had persuaded to leave St Petersburg for London. The first of them was *La scola de' maritati*, in which Morichelli sang the chief role. The plot is nonsensical but the libretto is entertaining, and the opera was received, the *Morning Chronicle* declared, with 'rapturous applause . . . Though very long, there was not one single scene or song that dragged.' 'So perfectly has [Soler] adapted his airs to the character of a nation where he has been so short a time a resident,' the same paper wrote a few days later, 'that many pieces of his first essay will assuredly come to the barrel organ.' The opera was often performed at the King's Theatre, as well as abroad, under a variety of names – *La capricciosa corretta*, *Gli sposi in contrasto* and *La moglie corretta*.

La scola de' maritati led to another brisk and venomous exchange between Da Ponte and his old foe Badini, for the ex-poet made a fierce attack on Da Ponte for what he described as the indecency and plagiarism of the opera. Da Ponte hit back robustly, calling Badini every insulting and obscene name he could think of.

The next venture of composer and poet was less happy, and brought their friendship to an end, as Da Ponte told Casanova – the last letter, so far as we know, that he was ever to write to him (Casanova died three years later). He begins with light-hearted excuses for not having written before. 'I'm well,' he goes on, 'I enjoy perfect health, and except for the fact that I've got twenty-four or twenty-six teeth missing, which for some crazy reason didn't want to remain with me, no one would think I was forty-six. My Nancy is with me; I love her, and she loves me; and I could be perfectly happy if I weren't one of those men whom fortune and evil friends enjoy treating badly.'

The opera was called *L'isola del piacere*, *The Island of Pleasure*, and the first act was written in perfect harmony. But then things went wrong. According to the memoirs (where the account is slightly different from the explanation which Da Ponte gave Casanova), Martin y Soler ('Oh! what a monster, without moral character or heart!') showed himself in his true colours, paying court to Morichelli and eventually going to live with her, spreading lies about Da Ponte even while he was staying in the Da Pontes' house, making pregnant their young but ill-favoured servant and declaring that Da Ponte was the guilty man. 'Our long, delightful and enviable friendship grew cold, and the second act of *L'isola del piacere* was written entirely on an island of ice: it seemed to me, as I wrote it, that I was writing for Righini, not for Martini or the composer of *Una cosa rara*.' Matters were not improved when Morichelli, singing the chief role, introduced a mad scene from another opera which she had sung in Paris with great success, but which 'fitted in as well as Pilate would have done in the Credo'. The opera was performed only four times, though it was more popular on the Continent, and was translated into German, Spanish and Hungarian. Haydn thought little of it – 'The overture from *L'arbore di Diana*, and a lot of old stuff from *Cosa rara*.' Soler returned to St Petersburg, and Morichelli, defeated by the strength of her opposition, departed for Venice. (On the second night of *L'isola del piacere* a one-act comic intermezzo, *Le nozze dei contadini spagnuoli*, with music by Martin y Soler and words by Da Ponte, was performed for the composer's benefit. The libretto is competent but of no particular interest, no doubt scribbled down in an hour or two for the occasion.)

It seems that Soler's advent in London was not welcomed by the rival factions at the King's Theatre; Da Ponte's championship of the composer gave a handle to his enemies, who persuaded Taylor to force him to accept less favourable terms of employment in his second year. To save the family finances, he rented from Taylor the coffee-room, which Nancy supervised. She seems once again to have been pregnant, since Da Ponte asked Casanova for permission to call their second child Giacomo – their first, Louisa, had been born in 1794. However, the next baby whom we know about was not born until 1799, another girl, and was christened Frances, presumably after the reigning Emperor Francis, so it is possible that Nancy had a miscarriage, or a second child who died young.

Nancy ran the coffee-room with her sister Louisa, and they managed to save a good deal of money. Here the opera audience assembled after each performance, and 'all the first society are regularly to be seen there'. Periodic advertisements extol the delicious refreshments which 'Madame Daponte' offers to the nobility, gentry and public. Still extant is her husband's receipt for refreshments provided at the benefit concert of Domenico Dragonetti, the double bass at the King's Theatre and the finest player of the instrument then living. He too was a Venetian, and had been engaged for London on the recommendation of Banti, at a rate of pay several times higher than that of the other players.

During the next season, 1795–96, Da Ponte again had a hand in many of the twelve operas which were staged. The first of these was *La bella Arsène*, with music by Monsigny, additions by Mazzinghi and a text by Favart 'improved' by Da Ponte (the changes are considerable). 'Pleasing but not great . . . gay, and slight, but not striking' wrote one newspaper; while the management apologised for any deficiencies by explaining that 'at the pressing desire of the Subscribers' the theatre had been opened 'without waiting for the arrival of the Performers from abroad; consequently the Entertainments cannot be expected to be so complete as otherwise they would have been if the opening had been delayed until the arrival of all the Company'.

Next came *Ifigenia in Tauride* by Gluck, whose *Alceste*, in a shortened version for which Da Ponte was responsible, had been performed with great success the previous year, with Banti singing the principal role. For both operas Da Ponte made typically workmanlike translations, and both were greeted with much applause. Gluck's music was new to London opera audiences, and the effect was stunning. Of *Alceste* one paper wrote, 'The most splendid opera we ever saw . . . The best of the kind, so different from the common race of operas, that it requires to be judged of, only, by a master in the science . . . It is truly difficult to the performers, and so original in its kind, that it will require several repetitions to make it familiar to the orchestra and to the audience.'

Later in the season there followed the first of many collaborations between Da Ponte and Bianchi. *Antigona*, the result of their partnership, was performed several times during the season, but the press notices were mainly taken up with comments on the presence or absence of Caroline of Brunswick, the new Princess of Wales, and of her husband, the future George IV. They had separated very soon after their marriage, and their respective supporters were vociferous in praise or abuse. The Princess of Wales was frequently at the opera – she was genuinely fond of music – and was always received with loud and long expressions of loyalty.

Antigona was succeeded by *Il tesoro*, with music by Joseph Mazzinghi. This was just the kind of story Da Ponte enjoyed working on – light, entertaining, with plenty of intrigue and misunderstanding which all come right in the end. *The Times* acknowledged his contribution by commenting that 'the tale is a tolerable one for the Italian stage', and the music was described as 'adapted to the season, light and airy'.

Finally there was *Zemira e Azor* with music by Grétry, for which Da Ponte provided a translation from the French text of Marmontel. 'For some mysterious reason,' he wrote in 1819, 'the French piece was given to Messrs Bonajuti and Baldonotti (two poets both aspiring to the honour of the dramatic crown) with the order of translating it into Italian. There was no dialogue to be curtailed, no dramatic personae to be rejected, no air to be introduced, no plan to be changed. The drama was written originally in verse, and was to be translated into Italian. A good premium was offered for the work. But who would believe it? Messrs B and B after a hard but fruitless labour of twenty days, returned the book to the prompter, and the poet of the opera house was ordered to make the translation.' In the memoirs he goes on to say that after completing the task he 'went to see a friend who knew music well, tried out the score with the words, and with a few small changes we found that it matched perfectly with the composer's notes.'

When the opera was repeated the following autumn it was chiefly notable for the first appearance of the tenor John Braham, who became Nancy Storace's lover. His talent and beautiful voice inspired one paper to hope that he would 'induce us to chace from an English stage the degrading and disgusting form of a *Castrato*'. Until the end of the century castrati were familiar objects on the operatic stage, but public opinion was gradually coming to feel that the convention of using them was cruel and barbaric, and they were soon to be replaced by tenors. [1]

Da Ponte does not say exactly when he began to get into even greater financial difficulties than usual, but it was probably some time during the next season, when the papers were full of Taylor's money problems. As he tells the story,

Signor Taylor, meanwhile, either because of the happy result of my first opera, or because of some other reason which is unknown to me and which I have never been able to fathom, seemed extremely anxious to become friendly with me. He began to come to my house a great deal and went for long walks with me; he asked my advice on various matters connected with the theatre or of a pecuniary nature, and seemed to me to be very satisfied not only with my observations but also with my calculations. One day when I was with him and Banti, rather overheated with wine, he asked me laughingly whether I thought I could get him some money. 'How?' I asked. He brought out of his pocket various bills of exchange which Federici [2] had endorsed and accepted. I took one of them to the value of £300 and without giving it much thought said that I would try, and hoped to succeed. 'If you can,' said Banti, 'your fortune is made.' I went out of his house, asking myself, 'How could I undertake such a thing? Where can I find money, I, who by profession am a poet, have only a modest salary, and barely understand the meaning of the words "acceptance", "endorsement" or "bill of exchange"?' I do not

[1] There used to be a superstition that the necessary operation should not be performed in bad weather, as the castrato never thereafter sang in tune.

[2] Vincenzo Federici was another of Da Ponte's *bêtes noires*. A teacher of music and composer of moderate talent, his main work at the King's Theatre was to preside at the harpsichord and write music for inserting in the operas of other men. Da Ponte describes him as a monster of perfidy. But as a director of music at the theatre, a friend of Taylor and one of the sources through whom the impresario obtained funds, he was a powerful adversary.

ABOVE LEFT: Lorenzo Da Ponte as a
young man, a watercolour
probably painted while he was
at Treviso.

ABOVE: Ceneda piazza around the
middle of the eighteenth century.
From an engraving by
Sebastiano Giampiccoli.

RIGHT: Bishop Lorenzo Da Ponte.
Artist unknown. The portrait
hangs in the cathedral in
Vittorio Veneto (formerly Ceneda).

ABOVE: The Da Ponte family house,
according to local tradition.
A modern photograph.

LAURENTIUS
DE PONTE
EPŪS ET COMES
CENETEN,
1759

Joseph II.

The Burgtheater, Vienna.
Engraving by Karl Schütz, 1783.

ABOVE: Anton Salieri.

ABOVE RIGHT: Wolfgang
Amadeus Mozart.
Silverpoint drawing by
Doris Stock.

RIGHT: Nancy Storace
from a painting by
De Wilde.

ABOVE: Adriana Gabrieli Del Bene, 'La Ferrarese' (second from left). Drawing by Antonio Fedi.

LEFT: Leopold II.

LEFT: Nancy Da Ponte.

BELOW: King's Theatre, Haymarket, after 1790, with front decoration by John Nash.

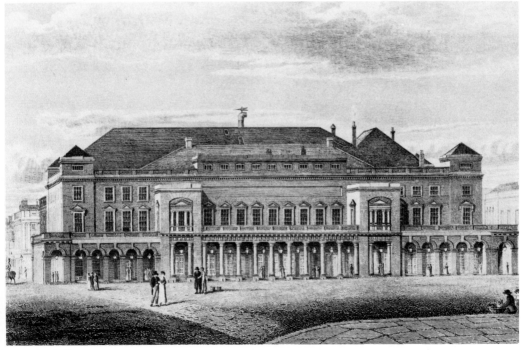

ABOVE: Fanny Da Ponte.

LEFT: Brigida Banti, negligently holding a copy of 'God Save the King'. Painting by J. Hopkins.

BELOW: Park Theatre, New York.

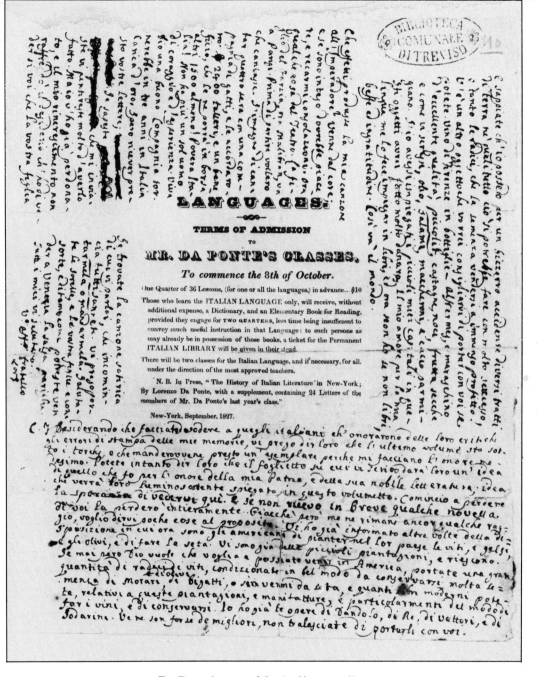

LANGUAGES.

TERMS OF ADMISSION

TO

MR. DA PONTE'S CLASSES.

To commence the 8th of October.

One Quarter of 36 Lessons, (for one or all the languages,) in advance... $10

Those who learn the ITALIAN LANGUAGE only, will receive, without additional expense, a Dictionary, and an Elementary Book for Reading, provided they engage for TWO QUARTERS, less time being insufficient to convey much useful instruction in that Language: to such persons as may already be in possession of those books, a ticket for the Permanent ITALIAN LIBRARY will be given in their stead.

There will be two classes for the Italian Language, and if necessary, for all, under the direction of the most approved teachers.

N. B. In Press, " The History of Italian Literature in New-York; By Lorenzo Da Ponte, with a supplement, containing 24 Letters of the members of Mr. Da Ponte's last year's class."

New-York, September, 1827.

Da Ponte's appeal for Italian pupils,
framed by a letter to his brother
Agostino.

Da Ponte in old age.

know whether it was a good or evil spirit which made me remember that when we first came to London I had been obliged to sell a diamond ring, and had gone into a shop over the door of which was written '*Money*', and a very polite young man had lent me six guineas for a ring which was worth nearly twelve.

I went to this shop, found the same young man and gave him my card, and he said that if I wanted to buy a ring or a watch he would give me the rest in cash. He showed me various things and I chose a repeater, which he put at twenty-two guineas and which was perhaps worth fifteen, and gave me an order on the Bank of England for the rest. When I held out my hand to take it, he gave me a pen instead and made me write my name below Federici's on the bill of exchange I had brought him. Not realising the significance or the consequences of such a signature, I thought that it was nothing more than a formality or a receipt: but as soon as I saw my name on this piece of paper it flashed through my mind that one of the three pieces of advice Casanova had given me was never to write my name on bills of exchange in England. I trembled like a leaf, and at that moment a deadly presentiment seemed to speak to me: 'You are lost!'. Nevertheless I went back to Taylor and showed him the cheque from Parker (this was the money-lender's name) and the repeater which he had given me. Taylor, who had already procured money from other bills of exchange through Federici and Gallerini, [1] and who was used to losing seventy, eighty and even a hundred per cent through these scoundrels, was pleasantly surprised to see how quickly he had been served and how small was his loss. In a transport of joy Banti exclaimed, 'Bravo, poet!', and graciously pocketed the repeater, which Taylor was about to present to me, crying with a second transport of joy, 'Oh, that's just right for me!'

The immediate result was that Taylor gave him an improved contract and other favours, but the longer-term ones were that he became hopelessly embroiled in the manager's pecuniary disasters. The situation was made still worse when the wily impresario, 'to the surprise of everyone', as *The Times* put it, managed to get himself elected for Parliament in 1797 for the borough of Leominster, after several unsuccessful efforts to find a seat (in the end he was recommended by the Prince of Wales and the Duke of Norfolk). This meant that he could not be arrested for debt – and he remained a Member until 1802. (Members of Parliament were immune from arrest, not only when parliament was sitting but also for forty days after prorogation and forty days before each new session. Since by

---

[1] This is 'Sir' John Gallini (his knighthood bestowed by the Pope), who had come to London some years before as a ballet dancer and had gradually worked his way up to a position of influence at the King's Theatre. Da Ponte hated and distrusted him.

the end of the eighteenth century parliament was rarely prorogued for more than eighty days, the practical result was that the immunity was constant.)

Unhappily, anyone whose signature appeared on a bill of exchange was liable for payment; and as, during the next few years, Da Ponte signed many of them for Taylor, often for large amounts, he was held liable when they became due and the impresario could not pay them. So he would run from money-lender to money-lender, 'until, either to pay what was due, or to satisfy the needs, the caprices and the appetites of the insatiable she-wolf of the theatre, the sum which I found in less than a year amounted to six thousand five hundred guineas. So I was the treasurer, the disburser, the agent, the paymaster and the favourite of Taylor. Did they have to go to the country while the theatre was closed? Da Ponte will find the money. "There is no wine in the cellar," says Banti. Da Ponte will get it on credit from the wine merchants. Signor Taylor needs hose, shirts, handkerchiefs, etc. etc.? He tells Da Ponte. The theatre ushers, the actors, the ballet-dancers, the singers, need money? They go to Da Ponte.' His role as general procurer and disburser of money was no doubt responsible for the comment in one contemporary squib that 'Signor Daponti, the poet, a Genoise jesuit, and Signor Gallerino, prompter thereto, a Neapolitan negociant, were appointed brokers and agents' for the theatre.

Da Ponte's protestations that he became embroiled in Taylor's financial embarrassments through innocence and ignorance should be taken with a certain reservation. In the ups and downs of life he must on many occasions have had to borrow money (he himself says that he raised funds while he was in The Hague by means of a bill of exchange), and Nancy's father and brother were both usurers. As so often in his life, it is likely that his inability to refuse Taylor was due to a combination of credulity, eternal optimism that everything would come right in the end, the desire to ingratiate himself and to show his rivals that *he* was the impresario's favourite – and surely, also, to a genuine warm-hearted impulse to help Taylor out of a jam.

Interestingly, Da Ponte gives us another aspect of Taylor and the ferocious Banti which helps to explain his loyalty to the manager. It seems that Banti (who 'changed her secret Adonises as often as most ladies change their hats') and Federici had been lovers, but the *diva*

... either because she wanted a new lover (a secret one, of course) or from some supposed injury which she had received at his hands, became such a bitter enemy of his that she couldn't bear to see him or hear his name. The favours of this capricious woman then fell entirely on me. She seemed to be happy only when I was with her; to her friends and the impresario himself she spoke of no one but me; she praised my goodness, my energy, my disinterest, my talent, and sometimes she even praised my beautiful eyes! At that time I was forty-nine, with a wife whom I loved and who was considerably younger and more beautiful than she was; so it is no marvel that I played deaf and blind, and feel I deserve no merit for doing so. But the more I tried not to understand, the more this she-wolf seemed to want to make me do so.

Taylor meanwhile decided to go to his house in the country and to take Banti and her family with him. As soon as this had been decided Banti sent for me; and since I had the bad luck to find her alone she ran towards me and said, 'Signor poet, you must get ready to come to the country with us. I have something very important to tell you. Come, my dear, give your good friend Banti this pleasure.' She took my hand as she said this, with a look which would have frightened the chaste Joseph . . .

Prudently, Da Ponte took Nancy with him, which infuriated Banti. 'But after spending three days with Taylor, and having the opportunity to observe him from close to, I was so convinced that left to himself, and with plenty of money, he would have been one of the best men in the world, that truly I often shed tears of compassion. As for Banti, who in the theatre was a veritable viper and made him the same, at Holywell she was affable, gentle and positively amiable. The constant attention which Taylor paid her, his generosity without show, his simplicity of manner and his hospitality towards everyone who turned up, made even Banti quite different from what she truly was.'

With his fertile, active brain, Da Ponte now thought of another scheme which – as always – he was confident would make money: he would set up his own printing press, and himself print the libretti which were sold in the theatre, thus making a double profit. So far as we know, the first of them was *Evelina*, which he skilfully translated from the French of N. F. Guillard, turning the rhyming verse into blank verse. The music was by Sacchini, adapted for the occasion by Mazzinghi. Staged early in January 1797 and performed before 'the most crowded and brilliant audience we have witnessed this season', it was a triumph, often repeated, and for once the librettist, who was usually mentioned only to be scolded, was praised for the fidelity of his text.

Earlier in the season he had written the libretto for *Il consiglio imprudente*, with music by Bianchi. The light but clever and amusing story, based on a play by Goldoni called *Un curioso accidente*, is set in The Hague, so perhaps he was inspired to choose it by his visit there three years earlier. This is probably the opera to which he refers in his memoirs as 'an *operetta buffa* in one act which was one of the best things Bianchi ever wrote in the *buffa* style'. 'The success of this piece,' *The Times* proclaimed, 'from which the ribaldry and buffoonery that in general debase similar productions are excluded, holds out a pleasing prospect to the *Amateurs* of rational music.' It was followed as a double bill by another heroic cantata, *Le nozze del Tamigi e Bellona*, to celebrate 'the Glorious Victory of His Majesty's Navy' off Cape St Vincent on 14 February. This was an adaptation of a cantata originally written to celebrate the wedding of the future King George IV and Caroline of Brunswick; it seems an incongruous metamorphosis, and presumably was botched together for the occasion.

Two other operas for which Da Ponte wrote the libretti were performed this season. The first was *L'albero di Diana*, which, though a favourite on the Continent under its original title of *L'arbore di Diana*, had never been seen in England. It was a great success, affording Nancy Storace, as Amore, a chance to delight the audience, not least because, 'in order to give [her] an opportunity of displaying the graces of her person, as well as the charms of her voice, the celebrated air of the *Negro Dance* in *Paul et Virginie* was introduced'. Finally there was *Merope*, another collaboration between Da Ponte and Bianchi, a heroic opera based on a text by Voltaire to which many librettists had helped themselves. Da Ponte's adaptation was very free, and in no way simply a translation. One newspaper praised his 'most admirable dramatisation' and *The Times* wrote of 'the skilful and affecting manner in which it has been introduced on the Italian Stage'.

The next season opened with a number of revivals, and Da Ponte had a major hand in only two new productions (and one of them new only to English audiences): *Cinna*, with music by Bianchi and an absurd classical plot which must, however, have been a marvellous vehicle for Banti; and, three weeks later, *La cifra*, originally seen in Vienna.

The theatre was badly in need of a prima donna to sing the main *buffa* roles for the following season, since Nancy Storace had departed to the Continent with her lover, John Braham, and Taylor was apparently unable to find a successor. So he asked Da Ponte whether he would like to go to Italy to find two singers, a man and a woman, of the first rank. Da Ponte, who was longing to see his family, jumped at the offer. Taylor provided a hundred guineas towards the cost of the journey, and Da Ponte, who had somehow managed to save £1,000 in jewels and money (mainly, one feels, through Nancy's hard work and prudence), bought a modest carriage. Early in

October 1798 they set out – presumably leaving the small Louisa with her aunt – on an expedition which, although it was disastrous for his future at the theatre, nevertheless provided one of the most delightful and rewarding experiences of his life.

XI

Nancy and her husband disembarked at Hamburg and made their way to Castelfranco, some thirty miles distant from Venice. Here Da Ponte left Nancy, arranging to rejoin her in Treviso two days later, and went on to Ceneda.

When my feet touched the ground which had cradled me, and when I breathed the air of that sky which had nourished me and given me life for so many years, I trembled in every limb, and through my veins there ran such a feeling of gratitude and reverence that for some time I could not move. I cannot tell how long I should have remained like this if I had not heard a voice at the window which I seemed to know, and which went straight to my heart. I had alighted from the post-coach some distance from the house, so that the noise of the wheels would not betray my arrival, and had covered my head with a handkerchief to prevent anyone from recognising me from the windows by the light of the lanterns. When I knocked at the door I heard someone call from the window, 'Who is there?' I disguised my voice and replied only, 'Open the door!', but these words were enough for one of my sisters to recognise my voice. She cried to her sisters, 'It's Lorenzo!'. They all flew downstairs, threw their arms round my neck and almost suffocated me with their caresses. Then they took me to my father, who when he heard my name and saw me was absolutely motionless for some minutes.

The scene in which Da Ponte describes his return home is one of the most touching and genuine in the whole of the memoirs, even though he spent only two nights under the paternal roof. His family – especially his father, now seventy-six, who still deeply mourned the loss of Girolamo and Luigi – were enraptured to see him, and old friends came from every quarter of the town to join in the celebrations, including two who were especially close, Antonio Michelini and Girolamo Perucchini.

His stepmother had died in 1790, but his stepbrother Paolo, whom he had last seen in Trieste, was there to welcome him, as well as his youngest stepsister, Faustina, whom he met now for the first time, since she was not born until early in December 1779, when he had already escaped to Gorizia. He conceived a special affection for her, describing her as a true angel of beauty; he hoped to take her back to England with him, but this was not to be. His partiality, then and later, was so marked that it makes one wonder. Early in 1779 he had spent some weeks with his younger brother Luigi, Angioletta, and his stepmother, first in Venice and then in Ceneda. Is it possible that he and his stepmother became lovers and that he thought Faustina was his daughter? There is no proof of this hypothesis, and the relevant dates are not known with sufficient exactness to advance it with confidence, but in his letters and memoirs his references are so tender as to imply a feeling deeper than that of a brother for a stepsister whom he saw for only a few days.

During his brief stay his father described one incident which had taken place as the French armies swept through northern Italy:

> Bonaparte, who was the general of this division, had come to Ceneda. Since there were no barracks, he ordered that his soldiers and officers should be lodged in people's houses. The very first sight of these young Frenchmen, gay by national character and full of fire after the victories they had won, put the women of the city under a spell. As soon as my old father heard of Bonaparte's orders, he shut the door of the house and waited by a window for him to pass. The house stands in the centre of the great piazza, near the café where most of the people go.[1] After a few minutes Bonaparte appeared with his officers and sat down in the café to take some refreshment. My father, without losing any time, chose an opportune moment, and leaning out of the window asked permission to speak.
>
> 'Who is the general of the French?' he said. 'I am,' Bonaparte called. 'General, the old man who is speaking to you is the father of seven honest daughters who lost their mother many years ago. Only two are married, the others are with me. Their older brothers are not with them now to protect them, and I, their father, must leave the house to get bread for them. I respectfully ask that your order that your brave warriors should be taken into our houses should not extend to me. I beg that you will protect my white hair, the innocence of these young girls and the honour of my sons. If you will grant me this, I will pray to God at the foot of this crucifix' – and as he spoke he took from his bosom the crucifix which he carried everywhere – 'for your prosperity and that of your armies; if you will not grant my prayer, I will not open the door of my house, but, at

---

[1] According to local tradition, when the Da Ponte family left the ghetto they moved to a house facing the piazza and opposite the cathedral. The site is now occupied by a tobacconist's, but there is still a café next door.

the first sign which your soldiers or officers give that they intend to open it, I have a barrel of gunpowder in the house, and I swear on this same crucifix to save with it the modesty of my daughters.'

The old man's eloquence gained his cause, and his was the only house which was not prostituted by the French.

Doubt has been cast on this story because, although Napoleon was in the neighbourhood, he did not actually pass through Ceneda. However, one of his generals, Andrea Massena, was quartered there for some days, requisitioning for his troops private houses, public buildings and even the seminary, a terrible experience which was long remembered by the citizens. All the French soldiers were noted for their brutality and their ruthless depredation of the countryside, and Massena's troops were especially infamous for this, so Gasparo Da Ponte had good reason to be fearful for his daughters.

Da Ponte roused the curiosity of his family with the teasing remark that he had brought with him a beautiful young girl who had danced in the opera, and promised that they would soon see her. After a day of feasting and rejoicing he told them that the next day he must leave for Treviso, and perhaps also for Venice, but that he would return with his lovely companion. Taking Paolo and Faustina he travelled the short distance to Treviso, where again he had a tremendous welcome, especially from the pupils who still remembered his inspired teaching. Giulio Trento was there, and, by a stroke of fortune, Bernardo Memmo and his Teresa: 'widowed, ugly, fat and aged, she was nevertheless the idol of this man and the absolute mistress of his will!'

Nancy joined them – rather later than she was expected, and Paolo teased his brother for his anxiety when she did not turn up on time. Paolo had become very fond of Nancy while they were all living in Trieste, and he had been asking his brother a hundred questions about her. Lorenzo did not reveal the identity of his companion, but 'always replied in general terms, without giving him either hope or a suspicion that he would in fact see her again as my wife'. So when she did turn up Paolo was infinitely pleased to find who the young 'ballerina' was.

Da Ponte, as he writes with a certain disingenuousness, was about to return with them to Ceneda when he 'suddenly remembered' the reason for his journey to Italy. Hearing that there were two excellent *prime donne* in Venice, he sent Paolo, Nancy and Faustina back to Ceneda while he went on to the city he loved so dearly. Alas for Venice. A year and a half earlier the Doge had abdicated and French troops had taken possession. Five months later Napoleon had handed the government over to Austria by the Peace of Campoformio, and Austrian troops replaced the French. The city was a scene of desolation; in the Piazza San Marco all was sadness, silence, solitude. The coffee houses were deserted, and Da Ponte was warned never to discuss politics, for more than ever were spies lurking at every corner. All the talk – but secretly, behind closed doors – was of the high price of food, the barbarity of the German troops, and the poverty and hopelessness of life.

During his two days in the city he had joyful encounters with old friends, including the lawyer Lucchesi, who had been so charitable to him in Trieste. Some of these meetings were more curious than happy. He met the Ferrarese, and, though he found her appearance and her voice much the worse for wear, nevertheless he took her to the opera to see Casti's *Il rè Teodoro in Venezia*. In the fish-market he met an old man with a white face, thin, dirty, grey, who looked like a beggar but who cried out in stupefied tones, 'Mother of God! Lorenzo Da Ponte!' It turned out to be the brother of his old love Angiola Tiepolo, who had once tyrannised over him but now, deprived of his income by the new rulers, was reduced to destitution. Da Ponte took him back to his inn and provided him with food and clothes. The wounds of the past forgotten, they spent some pleasant hours together.

But his most significant encounter was with Gabriele Doria, the brother-in-law of his disreputable love Angioletta. According to Da Ponte he was a spy of the Inquisitors, though no evidence of this has come to light. (The stupendous Venetian archives may still yield up the proof of Da Ponte's accusation.)

And now, for the first time in the memoirs, Da Ponte refers to his affair with Angioletta, twisting events to make both his rôle and hers considerably more respectable than they in fact were. Concealing much, he writes with an apparent frankness which may or may not have deceived his readers. According to this bowdlerised account, the part he played was to rescue Angioletta, a pure and misused young woman, from a husband who had planned to murder her. When he comes to the point at which he must reveal that his relationship with her was not platonic, he resorts to a device which he uses on two other occasions. 'By a strange accident,' he writes, 'a page of this story is missing. I had already written it, and was about to dry it with sand, when instead I took up the inkwell and spilt ink on it. Since I have no time to copy it, I will leave my readers to write what they please.' So, in the memoirs, he ends this partial and distorted tale of the events of twenty years earlier.

Coming to the present visit, he relates how Angioletta and her husband, Carlo Bellaudi, visit him at his inn, where they have an emotional reunion. But Angioletta slips him an affectionate note saying that Doria is now her recognised *cavaliere servente*, forced on her by her husband and his family, though she loathes him. He is, the letter goes on, bitterly jealous of Da Ponte, who will be in danger if he stays longer in Venice.

That same evening Doria, heralded by the enormous nose to which Da Ponte draws attention and accompanied by another messenger, came to the inn and delivered an ultimatum, 'by order of His Imperial and Royal Majesty', commanding Da Ponte to leave the city before the evening of the next day. Spy? Jealous lover? A story invented by Da Ponte? We shall never know. The only clue consists of documents in the Austrian police records showing that on 7 November the assistant commissioner of police in Treviso expressed interest in Da Ponte, who had arrived there from Ceneda three days earlier. On 13 November the commissioner was given orders to evict him. Four days later he acknowledged these instructions, but by then Da Ponte had already gone to Venice. It seems quite possible that, since Venice was also under Austrian jurisdiction, the order was passed on to the police there.

However this may be, the banishment not only forced him to leave the city (before daybreak he had departed for Padua), but made it impossible for him to carry out his plan of returning to Ceneda to fetch Nancy and say goodbye to his family. According to his own account, he was unable to do so because fighting was expected to break out at any moment between France and Austria, and his journey from Padua to Ceneda would have been difficult in the midst of hostilities. Moreover, he was afraid that his family might detain him. There were, however, no armies in the vicinity at that time. Whatever the reason, he did not go to Ceneda, and never saw his family again. Nancy came to him, and, once reunited, they set out for Bologna, then the most important market-place for artists in Italy, where agents provided singers, dancers and musicians for all the opera houses in Europe.

On the way they stopped in Ferrara, where, to Da Ponte's immense delight, he met the young poet Ugo Foscolo, who was to become one of Italy's foremost writers. They often talked together, and Da Ponte proffers the dry comment that Foscolo's final visit to him must have made a lasting impression on the young poet. 'He very much wanted some fine lawn shirts which he saw in my room: perhaps that is why he must, it seems to me, have remembered me for at any rate a number of years.' But this made no difference to Da Ponte's deep

155

admiration for his work; personal reservations never affected his recognition of true literary merit, and reverence for it.

The days passed happily in Bologna, not least because his operas were popular there and he was suitably fêted. Once more he forgot the reason for his journey, until a letter arrived from London saying that Banti and Federici had patched up their quarrel. This endangered his own position, for they would again unite to undermine it. So, no singers being available in Bologna, he decided to go to Florence, not only in search of singers but also because he longed to see that beautiful city, which he had never visited. He left Nancy behind, for winter was biting deep, the journey through the Apennines was long and treacherous, and she was pregnant. He was enraptured by the buildings and ancient monuments of Florence, the statues, gardens and pictures. And he found there such culture and friendly warmth, especially among the lovely women, that he was in ecstacies. The soirées were devoted to literature; one evening it fell to his lot to read the part of Aristodemus in a tragedy by Monti,[1] and on another occasion his own early poem *Sugli odori*. He also listened with rapture to a reading of *Saul*, one of the most popular plays of the famous poet and dramatist Alfieri.

It is possible that he met Alfieri face to face during his stay in Florence. Years later he wrote, 'Finding myself one day in London with the great Alfieri I had the courage to give him my tragedy [*Il Mezenzio*]. He read it and on returning it said smiling, "You have read Metastasio too much." "And whom should I read," I replied, "before an Alfieri existed?" *Laudes placant hominesque deosque* – "Read the Greek tragedies," he answered, "and continue to write." I read Sophocles, Euripides and Aeschylus, but I never wrote, or shall write, another tragic verse.' This encounter could not have taken place in London, as the poet was not in England during Da Ponte's own stay there. But he was living in Florence when Da Ponte paid his brief visit, and they may well have met then.

No singers were to be found in Florence, and he returned through the bitter cold to Bologna, at one point being catapulted out of his carriage into the deep snow when his rickety vehicle capsized. He was taken to a nearby inn, more dead than alive, where the good landlady rubbed his arms and legs with snow and revived him with

[1] In the first edition of the memoirs Da Ponte wrote that the play made all these beautiful women weep. 'When a tragedy is being performed,' he went on, 'I have often seen people weeping who would not give way to tears at the most terrible misfortune. I believe the reason to be this: in the latter case the tears are the result of wretchedness, and betray weakness; in the former they flow from a pleasurable emotion, and are a sign of a gentle and compassionate spirit.'

chianti and Alkermes (a liqueur now based on herbs and spices, but originally made from Kermes, or scale-insects, found on oak trees; mixed with vinegar, it used to be a well-known, widely-used astringent).

Back in Bologna, he went hastily to an agent and hired, as he mendaciously describes them, 'two singers of the first rank and the only ones I found unemployed in Italy'. One was the soprano Maddalena Allegranti. The daughter of a Florentine innkeeper, as a young woman she had fascinated Casanova: 'Her appearance, her grace, the sound of her voice,' he wrote in his memoirs, 'were more than I could resist.' The second was Vitale Damiani, who was a reliable singer of the second rank, but who never took leading roles.

With rumours of war growing, they left at once for London, through a countryside which was often devastated by the passing of Napoleon's troops. The party consisted of Da Ponte and Nancy, Allegranti, her husband and their child, and Banti's son, whom Da Ponte had been commissioned to bring back, and who made something of a nuisance of himself on the journey. (Damiani came separately.) This ill-assorted little group set out towards the end of December, and had a cold and uncomfortable journey to Hamburg, travelling for the last stage of it over the frozen Elbe, as many other travellers were doing. Da Ponte describes vividly their horror as they sped past the place where not long before a coach drawn by six horses had plunged through the ice, drowning all the passengers. Part of the coach was still visible, a grisly reminder of the fate which might overtake them also, but which happily they escaped. In Hamburg, where all the inns were packed with travellers held up by the freezing weather, they were forced to stay for a month, as the harbour was ice-locked. The delay almost emptied Da Ponte's purse. But he did not regret a penny of the money which the journey had cost him, 'so much and so great was the pleasure that I experienced . . . which was worth more than all the gold in the universe'.

Taylor received him without any signs of welcome, and nothing was said about his reinstatement as poet to the theatre. On this occasion the impresario can hardly be blamed, for Da Ponte had long since been expected back, and the theatre had been in great difficulties for lack of a leading *buffa* singer. 'We understand that by the confusion which reigns in Italy,' the *Morning Chronicle* had written in December, 'through the revolutionary system, the first comic woman, whom the Agent of the Theatre is now actually gone to conduct to England, is not yet arrived.' And two days later, 'The accident of the first comic woman not being arrived is not to be imparted to the direction of the

Opera, whose interest suffers by her absence, but to the deranged circumstances of that part of the Continent from which she is to come, and where there has been an agent, at a considerable expense, some months ago, sent expressly to bring her over.'

When Allegranti and Damiani did at last arrive, they were disastrous failures. Twenty years earlier Allegranti had been idolised on the London stage, but now, as Mount Edgcumbe wrote, 'she had scarcely a thread of voice remaining, nor the power to sing a note in tune'. She appeared four times, and then deserted the stage for ever, leaving the theatre once more in disarray for want of a *buffa* singer. The invaluable and versatile Banti held the fort on several occasions, though she had to 'make a temporary retreat from the Stage' in order to have her twelfth child.

Damiani never appeared at all. Without authorisation from Taylor, Da Ponte had agreed to the insertion in his contract of a clause giving him the right to choose the opera for his debut. He also demanded the freedom, when he was not singing at the King's Theatre, to do so at 'any other place in town for his own benefit' (a privilege for which all the leading singers fought, and which was fiercely contested by the management, since it meant that they tended not to be available for the theatre when they were wanted); the liberty to change the music in any opera; new clothes for every opera; and four tickets of admission every night for the gallery and two every Tuesday night for the pit. The squabble went on for weeks, and in the end Damiani departed back to the Continent.

As for Taylor, he was immersed in yet another of his great schemes, since he had applied for permission to widen the approaches and avenues to the theatre, and in particular the east end of Pall Mall, by opening up a new street from the Haymarket to Charles Street. Early in 1799 a bill was brought before Parliament for this purpose, and on 12 July the royal assent was given and the bill passed into law. Taylor had all kinds of grandiose plans for extending the lease of the theatre to ninety-nine years and for rebuilding the streets and houses in the neighbourhood, and for months was involved in furious quarrels and arguments about the project.

From this time onwards, Da Ponte's association with the theatre was much looser and he wrote very few operas. But he was as active as ever with other projects. Since 1797 he had been printing opera libretti, and by 1799 he was registered as a master printer and Italian bookseller, with one press, operating from 5 Pall Mall. In 1803 he moved to the Haymarket, a flourishing centre for tradespeople, especially Italians. 'On the east side,' said one guide, published in 1793, 'was the Orange coffee house, which was chiefly used by opera dancers, and castratos.' This was certainly the notorious caffe degl'Italiani which Casanova had warned his friend never to enter. But how could a man of his temperament resist it? And how vividly can one imagine him moving easily between the opera house, his printing shop and the noisy, crowded café, where he must have met so many of his countrymen who had flocked to London!

During the next few years he continued to print the libretti of operas which were being performed at the King's Theatre, and, amongst his other publications, an expurgated edition of Ariosto's *Orlando furioso* for the benefit of young English ladies whose delicate sensibilities might have been shocked by the full version. This, he claims, sold 1,000 copies in less than two years.

It was as a result of his printing operations that he once more made contact with Casti, now a very old man and living in Paris. In 1802 Casti published a poetical allegory entitled *Gli animali parlanti*, ridiculing the defects of various forms of government in Europe. It caused a sensation, and was translated into many languages. Da Ponte brought out an annotated and slightly expurgated edition, and rumours of this reached Casti. He was greatly alarmed, since amongst other thinly veiled targets his poem condemned the massacres which had been perpetrated in Europe by Napoleon, thereby incurring the displeasure of the Emperor. The last thing Casti wanted was an annotated version which would broadcast the significance of his allegory, and he wrote a lengthy and indignant letter to Da Ponte. Whether he ever received Da Ponte's reply is not known, since he died not long afterwards, of indigestion after a tremendous dinner at the Spanish Embassy.

Da Ponte's printing operations led him into still greater financial embarrassment, partly as a result of his partnership with Corri and Dussek, who for some years had been registered as music sellers and printers. This is how Da Ponte himself describes his struggles during this period, in a booklet published in 1807 called *Storia compendiosa della vita di Lorenzo da Ponte* (see p.174.):

In spite of satires, libels and a thousand other dastardly attacks by my poetical rivals, for eight years I remained [at the King's Theatre] with much gain and not without glory. Various female intrigues [1] deprived me of the post at a moment when I had least reason to fear losing it . . . A rogue from Florence persuaded me to associate myself with him in a printing business which he could not manage on his own, but he took ungenerous advantage of my credulity. My unbounded love of doing good was the principal cause of my undoing. It was a torment for me to

[1] Da Ponte clearly means Banti.

be happy when my friends were unhappy. How little I knew them! . . .
One absconded, one failed, one went to jail, one laughed at me, one tried
to make people believe that I had defrauded him.

As so often, it is impossible to pin Da Ponte down to precise dates
and facts, and his memoirs at this point are a confused tale of
attempts on the part of Banti, Gallini and Federici to swindle him,
depose him as poet, and take advantage of his credulity. To com-
pound his difficulties, in 1800 Corri and Dussek went bankrupt.
Dussek escaped to Hamburg to avoid prison, and, *The Times* remarked
sarcastically, 'during the short time he has been there his *notes* have
had such a currency that they have cleared him several hundred
pounds'. Corri, on the other hand, went to Newgate, but was soon
released by special pardon, and at once established in the Haymarket
a music and instrument warehouse.

It was Da Ponte who was left to bear the brunt not only of their
debts but also of all the notes which he had endorsed for Taylor. The
impresario was particularly hard-pressed for funds at this time, and
in January 1800 the Lord Chamberlain refused to license the theatre
for the season because Taylor had not paid the salaries for the
previous year; as a result the opera house opened a week late.

Da Ponte's appeals to the impresario to reinstate him as poet,
prayers, pleading, tears, were all in vain, and Taylor burned unread
his despairing letters. In February Da Ponte too was forced to declare
himself bankrupt. This was a favourite device of traders whose
financial affairs were in a tangle, since it prevented or delayed their
creditors from collecting the sums owing to them. Other roads of
escape were to flee abroad, stay away from work or venture out only
on Sundays, become a member of parliament (as Taylor had done)
or lie low in prison. So no doubt Da Ponte saw in his declaration of
bankruptcy a means of winning a little breathing-space; 'and I
believe,' he writes, 'that I was the first person in England to set the
example of an unfortunate man who went bankrupt without owing a
farthing to anyone.'

A declaration of bankruptcy did not immediately bring immunity,
for various legal formalities had first to be completed. So, as Da
Ponte lay in bed on 10 March, receiving Nancy's congratulations on
his fifty-first birthday, there was a thunderous knock on the door
and he was arrested. He found a friend to stand bail for him and was
released, but, he claims, was arrested twice more in the space of
twenty-four hours and thirty times in three months. It must have
been during this period that he spent his 'last halfpenny to pay for
the expenses of the judges, constables, confinements, lawyers for and
against, carriages, messengers, etc. etc.'

At last, on 27 May, a docket of conformity was struck: this protected him from being arrested for the thirty-first time. But what was there for him to live on? His printing press was mortgaged, and it was not for many months, paying a guinea a week, that he was able to reclaim it. 'All my hopes, therefore, rested on my salary as poet and on the sale of the opera libretti which I had written. But even this salary had been mortgaged to a merchant who had advanced Taylor money; and only old works were put on at the opera, so that the profits should go to Federici.'

Gallini and Federici, who had also endorsed many of Taylor's notes, went bankrupt in 1800 as well. According to Da Ponte they were imprisoned, and he went to great lengths to secure their release, but was rewarded by both with stabs in the back. Yet somehow, even when the clouds were darkest, he always managed to keep a reservoir of buoyancy and determination. Just as in Vienna, when, though oppressed by the intrigues of his enemies and the mortal illness of his protector, the Emperor Joseph, he had written the miraculous libretto of *Così fan tutte*, so now he boldly advanced on a new enterprise.

One day, when he was walking along the Strand, a bull came charging up the street and he took refuge in a nearby shop. It happened to be a bookshop, and the idea sprang into his mind of opening in London a shop for the sale of Italian books, 'so returning to its former glory the literature of Italy, which was no longer esteemed in this most noble city, as it used to be in the days of Gray, of Spencer, of Dryden, of the great Milton, and so many others'. The owner had a whole roomful of such books, dusty and neglected, which he was delighted to sell at a bargain rate, and without pausing to examine them Da Ponte bought the whole lot for thirty guineas. After an initial qualm he realised that many of them were rare and valuable, and he disposed of them at a good profit, and of others which he bought at auction sales or ordered in large numbers from Italy. In November of that year (1800) he issued a carefully compiled catalogue. There are many treasures, including a 1584 *Orlando furioso*, works by Dante, Metastasio, Goldoni, Machiavelli and Petrarch, dictionaries, grammars and schoolbooks.

His customers were equally distinguished: he mentions by name 'Lord Spencer', presumably the George Spencer who later became Duke of Marlborough, a noted bibliophile and the possessor of a splendid library; and 'the Marquis of Douglas'. This must have been the Duke of Hamilton, who had spent his early life in Italy, when he was given this courtesy title. Many years afterwards he was elected as a trustee of the British Museum. Other patrons included the

Duchess of Devonshire, Ferrari's protector, queen of high society and famous for her charm and intellect; William Payne, perhaps the same William Payne who was the expert on whist; and the historian William Roscoe, who had a magnificent library of Italian books, many of them bought from Da Ponte's shop. How he must have revelled in this aristocratic clientèle, and what must have been his true delight in talking to people who knew and loved Italy, who were so cultured, and so learned in the Italian writers whom he adored.

Another cherished visitor to his bookshop at this time was his old and dear friend Michele Colombo, on a trip to England with three young men after a long tour of the Continent. He stayed for several months, seeing the sights and often coming to visit Da Ponte, kept in London by the haemorrhoids which tortured him, making the jolting of a carriage an unbearable torment.

Best of all was his friendship with Thomas James Mathias, now forgotten, but in his day one of the finest Italian scholars living – W. H. Prescott bracketed him with Milton. Mathias, who later became the Queen's Treasurer and also, it would seem, librarian at Buckingham Palace, had published anonymously in 1794 the first of many volumes of *The Pursuits of Literature*, a satire which savagely attacked many of his fellow-writers, and was bitterly attacked in its turn. One day he came into Da Ponte's shop, and his eye fell upon an edition of the librettist's own poems, *Saggi poetici*, which Da Ponte brought out in 1801. He was deeply struck by it, particularly by the ode on the death of Joseph II, which he compared with Dante and Petrarch, not to the discredit of Da Ponte. He was amazed to find that a man who was capable of writing such a poem was also the poet to the opera house, the meanest of occupations. When, the following year, he sent a copy of *Saggi poetici* to the writer and scholar Samuel Henley, he described Da Ponte as 'a man of genius, learning and taste', and the ode to Joseph II as 'one of the finest lyrical compositions in the language. I am sure,' he went on, 'you will feel interested in a man of genius and an original Poet – in *catene servili dell'Opera*, sotto la *protezzione* or *maledizione* del Signor Taylor, brutto Impresario.' And later he wrote, 'I believe that if Petrarch had heard [the ode], he would have given the author a place quite close to his own, without asking for any other proof of his lively, fertile, cultured and sublime mind.' However exaggerated Mathias' view of Da Ponte's poetry, it shows how highly it was valued by a man who was himself a brilliant, widely read Italian scholar.

The two men struck up a warm friendship, and many years afterwards, when Mathias was living in Italy and Da Ponte in America, resumed their friendly contact. Da Ponte's feelings for

Mathias, and his gratitude for all his friend did in the cause of Italian literature, fell little short of idolatry, and it is tempting to think that the copy of *Saggi poetici* in the British Library, inscribed in his elegant hand '*offerta dell'autore al Protettore della Letteratura Italiana*', is Mathias' own copy.

1800 was altogether an eventful year for Da Ponte, for in February he wrote to his young stepbrother Paolo, then living in Ceneda, to ask whether he would like to come to London to work in a piano business in which Da Ponte was interested. 'If it doesn't ruin me, perhaps it will make my fortune. Well, who knows? God is more powerful than all the devils. Let us continue to put our faith in his providence.' In this letter Da Ponte bitterly reproaches a young man by the name of Michele, who had returned to Italy without repaying money which Da Ponte had lent him and which he had faithfully promised to refund; and he also mentions harp and violin strings that he appears to have asked Paolo to send him, so it seems likely that both these and the piano business were bound up with his partnership with Corri and Dussek. Mindful too of his family, whose fortunes were at a very low ebb, he asked Paolo to give his father money from the sum owed by Michele.

Paolo duly came, and his presence and help were a great consolation to his older brother, who always got on well with him – as he signally failed to do with his stepbrother Agostino, who went from one scrape to another. Only a few years earlier he had got into trouble yet again in Venice, when he was accused of fleecing a German merchant with whom he was in company.

In general, Da Ponte disliked and suspected his fellow expatriates, whether in Vienna, London or America. But for some he had great respect, 'cultured, gifted and honourable, expert linguists, superb grammarians and good poets who . . . instead of slandering and envying . . . my zeal and my hope of disseminating and elevating our language, from patriotism and goodness of heart did everything they could to help me.' Among them was Filippo Pananti, a Tuscan, who came to London in 1802 and became an Italian teacher – one of his pupils was the Princess of Wales. In 1805 he succeeded Da Ponte as poet to the theatre, a post which he held until he returned to Italy nine years later, and he encapsulated the disagreeable experience in a witty poem, *Il poeta di teatro*, published by Paolo in 1808, which gives a vivid description of the humiliations that have to be endured by the librettist at the opera house, of the pride, power and vanity of those whom he has to satisfy, the lack of dignity attached to the position, and the servile attitude he must affect in order to keep his place. All these humiliations Da Ponte suffered too.

In later years Pananti expressed great admiration for Da Ponte's writing: for his libretti, especially *L'arbore di Diana*, *Una cosa rara* and *Proserpina* (first performed in 1804), which 'excell in vis comica and elegance: possess the vivacity and taste which true comic and tragic actions require, and are the exact opposite of those plays which disgrace the theatre, Italy and the art of poetry'; for his 'curious and beautiful' memoirs; for his lyric poetry; and for his efforts to establish in America a love of the language and literature of Italy.

One of Taylor's friends whom Da Ponte got to know was James Perry, editor and owner of the influential *Morning Chronicle*, the leading mouthpiece of the Whig party. Perry, like Taylor, was a native of Aberdeen, with the same harsh brogue. He was a lively, highly cultured man, an excellent talker, who liked to stroll along Pall Mall and St James's collecting valuable scraps of news and gossip for his paper, and Da Ponte must often have met him. On one occasion, he writes, Taylor got into a particularly bad scrape, when hordes of creditors descended upon him. Da Ponte flew to Perry, who had some connection with the King's Theatre,[1] and the two men devised a scheme which saved the impresario. Taylor, to Da Ponte's disgust, repaid his one-time librettist with nothing but ingratitude.

When Da Ponte was sacked in 1799 his place had been taken by Serafino Bonaiuti, whose libretti Da Ponte despised so heartily. Pananti's opinion was no higher: in *Il poeta di teatro* he wrote scathingly of Bonaiuti's audacity in 'improving' a text by Metastasio. Opening a libretto, he says, he reads, '"*Didone abbandonata* by Metastasio, corrected and embellished, and adapted for the modern theatre by Buonaguti". This is a trifle bold – Metastasio, corrected and refurbished by Buonaguti? But the man is mad.' Bonaiuti did not hesitate, either, to bring his 'improvements' to bear on the text of *Le clemenza di Tito*, the first Mozart opera ever to be heard in London.

---

[1] This, no doubt, was one reason why the *Morning Chronicle* was generally so kind both to Taylor and to his opera house. In 1796, for instance, it wrote, 'We have witnessed the exertions of the proprietor of this Theatre under circumstances of opposition, or rather of persecution, that would have sunk almost any other man in despair. He has by an energy of character that does him honour put this very fine Theatre on its present establishment with no assistance but from his own constancy and vigour ... Out of the ashes of the old Theatre, he has not only raised this grand structure which, as a Theatre, has not its parallel in England, but notwithstanding the lack of success, has collected a Company which no Stage in Europe can rival.'

While Bonaiuti was enthroned as poet hardly any of the operas with libretti by Da Ponte were performed, but between 1801 and 1804 he was reinstated at least in name, and though he wrote few new operas his old ones were constantly seen: during the 1800/1 season, for instance, performances were given of *Il consiglio imprudente*, *La bella pescatrice*, *Alceste*, *L'isola del piacere*, *Il capriccio drammatico*, *Semiramide*, *Le gelosie villane* (this was a slightly amended version of *I contadini bizzarri*), and the ever-popular *La scola de'maritati*.

The first new libretto – new to the King's Theatre, that is – in which he had a hand was *Angelina*, set to music by Salieri. The text, by Defranceschi, was already in existence and simply had to be altered. The opera is of no particular interest, except that, for those following Da Ponte's career, it is perhaps worth remarking that the story has a certain cold-blooded brutality which is quite atypical of the librettist's usual work.

It was just about this time that William Taylor made a hasty exit from the country. He had already been ousted from the managership of the theatre in favour of William Jewell, and now he was ejected from the House of Commons when parliament was dissolved and he found it impossible to secure another seat, in spite of the disbursement of large sums of money and appeals to all his influential and titled friends. Since he was no longer immune from arrest for his mountain of debts, he fled to Paris, remaining there for several months. 'The Sheriffs' office perhaps never was so full of writs against one person,' a contemporary satirist wrote, 'but before the Royal Message arrived, the person was off to Calais, Boulogne, and St Omer.' In 1803 he sold a third of his interest in the theatre to Francis Goold, who in the following year acquired further control. For the remainder of Da Ponte's sojourn in London Goold remained in charge of the theatre, with Jewell and Kelly acting respectively as director and stage manager.

The change must have been welcomed by opera lovers. 'We rejoice to see,' the *Morning Chronicle* wrote, forsaking its usual loyalty to Taylor, 'that under the management of Mr Goold [the King's Theatre] is so perfectly relieved from all its embarrassments, that the Opera season is made to commence at its accustomed time . . . We have reason to believe that it will now be conducted with a spirit, taste, and magnificence, that will be truly favourable to the arts.'

It was Goold who in 1802 secured for the theatre the services of the English soprano Elizabeth Billington, one of the finest singers living. She had been working on the Continent for some years, and was at the height of her fame. George Hogarth, a noted music critic, commented that she had become too fat, and though her features were beautiful her expression never varied and she had no talent as an actress. But 'her voice was a pure soprano, not remarkable for volume, but very sweet and flexible, and of extraordinary compass in its upper extremity. Her rapidity was amazing, and nothing could exceed the finish and delicacy of her execution. She was, too, a thorough musician, having been in her youth a great performer on the pianoforte.'

Her coming did not please Banti, for now there were two top singers for serious opera – and Banti's protector was no longer on the spot to support her. There was friction almost at once, and this time it was Banti, after so many years of supremacy, who gave way, departing at the end of the season for the Continent, never to return. 'This incomparable artist,' the *Morning Chronicle* wrote, 'after sustaining our Opera with undiminished attraction for eight years, takes leave of the London Theatre after her next performance . . . and never, we will venture to say, did any performer quit a Theatre with such universal regret from all who know how to estimate talents, zeal and attention to her duties.' Her larynx, which had so amazed Madame Vigée-Le Brun, she bequeathed to the municipality of Bologna, where she died in 1806.

Before she left she sang in *Armida*, with music by Bianchi and a libretto by Da Ponte – the last time composer and poet were to work together. This had a mixed reception (*The Times* damned it as 'certainly one of the worst [operas] which has of late been exhibited'), but it is a dramatic tale which must have given Banti an excellent opportunity to display her talents.

For the 1802/3 season, under the new management, the King's Theatre took on a fresh lease of life. Not only was Billington there, crowding the house every time she sang, but in the following year Goold also brought over the excellent contralto Josephina Grassini. Hogarth, a passionate opera-goer, described her as strikingly beautiful, with the gait and attitudes of a Greek statue. Her contralto voice was not, however, always popular and it used, unkindly, to be said that audiences would do best to listen to Billington with their eyes shut and watch Grassini but block up their ears. Hints were also dropped that perhaps in combination they would be better suited to the public weigh-house than to the opera house.

Another newcomer was the clever, versatile composer Peter von Winter, who, writes Hogarth, 'on the death of Mozart, had been left without a rival in Germany, and, when he came to England, was the most eminent composer of his time, for the Italian as well as the German stage.' Mozart loathed him, and Winter returned his dislike with interest, accusing him of stealing from Handel. Though the

German had a reputation for being mild and inoffensive, people who knew him well regarded him as unstable, difficult and not above intrigue.

However this may be, it was for Winter that Da Ponte wrote his last three operas – and splendid successes they all were, a fitting climax to his twenty-two years as a librettist. The first was *La grotta di Calipso*, which had its *première* at the end of May 1803. The plot, as so often, is farcical, but the libretto is readable and entertaining, and with Winter's music and Billington singing Calipso the large and stylish audience greeted it with immense enthusiasm. It was repeated many times.

The season of 1803/4 was one of the most brilliant in the annals of the opera, 'memorable,' wrote Hogarth, 'not only for the production of the *chefs d'oeuvre* of Winter, but for the simultaneous appearance of Billington, Grassini, and Braham'. First came *Il trionfo dell'amor fraterno*, based on the story of Castor and Pollux and adapted by Da Ponte from a French text. His share was for once acknowledged: 'The invention of the Poet,' *The Times* wrote, 'has embellished the ground-work with several incidents which, although not strictly classical, may be fairly allowed.' Winter's music was rapturously applauded, and the opera was often performed.

Even more successful was *Il ratto di Proserpina*, put on six weeks later. It is said to have been written in only three weeks, for Grassini's benefit. Nervous of giving it on her own, she asked Billington to support her; she herself took the part of Proserpina, while Billington sang that of Ceres. 'The Music of each of the parts,' wrote Hogarth, 'was adapted with consummate skill to the different powers of the performers; and Grassini, if she did not carry away the palm from her rival, at least divided it with her . . . For this, and the two following seasons – as long as Billington and Grassini remained upon the stage – this opera drew crowds to the theatre.' Once more, too, the despised librettist came in for a share of the praise. 'It is a grand and sublime production,' the *Morning Chronicle* said, 'and in every point – in the composition both of Music and Poetry . . . is altogether without a parallel.' When it was revived in 1815 *The Times*, too, praised 'the language in which the story is written, [which] must, on comparison with the trash we have sometimes swallowed, be considered rather creditable to the poet employed.'

In his memoirs Da Ponte makes only a passing reference to these operas, and says nothing at all of his collaboration with Winter. Once again he was embattled with his creditors, who assailed him on all sides, and the memoirs are a confused jumble of writs, promissory notes and threats of imprisonment. Taylor returned secretly from France and went into hiding. According to Da Ponte his whereabouts were betrayed by Gallini and he was handed over to the constables, who took him into custody; he was only released when the librettist found the money to pay the most pressing of his creditors, rushing off on his rescue mission despite the cries and protestations of his wife, his family and his friends. (This is almost the only occasion when we hear of Nancy trying to dissuade her impetuous husband from some quixotic and foolish act, though the times when she did so must have been legion.) Having bailed Taylor out, he looked after the one-time manager for some months, providing him with the necessities of life and somehow finding the means whereby to satisfy his innumerable creditors, while Taylor perforce remained in hiding.

It is a long story of woe, for at various times during these final years in England he was, he writes, let down by one after another of his colleagues; the newspapers are full of the names of those with whom he was associated in his various projects, who are reported (often more than once) as going bankrupt, being imprisoned, or summoning meetings of their creditors: Gallini, Federici, Corri, Dulau and Nardini (both printers and booksellers with whom at different times Da Ponte went into partnership), and Gameau, another bookseller with whom he also had dealings which left him financially a good deal worse off.

In order to pay his debts he was obliged to sell many of the books in his shop, which had been flourishing to a marvellous degree. On a previous occasion, when this had seemed the only solution to his troubles, Mathias had come to his rescue; but in the spring of 1804 he shrank from once more involving his friend. The sale took place between 16 and 26 April, and the catalogue, which is in the British Library, shows what a remarkable collection it was, 'consisting of almost every Author in the Italian Language many of which are of the greatest rarity, and some Editions may be said Unique in this Country . . . the which forming one of the finest Collections of Books which has been offered to the Public for many years, being the first and scarce Part of the genuine property of Mr. L. Daponte, Bookseller (Retiring from the Bookselling Business) . . .' The collection ranged from rare editions of Boccaccio and Petrarch to Swift's works in twelve volumes, *Robinson Crusoe* and *Sandford and Merton*. They fetched, Da Ponte declares, only a fraction of their real value.

Soon afterwards Nancy went to America to visit her family, who had settled there a few years earlier. Some mystery attaches to this venture. She took with her the considerable sum of money which she had saved while she was looking after the coffee room at the King's Theatre, so did Da Ponte send her out of the country in order that such capital as they possessed should not come into the clutches of his creditors? Or – which also seems entirely possible – did Nancy herself decide that enough was enough, and that she could no longer put up with the uncertainties of life with her volatile husband? Whatever lay behind her decision, this is how Da Ponte describes their parting:

> The day of her departure was fixed, and on the 20th September in the year 1804 she left London with her four children. [1] I accompanied her as far as Gravesend, where she embarked on a ship which was leaving for Philadelphia under the excellent Captain Collet. From London to Gravesend our journey was nothing but tears; but at the moment when I left the vessel to which I had accompanied her, at the moment when I embraced her for the last time, turning my gaze from her to the four children, I seemed to feel a hand of ice seize my heart and tear it from my breast, and my contrition and grief were such that for more than half-an-hour I was unable to decide whether to take the family back to London or go to America myself and leave the rest to providence.

He then recollected, curiously enough, that he had promised to help the principal bass at the King's Theatre, Rovedino, who was also being pressed by creditors – and what would Taylor do without him? So he decided to go back to London, 'and to part from five people who took with them almost the whole of my heart. I would have said "all": but Paolo was still with me. He united his tears with mine, tried to console me, then began to weep again himself, and in the end had as much need of consolation as I did . . .'

> I had given my wife permission to stay in America for a year; but as soon as I found myself without her and without my dear children, the house where I lived, the city where I dwelt, in truth everything which surrounded me became so hateful and insupportable that many times I was on the point of leaving everything and of fleeing to America. My brother and Mr. Mathias, whom I loved as dearly as myself, and whose affection for me and for my family was worth everything, were the only objects which held me back from this resolution, keeping me locked for another six months in a kind of hell.

He longed to have his family back again. 'I wrote, and wrote again, to my wife, telling her to come back to England without delay, and

[1] Da Ponte is getting mixed up. 20 September is the date when the ship reached Philadelphia; it had left Gravesend on 1 or 2 August. The two younger children were Joseph, born in 1800, and Lorenzo, who appeared three or four years later.

towards the end of February I gave her explicit instructions to leave America.' Whether Nancy would have obeyed was not put to the test, since the worsening of his own situation forced a change in his plans. A great rain of promissory notes which he had signed on behalf of Taylor, Corri and Rovedino descended on him, and these, together with various debts incurred by his bookshop, amounted to a large sum.

> Seeing no way out, I decided to call all my creditors together, explain my situation and put everything in the hands of two honest men, who, when all my accounts had been balanced, would have enough left to pay everyone to the last farthing. The day of the meeting was fixed, and meanwhile I took care to see Taylor and asked his opinion. He thought that my plan was ridiculous. 'You've lived in London for all these years,' he said, 'and haven't discovered yet the kind of men you've been dealing with?' In fact all my creditors, or rather those of Taylor, Corri and Rovedino, were lawyers or usurers. 'You can try,' he went on, 'and if it's no use, as it won't be, go to America, stay there until my affairs are settled . . . and then don't be afraid to return to London. Meanwhile, so long as you are there, I promise to send you your salary as poet, and you can write some operas for my theatre.' I was delighted by his words, but all the same I wanted to see if it was possible to make these hard-hearted people see reason. On the first day of March [in fact April] in the year 1805, towards six in the evening, they all met. My lawyer showed them my accounts and offered to collect what was owing to me and to pay what I owed. They heard him out patiently, drank twelve bottles of wine which, as a gracious gesture, they allowed me to pay for, and after many murmurings of 'We will see', 'We will calculate', 'We will talk about it' and similar meaningless phrases, bade me goodnight and left towards nine o'clock. I began to feel that Taylor had spoken the truth, went home and to bed, and after some hours fell asleep.

He was woken by a banging on the door, and found outside a friendly constable who told him that he was about to be arrested. He dressed and went quickly to Goold's house. Explaining his dilemma, he obtained an advance of 100 guineas on his salary.

> I returned home, went to bed for a few hours, and towards dawn dressed and ventured out into the city to look for a passage. I did not have to seek long; in the shop where I went to ask about ships which were leaving for America I found Captain Hyden,[1] who had put up a card giving notice of his departure for Philadelphia, which would take place on the fifth day of the same month.
>   There was no time to lose. I went to the Alien's Office, shut myself up

[1] Captain Abishai Hayden, master of the *Columbia*.

with the director and told him everything, and he, with a kindness and dignity worthy of him, ordered that I should be issued with a passport immediately, and gave instructions that no one in the office should breathe a word about my departure. I then took a postchaise and went to Gravesend with my brother. When I told him that I was going to America his grief was so great that I thought he would die. But through prayers and reasoning he seemed to become a little calmer, above all when I solemnly promised either to return to London in six months or send for him to join me in America. But neither the one nor the other took place. He died in London two years after my departure; and I am still in America.

Paolo was declared bankrupt on 29 April, and was hounded to his death, Da Ponte believed, by merciless usurers who took advantage of his credulity. In the unreliable directories of the day the firm is registered as booksellers and printers until 1811, and Paolo's imprint appears on the libretti of several of the operas which were put on at the King's Theatre between 1805 and 1809, including Mozart's *La clemenza di Tito*. The date of his death is not known, but Lorenzo was in touch with him in 1808.

Soon after Da Ponte had landed in the new world John Braham chose for his benefit at the King's Theatre *Una cosa rara*, which had not been performed there since 1789. The splendid cast included Braham himself, Nancy Storace, Billington and Kelly, while Grassini sang a solo between the acts. It is puzzling that the opera was never put on while Da Ponte was poet to the theatre, for when it was first seen in London it was so popular that it was repeated more than any other opera that season. Now, fifteen years later, the reviews were brilliant, and it was given on several subsequent occasions. Probably the news of this triumph never reached Da Ponte, for, although *Una cosa rara* remained one of his favourite libretti, in his writings he never referred to Braham's revival.

And so ended his career as a librettist, which has brought him such renown, if not in his lifetime, at least in the century and a half which have elapsed since his death. During his two decades as poet successively to the Vienna opera house and to the King's Theatre he wrote, adapted or translated nearly fifty operas, as well as having a hand in many others that were staged; and both theatres owed much of their success during this period to his intelligence, energy and skill.

Few of these operas are heard nowadays, since the composers who wrote their music are largely neglected. The shining exception, of course, is Mozart, the sublimity of whose operas soon began to be recognised by English audiences as well as by Continental ones (though it was still some time before they became as popular as those of Rossini, who was then the rage). *La clemenza di Tito*, in 1806, was followed by *Die Zauberflöte*(in Italian) and *Così fan tutte* in 1811, *Le nozze di Figaro* in 1812 and *Don Giovanni* in 1817. By this time the librettist himself was thousands of miles away, vigorously carving out an entirely different life for himself in the new world. Though it is as Mozart's librettist that we know his name today, perhaps Da Ponte himself might have preferred to be remembered as the indefatigable pioneer who gave to Americans an awareness of the literary and musical heritage of his native land, opening their eyes to splendours they had never seen or dreamt of before.

XII

Da Ponte had an uncomfortable voyage, which in later years he remembered as having lasted for three months, though in fact it took less than two. Impetuous as always, he paid the captain 44 guineas for his passage without enquiring what he would get in return, and found that he was provided with neither mattress nor bed-linen. At his first meal he, the captain and his fellow-passenger, one Richard Edwards, a merchant (both of whom Da Ponte describes in the most scathing terms), sat down at a dirty table to a bowl of thin and repulsive soup, with a chicken floating in the middle which more nearly resembled a crow that had come off second-best in a fight with a cat. What a hideous penance for someone who enjoyed his food so much, as Da Ponte did throughout his long life!

Worst of all, to while away the boredom of the voyage he and Edwards gambled steadily, and he lost all his money. When at last they reached Philadelphia he did not even have enough to pay the duty on the few possessions he had brought – a violin and some violin strings, a tea-urn, a carpet and some books – and Edwards had to lend him the $32.31 which he needed to rescue these goods from the customs officials.

The ship docked on 4 June 1805, and Da Ponte set out in search of his family. From the captain who had brought them to America the year before he learnt that they were living in New York, and hurried to join them. Since we know so little of Nancy, it is impossible to guess her feelings when her husband turned up, penniless as usual. He himself writes that she received him 'with every mark of tenderness, although I came destitute of all those blessings of fortune, of which I should not have been deprived had I attended to her counsels', and she seems to have been such a tender-hearted, long-suffering, patient person that this may indeed be true. What is more, she entrusted to him her own savings – the money she had brought from England, what she had earned in America (how, Da Ponte does not say), and sums which her sister had from time to time sent her from London, a total of $7000. With this Da Ponte turned to business.

When Nancy's family emigrated to America they went first to Pennsylvania – her parents, John and Antoinette Grahl, and her brother Peter and his wife Elizabeth, who in Trieste had been very fond of Da Ponte. It seems probable that Antoinette died some time before 1799. The rest of the family were engaged in profitable land speculation and trading, while John and Peter, with their expertise as chemists, both assumed the title of 'Dr' and added the practice of medicine to their other occupations. Peter, unqualified though he was, became a well-known physician.

Charles Niccolini seems also to have gone to America in 1799, leaving Louisa in London, but if so he soon returned to England, for in 1800 he was involved with Da Ponte in printing opera libretti: *Alessandro e Timotea*, published in that year, bears the imprint 'C. Nicolini'. (His imprint on the libretto may be connected with the fact that this was the year Da Ponte went bankrupt.) Some time afterwards both he and Louisa emigrated to America, joining the rest of the Grahls. Increasingly Da Ponte grew to dislike and distrust Nancy's family, while the Grahls, who managed their affairs with much greater acumen than he did, must have watched aghast as he became involved in one catastrophic business deal after another. Da Ponte, on the other hand, held them responsible for many of his misadventures, and after Nancy's death wrote of them with great bitterness.

But in the early days relations were amicable, and on the advice of John Grahl he invested his capital in a grocer's shop. 'Anyone with a grain of sense,' he writes, 'can imagine how I laughed to myself every time my poetical hand weighed out two ounces of tea, or measured half a yard of plug tobacco for a cobbler or a carter, or a morning dram costing three cents.' After a few months he and Nancy left New York, and with their four children – Louisa, Frances, Joseph and Lorenzo – moved to Elizabethville to join Charles and Louisa Niccolini; here he bought a small house and a plot of land, and continued his new vocation of merchant. But, he says, everyone cheated him, and his kindnesses were repaid by villainy. 'I was

173

sometimes obliged, rather than lose everything, to take for notes, due long since, lame horses, broken carts, disjointed chairs, old shoes, rancid butter, watery cider, rotten eggs, apples, brooms, turnips, potatoes.' The whole venture was a disaster, and within a year he lost $6000. He sold the house and land, paid his debts, and early in 1807 returned to New York. Before this, however, his and Nancy's last child, her 'Benjamin', had been born; he was christened Charles Grahl, and Da Ponte always referred to him as Carlo.

At this point Da Ponte very sensibly decided that trading was not his forte, and set out to discover whether he could earn a living through his knowledge of Italian literature and Latin. The Americans, he found, knew nothing about the former and cared less, while they had no intention of learning the latter from a foreigner. He was on the point of giving up when one day, in a bookshop on Broadway, he met the man who for the rest of his life was to be one of his best and truest friends – Clement Clarke Moore, known to untold numbers of children as the author of *The Night Before Christmas*,[1] and at this time in his late twenties (he was exactly thirty years younger than Da Ponte). They had a lively discussion on Italian literature, in the course of which Da Ponte declared that it would take him a month to list his country's greatest writers during the preceding six centuries.

The upshot was that on 15 December 1807 he began his last, longest and most glorious career, as a teacher who was to bring to the new world, for the first time, a knowledge and understanding of the greatness of Italian literature, and especially of Dante. On that day he held his inaugural class in the house of Clement Moore's father, Bishop Moore, then president of Columbia College. His pupils included his host's son Clement and his nephew Nathaniel, and another young man, John MacVickar, who was to become a great friend of his own son Lorenzo.

Within a month, he writes, the number of his pupils, young men and women, rose to twenty-four, and thereafter steadily increased. He pays the most generous and grateful tribute to all these benefactors. During this year, too, he wrote the first of the many compositions which he was to publish during his years in America: this was the *Storia compendiosa della vita di Lorenzo Da Ponte*, a forerunner of the

[1] Originally entitled *A Visit from St Nicholas*. Countless adults remember how, as children, they listened entranced to the opening lines –
Twas the night before Christmas,
when all through the house
Not a creature was stirring,
not even a mouse . . .

memoirs, written in Italian and translated by his pupils into some-what shaky English. To this he appended the text of a *conversazione* held in his house, which he clearly hoped would be the first of many, and which was surely intended to emulate the Arcadian meetings in Gorizia. On this occasion Nancy, dressed as Venus, recited a poetic epilogue written by her husband and translated by Clement Moore. What a picture this conjures up, and how one longs to have seen her, still, in her late thirties, a lovely woman.

Advertisements began to appear in the New York papers announc-ing the Manhattan Academy for Young Gentlemen and the Manhat-tan Academy for Young Ladies, the latter under the direction of 'Madame Duponte', who undertook to instruct her pupils in French and Italian and the art of making artificial flowers, and to give them the benefit of instruction by the most able music and dancing masters. Nancy was an accomplished linguist. During their journey to Italy in search of singers for the King's Theatre, Da Ponte relates that on one occasion they were stopped by officials who suspected that she was a French spy. They began to question her in various languages, and became even more suspicious when she replied to every question in the language in which it was put. 'This young lady,' one of them said sarcastically, 'is very gifted in a number of tongues.' 'Oh sir,' Nancy replied, 'I speak others as well, among them my own.' 'What is your nationality?' 'I am English, sir! And I speak French because I lived for some time in France; German, because my father was born in Dresden; Dutch, because I lived in Holland for some time; and Italian because that is the language of my husband.'

For his part, Mr Da Ponte announced that he would teach his young gentlemen French, Latin and Italian, and that 'a very able person' would instruct them in writing and ciphering, English grammar, geography and other juvenile rudiments. Since the adver-tisement also stated that 'every attention will be paid to the morals of those entrusted to his care', it seems as if some of the young gentlemen boarded with him, as they were certainly to do later on.

Not a single bookshop in New York, he declares, stocked Italian books. Unable to obtain them from Italy, he appealed to Paolo in London, who sent him an excellent collection of Italian classics, even though he was in very great difficulties himself at that time – as Filippo Pananti writes in a later edition of *Il poeta di teatro* – persecuted, like his brother, by merciless creditors. '"Let the printer go to the devil,"' Pananti accuses the management of the King's Theatre of saying, '"we want to see no more of this race of Da Ponte." But why didn't you want Paolo Da Ponte any longer?'

Pananti continues rhetorically. 'He was an honest man and a skilled printer, he had served you loyally and efficiently. The wrong you did him perhaps contributed, with other tribulations, to hasten his premature death. The city has lost a good printer, and I have lost a friend.'

As Lorenzo Da Ponte had shown in his younger days, he was a teacher of genius, and he had not lost his skill with the years. 'The sweetest moments of existence,' one of his pupils said many years later, 'were those passed in literary conversations and sympathetic study of the leading authors of Italy with the *caro maestro*'. And Arthur Livingston, to whose wide-ranging and dedicated research we owe so much of our knowledge of Da Ponte's American life, writes in a similar vein:

> There is no doubt at all that this was an important moment for the American mind. Da Ponte made Europe, poetry, painting, music, the artistic spirit, classical lore, a creative classical education, live for many important Americans as no one, I venture, had done before. And his classical scholarship, his competence as a creative Latinist, dazzled quite as much as his fame as an Italian poet . . . It was not so much Da Ponte, as Da Ponte and his setting – the cultural atmosphere of his home that survived in his children and thereafter . . . It has happened to me thrice, a near century after Da Ponte's death, to hear some New Yorker boast, not knowing quite the significance of the words, that his grandmother, or his mother, 'studied with Da Ponte'.

He established 'day-time and evening assemblies when only Italian was spoken, where [my pupils] read and repeated by heart the most beautiful passages of our orators and poets, or little comedies or plays which I wrote . . . On one occasion, in a small theatre which I had built in my own house, we recited the great Alfieri's *Mirra*: our audience consisted of 150 people whom in the space of only three years I had initiated into the Italian tongue . . .'

In 1808 he wrote a poem entitled *Agli Stati Uniti d'America*, an appeal to his adoptive country to take up arms in support of England, threatened by Napoleon's fleet which was standing off the French coast awaiting the moment to invade. This he sent to Paolo to be published. Ten years afterwards it also came out in Italy, and both there and in London it had some success. Some time later his friend Mathias wrote to him to ask for a copy 'of your marvellous canzone . . . It was very much admired in London, as I know for a fact.' Da Ponte replied that he did not possess one and had written it so long ago that he doubted whether he would be able to rewrite it even if he tried – and, with a rare burst of modesty, that he didn't particularly care for it because it seemed to him insufficiently Petrarchian.

In 1809 little Louisa, now fifteen, was married by Bishop Moore to Miles Franklin Clossey, a lawyer and the son of a New York shopkeeper, who seems already to have been part of the Da Ponte household. Immediately after the wedding his new father-in-law wrote to a former pupil, 'My wife, my daughter and our friend Clossey send a thousand warm greetings. I am much indebted to the good youth, and want him to be happy, and begin to hope he will be. I do not know what would have happened to me without the repeated marks of his friendship.' Perhaps Da Ponte had touched Clossey for a loan, as he did others of his pupil-lodgers.

The number of his students increased so happily that he could have kept his family on the fees they paid him. Unfortunately, he writes, he met certain 'bloodsuckers', with one of whom he entered into a partnership in the distilling business. For some time all went well. But then not only did he become disgusted with his partner, who he was firmly convinced was becoming rich at his, Da Ponte's, expense, but the enthusiasm for Italian which had brought him so many pupils showed signs of waning. Simultaneously he and Nancy received a letter from Louisa Niccolini giving such an enthusiastic account of Sunbury, the little town in Pennsylvania where the Grahls were now living, that he decided to move there. Nancy must certainly have been in favour of such a plan, for all the evidence shows that she was extremely fond of her family and able to live with them in harmony – which her erratic husband became increasingly unable to do.

'We arrived, and in three days I fell in love with it so completely that I decided to settle there . . . I had saved between three and four thousand dollars: I hoped therefore that an ounce of good luck, and two of brains, would be enough to set me going in some kind of trade, from the profits of which I could keep my family in comfort.' On the advice of 'Dr Grahl' (presumably his father-in-law) he invested his capital in a variety of merchandise, mainly medical supplies of one kind or another, and set himself up as a trader.

At first all was rosy, and he paints an idyllic picture of Sunbury – the only occasion in the memoirs when he describes his surroundings – verdant with bushes and shrubs which made the countryside look like one enormous garden, with streams, waterfalls, little hills, outcrops of rock, ravines and distant mountains. 'Here and there are small houses, shepherds' huts, immense coal and lime quarries, stretches of cultivated land, comfortable inns, and an enormous number of deer, wild boar, partridges, pheasants and every sort of game, wolves, foxes, bears and rattlesnakes, which, although they rarely attack the walker, nevertheless add a kind of agreeable terror, a certain air of solemnity to this majestic solitude. The water is clear, fresh and sweet, like that in which the divine Laura dipped her beautiful limbs, and at certain periods of the year one can find there trout so tasty that the lakes of Como and Garda yield no better.'

In the pleasantest part of the town, overlooking the noble Susquehanna, he rented a house and quickly became friendly with the foremost families. The evenings were passed delightfully in *conversazioni*, country dances, banquets and games.

For the next seven years, from 1811–18, he traded in Sunbury and Philadelphia, dealing in a great variety of goods – wheat, distilled liqueurs, medical supplies, spices, indeed, virtually anything that could be bought and sold. No fewer than seventy-two times, he tells us, he crossed the mountain between the two towns, 'and not always when the flowers were blooming'. 'L. de Ponty's wagon' became a familiar landmark on the well-trodden road. He taught some of the young ladies whom he always found so irresistible, and some of the young gentlemen too, and opened a millinery shop in Philadelphia. Presumably Nancy's expertise was useful in this venture, though their second daughter, Fanny, may also have taken a hand, as she was in Philadelphia a great deal.

In 1814 he built a spacious dwelling, known as Brick House, which for thirty years was the only three-story residence in Sunbury. At this period he was the largest tax-payer in the town except for Charles Hall, a lawyer and one of the foremost citizens. Hall and his wife Elizabeth became great friends of the Da Pontes and the Niccolinis, and Da Ponte coached their son Robert for Princeton. Louisa Niccolini made Charles Hall her executor, a trust which Robert took on after his father's death.

Such a story of prosperity one would in no way guess from the woeful account which the memoirs, at inordinate and tedious length, provide of one transaction after another with rogues who swindle him out of his money and possessions, have him arrested for debt and lodged in Sunbury jail (albeit for only one night), and steal from among his papers a promissory note which he had signed for William Taylor many years earlier. As always, he is the honest man who is duped by the perfidy of those who declare themselves to be his friends. He was forced to sell Brick House, to the great sorrow of his family, and build another, smaller one close by, but still he was cheated by colleagues and rivals alike. He wrote little in those years, but one canzone, dating from 1816, was dedicated to Mathias.

His anger is directed not least against the Grahls. During the

Sunbury period four of them died – Nancy's father John, her brother Peter, and Charles and Louisa Niccolini. At the time of her death Louisa Niccolini was a rich woman, her money the reward of prudent investment, careful savings and hard work. Da Ponte considered that by rights some of it, at least, should have come to him. 'This woman,' he writes, 'had been a widow for some years, and was absolute mistress of a considerable fortune which she had acquired almost entirely through my charity and through the industry and talents of her sister; she had no children, and, although I knew that she did not particularly like me, nevertheless I hoped that on her deathbed she would not dare to be so unjust as to deprive me entirely and for ever of property which her sister, through exaggerated caution and too much sisterly confidence, placed in her hands.'

Louisa had, in fact, drawn up her will in such a way that Da Ponte had no hope of ever laying claim to any of her inheritance. Most of her money she left to Nancy, who inherited $5000 through a trust fund which was administered by Charles Hall. The interest was paid to her, and on her death the principal was to be divided among her children, who were also each to receive $600 on their majority, the interest meanwhile to be paid to Nancy. She left her furniture to her niece and namesake Louisa and her wardrobe to Nancy. Thus she did everything in her power to safeguard the future and wellbeing of her sister, nieces and nephews.

Peter died in the following year, and Da Ponte, who had borrowed $500 from him and perhaps hoped that he would never have to repay it, found himself dunned for this sum by the man to whom Peter had assigned all his property. In retaliation he brought a suit against Elizabeth Grahl, Peter's widow, for jewellery which she had inherited from Antoinette, on the grounds that Nancy had never had her share. 'My poor brother-in-law,' he wrote, 'was no longer, in Sunbury, the man I had known in Trieste. The unhealthy side of this town had corrupted his good character and hardened his heart.'

But there were bright sides to the picture too. In 1815 Da Ponte's beautiful and talented grand-daughter, Matilda, was born to Louisa and Miles Clossey, and she became the joy and pride of his heart. In the same year Fanny married. This, however, turned out to be less happy, for her husband was a layabout – Da Ponte, so tirelessly active during the whole of his life, describes him as a miserable parasite – and three or four years later Fanny divorced him and went back to live with her parents.

Da Ponte's disillusionment with Sunbury became so complete that he determined to settle in Philadelphia and try to earn a living by teaching. Though he left the town respected and financially in credit, there is no doubt that, incontrovertibly one of the worst businessmen in the world, he felt increasingly desperate as he found himself trapped in an uncongenial occupation and surrounded by rogues, of whom there were plenty in Sunbury, then still a frontier town filled with adventurers and fortune-seekers. 'When I left New York,' he writes, 'I took with me merchandise worth over $3000; when I departed from Sunbury, an old carriage, a broken-down horse and 12 thalers constituted all my possessions.' He had, he told his one-time pupil Nathaniel Moore, lost at least $12,000 during his eight years there.

So on 24 August 1818, taking Joseph with him and leaving Nancy to settle their affairs and collect money owing to him, he set off for Philadelphia.[1] He took with him enough money, as he thought, to tide him over before Nancy joined him, but towards the end of September she wrote that she would have to stay another two weeks. She was, in fact, writing urgent letters to Charles Hall, begging him to pay in advance interest not yet due. Meanwhile Da Ponte's money had vanished; he had neither friends nor credit in Philadelphia; in the space of a month he had found only two pupils; and he and Joseph were lodging with an old woman who was pestering him for the rent.

In this crisis he was relieved beyond measure to receive a letter from Nathaniel Moore, gratifyingly written in Italian. Da Ponte replied at length explaining his predicament: 'I have many creditors who owe me money, a capital of about $10,000 which yields an interest of 6% to my wife, and a great deal of land to sell. But the immediate emergency is dreadful.' Might it be possible, he went on, for a New York bookseller or some of his friends there to advance money on the book he was writing, which he hoped to publish in the new year? By this he must have meant *An extract from the life of Lorenzo Da Ponte with the History of several dramas by him, and among others, il Figaro, il Don Giovanni and La scola degli amanti; set to music by Mozart*, which was published in 1819. Like the *Storia compendiosa* of twelve years earlier, it was a forerunner of the memoirs. It ran to 46 pages, and was in English, almost certainly translated from the Italian by his pupils or one of his children.

Another correspondent to whom he mentioned the memoirs at this time was his friend Michele Colombo, of whom he had news through

[1] His Sunbury physician, Dr Jackson, describes him at this time as having 'a good figure, very handsome, and with a noble manner. An extremely honest man, delightful company, witty, and often deceived by rogues into embarrassing situations.'

an Italian traveller. 'With what transports of joy,' he wrote to Colombo, 'did I learn from Signor Luigi Pittori that you are alive, well and happy . . . I have written a large part of my life,' he wrote in this same letter, 'and shall perhaps publish it.'

Meanwhile, Nathaniel Moore must have sent him some money, for early in October he writes – still from Philadelphia – to say that he does not know how to express his gratitude for such boundless generosity. He congratulates his one-time pupil on his metamorphosis from lawyer to professor (Moore became Professor of Greek at Columbia College, and this connection was to be very important to Da Ponte). 'How I should love in my old age to find a similar post in Italian literature! This dream often haunts me; but I am very much afraid that in America it will never be anything but a dream . . .'

By the end of March he is writing again to Nathaniel to say that his hopes of establishing himself as a teacher of Italian in Philadelphia have faded. At first he was optimistic, and the only thing that gave him pause was the high cost of Italian books, of which there were in any case very few. 'By chance I came across an Italian traveller who had in his possession an entire set of all our classics in the Milan edition,[1] a veritable treasure house of literature, which you will certainly have seen, and with some difficulty I persuaded him to part with it. I immediately managed to see the director of the public library, and, convinced that I was conferring a real benefit on the city, tried my utmost to persuade him to buy it. He did me the honour of accepting four volumes which I donated to the library . . . For two and a half months this gentleman spoke fair words, and they seemed to be on the point of assuring me that they would buy, if not all the collection, at least a good part of it. So I took the plunge and bought them from the Italian traveller, who was on the point of going away, and since at that time I hadn't enough money to pay for them I gave him a note payable at three months . . . A few days before the note fell due the director of the library told me drily *We do not buy the books.*'

Da Ponte then had the idea of trying to sell them in New York, and despatched Joseph with half of them. For the time being he kept the remainder, overwhelmed by the boldness behind the whole conception of the series, the excellence of the annotations, and the sublime beauty of the contents. Soon Joseph returned with all the books sold at a good profit, and with a warm invitation from Clement Moore to Da Ponte to come to New York and teach Italian there.

[1] Some years earlier a firm of publishers and booksellers in Milan, Fusi e Stella, had begun to bring out an important series of Italian classics, which they called Classici Italiani di Milano. Da Ponte was enraptured by it.

Joyfully Da Ponte packed his bags. At some point his family had joined him in Philadelphia, but once again he decided to take only Joseph with him, leaving Nancy and the other children behind until he was sufficiently established to bring them to New York.

XIII

Da Ponte was to spend the rest of his life in New York, buying and selling Italian books, writing prose and poetry and letters, and above all teaching.

His first concern, when he arrived in the spring of 1819, was Joseph. He was worried about his eldest son, who seems to have got into wild company in Philadelphia, and the wisdom of putting a certain distance between that city and his family was one of his most urgent reasons for deciding to return to New York, since 'the dissipations of the young men of that city frightened me so much that I felt it would be dangerous to leave him there for long without a father to look after him'. Joseph was studying law, but since starting to do so had entirely neglected the Greek and Latin which were essential for a legal career. Da Ponte found him an excellent tutor, and with a light heart went to visit his friends, his 'dearest cousins' Clement and Nathaniel Moore, and the rest of their family. Once more he began to follow the career of teacher, and by the end of the month he had a sizeable class, to whom he sold the rest of the Italian classics that he had bought in Philadelphia. At his suggestion, his students presented sixty of them to the New York public library, which at that time possessed no Italian books, while Da Ponte gave them some magnificent volumes on his own account.

He rented and furnished a small house, sent for his family, and entered Joseph at Columbia College. At first there was some difficulty about this, for in the Butler Library there is a letter in Da Ponte's hand to Dr Harris, president of the college, written with particular care and in English. It has to do with the payment of the fees. 'I offered to Mr Livingston,'[1] he wrote, 'an order on the mechanic's bank, (in which I hold stock) for the amount of eighty Dols, which would fall due on the first day of February next, or orders upon any

[1] Perhaps John R. Livingston, a wealthy and hospitable New Yorker whose three daughters Da Ponte taught.

of my scholars of the first families of Newyork payable in less than three months. He however told me that there was but one method, which was to obtain an order from the President or one of the Professors of the college to place such an amount to my credit on his account. As this is a favor which I dare not expect from any one, I shall be under the necessity, you may suppose with how much regret, to deprive my son of the benefit of tuition in the College.' The difficulty must have been cleared up, for in the autumn Joseph duly became a scholar there.

In his teaching Da Ponte was once again held up by the lack of Italian books. Every other product of his native land was to be found in America – wine and grapes from Sicily, oil, olives and silk from Florence, marble from Carrara, golden chains from Venice, gut from Rome and Padua, rosolio (a kind of liqueur) from Trieste, salami from Bologna, pasta from Naples and plaster figurines from Lucca. But nowhere was there an Italian bookseller, and in the one shop in New York where a few Italian books were to be found the prices were so outrageous that they discouraged anyone from studying the language. Da Ponte, with his usual energy and refusal to admit defeat, wrote to a number of booksellers and publishers in Genoa, Venice, Florence, Leghorn and other cities, but all of them demanded payment in advance, which he was not in a position to make. So for the moment nothing came of this plan.

He was vexed also by a running battle with some of his compatriots who had come to New York to seek their fortune. Since his last sojourn, the city had been invaded by 'a whole stream of exiles . . . who, without careers, means, or – unfortunately for them – talent, had exchanged guns and bayonets for dictionaries and grammars, and begun to teach languages'. Some of them, he declares, envious of his success as a teacher, became his bitter enemies, and one, Marco Antonio Casati, a defrocked abbé, circulated to the parents of all his pupils an anonymous letter accusing him of every crime under the sun – adultery, homicide, swindling, cheating, intrigue and debauchery – and attacking his birth, education, poverty, pronunciation, habit of plagiarising, teeth, servants, vicious behaviour, heartlessness and duplicity towards his compatriots, and, for good measure, his family's morals also. 'His son [Joseph] . . . is familiar to every vice,' the letter said, with what truth we do not know.

The assault was so wild that it cannot have done him much harm among his friends and pupils. But it was not in his nature to let anything of this kind rest. In the first edition of the memoirs he included a long account of the affair, setting out the twelve most serious accusations and his refutation of some of them (but not all –

about the charge that 'He was obliged in his early life to quit Venice for his misbehaviour' he must have felt it wisest to say nothing, and he quietly let it disappear into thin air). In addition, he appealed to as many people as he could who were in a position to rebut Casati's accusations. One of them was a former pupil, Professor Samuel Jarvis, now teaching at Yale, whose reply was eminently satisfactory. Another was a doctor whose name Casati had used to support his accusations, and who replied to Da Ponte's appeal that he remembered him as 'firstly, a man of letters; second, a good husband, blessed with a loving wife, and a good father; and thirdly, a complete gentleman.'

In his answer to Casati's polemic Da Ponte made one claim which was uncharacteristic – that he had been 'imperial poet' in Vienna, which of course was incorrect; he had been poet to the theatre. Generally it was the other way round; when people erroneously gave him the grander title, he took care to correct them, as in this passage in the first edition of the memoirs: 'I was never Caesarean poet for very good reasons: first, because I had neither the talent nor the experience to occupy a post which had formerly been filled by those two pillars of the Italian theatre, Zeno and Metastasio; and secondly, because Joseph had resolved not to have one.'

Early in 1821 he once more indignantly took up his pen, this time in defence of his native land. One Charles Phillips, a lawyer and a member of the New York City Council, had published an open letter addressed to the King of England. It began as an attack on the morals of Queen Caroline, who during an extended visit to Europe had, it was said, taken her courier, Bartolomeo Pergami, as her lover; when she returned to England in 1820 she had been put on trial for adultery. Phillips' letter then broadened out into an attack on the whole Italian nation. 'This barbaric diatribe,' wrote Da Ponte, 'appeared in the public journals, with all the usual sarcastic observations of various journalists from Ireland, England and America.' Enraged, he sprang to the defence of the Queen; perhaps with a vivid memory of how he would once have been grateful for a little discretion, he wrote that Pergami became 'her counsellor, companion, guest, confidant, friend . . . Here let it rest.' Then, in a reply which shows how carefully he had followed events, he went on to refute the attack on Italy, which, 'though an ungrateful and cruel stepmother towards me, I have loved and shall always love with the most tender filial affection, until the last moment of my life.'

This *Discorso apologetico* he read to a gathering of over two hundred people, the audience being 'one of the most numerous . . . of wit and fashion, which ever graced an apartment in this city'. The occasion was a triumph: the company 'listened with delighted attention' – not least because he gave the address in English, as we know from two of those who were present, H. T. Tuckerman and Dr John Francis, his New York physician, both of whom wrote about it afterwards. He delivered his discourse, Dr Francis remembered, 'with the earnestness and animation of a great speaker'. Da Ponte says that in order to make it more accessible to his audience he *had it translated* into English, and it was published both in this language and in Italian.

How good a command of English he had by this time we can only guess. Arthur Livingston, describing the first meeting with Clement Moore, says that he 'spoke English fluently, but with a trace of a defect in his speech – if with a foreign accent'. But Livingston gives no documentary evidence for this statement and, as elsewhere in his informative annotations, this may be a small picturesque addition to the known facts. All the same, after thirty years in London and America – especially the latter, where he would have met relatively few compatriots – Da Ponte must have acquired a good working knowledge of English. During his schooldays and the years which he had spent as theatre poet, poring over hundreds of libretti and plays in a variety of tongues, he had acquired a familiarity with many languages. This is shown not only by his wide reading in their literature but also by a passage from the *Discorso apologetico*, in which he speaks of the sublimity of Greek, the magnificence of Latin, the grandeur and conciseness of Hebrew, the boldness of German, the majesty of Spanish and the vigour of English.

But speaking and writing a foreign language are not the same thing, and to the end of his days Da Ponte, with his passionate love of his native tongue and his ease in writing it both for verse and prose, preferred Italian. Several members of his family were skilled linguists, and he could always call upon them, or upon his pupils, if he needed help with translations – for, in typical Italian fashion, the Da Ponte enterprise was run as a kind of family co-operative, with everyone lending a hand. Apart from the letter to Dr Harris, he resorted to English while he was in Sunbury to write some of his business correspondence and make out invoices, but these seem to be the only exceptions. Certainly all his literary work was in Italian.

Triumph was followed by grief. Joseph was nearly at the end of his first year at Columbia, and was doing well. But one day Da Ponte went into his room and found him in a state of profound melancholy. Joseph, with an expression which terrified his father, presented him with a letter in which he begged to be allowed to finish his legal studies in Philadelphia, on the grounds that he would thus obtain his degree in one year, whereas in New York it would take two. 'I understand why you took me away from Philadelphia,' Joseph said when his father had finished reading the letter. 'Dear father, don't be afraid. I know what I owe to you, to my family, to myself. If I long to return there, it is because I want to please you and give you joy, not to make you desperate and in the end kill you.' Da Ponte did not have the heart to refuse him, and Joseph departed for Philadelphia.

For six months he wrote only good news, and his parents had no reason to guess that his letters were so cheerful in order to make them believe that all was well. They were horrified when, in December, he unexpectedly returned home, thin, pale, exhausted, 'so that it needed only a moment to know that he was doomed'. Six months later, in his twenty-first year, he died. To his parents' grief was joined anxiety, for his illness (which was consumption, although the disease was still unrecognised; Da Ponte describes it as 'a strange and most grave illness, which the most experienced doctors either did not identify or found greater than their art') entailed a good deal of extra expense. Moreover, Joseph had contracted debts in Philadelphia of which his father knew nothing and which honour demanded that he should pay. To his fury, he was not allowed to use Joseph's inheritance from Louisa for this purpose.

Typically, he says nothing about Nancy's grief at the death of her son, though the loss must have been indescribably painful to her. Even as a boy he had been her prop and mainstay; from the age of twelve he had witnessed deeds and mortgages for his parents, and much of Nancy's business correspondence is in his handwriting.

Da Ponte was consumed by his own sorrow. One of his pupils, hoping to provide him with some distraction, gave him a copy of Byron's poem *The Prophecy of Dante*, written two years earlier when the poet was living in Ravenna in a house close by Dante's tomb. Da Ponte, seeing a similarity between Dante's situation and his own – both men were old, exiled, unrecognised, longing for their homeland and filled with patriotic feelings – decided to attempt a translation, or rather, as he put it, an imitation. To this end he spent the following summer on the country estate of John R. Livingston; the family were amongst his closest friends, and he seems often to have stayed with them during the summer.

Here he retired with his own family and a few students. 'I rose with the sun and spent an hour reading Italian poetry or prose, sometimes with my students and sometimes with my children. With them I ate breakfast out of doors, and half-an-hour later lay down (always weeping) under a peach or apple tree and translated a passage of the poem, which sweetened my tears ... In this way almost two months passed, and although my grievous wounds were not healed, nevertheless I found enough strength and courage to bear them.'

Back in New York, he published his translation, which contains a great number of notes, included for the benefit of his students 'and above all for those who, in reading this translation through with me, seem not to understand the words and phrases which I have explained here'.

According to the usage of the day, his friends and pupils subscribed to buy the little book; their names are printed at the end, and they include President Harris, Professor Jarvis, a whole covey of Livingstons, and John MacVickar, one of his first students, by then Professor of Philosophy at Columbia College.

Both the translation and the *Discorso apologetico* reached Italy, for he received a letter from a Signor Giacomo Ombrosi, the American vice-consul in Florence, who told him that a copy of *La profezia di Dante* had been presented to Byron while he was in Leghorn, and that he had received 'your worthy offering with much satisfaction'. It is perfectly possible that Byron did in fact see the translation, for at this time he was living in Pisa and paying visits to Leghorn, where he had taken a villa for his mistress.

The 'Letter to Lord Byron' which prefaced the main text was rendered into excellent English 'by the translator's daughter'; this must have been Fanny, now living with her parents. The second edition, published a year later, contains some interesting and unexpected items: a gay and delightful little poem thanking one of his 'damigelle' – as he loved to call his young lady students – for the delicious fruit tart she had given him for Christmas; another entitled *'L'amante discreto'*, charmingly written and with a free but beautiful translation by his daughter; a tender *canzonetta* 'from a father to his daughter' on the occasion of her marriage (written years earlier, perhaps, for Louisa or Fanny), and another 'from a father on the arrival of his dearly-loved daughter'.

Da Ponte is often accused, and justly, of writing about himself at extreme length and rarely about his family. Such poems as these help to redress the balance, for they show him, as do comments here and there by his friends and by other people who came into contact with him, as a loving, often playful father who was always deeply concerned for the well-being of his children. With all his egotism, his passionate longing for glory and his obsession with what he saw as his divine mission to bring to America an awareness of the sublimity of Italian literature, his family were at the centre of his life and he could not have managed without them, as he very well knew. What he never seemed to realise was how much they suffered because of his self-absorption. When from time to time he was forced to sell houses, furniture and other necessities or amenities of life, or uproot the whole family for a plunge into the unknown, it was always himself he was 'depriving'; rarely does he express regret at the sacrifices which his family, and especially Nancy, constantly bore because of his imprudence or rashness. But that he loved them deeply and genuinely there is no doubt.

One such occasion of 'sacrifice' arose as a result of Ombrosi's letter; Da Ponte, 'depriving' himself of 'many articles necessary to the decorum of the family', managed to scrape together a hundred dollars, and these he sent to Ombrosi, asking him to use the money to order books on his behalf from Florentine booksellers. From this time he began to trade regularly with Italy, and first of all with Fusi e Stella, who after the *Discorso apologetico* reached Italy had spontaneously offered to supply him, and who gave him excellent terms. Da Ponte had a very close relationship with them over the years. Quite unexpectedly, too, he received a consignment from Bossange, well-known booksellers in Paris, to whom he had written some time earlier. So he was able to embark on his project of setting up as a bookseller in New York, which he had long had in mind.

In the spring of 1821 he and Nancy had begun to take some of his pupils as lodgers so that, by living *en famille*, they would improve their pronunciation. The first of them was Henry James Anderson, later to become professor of mathematics at Columbia College and an eminent astronomer. His two brothers came with him, and four more young men as well. They, and their successors, stayed for one, two or three years, before leaving to take up whatever profession they had chosen, but Henry Anderson lingered on, for a very good reason – in 1831 he became Fanny's second husband. Nancy did not approve of the marriage, as Da Ponte wrote to Dr John Francis – 'The same thing happened to me with my wife's mother, and I find it quite natural' – but he does not give the reason for Nancy's concern.

'As you know, I am an old man,' Da Ponte wrote in the spring of 1822 to his schoolfriend Girolamo Perucchini. 'Nevertheless, though seventy-three years have passed, they don't weigh very heavily yet, either on my mind or on my back; I still eat well, drink well, sleep peacefully, and – which amazes people – spend six, eight, ten and sometimes twelve hours a day working, and writing poetry too. I don't claim that it is good, and I don't dare to believe my friends when some of them say it is, because, after more than forty years' absence from Italy, I can't believe that I haven't entirely lost what little skill I perhaps once had . . .' As he always did in letters home, he begged for news of Ceneda, which never lost its place in his heart.

The next year, 1823, began prosperously and was a landmark for Da Ponte, since in the course of it there appeared the first volumes of the memoirs, on which he was to be busily engaged for the rest of his life. He had, he wrote five years later, felt some diffidence about publishing them, not knowing whether the public would find them interesting and enjoyable. But a number of his friends tried to persuade him to print them; he read them again; and little by little he changed his view. Writing with his students in mind, who often had no dictionaries or, even if they had, would not have wanted to look up every other word, he adopted an easy, spontaneous style. Above all he strove for clarity, 'in my opinion the noblest prize of every writer'.

The memoirs were published over the imprint of Lorenzo and Carlo Da Ponte, and at the end of the second volume 111 names appear as subscribers: they include Da Ponte's Sunbury physician, Dr Jackson, Dr Harris, and the ex-King of Spain, Joseph Bonaparte, who, under the alias of the Count of Survilliers, was at that time living in America, and who ordered a grand total of fourteen copies.

In this same year Da Ponte and Carlo – who was helping his father in his bookselling enterprise – brought out a list of the books that were to be found in their shop. This was an expanded version of a descriptive catalogue which Da Ponte had composed for his sons while the family was living in Sunbury. Written from memory, since he then had no reference books to consult, it not only contains hundreds of Italian titles and authors but in many cases gives detailed descriptions of the various editions available, showing an extraordinary knowledge both of the works listed and of the relative merits of the different editions. Da Ponte was delighted because it encouraged librarians in other American cities to order Italian books, and also led to the spread of Italian literature in Mexico, where the catalogue was taken by a highly cultured traveller, Signor Rivafinoli.

Nancy and her husband lost another child this year, for their elder daughter Louisa – 'the ornament of the family', as Da Ponte calls her – died in the summer at the age of twenty-eight, like Joseph of consumption. Her second baby, a boy, had lived for only five months, so the beautiful and gifted Matilda was the sole issue of the marriage between Louisa and Miles.

Back in Ceneda, in 1806, old Gasparo Da Ponte had died also. To what extent Da Ponte had remained in touch with his stepsisters since then we do not know. He had faithfully helped to support them during his Vienna days, but there is no evidence that he was able to go on doing so when he moved to London, except for the small sum which he tried to send through Paolo in 1800. Now, in the mid-twenties, perhaps through a friend or pupil who was travelling to Italy, he sent them a copy of the memoirs, enclosing with the small volumes one of those gay and charming rhymed letters which often give so much more vivid a picture of his life, and so much truer a portrait of Da Ponte himself, than do the memoirs themselves.

Tell me what you are doing, he writes, how you are, whether you are married and have sons and daughters, if your husbands are alive and whether they are honest or not, rich or poor, ugly or handsome. What has happened to my friends, and especially to two who are always in my mind, Michelini and Colombo, whom I have never stopped loving even though the ungrateful old men have forgotten how much I loved them? But if they are dead I will excuse them.

Next, he goes on, I will tell you about my own life, and don't interrupt.

I have lived in this country for twenty years, and although it is large it isn't so different from the world I came from; there are arts and sciences, vices and passions, bad men and good, woods and rivers, roses, thorns, horses, dogs and cattle. And there are ladies like you, who sleep when they are sleepy, drink when they are thirsty, and can do – or almost – everything you can. Whether I did well in coming here I don't know and don't want to: it isn't always carnival time, and we can't always be laughing.

Now let me tell you what I do. I get up early, before my cock wakes, and at the first cock-crow I take my horse and my German servant and buy food for ten or more people. Back home again, I drink tea or coffee, perhaps two or three cups, with some biscuits. Then I set out once more in my gig and go from house to house selling merchandise which I've imported into America – Dante, Petrarch, Boccaccio, Machiavelli, Casa, Ariosto, Tasso and a hundred others: criticism, mathematics, history, grammar, politics, poetry. I've opened my first bookshop and sell from morning to night; and here is a list of all the wonderful poets whom my scholarly young pupils read . . . Here too are six kisses to divide between you. If there is one left over, dress it in black and take it to the tomb of her who is dead.

To the youngest, Faustina, for whom he had such a soft spot, Da Ponte sent a lock of hair from a certain charming girl who, like her, had beautiful eyes and was altogether beautiful, and who was, in fact, so like Faustina that she might have been her twin sister. And he asks Faustina to let him have a lock of her own hair in return, which he will make into a ring for 'Franceschina' (Fanny).

Not long afterwards he heard, with a delight which can be imagined, that an Italian opera company was coming to New York.

The city, like other large towns in America, was no stranger to opera of a kind. From the mid-eighteenth century New York audiences had become familiar with ballad operas, massacred versions of Continental operas, and plays with incidental songs, sung in English and supplemented with fore and after pieces and farces. Samuel Arnold, Henry Rowley Bishop, Michael Kelly and Joseph Mazzinghi were all favourite composers, as was Stephen Storace, whose works were especially popular. But these were 'makeshifts adapted, pruned and spliced to fit the exigencies of the companies performing them. They were, in form, little better than modern musical comedies, abounding in spoken dialogue and other stage business. Arias which taxed the powers of the singers were omitted and popular airs of the day inserted to replace them.' New Orleans was exceptional in having a permanent opera company – the first in the North American continent to do so – which since 1791 had performed French operas, drama and ballet, and which went on regular and successful tours. Their performances were popular, but Da Ponte had a low opinion of the singers, referring to them scathingly as 'howling *Galli* or rather *Gatti*'.[1] Nothing had been seen which could prepare New York audiences for what they were about to witness, for the few Italian operas that had been attempted would almost certainly have been disowned by their creators. Sung in bad English translations, they were invariably cut to ribbons in order to leave room for the additional entertainment which the audience expected. However, many of the pasticcio English operas performed at this time included extracts from Italian operas, and in this way American audiences, whether or not they realised what they were hearing, would have acquired at any rate a little familiarity with the music of these composers.

Now, in 1825, an Italian opera company – the first ever to perform in America – had been persuaded to make the long and uncomfortable journey to New York, with a doubtful financial result at the end, by a certain Dominick Lynch, a wealthy wine-merchant with a passion for music and especially for opera and *bel canto*. He went to London to induce Manuel Garcia, a famous Spanish tenor, to bring his company to the Park Theatre, one of the only two theatres in New York, whose manager, Stephen Price, was equally keen on the

[1] A pun on the Italian for 'French' (Gauls) and 'cats'.

project. Garcia's singers consisted of himself, his wife, his son and daughter, a second soprano and tenor, and two basses.

On 29 November 1825 the season opened gloriously with *Il barbiere di Siviglia* by Rossini, then the most popular and influential composer living. Garcia himself sang the role of Count Almaviva, which he had created at the first performance of the opera nine years earlier. 'In what language shall we speak of an entertainment so novel in this country?' the *New-York Evening Post* asked its readers next day. 'All have obtained a general idea of the opera from report. But report can give but a faint idea of it ...' Among the audience – which included an assemblage of ladies the like of which, 'so fashionable, so numerous, and so elegantly dressed, was probably never witnessed in our theatre', were the novelist Fennimore Cooper, the poet Fitz-Greene Halleck, who had once learnt Italian from Da Ponte and always kept in touch with his old master, and Joseph Bonaparte, who had taken a box for the season. The evening was a triumph – 'Bravo! bravissimo!' the audience cried.

Da Ponte says only that he took some of his pupils to the fifth performance, but it is inconceivable that he missed this splendid *première*. There is a legend that, when he and Garcia met, the singer embraced the seventy-six-year-old librettist, singing the first lines of the 'champagne aria' from *Don Giovanni*. His daughter Maria, then at the beginning of a career which was to make her famous wherever opera was sung, took the town by storm. She was seventeen, lovely, wayward, passionate, full of charm, with a beautiful voice of great range and a soul of fire, as the violinist Ole Bull said. But she was to have a short and often sad life. While she was in New York she married one Eugène Malibran, a French merchant many decades older than she was and saddled with debts. In 1827 she escaped from him and returned to Paris, where she made a brilliant reputation as Madame Malibran and fell in love with a young violinist. Eventually she obtained a divorce and married her lover, but she had only a brief period of happiness, for six months later she died after a fall from a horse.

Garcia had brought with him five operas by Rossini, four of them *opere buffe* – *Il barbiere di Siviglia*, *Tancredi*, *Il Turco in Italia* and *La Cenerentola* – and the fifth, *Otello*, an *opera seria*. His company also performed Zingarelli's *Romeo e Giulietta* and two operas of his own (he wrote about fifty, all of them now forgotten), set to libretti by Paul Rosich, the *basso buffo* of the company. There was too – and how Da Ponte rejoiced – 'his' *Don Giovanni*. With this, and with *Le nozze di Figaro*, New York audiences might have been familiar to some extent, as both had been performed, but in much shortened versions and in wretched English translations by Henry Rowley Bishop (as had *The Barber of Seville*, under its alternative title *Almaviva*). The company lacked a suitable Don Ottavio, so the librettist himself found a singer for the part, and with his pupils and some friends provided the fee. *Don Giovanni* was a success and was repeated three times, though legend has it that on the first night Garcia, who was singing the Don, 'exerted himself in vain to keep the singers and orchestra in time and tune, until at last, sword in hand, he came forward and, commanding silence, exclaimed that it was a shame to murder a masterpiece. They began again, collected themselves, and took pains, and the finale came happily to an end.'

Da Ponte brought to New York his great friend Filippo Traetta (son of the famous Venetian opera composer), who had studied in Naples with Piccinni and directed the Conservatorio dell'Ospedale in Venice shortly before Da Ponte's first visit there, and who was now running a conservatory of music in Philadelphia. The idea was that they should write an opera together for Garcia. The project came to nothing, but that Da Ponte was striving to keep his hand in is shown by a letter which he wrote in 1829: in it he said that he was writing both a serious and a *buffo* libretto (he was then seventy-nine!); was there, he asked, an impresario in Trieste who would have the courage to put it on?

The Garcia season closed on 30 September 1826, just ten months after it had begun, and the company departed to Mexico to give a season there. On the whole they had a good press in New York, but Hogarth (who referred to Garcia as 'a man of brutal temper, but a thorough musician') said that apart from the tenor himself and his daughter, who captivated the Americans with her voice, beauty, and vivacity, the company was wretched. Four years later *The Harmonicon* declared that Garcia, now fifty, was 'half worn out; if he had ever possessed the power of sustaining a note, it is now entirely gone, and he endeavoured to conceal the defect by the utmost profusion of florid ornament. It must be acknowledged, however, that in the novelty, variety, and taste of his divisions, he has been excelled by no tenor of his time.'

Whatever the criticisms of the *cognoscenti*, New Yorkers had had their first taste of Italian grand opera, and had revelled in it. In the words of one eminent citizen, these 'musical creations rendered the winter of 1825–6 an epoch in the history of New York society'.

Da Ponte seized the opportunity provided by Garcia's company to publish the libretto of *Don Giovanni* with a translation 'of the poetical part' by his son Lorenzo. This was put on sale both in the theatre and in bookshops, and, he says, an enormous number was sold. He also published *Una tragedia et tre drammi*, dedicated to 'three lovely flowers of my Tuscan garden', as he liked to call the young pupils whose beauty and grace so intoxicated him. The play was *Il Mezenzio* and the operas were *Le nozze di Figaro*, *Il Don Giovanni* and *L'Assur Re d'Ormus* – the only libretti, amongst all those he had written, which he had brought to America, and even these he possessed by accident. This little publication includes some interesting references to his Vienna operas, as well as the caustic comments on Michael Kelly which have already been quoted.

In the introduction to *Don Giovanni* he bitterly accuses the theatre impresarios in Italy of cheese-paring and of not understanding the importance of the libretto if the music is to make its proper effect:

> Good poets must be honoured and paid properly, as they are in other countries, and especially France. If our composers steadfastly refused to adorn with their melodies the tasteless rubbish of these insipid pieces; if the directors of Italian opera in foreign countries chose only those which are good (and even we have some which are); if the translations made sense; if, finally, the original texts were not mutilated, emasculated and adulterated at the caprice of every singer, and not distorted by a charming patchwork of some six or seven hundred printing errors which nullifies anything good there may be, we should see on our stage not melo-monsters but melo-dramas; and the nation which in the arena of poetry – tragic, comic, pastoral, and in every other genre – can present itself without blushing, could boldly and without shame show itself on the field of opera also. Zeno, Metastasio, Calsabigi, and – for the charm of his style – the Abbé Casti in Vienna; Migliavacca and Mazzolà in Dresden; Caramondani in Berlin; Coltellini in St Petersburg – all of them, because they were properly rewarded, wrote texts in this genre as excellent as anything the Italian genius could provide. These plays, set to the marvellous music of Sarti, Burenelli, [1] Piccinni, Sacchini, Anfossi, Guglielmi, Paisiello, and other excellent composers of the last century, are no longer performed, just as the Greek tragedies are no longer seen, or the comedies of Macchiavelli and of his contemporaries, or the pastoral plays

---

[1] Baldassare Galuppi, known as 'Il Buranello' because he was born on the island of Burano. He wrote a number of operas for the Venetian opera houses, and set to music many of Goldoni's plays. In 1740 he was appointed director of music at the Ospedale dei Mendicanti, where thirty years later the Ferrarese was to be a pupil, and between 1768 and his death in 1785 was choir-master at the Ospedale degli Incurabili. He was also first choir-master and then director of music at San Marco. So he was active in Venice all the time Da Ponte was there, and the librettist must have known his operas well, and perhaps the composer himself.

of Tasso or Guarini, not because they are no longer patterns of true
beauty but because

> Ut silva foliis pronos mutantar in annos
> Prima cadunt.

Since everything depends upon taste, after a while changes come; and
although the prevailing taste is not always the best, nevertheless it robs
the light from those which reigned before, until a new taste is born which
seizes the throne in its turn. How marvellous, then, that with such a
succession of changes the three operas of Mozzart [1] are almost the only
ones which no modern Composer has succeeded in supplanting; the only
ones which with every day that passes are more highly esteemed and
valued, in every theatre in Europe; the only ones which can cry out in
triumph, WE ARE ETERNAL.

The words of these operas were written by me. To that immortal
genius I gladly yield all the glory which is due to him for writing such
miraculous works; for myself, may I hope that some small ray of this
glory may fall on me, for having provided the vehicle for these everlasting
treasures, through my fortunate poetry.

The introduction to *Le nozze di Figaro* calls Mozart and Salieri 'the
two most renowned geniuses of the musical kingdom [who] will
indubitably live as long as music and poetry delight those hearts
which are tender and capable of feeling noble sentiments.' And Da
Ponte describes *Don Giovanni*, *Figaro* and *Assur* as 'the three most
precious gems of the lyrical/comic theatre of Italy'.

He seems not to have kept abreast of what was happening at the
Burgtheater, for in 1828 he wrote to a correspondent in Trieste, 'I
should love to know how the theatre in Vienna is doing; who is
singing there; if the great author of the Corneide is still Poet
Cornilaureate [2] and if Weigl is still alive. How gladly I would write
an opera for him! Old as I am, I would take my courage in my
hands and fly to Vienna to write it!' He was, however, well informed
about the growing popularity of Mozart at the King's Theatre, of
the wretched English version in 1812 of *Le nozze di Figaro* (which, he
believed, had been badly translated on purpose), and of the performance there in 1817 of *Don Giovanni*, which, wrote *Blackwood's Edinburgh
Magazine*, 'did more for the proprietors than all the efforts of several
years'. Da Ponte bitterly attacked this review, which had failed to
mention his name:

[1] '*Le nozze di Figaro, il Don Giovanni, e la scola degli Amanti.*' (Da Ponte's footnote)
[2] Giovanni de Gamerra, who had followed Bertati as poet to the Italian opera in
Vienna but had long since lost his post. Between 1770 and 1781 he had written a
long and obscene poem entitled *Le Corneide*.

No one can be surprised if when these dramas are spoken of by a public character, I expect to see the name of Mozart entwined with that of Da Ponte, as the ivy with the oak ... As to the merits or defects of my operas, I shall say nothing: but whether you give to my verses the name of poetry, of measured prose, *or of vehicle*, etc., I will only observe, that Mozart must have been pleased with them, because after the first and second of my dramas, he was happy to have the third; that he ennobled them with *a load of delightful notes*, with which you were equally pleased; and that on other words he undoubtedly would have composed another music; better, perhaps; but this is problematical!

In all likelihood – since he does not mention them – he never knew about two earlier performances in London of *Don Giovanni*. The second of these took place on 23 May 1809, at the Hanover Square Rooms, under the direction of the pianist and composer George Eugene Griffin. (There was a postponement from 20 April, 'in consequence of an event of the most melancholy nature' – the death of the conductor's father.) Much of the recitative seems to have been omitted, but otherwise the greater part of the opera was performed, the excellent cast including John Braham and Mrs Bland, a noted soprano. Mr Griffin played a piano concerto of his own composition, and the great Mrs Billington sang a recitative and an aria.

The first performance of all, which presumably also took place as advertised, was on 17 April at the Old London Tavern, Bishopsgate-street. This was for the benefit of the violinist Spagnoletti, and again there were some noted singers. The press announcement stated that the audience would be able to enjoy 'the Grand Opera of DON JUAN by Mozart, never performed in public in this country'; but no doubt on this occasion too extracts, rather than the whole opera, were given.

It was during the eighteen twenties that Da Ponte's career as a teacher flowered most gloriously; his happiest hours were spent with lively, intelligent students anxious to learn (there was a preponder-ance of young ladies – the young gentlemen, disappointingly, were less eager to sit at his feet). 'My house is a little school,' he wrote to Mathias in 1827. 'Every morning before nine o'clock, with the excellent help of two members of my family,[1] I start my Italian lessons, both in my own house and elsewhere ... From 12 until 3 two teachers, both carefully chosen, teach Spanish and French to a large class of lively young ladies, and almost the whole of the rest of

---

[1] Da Ponte uses the female gender, and he is almost certainly referring to Fanny and Matilda, who, despite her youth, took an active part in his lessons.

the day is spent in scholarly discussion or in reading the classics. With me they talk Italian more than any other language, and if I had my way it would be the only one that was ever spoken.'

One of his 'lively young ladies' has left a description of his method:

> I began straight away with the verbs: right from the beginning I learnt a great number without difficulty, following a rule which my teacher had himself discovered, which taught in a flash more than five hundred irregular verbs.[1] After about ten lessons I began to translate a story from French into Italian, and in this way, without actually studying it, I learnt almost all the grammar, because when Signor Da Ponte corrected my translation he explained the reasons for his alterations and showed me what I should have done, so that I could avoid the same errors in future.
>
> At the same time I began to read with him the lovely plays of Metastasio, the easiest of the Italian poets, and little by little in six months I read almost all the classics.

She learnt by heart Petrarch's sonnets, Tasso, and Dante, as well as 'the poetry of my kind master, who wrote such elegant verse. After twenty-four lessons I wrote my first short letter in Italian, and in four months at the most I wrote forty more, which Signor Da Ponte gave back to me so that I could note the corrections. In this way I learnt everything I know of the Italian language, which is rightly called the most beautiful in the world.'

Da Ponte expected his pupils to work hard, and above all to read and study the great writers – Dante, Tasso, Monti, Metastasio, Petrarch, Alfieri – for several hours each day. When he first lived in New York he wrote to one former student, now at Yale, to say how glad he was to hear that the library there possessed so many Italian books (in contrast to Columbia, where, when he came to America, only a tattered copy of Boccaccio was to be found, while Harvard was no better off – as late as 1814 it had neither a good teacher of German, nor a German dictionary, nor even a German book of any kind). 'Read them all indiscriminately,' he went on, 'because there is much of value to be found in all of them. Study, criticise, comment on them, and absorb them, as it were, into your very being.' One sign of his skill and dedication as a teacher is that when later some of his pupils went to Italy they were praised for the purity of their style.

How passionately he wanted to share with them his own joy in

---

[1] Perhaps she used *A General Table of the Italian Verbs, regular and irregular, by which the formation of any tense or person may be immediately found. Republished by L. Da Ponte, for the particular use of his Scholars.* A copy of this huge and very clear chart – a boon to anyone who is trying to thread his way through the maze of Italian irregular verbs – is in the Houghton Library at Harvard University.

Italian literature! 'What ecstasy would someone feel who had been blind from birth,' he wrote, 'and who suddenly opened his eyes and saw the sunrise, the sky studded with stars, a meadow covered with grass and flowers and many other beauties of the universe! Study our great writers, learn to know them well, and I promise you that you will feel the same delight, the same sense of the miraculous, that such a man would experience.'

In addition to his private lessons he taught in a number of schools – at various times he seems to have been employed in eight – but by the end of the twenties he had lost his connection with all of them. French and Spanish were becoming popular because they were of greater practical use, especially with an increase in trade between America and Mexico, and dancing, music and drawing had irresistible attractions. For the same reason his private pupils, too, began to dwindle.

In 1825 a signal honour, but as it turned out an empty one, was bestowed upon him: he was made Professor of Italian at Columbia College. By now several of his ex-pupils occupied posts there, and it was no doubt their influence which secured his appointment. Clement Moore was a trustee and on the books committee (he was also Professor of Biblical Learning and later of Oriental and Greek Literature at the General Theological Seminary, which he had himself founded); Nathaniel Moore was Professor of Greek and Latin; and Henry Anderson was Professor of Mathematics as well as librarian. No salary was attached to Da Ponte's post, although he was required to make a reasonable charge, and the attendance of the students was voluntary (other modern languages were treated in an equally cavalier way). Da Ponte did not care a fig about the salary, and would have preferred to teach without payment, but this the directors would not allow him to do.

In the first year he had twenty-eight students, but the number steadily dwindled, and those who did attend made no progress. It was a disheartening business, and he resigned. Two years later he reluctantly allowed himself to be reinstated, when a new course of studies was being discussed, and theoretically he remained a professor of the college until the day of his death, though still without pupils. He continued to press for the establishment of a chair of Italian, sometimes wearying even his most loyal friends with his insistence. 'For what you have done for Italy and the cause of letters,' Clement Moore wrote to him, 'so long as there remains a spark of taste among us for the belles lettres, the name of Da Ponte . . . will be held in veneration . . . and it is therefore, my dear sir, that I pray you to let this suffice, and not aspire to acquire for yourself alone the whole glory of the universe.'

He did, however, inaugurate a series of Dante lectures which were full of interesting, thoughtful, sometimes provocative comments. These lectures laid the foundations for the subsequent study of Dante in America, and in the words of Krehbiel, 'Da Ponte lives in the respect and admiration of Dante scholars as the first of American teachers and commentators on "The Divine Comedy".'

He also made a determined effort, through Clement Moore, to persuade the college to buy some of his store of Italian classics, and in this he was at any rate partially successful. Early in 1826 they bought 263 volumes for $364, and three years later a second, smaller consignment. They also commissioned him to catalogue not only these but other books in the college library, for which he was paid an additional $50. In a report to President Harris, Henry Anderson said how well he had done the work, which occupied him for an average of not less than four hours a day over a period of six months.

Though Columbia refused to buy any more of the books which he offered them, through another of his pupils, Gulian Verplanck, a Congressman who was living in his house, he sold many fine and costly works to the Library of Congress; they included magnificent editions of *The Divine Comedy*, Ariosto and Alfieri.

He conceived an ambitious project of setting up a permanent Italian library in New York, where students would be able to read the glories of his country's literature, and hoped that many living authors would donate their books. To this end he wrote an ode *'per lo stabilmento d'una permanente libreria'* in New York. Though the subscription was modest, the results of his appeal were bitterly disappointing, for only four or five potential readers offered themselves. Other 'bargain offers' were equally unsuccessful, including an attempt to lure pupils to his classes at Columbia by offering them free a 'Dictionary, and an Elementary Book for Reading, provided they engage for Two Quarters, less time being insufficient to convey much useful information in that Language; to such persons as may already be in possession of those books, a ticket for the Permanent Italian Library will be given in their stead'.

His friend Mathias wisely advised him not to become involved in business and speculation but to stick to literature. 'Live for the Muses,' he wrote, 'for your family, for the well-being of your Language and of beautiful literature. You have sown the seed and seen the flowers blossom, and I hope that you will gather the fruit . . .'

During this decade he was tirelessly writing and translating. He crossed swords in a sharp battle of words with a writer in the *North American Review* who did infinitely less than justice, he felt, to the glories of Italian literature. (The writer was W. H. Prescott, then still a young man, but already known in Italy.) He translated into Italian part of a play written by the father of one of his pupils, *Scena quarta del quinto atto di Adad* by J. A. Hillhouse, and also a small book by an English writer, *Economia della vita umana*, his comments showing that he was familiar with the works of Shakespeare, Chaucer, Wycherley, Congreve, Beaumont and Fletcher, Dryden, Pope and Byron. He embarked on a verse translation of Le Sage's novel *Gil Blas*, and, like Carlyle, suffered from loss by fire when a great part of the manuscript was burnt in a sudden blaze at his printers. And he wrote a long pamphlet on the subject which perennially engaged him, *La storia della lingua e della letteratura italiana in New-york*, relating at great length the heroic efforts he had made to introduce both to the city, and the opposition he had encountered from jealous rivals and indifferent citizens. Two editions of poetry came out, and on the evening of his seventy-ninth birthday, at the party with which his friends customarily marked the event, he delivered a long oration on the glories of Italian literature. [1]

One can imagine his audience inwardly groaning as he embarked on yet another enormous exposition of the theme which they must already have heard on umpteen occasions – with no concessions this time for those whose Italian was weak or non-existent, since an English translation was not provided. Nevertheless, it is impossible not to be filled with astonishment and admiration for this scholarly discourse (which is omitted from English translations of the memoirs), showing such breadth of knowledge of a vast number of ancient and modern writers on the widest variety of subjects: poetry, history, military and civil architecture, all branches of mathematics and medicine, the law, politics, hydraulics, political economy, translations, and various other topics. As usual, his opinion of them was much too high, but nothing gives better proof of his wide-ranging, passionate reading, of his scholarship and phenomenal memory, of his deep, enduring love of learning, and of the interest with which he followed contemporary literature on both sides of the Atlantic. For anyone in the prime of life it would have been an amazing performance; for a man of seventy-nine it was almost unbelievable.

---

[1] Guido Bustico writes that between 1825 and 1830 Da Ponte published beautiful editions of Italian classics, including Dante and Monti, 'little jewels of typography', but I have never been lucky enough to come across any of these, and have seen no other reference to them.

In his lessons he made full use of the memoirs; he also sent many copies to friends in Italy, and was overjoyed when a lengthy critique appeared in the prestigious Florentine journal *Antologia*. The two articles were written by G. Montani, one of the chief contributors, who had stayed with the Da Pontes in New York, and who wrote in his review, 'I can say much of how excellently [Da Ponte] is endowed in both his intellect and his heart.' The memoirs had been brought to his notice by Pananti, and also by Dr Giuseppe Gherardi, a young Florentine who had taught for some time at Harvard; he too had enjoyed Nancy's hospitality, and all the family became very fond of him. On the whole the review was very favourable, praising, amongst other felicities, Da Ponte's description of Venice in her last years as a republic. It was Pananti who sent the articles to Da Ponte, and he was rewarded with a charming and generous letter of thanks.

It must have given Da Ponte infinite pleasure at last to see his name in print in his native land, for he never ceased to marvel at the frivolities with which the papers were filled, while matters of importance, such as his contribution to the dissemination of Italian literature in the new world, went unrecorded.

'Count Such-and-such [he quotes] arrived yesterday from London with six horses of the king's stud.' 'Such-and-such a locksmith,' another informs us 'has invented a key which will open all the doors of the city.' This one writes a three-page article in praise of the wrinkled throat of a eunuch; that one announces the arrival of an elephant and two monkeys in such-and-such a town; and a hundred similar things of no account; and in more than twenty years not one charitable writer has been found who has deigned to put down in black on a small piece of paper, so that the literary world, and in particular the Italians, may learn about it, what I have done in America!

But, he went on, if he found himself becoming too resentful, he would hurry to his bookshop and chastise his inflated ego by reading some of the wonders that were to be found there.

His delight in the review was tempered by a certain annoyance at the comparison between his memoirs and Goldoni's, and by some criticism of his style. All the same, he arranged for his son Lorenzo and some of his pupils to translate the articles into English, and this translation – annotated as usual – he published in 1829.

Copies of the memoirs went to London, to the firm of Colnaghi, to sell on his behalf, and to Venice. From Agostino there came a dusty reply, saying that they did him little credit, for everyone was complaining about the printing errors, of which there were legion. (Da Ponte, not a good proof corrector at the best of times, remarks more than once how expensive printing was in New York, and how impossible to get it done properly, since none of the printers had the foggiest knowledge of Italian.) Every paper in Europe, he wrote bitterly, was full of praise of Michael Kelly's reminiscences, 'a collection of rubbish, puerility and foolishness, invented by a deranged, swollen-headed mind without a vestige of knowledge or culture'.

As soon as Montani's review appeared the memoirs were banned in Venice, Trieste, Naples and the Austrian empire. The censorship did not apply to Tuscany, where the authorities were more liberal than anywhere else in Italy, and a year later they were selling briskly there. In fact, just because they were prohibited elsewhere they were eagerly devoured by anyone who could lay his hands on a copy. Despite the censorship Mathias – now living in Naples, where he had gone ten years earlier for reasons of health – found many subscribers both there and in England.

One great joy was that the memoirs renewed the links between Da Ponte and old friends, as well as bringing him fresh ones. After Vienna and London he had vanished from the horizons of most of them, and few people knew what had happened to him, though there was much curiosity about his fate. He had lost touch once more with Colombo, and was overjoyed to hear from him again, as well as from his schoolfriend Girolamo Perucchini. It was no doubt as a result of the memoirs that he exchanged letters with Anthony Panizzi, an Italian patriot who, condemned to death in 1823, had fled to London, where he became successively Professor of Italian at University College, Assistant Librarian of the Printed Books Department of the British Museum, Keeper of Printed Books, and finally Principal Librarian. It is Panizzi whose grand conception is responsible for the splendid reading-room, where thousands upon thousands of scholars and students from every quarter of the globe have passed happy and fruitful days.

But the new friend who was to make the greatest impact on his life was Dr Domenico Rossetti, a lawyer and one of the most eminent citizens of Trieste. Da Ponte, he wrote to the memoirist, had probably met his older brother in Trieste, at Pompeo Brigido's or Baron Pittoni's, while Domenico himself, as a small boy, remembered seeing him either in that city or in Vienna. Rossetti greatly admired the memoirs, and for some years he kept up a regular correspondence with Da Ponte, proving himself a model of helpfulness and loyalty, and dealing patiently with Da Ponte's frequent, often demanding calls for help.

It was Rossetti who sent Da Ponte a whole bundle of letters from his old friends, and Da Ponte wrote in reply that he was so overcome with joy and bewilderment that he hadn't known which to start with first but had read bits of each of them in turn, 'as I imagine a Turk must do when he is surrounded by the beauties in his harem and bestows his kisses and caresses first on one and then on another.'

Rossetti worked hard to arouse interest in Trieste in Da Ponte's efforts to establish an Italian library in New York; he encouraged Trieste writers to donate their books, and arranged for an article on Italian literature in New York to be published in the *Osservatore Triestino*.

Not all the comments from Italy were favourable, and Da Ponte, who always felt criticism to the quick, wrote to Colombo that he would rather sense than hear them. 'In this I am like certain women who, although they can see in their mirrors that they are ugly, all the same resent being *called* ugly.' He went on to ask Colombo to act as a sieve: 'Throw everything about me into it, and if in a great pile of rubbish you find some grains of good metal, quickly imprison them in a bottle and send them to your Da Ponte before they disappear!'

His friends wrote to advise him, in subsequent editions, to make some judicious cuts – as had the writer in the *Antologia* – in order to render the memoirs more acceptable to the censors. He quoted too much of his poetry *in extenso*, dwelt at wearying length on personal minutiae, especially his multitudinous grievances, which were of interest to no one but himself, and in particular was far too bitter in his criticism of Leopold, whose son Francis was now the reigning emperor. Most of this advice Da Ponte very sensibly followed, and he also gave three or four of his trusted friends authority to alter anything else which still seemed to them objectionable, if this might be a way of finding an Italian publisher. But, as Rossetti wrote to him, the chances of doing so were remote. His pessimism was justified: it was nearly half a century before the memoirs first saw the light of day in Da Ponte's native land.

XIV

Da Ponte's teaching was closely bound up with his activities in importing and selling Italian books, since both enterprises were at the heart of his determination – which dictated everything he did in the last years of his life – to give Americans an understanding of the glory of the literature of his native land. To further this aim, in about 1830 he

> . . . opened a little bookshop, where I betake myself at cockcrow, leaving it only for a few minutes, and staying there till late at night. Five months have passed since I became a bookseller.[1] It is true that I don't often have occasion to get out of my chair; buyers are very few; but instead I have the joy of seeing coaches and carriages come to my door, and sometimes the most beautiful faces in the world emerge from them, mistaking my shop for the one next door, where sweetmeats and pastries are sold. So people imagine I have a lot of customers, and I'm thinking of putting a notice in the window saying: 'Italian sweetmeats and pastries sold here', and if anyone comes into my shop as a result of this joke I will show them Petrarch and some of our other poets, and insist that these are our most delicious sweetmeats of all, for those who have the teeth to eat them.

The number of his pupils steadily dwindled, but this only spurred him on to greater efforts to spread Italian literature far and wide, not only in New York but also in other cities. In the *Storia della letteratura* he says that he has already placed in the New York public library six hundred books, and is awaiting another consignment of the same size on literature, physics, mathematics, hydraulics, politics, antiquity, military and civil architecture, medicine, chemistry and agriculture, as well as books which will give full information to those who want to know how to plant mulberries, vines and olives, rear silkworms, make silk, practise viniculture, forestry or agriculture, keep sheep, cattle and bees, or plant flax, hemp and cotton. He was, he told Rossetti, always ordering books from Italy or buying them at auction, and 'when I lack the money I sell, pawn, borrow, and, by heaven,

---

[1] Da Ponte means in a formal sense. As he wrote to Rossetti in 1829, he had been carrying on the profession of 'semi-bookseller' for twenty years.

work such miracles as neither St Francis nor St Anthony ever worked'.

By now he was ordering on a regular basis from several Italian booksellers, especially Fusi e Stella of Milan, who were always generous in the matter of discount and dates of payment. It was sometimes difficult trading at such a long distance: he was sent books which were unsuitable and impossible to sell, and no doubt the firms with which he dealt had their own headaches; but the lists which he gives from time to time in his letters cover an astonishing range of authors and titles.

One distinguished American with whom he came into contact through his bookshop was Longfellow, then in his mid-twenties. It seems that the poet, who had spent three years in Europe and become a dedicated student of Italian, contemplated revisiting that country in 1832 and spending some weeks in London on the way, for Da Ponte wrote for him a glowing letter of introduction to Panizzi, as he had done for other friends. The visit never materialised, but Longfellow kept the letter among his papers. The poet, by now Professor of Modern Languages and Belles Lettres at Harvard, also paid a visit to Da Ponte's shop and placed an order, and Da Ponte later wrote to ask him for help in selling in Boston some books which it seemed impossible to dispose of in New York. Two volumes of Da Ponte's collected poems, bearing the author's signature, were in Longfellow's library when he died.

Another distinguished contact was with Pietro Maroncelli, a composer and a famous Italian patriot who had been imprisoned for his part in fighting for the liberty of his country, and had taken refuge in America. Da Ponte quixotically wanted to print 1,000 copies of an English translation of his books *Mie prigioni* and *Addizione alle mie prigioni*. Maroncelli refused the offer, for, as he wrote to the translator, 'Signor Daponte would have had to give a surety of 2,500 dollars without having sold it [which], since he is not rich, is not a merchant by profession, and, in taking this gamble, might have won but might also have lost, would have caused me great distress'.

Every penny he could scrape together Da Ponte spent in buying books. But gradually interest waned – not least, he believed, because the craze for Italian opera which had seized New York with the coming of Garcia's company was gradually dying away. He was convinced that through the enjoyment of this art Americans would learn to love Italian literature; and the three heroic attempts which he made to establish opera on a permanent basis in New York and Philadelphia all sprang from this conviction, as well as from his longing to hear these sweet melodies once more – and perhaps even to see his own operas performed.

Very dear to his heart was a project to bring to America his half-brother Agostino, with his younger daughter Giulia. As early as 1823 Agostino had been trying unsuccessfully to get an American visa, to seek there the fortune which had eluded him in Venice, where he was now a kind of broker, with business interests throughout the Veneto and a pack of creditors always hot on his heels. Not only was Giulia extremely beautiful, but she was reputed to be an excellent singer – she had studied with Da Ponte's friend Antonio Baglioni, the first Ottavio at the Prague *première* of *Don Giovanni* and a noted teacher. Da Ponte, fired by Garcia's success, felt that her coming would bring glory to the Italian language, to Italian opera, and to himself, the bearer of Italian culture.

To overcome the difficulty of the visa, he wrote a *canzone* to the Emperor Francis, which Agostino had copied in a fair hand by a skilled calligrapher and sent to Vienna. Permission was at last given, but the Austrian authorities, their distrust of Agostino as acute as ever, still refused to issue a visa until he could prove that there would be sufficient funds to maintain his wife, Caterina, and their elder daughter, Pasquetta, while he was away. Agostino himself had no money, and as soon as his creditors heard of the proposed journey they pressed around him like locusts. So he appealed to his brother, as he had, it seems, on many previous occasions (Da Ponte wrote that he had had more than a hundred letters from him on the subject), and Da Ponte in turn asked his new friend, Dr Rossetti, for help.

The negotiations went on for years, with a great deal of misunderstanding between Da Ponte and Agostino and with the unfortunate Rossetti as middleman trying to smooth out the difficulties. Da Ponte declared that Agostino could not be trusted with money, and complained that he had used for other purposes a considerable sum which Da Ponte had sent him for the journey. Anxious to know whether Giulia's voice really was as fine as rumour said, he asked Filippo Traetta's brother, a noted horn player, to listen to her, and to urge her to come to America if he felt she was good enough. This Traetta's brother duly did, and back came the message that her singing had given him great pleasure.

Agostino and his family must have moved in excellent musical circles, for when Traetta visited them they were also entertaining not only Giovanni Battista Perruchini, son of Da Ponte's friend Girolamo and a well-known composer, but also the famous Velluti, the last great castrato, who often sang in Venice and who, like Perucchini, was a good friend of Rossini.

Da Ponte, meanwhile, was getting himself into difficulties by anticipating Agostino's arrival – though this time it seems not to have been entirely his fault. Convinced that his brother would reach New York by June 1829, he was persuaded by his son Lorenzo, who had a passion for the theatre, to enter into a contract to rent the Bowery Theatre in New York. Da Ponte describes this contract as iniquitous, and says that Lorenzo was inveigled into signing it by his wife's cousin, [1] the greatest rogue in the world. June came, but since Agostino and Giulia were still in Venice a considerable sum was forfeit, which Da Ponte was obliged to pay in order to save his son from dishonour or imprisonment. The whole fiasco, he wrote, had swallowed up half their entire capital, and Nancy had been forced to go to Sunbury – no doubt to discuss the matter with Louisa's executor – in order to rescue the whole family from total disaster. Nothing more is heard of this, so perhaps it was settled without too much damage. But Da Ponte continued to write frantic letters to Rossetti declaring that unless his niece came soon he and his family would be ruined.

At last all was settled: enough money was raised to keep Caterina and Pasquetta in reasonable comfort for the time being; Agostino's debts were paid; and Da Ponte guaranteed the cost of the passage. The captain of the ship on which the two travellers embarked undertook to provide them with drinking water, firewood, salt beef and pork, flour, potatoes, vegetables, rice, tea, coffee, brown sugar, butter and cheese. By now winter had come on, and though their journey was not unduly long it was very stormy, and poor Giulia must have suffered a good deal.

Da Ponte had given Rossetti authority to fix the best possible price for the voyage, but when he heard what it was he trembled from head to foot, not knowing how he would find such a large sum (and in fact he was forced to go to a moneylender and borrow at a high rate of interest, paying 30% to 40%, for, as he wrote to Rossetti, 'the Americans love usury as much as the Jews of Venice'). His anxiety left little room to anticipate their arrival with pleasure, for the money had to be paid as soon as they docked; but when on 18 February 1830 their carriage drew up at the door 'my infinite joy left no room for fear, and the caresses, the embraces, the questions to and fro, sometimes accompanied by laughter and sometimes by

[1] In 1826 Lorenzo had married Cornelia Durant, a niece by marriage of President Monroe.

207

tears, lasted the family for all the rest of the day and a good part of the night'.

The travellers had brought with them some of the delicacies for which Da Ponte longed, and which he had begged Rossetti to send – good Italian chestnuts (he had made a bet that one Italian chestnut was bigger than six American ones), rosolio from Trieste, and salame, half of it with garlic. 'It is many years, dearest Signor Rossetti, since I tasted such food, and to give me this pleasure would be a true favour to an octogenarian who has little appetite.' The parmesan he had asked for they could not bring, as it was sold in too large a piece, and would have deteriorated too much during the voyage.

Da Ponte, as we know, was enthusiastic about importing Italian products. Americans, he told Agostino, were receptive to the idea of planting vines, mulberry trees and olives, and of spinning silk. 'If ever it is the will of God that you should come to America,' he had written a few years earlier, 'bring with you a great quantity of vine roots, mulberry and olive seeds, silkworms, and as many modern books as you can about viniculture and the manufacture and storage of wine.' And he also advised him to bring wine from Florence (perhaps remembering the good chianti which had restored him on his wintry journey to Bologna), Alkermes, maraschino, pasta and parmesan. 'If I had used my small capital to buy these things, I should have made a lot of money.'

If Agostino came without all these goods, he did bring with him a cameo of Napoleon, which a publisher in Venice wanted Da Ponte to show to the ex-Emperor's brother, in the hope that Joseph Bonaparte would buy it. This led to catastrophe, for it was stolen from Da Ponte's shop while he was attending to a customer. Typically honourable in such matters, he offered to reimburse the publisher, even though the cameo had been sent unasked, but the documents do not reveal whether he actually had to do so.

Giulia, who was twenty-one, was greeted by everyone with rapture, and, said her father, treated like a princess. Until now she had sung only in private houses, since her family were reluctant that she should go on the stage, so it was decided that she should first give two or three recitals in the houses of friends; she also, to her uncle's delight, sang at his eighty-first birthday celebration.

She made her début at the Park Theatre at the end of March, sharing the stage with other singers in the usual mixed programme which began with a lecture and ended with a farce. She had (inevitably) a terrible cold, and though Da Ponte put a brave face on it, and some of the reviews acclaimed her performance, his letters to Rossetti give little indication of a true success (Ritter describes her as a third-rate singer). For her first operatic performance he put together an up-dated *Ape musicale*, with arias from various operas, but this was even less popular. However, Giulia earned an enormous amount of money – far more than the greatest singers of the day, such as Pasta, were making in Europe – and this helped towards the cost of bringing her and Agostino to New York, though Da Ponte complained that he had not been repaid nearly enough, and in Venice Caterina waited in vain for the money she needed to keep herself and Pasquetta. Giulia then went off to Philadelphia with her father and Nancy, but the little she earned there was swallowed up in expenses.

As Da Ponte soon realised, Giulia was not made for the theatre, or the theatre for her, and his hopes of reviving Italian opera with his niece as prima donna quickly faded. Before long, instead of singing, poor Giulia spent her days weeping bitterly. This was not, he believed, simply the result of her timidity; equally to blame was the type of music she had sung, which was too difficult and unfamiliar for American ears. To virtuosi who might contemplate following in her steps he offered some advice:

> Do not let them trust solely to their beautiful voices. *Vox cantat*, we say; and I would not deny that the voice is one of the first prerequisites of song. But if the voice is not accompanied by good music it will have the same effect as a coat of the finest cloth which makes people laugh because it is badly cut. It is therefore wise to be provided with a good repertoire of arias and so-called concert pieces with an easy, natural and melodious line which at the same time are not trivial and vulgar. Such melodies linger in the ears and heart of the listener, who sings them when he comes out of the theatre; publishers compete to publish them; and when they are published people buy them; those who can sing, sing them through again as well as those who cannot sing; they go back to the theatre several times to hear them again; and sometimes two or three pieces of this nature are enough to make an opera popular, to the honour of the singer, the glory of the composer, and – what is more to the point – the benefit of the impresario. Let us leave to those who enjoy it affected music, which forces the singer to struggle, to gasp for breath, to suffocate, in order to reach the notes and execute the trills demanded of her and to make her voice heard, now chained to the accompaniment, now drowned and blotted out by a storm of flutes, drums, horns, bassoons and trombones.

Relations between Da Ponte and Agostino deteriorated steadily as all the old antagonisms came to the surface. Da Ponte wrote to Rossetti that he should never have asked his brother to come: 'Our characters, our temperaments, our work have been not only different but directly opposed to one another, and at various times I have suffered at his hands too much torment, too much harm and too much ingratitude. I should have listened to the voice of prudence and to my friends. But I was moved by the longing, after so many years, to see someone of my own blood; by the hope of finding him changed now that he is older; and above all by the desire to make our language more beloved by Americans through the delights of song . . .'

In the end Agostino and Giulia left the Da Pontes' house, where they had cost a great deal of money during the months they had stayed there, taking up two rooms which would otherwise have been profitably let. Giulia married a Trieste merchant called Stafler who was visiting New York, and they sailed for home without even bidding Da Ponte farewell.

He seems to have had nothing more to do with Agostino, who died not long afterwards, no more successful in the remaining years of his life than he had been in the early ones and, it would seem, with the eyes of the law fixed steadily upon him to the last. So far as the disastrous visit to America is concerned, it is only fair to say that before setting off from Venice he had warned his older brother against being too precipitate, and had emphasised that he needed money before he could embark on the venture, that Giulia had no experience of the theatre, and that it would be madness to expose her to it straight away. As for Giulia and her husband, they soon made their peace with her uncle, for in September 1832 Da Ponte wrote a friendly note to Stafler, replying to one from him, in which – echoing the words of Joseph II so many years ago – he said, 'I should indeed have been glad to see you and Giulia before you left, but what is done is done, and cannot be undone.'

His distress at the whole episode may have been exacerbated because his normally robust health was temporarily failing him. He had a bad fall, and for a while was subject also to a great discomfort which perhaps indicated stones, though he prayed to God that this might not be the case. But this too seems to have passed, for there are no more references to it.

Da Ponte ended the fourth, and final, part of his memoirs on 14 September 1830, promising his readers a further instalment which, however, never appeared. To piece together the events of the eight years which still remained to him, we have to consult his letters and his published writings.

In general, his health continued to be excellent. 'When a man reaches a certain age,' he had written in 1828, 'he becomes a baby again. I am a baby in my gums because I have no teeth; [and] I am a baby in my legs because of an obstinate rheumatism which makes them weak.' But bodily failings made little difference to his vigorous life or to the endless stream of words which flowed from his pen.

In 1828 he had become an American citizen, for reasons which he does not explain. This, he wrote, made it possible for him to express his opinions freely on any subject he chose.

Three years later Fanny married Henry James Anderson, for so long a beloved inmate of the household. For a time he had been joint editor of the *New York Review and Athenaeum* (which, however, survived for only a year). He and Fanny had six children, four of whom died in infancy, and Fanny also reclaimed the son of her first marriage, who until then had been living with his father. Fanny herself died in Paris in 1844, on her way home from a trip to Europe.

As for the Da Pontes' son Lorenzo, after his disastrous fling with the theatre he settled down with his wife Cornelia. Like his father he became a teacher of Italian, first at Maryland University and then at New York University. A brilliant Greek scholar, as his father was a Latin one, he wrote a great deal, his most important work being a history of Florence. He and Cornelia had a warm friendship with Fanny and Henry Anderson.

Four months after Fanny's marriage came the unexpected death of the long-suffering, indomitable Nancy. She was sixty-two, and in excellent health. But she caught pneumonia, and was dead in six days. Da Ponte immediately published a small volume of poems, *Versi composti da Lorenzo Da Ponte per la morte d'Anna Celestina Ernestina, sua virtuosissima e adorata consorte*. The poems express very real sorrow, and reflect both his great love for Nancy and his understanding of her qualities (which he is rarely given credit for perceiving).

Preceded by a very brief account of his own life – as usual heavily edited – the eighteen sonnets and a longer poem which follow speak of the forty years that she spent with him, 'wife, friend, companion, consort, and a loving mother to her children – and to her everyone in distress was her child. Weep with me, for she is dead!' He writes of her lively eyes, her dear face in which was written, 'You are my only love', and of the honey of her chaste kisses. Though in the course of sixty years her golden hair had become silver and the bright colour had faded from her cheeks, she still moved with grace and vigour, and her industry and hard work, her every look, every gesture, every word mirrored her lofty mind. Kind, open, sincere, she was a mortal enemy to untruth, pious, charitable towards those in need, free from envy, virtuous, a humble daughter, a wise mother, a faithful friend.

Carlo, her youngest son, was in New Orleans when she died. 'We were all weeping round her bed, she uttered your name with a deep sigh, and with your name on her lips she died.'

Da Ponte's grief was no less real and deep for the fact that, as always with his pupils in mind, he appended footnotes on points of grammar. He sent many copies of the sonnets to his friends in Italy, writing to Colombo, 'It is impossible either for you to have an idea, or for me to put into words, my grief at her death'. To Gulian Verplanck he said, 'The death of this angelic woman has robbed me not only of peace of heart, but also of the means of supporting myself in my unhappy old age.' Presumably he was referring to the fact that Nancy's money, which had yielded a useful income, would now be divided between her children, in accordance with Louisa Niccolini's will. In this he was claiming a sympathy he did not entirely merit, for after Nancy's death he lived with his son Lorenzo and his daughter-in-law Cornelia, who continued to run the boarding-house, which was still flourishing in 1840. Da Ponte was, moreover, given an annual allowance of $200 by his son-in-law Henry Anderson.

The verses for Nancy contained not only a loving farewell to his wife but a virulent attack on her family, 'conjugal love and the desire for domestic peace' having until then sealed his tongue. In the next volume of his memoirs, he promises, he will reveal how for many years the perfidy and hostility of his wife's sister had been, and still was, fatal to his prosperity and peace of mind, and to the well-being of his family. Clearly, he still bitterly resented the fact that Louisa had made it impossible for him to win control of her money.

The next year brought another death, that of his adored grand-daughter Matilda, who died at the age of seventeen. From a very early age she had been one of the cornerstones of his household and his teaching. 'My husband and Signora B,' wrote one of his pupils in 1825, 'told me that your birthday celebration was very enjoyable, and that the charming and interesting Madamigella Da Ponte received her friends in the most charming and courteous way.' Da Ponte himself described her to Colombo as 'a true picture of beauty, grace and incomparable talent'; and he claimed that at the age of fourteen she recited the third canto of the *Divina commedia* from memory, a feat which lasted for more than three hours. She became engaged to a wealthy American, who intended to take her to Europe to restore her failing health. 'But I fear they are deceiving themselves,' Da Ponte wrote to Giulia's husband, 'and that it will please God to take from me in my old age this comfort as well.' The letter was already sealed when he reopened it to tell Stafler 'with trembling heart and hand that Matilda is no more!'

Grief, according to Livingston, did not prevent him from serving notice of Matilda's bill for board on Robert Coleman Hall, to prevent her legacy from going to her father, Miles Clossey, who had been struggling to make a success of law first in Sunbury, then in Philadelphia, and finally in New York. There had been some idea of his going to Washington to teach Italian, but after Matilda's death nothing more seems to have been heard either of this plan or of Miles himself.

From 1828 onwards Colombo and Da Ponte had been in regular correspondence, and luckily Colombo kept his friend's letters, which tell us so much of Da Ponte's life and thoughts. Each morning, he said, he kissed a portrait of Colombo which he had put in front of the book of household expenses. [1] And he fondly recalled the days of their youth, when he loved and imitated Colombo, when they made love and fought together, and played the fool. Colombo's health was not good, and he wrote to Da Ponte to say that he felt death was not far off. 'When you write of death,' Da Ponte replied, 'I swear that you make me laugh. You and I will only die when we are tired of living, and when you agree that I should die and I agree that you should. Do you know why? Because since I live in you, and you in me, you will not permit me to die without you, any more than I shall permit you to die without me.' Da Ponte's words were prophetic, for these good and true friends died within two months of one another.

Da Ponte kept in touch, too, with other friends in Venice and Trieste, and with booksellers in various parts of Italy. To them he expressed his longing to return to his native land, and to leave a country to which he was so little attracted.

In certain moods he enjoyed representing himself to his friends in Europe as impoverished, decrepit and put-upon, but this was not the impression he gave on the spot, as two remarkable operatic ventures show. Determined as ever to advance the study of Italian through the divine inspiration of its music, and to cover his own name with glory – since 'in every country throughout the world with pretensions to culture, [Italian opera] is the noblest and the most alluring of all the spectacles which human intelligence has invented' – in 1832 he brought to America a company of Italian singers under the management of the French tenor Giacomo Montresor, who had been recommended to him by one of his correspondents, the Dante scholar Alessandro Torri. This was a fearsome undertaking for anyone, let alone a man of eighty-three. It involved, amongst other things,

---

[1] A portrait of Colombo was offered for sale in New York in 1828. Da Ponte tried to buy it, without success.

getting promises of large sums of money from wealthy backers, and chartering a ship to bring the company over. His letters to Montresor are full of sound, practical sense – just as, years earlier, his suggestions for running the Burgtheater in Vienna had been. (Though, apart from the works of Mozart and Rossini, the operas which he suggested by now all belonged to a bygone age.) Do not come, he wrote again and again, unless you bring with you one really first-class singer, such as Grisi or Pasta, and do not bring a company of more than twenty. He also advised Montresor to put in his luggage a lot of arias, duets, trios and quartets, which it would be Da Ponte's task to knit into the parts. 'I know that every singer has his battle-horses; and if you bring them with you I will make them gallop, or rather soar to the heavens as if on the back of the hippogriff Ruggiero.' As for Montresor's expectations from the venture, 'The Americans are almost all business men, and they turn everything into business, even their amusements. Come, do your best to please them, and inspire in some of them the prospect of enjoyment, in others the hope of money.'

In fact, there was no 'star' singer, and instead of twenty Montresor brought fifty-three people with him. Financially the tour was a disaster; but from an artistic point of view it was another story. The orchestra, which was under the musical direction of Da Ponte's friend Bagioli and included two oboes, the first ever to be heard in the city, was acclaimed as 'the best . . . that ever played dramatic music in America'. About thirty-five performances were given at the Richmond Hill Theatre, which in a fit of euphoria changed its named to the Italian Opera House, as well as benefits and concerts. The operas included the first performances in America of two works by Rossini, *L'inganno felice* and *L'Italiana in Algeri*, of Bellini's *Il pirata*, and of *Elisa e Claudio*, the popular opera by Saverio Mercadante, who in his day was compared with Rossini, Bellini, Donizetti and Verdi. After the New York season the company went off triumphantly to perform at the Chestnut Theatre in Philadelphia.

Da Ponte wrote sadly that the venture, on which he had embarked with such hopes, had left him with nothing but debts and quarrels. In a long pamphlet that he wrote about the affair, *Una storia incredibile ma vera* (which Carlo translated into English, as he had done the preface to the *Sonnets to Ann*), he paid tribute to Montresor's ability as an impresario and to his goodness of heart and integrity, but said that he was much too credulous and gullible. And in farewell verses which he wrote for a friend, Armando Peremet, who was leaving for Italy – and how much, Da Ponte exclaimed, he longed to accompany him and say goodbye to the Hudson for ever! – he complained that

Montresor and his son, a medical student and a young man of great talent, had stayed with the Da Pontes for many months, and that this had entailed much expense, not least for tailors, lawyers, publishers, money borrowed but not returned and poetry written but not paid for.

As for Philadelphia, where he had gone with the company, that had been a disaster. First he suddenly learned that he was no longer to take any share in the management, which was put into the hands of a man whom Da Ponte describes as a rogue and a ruffian. Then he hurt his leg going through a door, and had to spend three weeks in bed. Though he was penniless the new manager refused to allow him any money, and no one helped him or came near him except Bagioli and one other member of the company, whose sympathy and kindness helped to restore his faith in his compatriots. At last he wrote to his son Lorenzo, who hastened to his rescue, and together they returned to New York, where he was welcomed by a loving daughter and two angelic grandchildren. [1]

Montresor went off to Havana, taking the scenery with him. There, says Da Ponte, he died, and his son sold the scenery before coming back to New York. In spite of many appeals, he repaid only a small part of the sum his father owed. So Da Ponte was left not only with debts, but also with 30,000 copies of the libretti which he had been authorised to print, but which the machinations of his enemies and the failure of the whole enterprise made it impossible to dispose of. His only recourse was to sell two-thirds of his beloved library of three thousand books, as he declared in a heart-broken poem. To Signor Fusi he sent a catalogue of the volumes he was selling, with a letter saying of his operatic ventures, 'No one is grateful, either the Italians or the Americans. What can I do? Weep, or laugh. And so that you may laugh too, I will tell you that in spite of so many tempests, so many misfortunes and losses, I believe I can say with Petrarch, *I shall be what I was, I shall live as I have lived*, and continue to write poetry, to love music, to bring good artists to America, and to follow the profession of bookseller and pay the booksellers who entrust their books to me.'

What irony that Da Ponte, the most gullible man in the world, should accuse Montresor of gullibility! In 1827 he had written severely that when you buy a horse you examine it carefully to see

---

[1] According to Arthur Livingston, Da Ponte wrote about this time a 'Hymn to America', with music by Bagioli, with which he opened concerts and closed seasons. It was sung by Montresor's company in Philadelphia, but no copies of it seem to have survived.

whether it is sound in mouth, eyes, feet and legs; that before you buy a house you check it for smoking chimneys and damp walls, and before you hire a servant you make sure that he is honest, capable, sober and loyal. Yet Da Ponte had spent his life being cheated by servants and taken in by rogues who sold him broken-down horses. Near the end of the memoirs, however, there is an interesting passage which seems to show that at last he had painfully become aware of this failing.

At some point in the late twenties, he writes, he was the victim of some unexpected and disagreeable event, the exact nature of which he does not specify (no doubt someone was dunning him for money).

Now, gentle reader [he goes on], listen to me for a moment. In the first three parts of my memoirs the cities where I lived, the posts which I filled, the various people with whom I came into contact, and a certain game of fortune, which seemed to want to subject me to the most extreme proofs of its capricious power, gave me ample and excellent material with which to hold the interest of my readers. Since the country in which I have lived for more than twenty-five years has provided no such adventures, I am in the situation of a botany teacher who goes on a journey with his pupils in order to instruct them in that science, and who, after showing them the attributes and virtues of plants and herbs and flowers, must next pass through sinister deserts and barren mountains and, so as not to waste any time, discusses the properties of the shrubs and brambles he has at hand. In the same way I, who now live in America, can write only of domestic doings and of events and happenings in this city, events in which nevertheless I have been, and am, if not the protagonist of the tragicomedy, at least one of the chief actors. From this, however, the wise reader may all the same draw something of value . . . For if, when I was young, I had read the story of a man to whom the things had happened which have happened to me, and whose conduct was more or less similar to mine, how many mistakes I should have been able to avoid, the consequences of which have cost me so many tears and are still afflicting me so greatly in my old age! Thus I can and must say with Petrarch,

I know my faults and do not excuse them,

but the damage, at my age, cannot be remedied, and all that remains to me is repentance. May others at least learn from my example what I did not have a chance to learn from others. Do not trust to honeyed words; do not open your heart to people whose character and ways you have not known for many years; turn a mind of stone and a heart of bronze to those who ask for pity with the voice of flatterers; do not measure the rectitude of others by your own rectitude; do not say, 'Such-and-such-a-one has no reason to deceive, to hate, to betray me, therefore he will not hate, or deceive, or betray me,' but say, on the contrary, the exact opposite, because the exact opposite is what happened to me; if you have been endowed by nature with some talent, make sure to hide it from others with great care; and finally, do not hope to change the souls of evil men with sufferance and benevolence.

Undeterred either by the disaster of the Montresor venture or by the laments and protestations of his family, who saw him putting his head (and their heads too) into yet another noose, he embarked on his next enterprise – a plan, which he had cherished for many years, to give New York a permanent home for Italian opera. To this end he raised large sums among wealthy New Yorkers, including Philip Hone, a former mayor of the city, and his friend Dominick Lynch. The building was conceived on splendid lines. Italian artists were brought over to embellish it and paint the scenery, and the décor was of a brilliance and beauty never before seen in an American theatre. 'The neatest and most beautiful theatre in the United States, and unsurpassed in Europe,' Hone wrote in his diary. Another admirer exclaimed, 'The whole interior was pronounced magnificent, and the scenery and curtains were beautiful beyond all precedent. The ground of the front-boxes [which were hung with crimson silk] was white, with emblematical medallions and octagonal panels of crimson, blue, and gold. The dome was painted with representations of the Muses. The sofas and pit-seats were covered with damask, and the floors were all carpeted.'

It was the first American theatre to have a tier of exclusive boxes; the rent for each one, for a season, was $6,000, and when they were drawn for by lot the excitement was tremendous.

The opera house opened on 18 November 1833, under the management of Da Ponte and the Cavaliere di Rivafinoli – presumably the same friend who had taken the *Catalogo ragionato* to Mexico. The season lasted for six months, with about sixty performances, one of them a benefit for Da Ponte. Then the management was reorganised and passed out of Da Ponte's hands. But the whole financial basis was hopelessly unsound, and the enterprise was quickly abandoned. In 1836 the Italian Opera House became the National Theatre, and three years later it was burned to the ground, having, as one writer put it, 'in its brief existence of six years brought misfortune upon all who had any connection with it'.

Philip Hone wrote that there were two reasons for the failure of Italian opera in America,

... both of which savour much of the John Bullism which we have inherited from our forefathers. The first is, that we want to understand

217

the language; we cannot endure to sit by and see the performers splitting their sides with laughter, and we not take the joke; dissolved in 'briny tears', and we not permitted to sympathise with them; or running each other through the body, and we devoid of the means of condemning or justifying the act. The other is the private boxes, so elegantly fitted up, which occupy the whole of the second tier. They cost six thousand dollars each, to be sure, and the use of them is all that the proprietors get for their money; but it forms a sort of aristocratical distinction. Many people do not choose to occupy seats (more pleasant and commodious than they can find in any other theatre) while others recline upon satin cushions, and rest their elbows upon arm-chairs, albeit they are bought with their own money. I like this spirit of independence, which refuses its countenance to anything exclusive. 'Let the proprietors,' say the sovereigns, 'have their private boxes and satin cushions; they have paid well for them and are entitled to enjoy them. We will not furnish the means of supporting the establishment, but go to the Park Theatre, where it is 'first come, first served'; where our dollar will furnish us with 'the best the House affords . . .'

Financially disastrous these operatic projects certainly were – Da Ponte declared that they had cost him over $4,000 – but on them were laid the foundations of opera in America. To Da Ponte himself, apart from the economic aspect, they brought immense pleasure and cachet. One contemporary writes, 'Some of our citizens yet describe his tall figure [1] and handsome face at the opera . . . infecting others with his enthusiasm, and serving as a vital bond between the musical strangers and the fascinated public'; and another also remarks that many of the audience will remember him, a 'stately nonagenarian whose white locks so richly ornamented his classical front and his graceful and elegant person'. 'At the age of ninety,' the first writer comments, 'Lorenzo Daponte was still a fine-looking man; he had the head of a Roman; his countenance beamed with intelligence and vivacity; his hair was abundant, and fell luxuriantly round his neck, and his manners combined dignity and urbanity to a rare degree.'

Despite all the honour and prestige which the opera ventures had brought him, Da Ponte himself felt acutely that all his great plans

[1] Dr Jackson, Da Ponte's doctor in Sunbury, also describes him as tall. Yet in 1871 Alfred Meissner, quoting his grandfather, says that he was small. Since the few portraits we have of him show only his head and the upper part of his body, posterity is unlikely ever to know who was right. Memories are unreliable things. On the one hand it seems likely that a Jew who had grown up in a ghetto in the Veneto, where overcrowding and interbreeding were prevalent and food was scarce, would be short; on the other hand, the testimony of two of his doctors would surely be more reliable – except that those who knew him later in life may have come, as they recalled him after his death, to equate his physical stature with his reputation.

had failed, and that he, who had done so much to bring an understanding of Italian culture to America, was neglected and unregarded – 'I, who have imported 26,000 volumes of excellent books to America,' (what a miracle that he had somehow managed to sell them!) 'who have taught Italian to 2,500 Americans!' Most of them, he complained, had forgotten him – 'I! The creator of the Italian tongue in America . . . I! the poet of Joseph the Second . . . the writer of 36 plays; the inspiration of Salieri, of Weigl, of Martini, of Winter, and of MOZZART! after twenty-seven years of labour, of effort and of service . . .' A lament in verse, dedicated to Colombo and written in the same year, echoes this cry:

> Yet to the hand which has those treasures given
> Ye have refused the cimbal and the lyre;
> And from *this* brow, the laurel crown have riven,
> Whose name has set the proudest stage on fire!

In 1828 he had written bitterly to Rossetti that of all his pupils he believed that no more than fifteen or twenty had bothered to read the memoirs from start to finish, and of these only eight to ten had found them interesting. It is not to be wondered at that Lucchesi and Rossetti, despite their admiration and their inexhaustible willingness to help him, agreed that he got too excited about things and carried them to extremes.

But these periods of depression alternated with days when life seemed rosy and when he echoed 'the words of my great Joseph, that if there are many evil men, there are also some good ones, and their goodness is of such a kind, and so great, that it counterbalances and compensates us for all the malignity of those who are evil'.

And here is another side of the picture, painted by one of the many younger friends who visited the household: 'No Italian or old habitué of that classic land . . . was likely to forget the soup, maccaroni or red wine, to say nothing of the bread and vegetables . . . indeed, to dine there, as was my fortune occasionally, and hear *la lingua Toscana in bocca romana* on all sides, with furious discussions of Italian politics and delectable praise of composers and vocalists or pictorial critiques – transported one by magic from Broome-street to the Piazza Vecchia or the Via Condotta . . . Corn-beef *versus* maccaroni, was the problem he loved to state and to solve.'

On one occasion this problem arose in quite another form, as he relates with much gusto. He was in company with four *sapienti* from four different countries – Spain, France, Germany and America. Each of them praised to the skies the literature of his own land, but when Da Ponte opened his mouth to speak of Italy they rose to go away, and the American said with a sardonic smile that, regretfully, after many years there he had discovered only two good things – pasta with parmesan cheese and beef *à la mode*. Da Ponte promptly invited them to dinner the next day, promising them just these dishes.

They arrived on the dot, and for an hour talked of nothing but

> . . . the extravagances of Dante, the conceits of Petrarch, the plagiarisms of Boccaccio, the follies of Ariosto, the counterfeit gold of Tasso and the sickly sweetness of Metastasio . . . At last we sat down to the meal, and as soon as they were seated one of my servants uncovered the dish of pasta generously sprinkled with cheese, and another the stew with garlic, whose fragrant odour would have excited the appetite of the dead. At this appetising sight the American cried, 'Bravo, Mr Da Ponte! This is what is good about Italy!' I was expecting a compliment of this kind, and had given one of the servants certain instructions. Accordingly he quickly took away the pasta and the stew, and replaced them with two great dishes of boiled corn. [At this point Da Ponte has the explanatory footnote: 'Corn: a favourite dish in America'.] 'And this,' I cried, 'is the one good thing in America.'

Despite the protests of his guests, the succulent dishes they had been longing for were not brought back. Da Ponte does not say whether the *sapienti* ever spoke to him again.

Sitting in his bookshop, or at home with Cornelia and Lorenzo – already seriously ill with the consumption which was to kill him – and with the few members of his family left to him (for Nancy, Louisa, Matilda and Joseph were all gone, and Carlo seems to have disappeared from the family circle some time in the thirties), Da Ponte, with his inextinguishable zest for life, enjoyed discussions with young and old. One of them was Dr Francis, who wrote:

> The opportunities which presented themselves to me of obtaining circum-stantial facts concerning Mozart from the personal knowledge of Da Ponte were not so frequent as desirable, but the incidents which Da Ponte gave were all of a most agreeable character. His accounts strengthened the reports of the ardent, nay, almost impetuous energy and industry of Mozart; his promptness in decision, and his adventurous intellect. The story of Don Juan had indeed become familiar in a thousand ways; Mozart determined to cast the opera exclusively as serious, and had well advanced in the work. Da Ponte assured me, that he remonstrated, and urged the expediency on the great composer of the introduction of the vis comica, in order to ensure greater success, and prepared the role with Batti, batti, Là ci darem, ec.

Da Ponte was concerned about his family in Ceneda, and his letters ask anxiously for news of them. To the composer Perucchini he wrote, 'I am overwhelmed by the wretched state of the Da Ponte family both in Venice and in Ceneda.' He sold the rest of his beloved books and sent the proceeds to Perucchini, begging him to divide the money between Agostino's widow Caterina, his oldest sister Angioletta, 'if she is still living, as I hope', and Faustina, 'who is not happily married, as I am told the others are'. In this same letter he wrote in grief that he now had only one pupil – perhaps it was a consolation that she paid him in kisses and caresses.

His last letter of which we know, written in April 1838, was to Stafler, once more asking for news of his 'poor and beloved sisters. Perhaps [they] think that I've forgotten them, but that isn't so, and I should have given them proof of it if God hadn't deprived me of the means of doing so. No, that's not right – it isn't God, but the cruelty, wickedness and ingratitude of men which deprives me of the means . . . Tell me if the poor things are still living, and how they are. I long to know all about them, but above all I long to have news of the one who is unhappily married. If twenty dollars can be of some use to them, please draw on me at eight days, and I shall glory in paying it. Greet my sister-in-law and Pasquetta, and kiss my dear great-nieces, whom God bless and keep.'

In this same letter Da Ponte tells Stafler that he is writing the fourth volume of his memoirs – 'God give me grace and strength to finish it!' – and hopes to be able to send it to him in August. Since it was never published, and no trace of it seems to have been found, the strong possibility is that his children destroyed it. In view of what he wrote in the sonnets composed after Nancy's death, it was presumably full of a bitter account of his dealings with her family; if so, how understandable their reluctance to allow this diatribe to see the light of day.

He died at peace with his church. Everything he wrote makes it clear that, renegade abbé though he was, he never for long lost his faith in a merciful God who kept a close eye on his errant children – or, it must be added, in a vengeful God who saw to it that those who had wronged Da Ponte sooner or later received their just punishment (which, oddly enough, often seems to have been the case: Doriguti, the jealous lover who in Vienna had been responsible for the loss of Da Ponte's teeth, some years later parted with several of his own in a fall; the one-time friend who refused to help the librettist during his poverty-stricken days in Trieste died with his son on the gallows; and, of the many merchants who at one time or another cheated him in America, one was eventually imprisoned and another struck dead by lightning).

In 1830, as a result of what Agostino had been telling him, he had addressed a poem to the Patriarch of Venice, Monsignor Jacopo Monico, who had followed him as professor of *belles lettres* in Treviso, later becoming Bishop of Ceneda. The Patriarch wrote him a charming letter in return, full of graceful compliments on his writings and his services to Italian literature, and making it quite clear that by this time, his youthful escapades forgotten, he was honoured by his compatriots. With infinite tact, Monsignor Monico ended his letter with a plea that Da Ponte would 'put his affairs in order in such a way that his last moments would not be embittered by remorse'. To Giovanni Battista Perucchini, whose father Girolamo had been a great friend of the Patriarch, Da Ponte wrote some five years later, 'Please have the goodness to remember my most humble name to his Eminence, and tell him that his holy counsels and Christian wishes had the effect which his charitable heart wished to evoke in my soul.'

As death approached he sent for the Rev. John MacCloskey, who received his confession and gave him absolution. His son Lorenzo and son-in-law Henry Anderson were walking in the Adirondacks when he breathed his last on 17 August 1838, but some of his closest friends were there, including Bagioli and Luciano Fornasari, one of the singers in Montresor's company. Three days later he was buried in splendour in the presence of a host of fellow Italians and American friends. Since the fact that he had been a priest was not generally known, it was decided that it was best to keep silent about this matter. After solemn obsequies in the cathedral, when Allegri's *Miserere* was magnificently performed, a vast procession followed the coffin to the Roman Catholic cemetery on 11th Street. The pall-bearers were his old friends Clement Moore, Gulian Verplanck and Dr Macneven, and Pietro Maroncelli, whose wife had been a leading member of Rivafinoli's company. Fitz-Greene Halleck was among those who followed the cortège to the grave. In front of the coffin was carried a splendid black banner with a Latin inscription in letters of gold.

Like Mozart, Da Ponte was buried in an unmarked grave, and the cemetery where his body was laid was not used after 1851. In 1912 it was dismantled and the graves were removed to Calvary Cemetery. Some years afterwards the Ceneda authorities – who by now realised that this one-time disreputable son of theirs had become something of a legend – wrote to New York to find out when he had died, as they wanted to put up a memorial to him. The memorial never materialised, but a street in Ceneda – merged since 1866 with the neighbouring town of Serravalle to become Vittorio Veneto – bears the name which he shared with the bishop who gave him his first chance in life.

Da Ponte was a complex man, full of contradictions, considerably larger than life, and perhaps influenced by his Jewish heritage to a far greater extent than he himself realised, or than he would have wished others to believe. Of himself he wrote, in his account of the Montresor venture:

I believe that my heart is made of a different stuff from that of other men. A noble act, generous, benevolent, blinds me. I am like a soldier who, spurred by the longing for glory, rushes against the mouth of the cannon; like an ardent lover who flings himself into the arms of a woman who torments him. The hope of giving, *post funera*, immortality to my name, and of leaving to a nation which I revere a memory of me which will not be ignoble; the sweet allurement of arousing feelings of gratitude and goodwill in those who follow an art that was not disgraced by my pen; the desire to awaken love for the beautiful language which I brought to America, and love too for our ravishing music; the longing to see once again on the American stage some of the children of my youthful inspiration, which are still remembered in the theatres of the Thames, the Danube and the Elbe; and, finally, a sweet presentiment of joy, encouragement and honour, based on the integrity of my actions, the reliability of my promises and the happy success of a well-organised spectacle, were the powerful spurs which goaded me to this delightful undertaking, and from which nothing, so far, has succeeded in deterring me. I dreamt of roses and laurels; but from the roses I had only thorns, and from the laurels bitterness! So goes the world!

But in the end Da Ponte, librettist and teacher of genius, dedicated scholar, eloquent champion of his mother country, has found the immortality for which he craved; for as long as the operas of Mozart are performed Da Ponte, too, will be honoured.

Chronological Table
of the Main Events of
Da Ponte's Life

1749 Emanuele Conegliano born
1763 Baptised and renamed
      Lorenzo Da Ponte; father
      remarries
1763
or
1764 Enters Ceneda seminary
1765 Takes minor orders
1768 Bishop Da Ponte dies
1769 Enters Portogruaro
      seminary
1770 First visit to Venice;
      probably meets Angiola
      Tiepolo
1773 Ordained; leaves
      Portogruaro and goes to
      Venice
1774 Engaged to teach at Treviso
      seminary
1775 Final break with Angiola
      Tiepolo
1776 Dismissed from Treviso
      seminary; returns to
      Venice
1777 Affair with Angioletta
      Bellaudi begins
1779 Letter of accusation
      deposited in lion's mouth;
      trial opens; escapes to
      Gorizia; sentence of 15
      years' banishment
      pronounced in Venice

1781 Leaves Gorizia and goes to
      Dresden; arrives in Vienna
1783 Appointed poet to the
      Italian opera at the
      Burgtheater; meets Mozart
1786 First performance of *Le
      nozze di Figaro*; first
      performance of *Una cosa rara*
1787 First performance of *Don
      Giovanni* in Prague and (1788
      in Vienna
1790 First performance of *Così fan
      tutte*; the Emperor Joseph
      dies; Leopold arrives in
      Vienna
1791 Dismissed as poet to the
      Italian opera; takes refuge in
      Brühl-bei-Mödling; goes to
      Trieste
1792 Marries (?) Nancy; leaves
      Trieste for London
1793 Journey to Brussels,
      Rotterdam and The Hague;
      appointed poet to the
      Italian opera at the King's
      Theatre
1794 Louisa born
1798 Leaves with Nancy for
      Italy; visits family in Ceneda
1799 Returns to London;
      dismissed as poet;
      connection with King's

Theatre thereafter much looser; Fanny born

1800 Declares himself bankrupt and is arrested; Paolo comes to London; Joseph born

1804(?) Lorenzo L. born; Nancy and children leave for America

1805 Da Ponte leaves for America; opens grocer's shop in New York; moves with family to Elizabethville

1806 Charles (Carlo) born

1807 Returns to New York; begins career as teacher

1809 Louisa marries Miles Franklin Clossey

1811 Moves with family to Sunbury

1812 Charles Niccolini dies

1814 John Grahl dies

1815 Matilda born; Fanny marries Coleman (?)

Freeman; Louisa Niccolini dies

1816 Peter Grahl dies

1818 Goes to Philadelphia

1819 Settles in New York

1820 Fanny divorces Freeman

1821 Joseph dies

1823 First volumes of memoirs published; Louisa dies

1825 Appointed Professor of Italian at Columbia College; Garcia company comes to New York

1828 Becomes an American citizen

1830 Agostino and Giulia reach New York; memoirs end

1831 Fanny marries Henry James Anderson; Nancy dies

1832 Matilda dies; Montresor company comes to New York

1833 Italian Opera House opens

1838 Lorenzo Da Ponte dies

Da Ponte's Works

For most of his life Da Ponte was a compulsive writer – of poems, opera libretti, translations, rhyming letters, polemics, various editions of his autobiography, and long screeds of accusation and self-justification. It is doubtful whether it would be possible to track down everything that flowed from his ready pen. Moreover, as the years went by he tended to publish and republish prose and poetry from his earlier collections. As much as possible of his work (mainly published but a little unpublished, such as the very early poems) has been included in the list given below, since it may interest readers to know exactly what his output was during his long life.

His writings are scattered in a variety of places on both sides o the Atlantic; libraries where copies are to be found are given in brackets (in a few cases two libraries, one in the old world and one in the new). The date of the first performance of every opera is given against the title of the libretto concerned. Some of his minor works are reproduced by Bernardi or by Gambarin and Nicolini, and this too is indicated.

1763–1766

Sonnet to his father, *Mandatemi, vi prego, o padre mio* (*Memoirs*)
Sonnets in honour of the Rector of Ceneda seminary, *Quello spirt divino, che, con l'ardente* and *Candido leggiadruccio cagnoletto* (*Bernardi*)
Perchè quel franco corridor, che senta (verses written in competition with his schoolmates) (*Gambarin and Nicolini*)
Verses for Pierina Raccanelli
Sonnet *Quanto è possente amor* (written with Michele Colombo (*Memoirs*)

1769

Anacreontica for Michele Colombo, *Quel chiaror di viva luce* (*Bernardi*)

1770

Canzone in praise of St Luke
Translation from Latin of a poem by a teacher at the seminary of
    Portogruaro (*Bernardi*)
Sonnets, *Nube che in largo umor dolce si scioglie* (*Bernardi*)
    Nè di frale beltà . . . (*Bernardi*)
Canzone anacreontica (*Bernardi*)

1771

Two sonnets: *Ei non morrà: se puote il sangue mio* and *Tu no'l vedrai: che'l
    glorioso aspetto* (*Elegia Celebrando la prima Messa il M. Rdo Sig. D.
    Gio: Batta Pelleatti, Maestro nel Seminario di Porto*) (*Biblioteca Comunale,
    Vittorio Veneto*)

1772

Egloga (*Bernardi*)
La fisica particolare (Portogruaro *accademia*. This includes his charming
    poem *Ditirambo sopra gli odori*) (*Bernardi*)
Various sonnets

1773

Canzone contro un Cenedese (*Bernardi*)

1776

Canzone: Se in core di donna si dia spirito virile (*Bernardi*)
Accademia poetica (Treviso seminary) (*Russo; Marchesan*)
Gozzi, se un cor gentil (*Saggi poetici*, Vienna 1788; London 1801)
Elegy, *L'Americano in Europa*

1779

Sonnet in Venetian dialect in defence of Giorgio Pisani, *Se'l fosse anco
    el Pisani un impostor* (*Memoirs*)
Le gare degli uccelli (*Biblioteca civica di Gorizia*)
Aurelio, ossia la gara della magnanimità (translation from the German of
    C. H. von Ayrenhoff)

1780

Il Capriccio (*Biblioteca civica di Gorizia*)
Il Cechino (*Biblioteca civica di Udine; Saggi poetici*, 1788)
Fasti Goriziani (translation from the Latin of Count Rodolfo Coronini)
   (*Biblioteca civica di Udine*)
La gratitudine o sia la difesa delle donne (*New York Public Library; Osservatore Triestino*, 8 October 1791)
Il conte di Varvic (translation by Lorenzo and Girolamo Da Ponte from the French of H. F. de La Harpe)
Sonnet: *Per la morte di Sua Maestà l'Imperatrice Maria Teresa*

1781

Setti salmi (*Russo; Saggi poetici*, 1801)
Filemone e Bauci (*Biblioteca civica di Udine; Saggi poetici*, 1788)

1782

Alla Santità di Pio VI (*Biblioteca civica, Treviso; Saggi poetici*, 1788)

1783

Preghiere che si cantano nella chiesa della Nazione Italiana, in tempo della Messa (translation from the Latin) (*Stadt Bibliothek, Vienna*)
A Sua Maestà Cesarea Giuseppe Secondo (*Biblioteca civica di Gorizia*)

1784

Al bel sesso (*Osservatore Triestino*, 15 January 1785)
Sonetti contro Chiovini e poesie contro altri
(?) *I bei capelli di Silvia* (with Casanova)

1785

A Sua Eccellenza Il Signor P. Z. [Pietro Zaguri] Patrizio Veneto e Senatore Amplissimo (*Saggi poetici* 1801)
Per la ricuperata salute di Ophelia (set to music by Salieri, Mozart and Cornetti)

1786

Sonnet: *Casti ier sera un'operetta fè* (*Memoirs*)
Gentil Casti, ho stabilito (*Saggi poetici*, 1788 and 1801)

1788

Saggi poetici (Two vols) (*Biblioteca civica di Treviso*)
A mio padre: Epistola (*Saggi poetici*, 1788)

1790

Morte dell'Imperatore e avvenimento al trono di Leopoldo II (*Saggi poetici*, 1801; *Gambarin and Nicolini*)

1791

Leopoldo, sei rè. Giustizia imploro (*Gambarin and Nicolini*)
Sonnet: *Sull' Ingratitudine dell'uomo* (*Saggi poetici*, 1801)
Il Mezenzio (with Girolamo Da Ponte) (*New York Public Library*)
Per l'insediamento di Sigismondo Antonio conte di Hohenwart (*Ziliotto*)
Per il giorno onomastico di S. E. la Sig.ra Teresa Contessa Brigido (*Ziliotto*)

1792

Sul proposito del sonetto 'Addio di Hebe' (*Ziliotto*)

1793

Il tributo del core (dedicated to the Duke of Choiseul) (*British Library*)

1795

Piacevoli noterelle sopra il turpe Libello, intitolato Breve notizia dell' opera buffa che ha per titolo La scola de'maritati, composto dal sedicente Vittorio Nemesini (*British Library; New York Historical Society*)
Six Italian Canzonetts (set to music by Martin y Soler)

1801

Saggi poetici (only Vol. I published) (*British Library*)

1807

Storia compendiosa della vita di Lorenzo Da Ponte (*New York Historical Society*)

1808

Canzone: Agli Stati Uniti d'America (Sterling Library, Yale)

1816

Al suo signore ed amico T. Mathias (Houghton Library, Harvard, in 'Alcune poesie')

1819

An Extract from the Life of Lorenzo Da Ponte, with the History of Several Dramas written by him, and among others, Il Figaro, Il Don Giovanni,& la scola degli amanti, set to music by Mozart (Yale; New York Historical Society)

1821

Sull'Italia. Discorso apologetico di Lorenzo Da Ponte in risposta alla lettera dell'Avvocato Carlo Phillips al Re d'Inghilterra (New York Public Library)
Apologetical Discourse on Italy: in answer to a letter addressed to the King of England by Charles Phillips, Counsellor at Law (translation of the above) (New York Public Library)
La Profezia di Dante di Lord Byron (translation) (Biblioteca civica, Trieste; New York Public Library)

1823

Catalogo ragionato de'libri che si trovano attualmente nel negozio di Lorenzo e Carlo Da Ponte (Columbia University)
Memorie di Lorenzo Da Ponte, da Ceneda, scritte da esso (IV Vols)

1825

Critique on certain passages in Dante (appeared in the *New York Review and Athenaeum*) (Cornell University)
Economia della vita umana, tradotta dall'inglese da L. Guidelli: resa alla sua vera lezione da L. Da Ponte (followed, amongst other items, by *Alcune osservazioni sull'articolo quarto pubblicato nel North American Review il mese d'ottobre dell'anno 1824*) (New York Public Library)
Letter to his sisters (*Biblioteca civica di Trieste*)
Scena quarta del quinto atto di 'Adad' by J. A. Hillhouse (translation)
Canzone all'Imperatore Francesco II ('Alcune poesie')

1826

Le nozze di Figaro, Il Don Giovanni e L'Assur re d'Ormus: tre drammi di Lorenzo Da Ponte (also contains *Il Mezenzio*) (*New York Public Library*)
Il Don Giovanni, with a translation of 'the poetical part' by Lorenzo L. Da Ponte (*New York Public Library, Music Section*)

1827

Storia della lingua e della letteratura italiana in New-york (*Gambarin and Nicolini; New York Public Library*)
Catalogue of Italian books, deposited in the New York society, for the permanent use of L. Da Ponte's pupils and subscribers

1828

Ode: *Per lo Stabilmento d'una permanente libreria di suoi allievi* (*Memoirs*)

1829

Memoirs (2nd edition)

1830

Alcune poesie di Lorenzo Da Ponte (Second edition also published this year under title *Poesie varie*) (*Houghton Library, Harvard* – this volume includes *Gil Blas*)
Memoirs (2nd edition, corrected and with 1 volume added) (*Library of Congress*)

1831

Anacreontica: Un doloroso addio a miei libri (*Rare Book and Manuscript Library, Columbia University*)

1832

Versi composti da Lorenzo Da Ponte per la morte d'Anna Celestina Ernestina, sua virtuosissima e adorata consorte (English translation by Carlo Da Ponte) (*New York Historical Society*)

1833

Storia della Compagnia dell'Opera Italiana condotta da Giacomo Montresor in America in agosto dell'anno 1832: Part II *Storia incredibile ma vera* (*Gambarin and Nicolini*)

1834

Il Mezenzio (*New York Public Library*)

1835

Frottola per far ridere (*New York Historical Society*)
Storia americana ossia il lamento di Lorenzo da Ponte quasi nonagenario al nonagenario Michele Colombo (*New York Historical Society*)

LIBRETTI

1781

Ati e Cibele (by Philippe Quinault, translation and adaptation by Mazzolà and Da Ponte)

1783

Ifigenia in Tauride (translation from the French of N. F. Guillard with Du Roullet) (Gluck) 14 December (*British Library*)

1784

Il ricco d'un giorno (adaptation of text by Bertati) (Salieri) 6 December (*Oesterreichische Nationalbibliothek*)

1786

Il burbero di buon cuore (adaptation of Goldoni's *Le bourru bienfaisant*) (Martin y Soler) 4 January (*British Library*)
Il finto cieco (adaptation of Legrand's *L'aveugle clairvoyant*) (Gazzaniga) 20 February (*Oesterreichische Nationalbibliothek*)
Le Nozze di Figaro (adaptation of Beaumarchais' *Le mariage de Figaro*) (Mozart) 1 May (*British Library*)

Il demogorgone ovvero il filosofo confuso (? adaptation of text by Brunati) (Righini) 12 July (*Oesterreichische Nationalbibliothek*)

Una cosa rara o sia Bellezza ed onestà (adaptation of Luis Vélez de Guevara's *La luna de la Sierra*) (Martin y Soler) 17 November (*British Library*)

Gli equivoci (adaptation of French translation of Shakespeare's *Comedy of Errors* entitled *Les Méprises*) (Storace) 27 December (*Oesterreichische Nationalbibliothek*)

1787

Il Bertoldo (adaptation of libretto by Brunati) (Piticchio) 22 June (*Conservatorio Cherubini*)

L'arbore di Diana (Martin y Soler) 1 October (*British Library*)

Il dissoluto punito o sia il Don Giovanni (adaptation of libretto by Bertati) (Mozart) 29 October (*Prague première*) (*British Library*)

1788

Axur, rè d'Ormus (adaptation of Beaumarchais' *Tarare*) (Salieri) 8 January (*British Library*)

Il Talismano (adaptation of text by Goldoni) (Salieri) 10 September (*Conservatorio 'S. Cecilia'*)

1789

Il pastor fido (adaptation of text by Guarini) (Salieri) 11 February (*Oesterreichische Nationalbibliothek*)

L'ape musicale (adaptation of text by Goldoni) (Various composers) 27 February (*Oesterreichische Nationalbibliothek*)

La cifra (adaptation of *La dama pastorella* by Petrosellini) (Salieri) 11 December (*British Library*)

1790

Così fan tutte ossia la scuola degli amanti (Mozart) 26 January (*British Library*)

Nina o sia la pazza per amore (adaptation of text by Lorenzi after Marsollier) (Paisiello/Weigl) 13 April (*Conservatorio 'S. Cecilia'*)

La quacquera spirituosa (adaptation of libretto by Palomba) (Guglielmi and others) 13 August

La caffettiera bizzarra (adaptation of libretto by Goldoni) (Weigl) 15 September (*Conservatorio 'S. Cecilia'*)

1791

I voti della nazione napoletana (Piticchio) 12 January
Flora e Minerva (Cantata) (Weigl) 17 January
Il Davide (?text after Antoni) (Composer unknown) 11 March (*Oester-reichische Nationalbibliothek*)
L'ape musicale rinnuovata (Various composers) 23 March

Date unknown (written between 1781 and 1791)

Il Sogno (Cantata)
Il sacrifizio di Jefte (Cantata)
Il ritorno felice

1794

Il matrimonio segreto (adaptation of text by Bertati) (Cimarosa) 11 January (*British Library*)
I contadini bizzarri (adaptation of text by T. Grandi. Also known as *Le gelosie villane*) (Sarti/Paisiello) 1 February (*Larpent Collection, Huntingdon Library; British Library*)
Il capriccio drammatico (adaptation of text by G. M. Diodati) (Cimarosa) 1 March (*British Library*)
Il Don Giovanni (adaptation of text by Bertati) (Gazzaniga, Sarti, Federici and Guglielmi) 1 March (*British Library*)
La bella pescatrice (adaptation of text by Maldonati) (Guglielmi) 18 March (*British Library*)
La prova dell'opera (Paisiello) 1 April
La Semiramide (adaptation of text by F. Moretti) (Bianchi) 26 April (*British Library*)
La frascatana (adaptation of text by Livigni) (Paisiello) 5 June (*British Library*)
La vittoria (Cantata. Text adapted by Da Ponte) (Paisiello) 23 June

1795

La scola de'maritati (also known as *La capricciosa corretta, I sposi in contrasto* and *La moglie corretta*) (Martin y Soler) 27 January (*British Library*)
Alceste o sio Il trionfo dell'amor conjugale (adaptation of text by Calzabigi) (Gluck) 30 April
L'isola del piacere (Martin y Soler) 26 May (*British Library*)
Le nozze dei contadini spagnuoli (Martin y Soler) 28 May (*Larpent Collection, Huntingdon Library*)

La bella Arsène (adaptation of text by C. S. Favart) (Monsigny/ Mazzinghi) 12 December (*British Library*)

1796

Antigona (Bianchi) 24 May (*British Library*)
Il tesoro (Mazzinghi) 14 June (*Larpent Collection, Huntingdon Library*)
Zemira e Azor (translation from the French of J. F. Marmontel) (Grétry) 23 July
Il consiglio imprudente (adaptation of libretto by Goldoni) (Bianchi) 20 December (*New York Public Library*)

1797

Evelina (translation and adaptation of French text by Guillard) (Sacchini) 10 January (*British Library*)
Le nozze del Tamigi e Bellona (Cantata) (Bianchi) 11 March
Merope (adaptation of text by Voltaire) (Bianchi) 10 June (*Larpent Collection, Huntingdon Library*)

1798

Cinna (? adaptation of libretto by A. Anelli) (Bianchi) 20 February (*British Library*)

1801

Angelina (adaptation of text by C. P. Defranceschi) (Salieri) 29 December (*British Library*)

1802

Armida (Bianchi) 1 June (*British Library*)

1803

La grotta di Calipso (Winter) 31 May (*British Library*)

1804

Il trionfo dell'amor fraterno (Winter) 22 March (*British Library*)
Il ratto di Proserpina (Winter) 3 May (*British Library*)

Acknowledgements

I am immensely grateful to the many people who have helped me in the research for this book, and especially to Prof. Lucio Puttin and Agostino Conti of the Biblioteca Comunale of Treviso, who started me on my way and were particularly generous in providing material which might not otherwise have been available. Dr Pianca of the Biblioteca Civica of Vittorio Veneto spared valuable time, and Riccardo Razza and Dr Bastian Dario cheerfully spent most of one morning tracking down the original of the photograph of Bishop Lorenzo Da Ponte. Dom Antonio Ornella, director of the Biblioteca del Seminario Vescovile di Concordia, Pordenone, put his archives at the disposal of my husband and myself, and although we found nothing relevant to our quest the visit was memorable because of our talk with him afterwards over a bottle of the delicious wine which the monks make. I had much help also from the Archivio di Stato in Venice, a veritable Aladdin's cave of wonderful material; the Biblioteca Seminario Vescovile of Vittorio Veneto; the Biblioteca Nazionale and the Conservatorio Luigi Cherubini of Florence; the Biblioteca Civica of Trieste; the Biblioteca Civica of Gorizia; the Biblioteca Civica of Udine; the Biblioteca Cini and the Biblioteca Marciana of Venice; and the Conservatorio di Musica 'S. Cecilia' of Rome. I should also like to thank Prof. Alessandro Vaciago and Signora Barzetti of the Istituto Italiano di Cultura in London.

For the Vienna research I am grateful to Dr Franz Dirnberger and other officials of the Haus-Hof-und Staatsarchiv and to Dr Günther Brosche and Dr Joseph Gmeiner of the Musiksammlung of the Oesterreichische Nationalbibliothek, as well as for the opportunity to consult books in the city and university libraries.

Much help came from the staff of the British Library, especially from Margaret Johnson, who very kindly prepared a long résumé of Guevara's *La luna de la Sierra*, and from D. L. Paisey and Pamela Willetts, who deciphered the German *Schrift* of the Vienna theatre accounts relating to payments to Da Ponte.

Albi Rosenthal generously lent me his copy of *Una cosa rara* and gave me copies of Da Ponte's letters to Armando Peremet and Signor Fusi. Gillean McDougall of the BBC arranged for me to hear recordings of *Una cosa rara* and *Gli equivoci*, and John N. Adams,

Senior Lecturer in Law at the University of Kent, took great trouble to furnish me with information about bankruptcy at the turn of the nineteenth century. Help in this complex issue came also from Miss J. Coburn of the Greater London Council Record Office and History Library, Dr J. B. Post of the Public Record Office and Robert Lewis of the Royal Courts of Justice. Dr Ursula Player very kindly vetted my translation of the extracts from *Rococo-Bilder*. I am grateful to P. W. Hasler, Secretary of the History of Parliament Trust, for allowing me to see the entry on William Taylor, and to Irene F. Pollock of the Guildhall Library.

A number of libraries in the United States possess holograph letters of Da Ponte which I was able to see, as well as other valuable material: The Library of Congress, Washington; the Houghton Library, Harvard University; the New York Historical Society (a treasure trove of Daponteana); the New York Public Library; the Rare Book and Manuscript Division of Columbia University; the Boston Public Library; the Huntingdon Library; the Sterling Memorial Library and the Beinecke Rare Book and Manuscript Library of Yale University; and the Pierpont Morgan Library. I was also allowed to consult books in the library of McGill University.

I am grateful to Dr Hans Moldenhauer for allowing me to see a letter from Da Ponte to Fortunato Stella, as well as the Dragonetti receipt from the Northwestern University Music Library Moldenhauer Archives; to Jack K. Hetrick of the Northumberland County Historical Society for his valiant attempt to trace Joseph Da Ponte's poem in the *Northumberland Times*; the Historical Society of Pennsylvania; the American Association for State and Local History; and Charles and Jo Sober for sending me George G. Struble's talk to the Northumberland County Historical Society.

David Osmond-Smith, Lecturer in Music at the University of Sussex, read the passages relating to opera in Vienna, London and America, and I am most grateful for his comments and suggestions, which saved me from many a blunder (any that remain are entirely my responsibility). With Dr Anthony Cox I had fascinating conversations about Da Ponte's complex psychological make-up. I am grateful to my friends Maria Theresa Starkie and Adriana Anichini for help with knotty problems regarding the Italian; to John Stone for the loan of his annotated version of *An Extract from the Life of Lorenzo Da Ponte*; and to Louis and Annette Kaufman for the libretti which they sent me from the Larpent Collection.

I wish particularly to thank Professor Robbins Landon for his kindness in writing the Foreword, and for the advice and encouragement which he and his wife gave me in Vienna; and above all I want to thank my husband, who for many years has lived uncomplainingly with Da Ponte as, so to speak, a third member of the household, who shared some of the research (which he found as fascinating as I did), and whose comments on the typescript were, as always, full of good sense and perception.

Notes and References

In order to keep the footnotes to a minimum I have listed below, rather than in the text itself, the origin of short quoted passages, giving the page number and the first few words for purposes of identification. Also included are a few other notes, sources and references which may be of interest.

Chapter I

p3   Ceneda no longer exists on the map. In 1866 it was united with its ancient neighbour, the town of Serravalle, in one administrative unit called Vittorio Veneto in honour of King Vittorio Emanuele II.

p3   The baptism is recorded in vivid detail in a 4-page printed pamphlet headed *Distinta Narrazione del solenne battesimo conferito nella Chiesa Cattedrale di Ceneda ad un padre, e tre figli del ghetto della città*, which is kept in the archives of Ceneda seminary.

p5   'Alas, that death robbed me . . .' From the *Canzone al suo signore ed amico T. Mathias*, written in 1816 and printed in *An Extract from the Life* . . . 1819.

p6   'with bitter shame . . .' 14 July 1763 (*Curia Vescovile, Vittorio Veneto*).

p7   'He was as dear to me . . .' and 'however crazy . . .' Letter dated 22 September 1827 to Daniele Francesconi, librarian of Padua Univesity.

p10   'My duties . . .' 23 April 1772.

p11   It is possible that Da Ponte dated some of these letters incorrectly, or that the dates have been transcribed wrongly, for on 29 January 1770 he writes from Portogruaro, yet five days later heads his letter 'Venezia', and it is in this letter that he says he has not been out of the house for ten days. Whatever the exact dates, it is certain that during this period he was in Venice a good deal.

p12   'why he left Portogruaro so hurriedly . . .' According to local oral tradition Da Ponte went away because he was told that he did not have a vocation for the priesthood. It seems likely enough!

Chapter II

p12 'Venice, dear beautiful Venice!' *Reminiscences*.

p13 'like one vast dwelling-place . . .' Molmenti.

p14 'In every square . . .' *Memoirs*.

p14 'Upon the Piazzi de S. Marco . . .' *The Present State of Music in France and Italy*.

p18 'Say nothing of this . . .' 19 January 1774.

p19 'Everyone in Treviso . . .' 8 October 1774.

Chapter III

p21 'extremely neat and pretty . . .' *Reminiscences*.

p22 'His poem was received . . .' 13 March 1776.

p23 'as one commentator remarks . . .' Toffoli, *Inediti dapontiani*.

p25 'every copy of the poems . . .' Possession of the confiscated verses was an offence attracting severe punishment. However, the bishop's chancellor hid all the papers relating to the trial in the chapter archives, for the illumination of future generations.

p25 'the bishop tried hard . . .' Giustiniani's letter dated 23 December 1776, quoted by Marchesan.

p28 '*La vera ragione* . . .' *Archivio Storico Italiano, Anno LXVII, Firenze, Serie VII, Vol. XIV*.

p32 'never to utter one word . . .' *Reminiscences*.

Chapter IV

p35 'descending rapidly . . .' *Fasti Goriziani*.

p36 'The innkeeper . . .' Gugitz throws cold water on this romantic tale of the Gorizian landlady by saying that the parish archives have no record of an innkeeper dying in 1779 or 1780. But she may have been buried elsewhere, or there may be some other explanation. Da Ponte tells the story so convincingly and with such feeling, and remembers his landlady so tenderly fifty years afterwards, that there is no reason to believe he was inventing the episode.

p38 'to smooth away . . .' Muratti.

p40 'he fixed the guilt . . .' Perhaps Da Ponte's conviction of Coletti's perfidy was not as unjustified as it seems. Years later, when he was living in New York, he exchanged many letters with Domenico Rossetti, a lawyer and one of the most respected citizens of Trieste. He told Rossetti all about the affair, and the lawyer replied that he knew Coletti, and did not disagree with Da Ponte's opinion of him; otherwise he would not have believed him capable of such an act of deception.

p41 The play by Quinault was *Atys*.

p42 In the memoirs Da Ponte incorrectly writes that the letter from his father announced the death of Girolamo, not Luigi. Later he corrects himself.

p43 'approaching my sixtieth year . . .' In a footnote to the memoirs Da Ponte writes, 'This was the age at which I began to write the story of my life. Now I am eighty . . .'

Chapter V

p44 'a terrible genius . . .' Macartney.

p44 'shortly, clearly, boldly . . .' *Autobiography*.

p45 'When I wrote about him . . .' Letter to Filippo Pananti, 28 November 1830 (*Scritti minori*).

p45 'very difficult of access . . .' Burney, *The Present State of Music in Germany, the Netherlands, and the United Provinces*.

p46 'All ranks of society . . .' *Reminiscences*.

p47 'the new poet to the theatre . . .' 7 May 1783.

p48 'To me, toleration . . .' Wangermann.

p49 'though he did make a translation . . .' Both Loewenberg and Pagnini include among Da Ponte's early libretti an Italian translation of the text of Gluck's *Iphigénie en Tauride*. Loewenberg says that this opera, performed in Vienna in 1783, was 'his first contribution to the Vienna stage'; Pagnini (apparently quoting from the title page of the printed libretto) that it had its first performance on 14 December 1783.

p50 'In the recitative . . .' From *La cantante e l'impresario*, quoted by Goldin.

p51 'First the *maestro di capella* . . .' *Epistola al Sig. Casti*.

p51 'a little man . . .' *Reminiscences*.

p52 'an impudent, worthless fellow' *Memoirs*.

p53 '*comme bouffon* . . .' *Ibid*.

p53 'energy, humour . . .' *The Present State of Music in Germany* . . .

Chapter VI

p56 'This young composer . . .' *An Extract from the Life* . . .

p58 'If a writer . . .' *Ibid*.

p59 'The success of this . . .' *Ibid*.

p60 'La Musique de Mozard . . .' 16 May 1788

p60 '[Mozart] has only one fault . . .' *Autobiography*.

p60 'has an enormous amount . . .' 7 May 1783
p60 'An Italian poet . . .' 5 July 1783
p62 'I should say . . .' 13 October 1781.
p63 'If the words . . .' *An Extract from the Life* . . .
p64 'the more comic . . .' 6 December 1783.
p64 'An opera is sure of success . . .' 13 October 1781.
p66 'the Emperor had given instructions . . .' In a letter to Count von Pergen, 31 January 1785.
p68 'I gave a copy . . .' Da Ponte quotes this letter in *An Extract from the Life* . . .
p68 'A comedy of 230 pages . . .' *Ibid*.
p70 'The marriage between . . .' 29 September 1786.
p70 'singular . . .' 4 July 1786.
p71 'a perfect model . . .' J. F. Reichardt, *Vertraute Briefe aus Paris*, quoted by Gugitz.

Chapter VII

p74 'a small book . . .' *Una tragedia e tre drammi*, 1826.
p78 'the most gifted . . .' and 'He retained . . .' *Reminiscences*.
p79 'Da Ponte's effort . . .' *The Monthly Musical Record*.
p79 'Joseph disliked one aria . . .' *Handbillet* 1786, quoted by Michtner.
p82 'one contemporary pamphlet . . .' Michtner.
p83 'One of [the girls] . . .' *The Present State of Music in France and Italy*.
p83 'The son of the Roman consul . . .' 1 November 1783.
p83 'I don't know . . .' 11 March 1784.
p84 'Elle a une voie . . .' *Joseph II als Theaterdirektor*.
p84 'Connoisseurs of music . . .' 15 October 1788, quoted by Michtner.

Chapter VIII

p95 'a certain special kindness . . .' 4 October 1788.
p99 'she knew how to sing it . . .' Salieri's comments, on the score of *La cifra* in the Oesterreichische Nationalbibliothek, Musiksammlung, are quoted by Michtner.
p103 'Twas then . . .' Published in *La profezia di Dante di Lord Byron*, 1821.
p104 'one of the greatest . . .' *Antologia*, No. 88, April 1828.
p104 'I'm dying to know . . .' To Count Collalto, 10 April 1790.
p107 'he tried to persuade Mozart . . .' Mozart is said – though not

by Da Ponte – to have replied in a letter written in September 1791, expressing premonitions of his death. But all the evidence indicates that this letter is spurious.

p107 'For a full account . . .' The events leading up to Da Ponte's dismissal are related with a wealth of documentation in Michtner's *Der Fall Abbé Da Ponte*, published in *Mitteilungen des Oesterreichischen Staatsarchiv*, 19 Band, Vienna, 1966. This was the first time these documents had been published; and to the best of my knowledge this fascinating material, which throws so much light on Da Ponte's banishment from Vienna, is quite new in an English version.

p110 'Everyone in the city . . .' Quoted by Michtner, *Der Fall Abbé Da Ponte*.

p112 Luigi del Bene's letter, which is undated but which must have been written early in February 1791, is in the records of the Archivio di Stato di Venezia, Inquisitori di Stato, Busta 257.

p112 'The Italian court poet . . .' 25 March 1791.

p112 The paragraph in *Gazetta urbana Veneta* is dated 7 April 1791.

p113 'his oldest stepbrother . . .' The correspondence about Agostino was between Count Breünner, Austrian Ambassador to Venice, and Count Giovanni de Cattaneo. See Archivio di Stato di Venezia, Inquisitori de Stato, Busta 576.

Chapter IX

p117 'Trieste . . .' In a letter to Casanova dated 13 July 1791.

p118 'he wrote from America . . .' To Domenico Rossetti, 26 July 1828.

p118 'On 5 July . . .' See Giuseppe Mainati's *Croniche ossia Memorie Storico sacro-profane di Trieste*, quoted by Pagnini in *Domenico Rossetti: Scritti Inediti*.

p118 'He was astonished . . .' 6 September 1791.

p119 'Everything I have ever heard . . .' *Antologia*, No. 88, April 1828.

p122 'two friends . . .' In a letter to Domenico Rossetti, 26 July 1828.

p123 'For what happened next . . .' The correspondence between Manolesso, Maffei, the Inquisitori and Da Ponte, and del Bene's letter to the Pope, are quoted by Franco Gaeta in his article *Un ignorato episodio della vita dell'Abate Lorenzo Da Ponte*, 1954. The exchange of letters between del Bene and the Ferrarese, del Bene and Da Ponte, and del Bene and de Corradini comes from the Venetian State archives (Archivio di

Stato di Venezia, Inquisitori di Stato, Buste 35 and 257) and is, I believe, quoted here for the first time.

p124 'The threat to Luigi's safety . . .' Letter from Count Breünner to Count Cattaneo, 3 April 1790.

p125 'If it is true. . .' 12 October 1791.

p125 'Da Ponte doesn't . . .' 14 January 1792.

p129 'Lorenzo Da Ponte . . .' Caprin, *I nostri nonni*, 1888, quoted by Pagnini.

Chapter X

p131 'a handsome . . .' Sheppard, *Survey of London, North of Piccadilly*.

p131 'So strange, so varied . . .' *An Extract from the Life* . . .

p132 'According to Badini . . .' *Il Tributo della coglionatura dell'Abate Vittorio Nemesini*.

p132 'the wittiest and most amiable. . . .' *Aneddoti piacevoli e interessanti*.

p132 'a profession . . .' 2 April 1793.

p133 'If you asked me . . .' 10 May 1793.

p133 'I enjoyed Da Ponte's letter . . .' 24 August 1792.

p133 'Da Ponte is completely mad . . .' 2 October 1792.

p133 'a violent and obscene lampoon . . .' Badini, *op.cit.*

p134 'Holland yielded nothing . . .' 9 November 1793.

p135 'arriving at a moment . . .' and 'So far as I'm concerned . . .' 17 November 1793.

p135 'harsh Scottish dialect . . .' John Taylor, *Records of my Life*.

p135 'One of the most singular . . .' *Seven Years of the King's Theatre*. All subsequent quotations from John Ebers are from the same source.

p137 'the rendezvous . . .' *Morning Chronicle*, 9 January 1797.

p137 'Every lady possessing . . .' Mount Edgcumbe, *Musical Reminiscences*. All subsequent quotations from Mount Edgcumbe are from the same source.

p137 'Whatever we may pretend . . .' 15 April 1795.

p137 'There has never been a dearth . . .' C. A. G. Goede.

p137 'Da Ponte had a low opinion . . .' According to his New York doctor, John W. Francis.

p139 'was throughout disapproved . . .' 10 March 1794.

p140 'she exhausted his patience . . .' Hogarth, *Memoirs of the Opera in Italy, France, Germany and England*. All subsequent quotations from Hogarth are from the same source.

p140 'attending to the business . . .' *Monthly Mirror*, February 1800.

p141 'How did the world . . .' 'Veritas'. According to John Taylor, 'He formed a connection with Signora Prudom, and there is reason to believe that he was actually married to her'. This may refer to a young singer of that name who sang leading roles at the King's Theatre between 1776 and 1781. By 1793 the liaison was presumably long since at an end, for Da Ponte does not mention her. From 1807 until his death in 1825 Taylor's common law wife was a Mrs Ann Dunn.

p143 'rapturous applause . . .' and 'So perfectly . . .' 26 January and 2 February 1795.

p143 'I'm well . . .' 25 August 1795.

p144 'The overture from . . .' Quoted in *The Collected Correspondence and London Notebooks of Joseph Haydn*, ed. H. C. Robbins Landon.

p144 'all the first society . . .' Mount Edgcumbe.

p144 'Pleasing but not great . . .' Unidentified cutting from King's Theatre cuttings book.

p145 'The most splendid . . .' 2 April 1794, unidentified cutting from King's Theatre cuttings book.

p145 'the tale is a tolerable . . .' and 'adapted to the season . . .' 15 and 20 June 1796.

p145 'For some mysterious reason . . .' *An Extract from the Life . . .* In the memoirs Da Ponte tells this anecdote in relation to *La bella Arsène*, whereas in 1819 he relates it to *Zemira e Azor*. Since both operas are translations from the French it is probably impossible to establish which is correct. However, as Loewenberg points out, *Zemira e Azor* had already been performed in London and two translations were available; it seems more likely, therefore, that the opera in question was *La bella Arsène*.

p146 'induce us to chace . . .' *Morning Chronicle*, 18 November 1896.

p147 'to the surprise of everyone . . .' 1 December 1798.

p148 'Signor Daponti . . .' 'Veritas'.

p149 'the most crowded . . .' Unidentified cutting from King's Theatre cuttings book.

p150 'The success of this piece . . .' 28 December 1796.

p150 'in order to give [her] . . .' *Morning Chronicle*, 9 April 1797.

p150 'the skilful and affecting . . .' 25 December 1797.

Chapter XI

p154 Angiola Tiepolo had died some years before. In March 1776 she had a child whom she called Pietro Lorenzo, though there is no suggestion that Da Ponte was responsible for it.

p156 'Finding myself . . .' Introduction to the American edition of *Il Mezenzio*, 1826.

p157 'We understand . . .' 18 December 1798.

p158 'Damiani never appeared . . .' The quarrel with Damiani is related in *Case of Signor Damiani of the Opera House 1799*.

p158 'On the east side . . .' *Roach's London Pocket Pilot*, quoted by Sheppard. That the 'Orange coffee house' and the 'Caffe degl'Italiani' are one and the same I deduce from the fact that Badini's lampoon *Il tributo della coglionatura* is addressed to 'those who frequent the caffe d'oranges'.

p160 'during the short time . . .' 31 January 1800.

p162 'a man of genius . . .' 16 March 1802 (*Reproduced by courtesy of the Trustees of the Boston Public Library*).

p162 'I believe . . .' *Canzoni e prose toscane*.

p163 'he wrote to his young stepbrother . . .' 18 February 1800. The letter was addressed '*Al Cittadino Paolo da Ponte, Ceneda*', refuting the statement which has sometimes been made that Paolo was living in Paris at this time (*Library of Congress*).

p164n 'We have witnessed . . .' 22 February 1796.

p165 'The Sheriffs' office . . .' 'Veritas'.

p165 'We rejoice to see . . .' 26 November 1803.

p166 'This incomparable artist . . .' 19 July 1802.

p166 'certainly one of the worst . . .' 2 June 1802.

p167 'The invention of the Poet . . .' 26 March 1804.

p167 'It is a grand . . .' 4 May 1804.

p167 'the language . . .' 20 July 1815.

p169 'I wrote, and wrote again . . .' *Storia compendiosa* . . .

Chapter XII

p172 'with every mark of tenderness . . .' *Storia compendiosa* . . .

p174 'sometimes obliged . . .' *Ibid*.

p176 'The sweetest moments of existence . . .' Quoted by H. T. Tuckerman.

p176 'day-time and evening assemblies . . .' *Storia compendiosa* . . .

p176 'of your marvellous canzone . . .' 11 August 1827.

p177 'My wife, my daughter . . .' To Professor Samuel Jarvis, 23 November 1809 (*Rare Book and Manuscript Library, Columbia University*).

p180 'When I left New York . . .' Quoted by Pagnini, *Scritti inediti di Domenico Rossetti*.

p180 'on 24 August . . .' See letter to Nathaniel Moore, 26 September 1818.

p180 'I have many creditors . . .' 26 September 1818 (*Reproduced by courtesy of the Pierpont Morgan Library*).

p180 'almost certainly translated . . .' This can be deduced not least from the fact that Mozart's name is spelt correctly, whereas Da Ponte invariably wrote Mozzart.

p181 'With what transports of joy . . .' 24 September 1818.

p181 'How I should love . . .' 2 October 1818 (*Rare Book and Manuscript Library, Columbia University*).

p181 'By chance I came across . . .' 27 March 1819 (*Ibid.*)

Chapter XIII

p182 'I offered to Mr Livingston . . .' 2 November 1819 (*Rare Book and Manuscript Library, Columbia University*).

p184 'one of the most numerous' and 'listened . . .' *The Columbian*, quoted by Odell.

p185 'with the earnestness . . .' *Old New York*.

p187 The letter from Ombrosi, dated 7 July 1822, is quoted in *Storia della letteratura italiana*.

p188 'The same thing . . .' July 1831. Quoted by Livingston.

p188 'As you know . . .' 4 April 1822 (*Reproduced by courtesy of the Oesterreichische Nationalbibliothek, Handschriftensammlung, Autogr. 42/76*).

p189 'in my opinion . . .' Letter to Colombo, 9 June 1832.

p190 'To the youngest, Faustina . . .' This last verse does not normally appear when the letter is quoted. It was, however, reproduced in a presentation booklet on the occasion of the marriage of Vittoria Morpurgo to Faustina's grandson, Luigi, by his three brothers (*Biblioteca Civica di Trieste*).

p191 'makeshifts adapted . . .' Mattfeld.

p191 'American audiences . . .' Sonneck, *Early Opera in America*.

p193 'exerted himself in vain . . .' Castil-Blaze, *Molière Musicien*, quoted by Jahn.

p193 'both a serious . . .' To Rossetti, 11 February 1829.

p193 'half worn out . . .' 1830, quoted by Mattfeld.

p193 'musical creations . . .' Ward.

p195 'I should love to know . . .' To Rossetti, 26 July 1828.

p195 'did more for the proprietors . . .' March 1819.

p196 'No one can be surprised . . .' *An Extract from the Life* . . .

p196 'My house is a little school . . .' 12 November 1827.

p197 'I began straight away . . .' Quoted in the 2nd edition of the *Memoirs*.

p197 'Read them all . . .' To Professor Samuel Jarvis, 23 November 1827 (*Rare Book and Manuscript Library, Columbia University*).

p198 'What ecstasy would someone . . .' *Storia della letteratura italiana*.

p199 The Dante lectures were published in the *New York Review and Athenaeum*, Vol i, 1825.

p199 'Live for the Muses . . .' Mathias' letter dated 11 August 1827, quoted in *Storia della letteratura*.

p200 Prescott's article, 'Italian Narrative Poetry', was published in October 1824.

p201 The *Antologia* articles were published in April and May 1828 (Tomo XXX, Fasc.88 and Fasc.89).

p202 'a collection of rubbish . . .' Letter to Rossetti, 26 July 1828.

p203 'as I imagine a Turk . . .' 26 July 1828.

p203 The *Osservatore Triestino* article was published on 15 January 1829.

p203 'In this I am like . . .' 20 June 1828.

Chapter XIV

p204 'when I lack the money . . .' 28 November 1828.

p205 The correspondence with Longfellow is in the Houghton Library, Harvard University.

p205 'Signor Daponte . . .' Letter to Professor Andrew Norton dated 6 February 1835. (A. H. Lograsso, *Rassegna Storica del Risorgimento*, quoted by Pagnini.)

p207 'the Americans love usury . . .' 18 May 1830.

p208 'It is many years . . .' 10 November 1828.

p208 'If ever it is the will of God . . .' 15 September 1827.

p209–10 'Our characters, our temperaments . . .' 19 May 1830.

p210 'I should indeed . . .' 30 September 1832.

p210 'When a man . . .' To Rossetti, 19 June 1829.

p211 'In 1828 he had become . . .' In a letter to Rossetti dated 30 February 1829 he remarked that he had done so 'a few months ago'.

p212 'It is impossible . . .' 9 June 1832.

p212 'The death of this angelic woman . . .' 18 March 1832 (*Reproduced by courtesy of the New York Historical Society*).

p212 'My husband . . .' Quoted in *Economia della vita umana*.

p212 'a true picture . . .' 1 August 1828.

p212 'But I fear . . .' 30 September 1832.

p213 'When you write of death . . .' 20 June (?) 1830.

p214 'I know that every singer . . .' and 'The Americans . . .' 1 August 1831, quoted in *Storia incredibile*.

p214 'the best . . .' *New York Mirror*, 3 January 1834.

p214 'And in farewell verses . . .' (undated) (*Reproduced by courtesy of Albi Rosenthal*).

p215 'No one is grateful ...' Letter dated 30 September 1834 (*Reproduced by courtesy of Albi Rosenthal*).

p215 'when you buy a horse ...' *Storia della letteratura.*

p217 'The whole interior ...' Ritter, *Music in America*, quoted by Mattfeld.

p217 'in its brief existence ...' White.

p217 'both of which savour ...' Hone's diary, quoted by Mattfeld.

p218 'Some of our citizens ...' Tuckerman.

p218 'stately nonagenarian ...' Francis.

p219 'I, who have imported ...' To Antonio Peremet (*Reproduced by courtesy of Albi Rosenthal*).

p219 'I! The creator ...' Undated letter to Bartolommeo Gamba.

p219 'the words of my great Joseph ...' To Rossetti, 31 December 1829.

p219 'No Italian ...' Tuckerman.

p221 'I am overwhelmed ...' 24 January 1837.

p221 'poor and beloved ...' 11 April 1838.

p222 'put his affairs ...' 12 September 1831.

p222 'Please have the goodness ...' 24 January 1837.

Note Regarding the Memoirs

The memoirs were not published in Italy until 1871, in the abridged version by Jacopo Bernardi (*Memorie di Lorenzo Da Ponte, e scritte vari in prosa e in poesia, Firenze*). Meanwhile a German translation had appeared, although this was also abridged: *Lorenzo Da Ponte, Memoiren, von ihm selbst in New York herausgegeben* (Stuttgart, 1847). A French version, *Mémoires d'un coureur d'aventures*, with a glowing preface by Lamartine but in a wretched translation, came out in Paris in 1860. The first complete Italian edition was published in 1915 in the Classici Italiani di Milano series for which Da Ponte had so much admiration. Not until 1929 did the memoirs become available in English: in that year translations came out on both sides of the Atlantic, in England in a condensed version by L. A. Sheppard and in the United States in a full edition by Elisabeth Abbott with annotations by Arthur Livingston. C. Pagnini, in *Scritti inediti di Domenico Rossetti* (Udine, 1944), provides very full bibliographical details of the various editions published both by Da Ponte and by other hands after his death.

Appendix

So much has been quoted in this book from Da Ponte's prose writings and letters, often in the nature of complaints, that it would be doing him an injustice not to quote also from his poetry. Here are two extracts from his Mozart operas; the first comes from *Le nozze di Figaro*, the second from *Così fan tutte*, in each case with a literal translation.

I. As a part of the plot to bamboozle the faithless Count Almaviva, Susanna has exchanged clothes with her mistress. Forsaking her usual no-nonsense mode of speech, she embarks on a delicious parody of the languishing airs in which an aristocratic lady might have expressed herself as she waited for her lover.

RECITATIVO:

Giunse alfin il momento	At last the moment has come
Che godrò senza affanno	When without reserve I shall rejoice
In braccio all'idol mio! Timide cure,	In the arms of my beloved; timid fears,
Uscite dal mio petto,	Flee from my breast,
A turbar non venite il mio diletto!	Come not to trouble my delight.
Oh, come par che all'amoroso foco	Oh, how the charms of this place,
L'amenità del loco,	Of the earth and the sky,
La terra e il ciel risponda!	Seem to respond to the flame of love!
Come la notte i furti miei seconda!	How the night favours my stealth!

ARIA:

Deh, vieni, non tardar, o gioia bella,	Oh come, do not tarry, oh lovely joy,
Vieni ove amore per goder t'appella,	Come where love calls you to rapture,
	While the torch of night shines not in the sky,
Finché non splende in ciel notturna face	
Finché l'aria è ancor bruna e il mondo tace.	While all is still dark and the world is silent.
	Here the stream murmurs, here the breeze is playing,
Qui mormora il ruscel, qui scherza l'aura	
Che col dolce sussurro il cor ristaura;	Restoring my heart with sweet whispers;
	Here the flowers are smiling and the grass is cool:
Qui ridono i fioretti e l'erba è fresca:	
Ai piaceri d'amor qui tutto adesca.	All is a snare to the pleasures of love.
	Come, my dearest; among these hidden trees
Vieni, ben mio: tra queste piante ascose	
Ti vo' la fronte incoronar di rose.	I will crown thy brow with roses.

II. This scene from *Così fan tutte* is a wonderful example of the consummate skill of Mozart and Da Ponte in taking off *opera seria*, and of the librettist's mastery of a complex rhyming

250

pattern. Ferrando and Guglielmo, as part of their plot to
seduce Fiordiligi and Dorabella, pretend to drink poison and
so arouse their pity.

FERRANDO E GUGLIELMO (*di dentro*)
Si mora, sì, si mora
Onde appagar le ingrate.

DON ALFONSO (*di dentro*)
C'è una speranza ancora;
Non fate, o Dei, non fate!

FIORDILIGI E DORABELLA
Stelle, che grida orribili!

FERRANDO E GUGLIELMO
Lasciatemi!

DON ALFONSO
Aspettate!
(*Ferrando e Guglielmo, portando ciascuno una
boccetta, entrano seguiti da Don Alfonso*)

FERRANDO E GUGLIELMO
L'arsenico mi liberi
Di tanta crudeltà!
(*Bevono e gittan via le boccette, nel voltarsi vedono
le due donne*)

FIORDILIGI E DORABELLA
Stelle, un velen fu quello?

DON ALFONSO
Veleno buono e bello,
Che ad essi in pochi istanti
La vita toglierà!

FIORDILIGI E DORABELLA
Il tragico spettacolo
Gelare il cor mi fa.

FERRANDO E GUGLIELMO
Barbare, avvicinatevi;
D'un disperato affetto
Mirate il triste effetto
E abbiate almen pietà.

TUTTI
Ah, che del sole il raggio
Fosco per me diventa!
Tremo le fibre, e l'anima
Par che mancar mi senta,
Nè può la lingua o il labbro
Accenti articolar!
(*Ferrando e Guglielmo cadono sopra i banchi
d'erba*)

FERRANDO AND GUGLIELMO (*Off-stage*)
Let us die, yes, let us die,
And so satisfy the ungrateful ones.

DON ALFONSO (*Off-stage*)
There is still hope;
Do not do it! Stay your hand!

FIORDILIGI AND DORABELLA
Oh heavens, what terrible cries!

FERRANDO AND GUGLIELMO
Leave me!

DON ALFONSO
Wait!
(*Enter Ferrando and Guglielmo, each carrying a
phial, followed by Don Alfonso*)

FERRANDO AND GUGLIELMO
May arsenic free me
From such cruelty!
(*They drink and fling the flasks away, then, turning,
see the two women*)

FIORDILIGI AND DORABELLA
Oh heavens, was that poison?

DON ALFONSO
Poison it was,
Which in a few moments
Will drain away their lives.

FIORDILIGI AND DORABELLA
The tragic spectacle
Turns my heart to ice.

FERRANDO AND GUGLIELMO
Draw near, cruel ones,
Marvel at the sad result
Of a desperate love,
And at least pity us.

ALL
How the sun's rays
Grow dark before my eyes!
I tremble, the fibres of my very being
Seem to fail,
Nor can my lips or my tongue
Utter any sound!
(*Ferrando and Guglielmo fall on to a grassy bank*)

DON ALFONSO
Giacchè a morir vicini
Sono quei meschinelli,
Pietade almeno a quelli
Cercate di mostrar.

FIORDILIGI E DORABELLA
Gente, accorrete, gente!
Nessuno, oddio, ci sente!
Despina!

DESPINA (di dentro)
Chi mi chiama?

FIORDILIGI E DORABELLA
Despina!

DESPINA (entrando)
Cosa vedo!
Morti i meschini io credo
O prossimi a spirar!

DON ALFONSO
Ah, che purtroppo è vero!
Furenti, disperati,
Si sono avvelenati!
Oh, amore singolar!

DESPINA
Abbandonar i miseri
Saria per voi vergogna.
Soccorrerli bisogna

FIORDILIGI, DORABELLA E DON ALFONSO
Cosa possiam mai far?

DESPINA
Di vita ancor dàn segno;
Colle pietose mani
Fate un po' lor sostegno
(a Don Alfonso)
E voi con me correte;
Un medico, un antidoto
Voliamo a ricercar.
(Despina e Don Alfonso partono)

FIORDILIGI E DORABELLA
Dei, che cimento è questo!
Evento più funesto
Non si potea trovar!

FERRANDO E GUGLIELMO (da sè)
Più bella commediola
Non si potea trovar!
(ad alta voce)
Ah!

DON ALFONSO
Since the poor wretches
Are on the point of death,
At least try to show them some pity.

FIORDILIGI AND DORABELLA
Help, someone, bring help!
Oh heavens, no one hears us!
Despina!

DESPINA (Off-stage)
Who wants me?

FIORDILIGI AND DORABELLA
Despina!

DESPINA (Enters)
What do I see!
I believe the poor wretches are dead,
Or near to dying!

DON ALFONSO
Alas, it is true!
Frantic, desperate,
They have taken poison.
Oh, strange love!

DESPINA
To abandon the poor unfortunate creatures
Would be a shameful act.
You must save them.

FIORDILIGI AND DORABELLA
But how?

DESPINA
They still show signs of life;
With pitying hands
Give them a little support.
(To Don Alfonso)
Come, hasten with me;
We will retun
With a doctor and an antidote.
(Exit Despina and Don Alfonso)

FIORDILIGI AND DORABELLA
Heavens, what a test!
A more dreadful event
It would be impossible to imagine!

FERRANDO AND GUGLIELMO (Aside)
A prettier little farce
It would be impossible to imagine!
(Aloud)
Ah!

FIORDILIGI E DORABELLA (*stando lontano dagli amanti*)
Sospiran gl'infelici!

FIORDILIGI
Che facciamo?

DORABELLA
Tu che dici?

FIORDILIGI
In momenti
Sì dolenti
Chi portriali abbandonar?

DORABELLA (*accostandosi un poco*)
Che figure interessanti!

FIORDILIGI (*c.s.*)
Possiam farci un poco avanti.

DORABELLA
Ha freddissima la testa.

FIORDILIGI
Fredda fredda è ancora questa.

DORABELLA
Ed il polso?

FIORDILIGI
Io non gliel' sento.

DORABELLA
Questo batte lento lento.

FIORDILIGI E DORABELLA
Ah, se tarda ancor l'aita,
Speme più non v'è di vita!

FERRANDO E GUGLIELMO (*sottovoce*)
Più domestiche e trattabili
Sono entrambe diventate;
Sta a veder che lor pietade
Va in amore a terminar.

FIORDILIGI E DORABELLA
Poverini! La lor morte
Mi farebbe lagrimar.

I suddetti; Despina travestita da medico, Don Alfonso

DON ALFONSO
Eccovi il medico,
Signore belle!

FIORDILIGI AND DORABELLA (*Keeping their distance*)
The unlucky creatures are sighing.

FIORDILIGI
What shall we do?

DORABELLA
What do you say?

FIORDILIGI
At a time
Of such distress
Who could abandon them?

DORABELLA (*Drawing a little closer*)
What interesting faces they have!

FIORDILIGI (*Doing the same*)
Let's go a little closer.

DORABELLA
His head is very cold.

FIORDILIGI
This one's too is as cold as ice.

DORABELLA
And his pulse?

FIORDILIGI
I can't feel it.

DORABELLA
This one's hardly beating.

FIORDILIGI AND DORABELLA
Oh, if help is much longer in coming
There will no longer be any hope of life.

FERRANDO AND GUGLIELMO (*Sotto voce*)
They have grown tamer
And more amenable;
We shall see whether their pity
Ends in love

FIORDILIGI AND DORABELLA
Poor things! Their death
Would grieve me.

(*Enter Don Alfonso and Despina disguised as a doctor*)

DON ALFONSO
Here is the doctor,
Charming ladies.

FERRANDO E GUGLIELMO (*fra loro*)
Despina in maschera!
Che trista pelle!

DESPINA
'Salvete, amabiles
Bonae puellae!'

FIORDILIGI E DORABELLA
Parla un linguaggio
Che non sappiamo.

DESPINA
Come comandano,
Dunque, parliamo.
So il greco e l'arabo,
So il turco e il vandalo;
Lo svevo e il tartaro
So ancor parlar.

DON ALFONSO
Tanti linguaggi
Per sè conservi;
Quei miserabili
Per ora osservi!
Preso hanno il tossico;
Che si può far?

FIORDILIGI E DORABELLA
Signor dottore,
Che si può far?

DESPINA (*toccando il polso e la fronte all'uno ed
all'altro*)
Saper bisognami
Pria la cagione
E quinci l'indole
Della pozione;
Se calda o frigida,
Se poca o molta,
Se in un volta
Ovvero in più.

FIORDILIGI, DORABELLA E DON ALFONSO
Preso han l'arsenico,
Signor dottore;
Qui dentro il bevvero.
La causa è amore
Ed in un sorso
Sel mandar giù.

DESPINA
Non vi affannate,
Non vi turbate:
Ecco una prova
Di mia virtù

FERRANDO AND GUGLIELMO (*Aside*)
Despina in disguise!
What a sad outfit!

DESPINA
'Salvete, amabiles
Bonae puellae!'

FIORDILIGI AND DORABELLA
He speaks a language
We don't understand.

DESPINA
As you command,
Then, we will speak.
I know Greek and Arabic,
Turkish and the Vandal tongue;
Swedish and Tartar
I know also.

DON ALFONSO
You may keep all these languages
To yourself;
Just now observe
These wretched men:
They have taken poison;
What can be done?

FIORDILIGI AND DORABELLA
Signor doctor,
What can be done?

DESPINA (*Feeling their pulses and foreheads*)

First I must know
The reason,
And then the nature
Of the potion;
Whether hot or cold,
Whether much or little,
Whether at one gulp
Or in several.

FIORDILIGI, DORABELLA AND DON ALFONSO
They have taken arsenic,
Signor doctor;
They drank it here.
The cause is love,
And they drained it
At one draught.

DESPINA
Don't be worried,
Don't distress yourselves;
Here is a proof
Of my skill.

FIORDILIGI E DORABELLA
Egli ha di un ferro
La man fornita.

DESPINA
(*Tocca con un pezzo di calamita la testa ai finti infermi e striscia dolcemente i loro corpi per lungo*)
Questo è quel pezzo
Di calamita;
Pietra mesmerica,
Ch'ebbe l'origine
Nell'Alemagna,
Che poi si celebre
Là in Francia fu.

FIORDILIGI, DORABELLA E DON ALFONSO
Come si muovono,
Torcono, scuotono!
In terra il cranio
Presto percuotono.

DESPINA
Ah, lor la fronte
Tenete su.

FIORDILIGI E DORABELLA
Eccoci pronte!
(*Metton la mano alla fronte dei due amanti*)

DESPINA
Tenete forte.
Corraggio! Or liberi
Siete da morte.

FIORDILIGI, DORABELLA E DON ALFONSO
Attorno guardano,
Forze riprendono.
Ah, questo medico
Vale un Perù!

FERRANDO E GUGLIELMO (*sorgendo in pedi*)
Dove son? Che loco è questo?
Chi è colui? Color chi sono?
Son di Giove innanzi al trono?
Sei tu Palla o Citerea?
(*Ferrando a Fiordiligi e Guglielmo a Dorabella*)
No, tu sei l'alma mia dea!
Ti ravviso
Al dolce viso
E alla man ch'or ben conosco
E che sola è il mio tesor.
(*Abbracciano le amanti teneramente e bacian loro la mano*)

FIORDILIGI AND DORABELLA
He's got
A magnet.

DESPINA
(*Touches the heads of the feigned invalids with a magnet and gently draws it down their bodies*)
This is a piece
Of magnet;
The philsopher's stone
Which had its origin
In Germany,
And which is now celebrated
In France.

FIORDILIGI, DORABELLA AND DON ALFONSO
How they are moving,
Twisting about, shaking!
Their heads are almost
Banging on the ground!

DESPINA
Ah, you must
Hold their heads steady.

FIORDILIGI AND DORABELLA
Here we are!
(*They put their hands on the foreheads of the two lovers*)

DESPINA
Hold tight!
Courage! And now you are
Freed from death.

FIORDILIGI, DORABELLA AND DON ALFONSO
They are looking round
And regaining strength.
Ah, this doctor
Is worth all the gold in Peru!

FERRANDO AND GUGLIELMO (*Getting to their feet*)
Where am I? What place is this?
Who is this man? Who are these people?
Am I before Jove's throne?
Are you Pallas or Cytherea?
(*Ferrando to Fiordiligi and Guglielmo to Dorabella*)
No, you are my heart's delight!
I recognise you
By that sweet face,
And by this hand which I know so well,
And which alone is my treasure.
(*They embrace the women tenderly and kiss their hands*)

DESPINA E DON ALFONSO
Sono effetti ancor del tosco;
Non abbiate alcun timor.

FIORDILIGI E DORABELLA
Sarà ver, ma tante smorfie
Fanno torto al nostro onor.

FERRANDO E GUGLIELMO
(*a Fiordiligi e Dorabella*)
Per pietà, bell'idol mio!
Volgi a me le luci liete.

FIORDILIGI E DORABELLA
Più resister non poss'io!

DESPINA E DON ALFONSO
In poch'ore, lo vedrete,
Per virtù del magnetismo
Finirà quel parossismo,
Torneranno al primo umor.

FERRANDO E GUGLIELMO (*da sè*)
Dalla voglia ch'ho di ridere
Il polmon mi scoppia or or.
(*forte*)
Dammi un bacio, o mio tesoro;
Un sol bacio, o qui mi moro.

FIORDILIGI E DORABELLA
Stelle, un bacio?

DESPINA
Secondate
Per effetto di bontate.

FIORDILIGI E DORABELLA
Ah, che troppo si richiede
Da una fida, onesta amante!
Oltraggiata è la mia fede,
Oltraggiato è questo cor!

DESPINA, FERRANDO, GUGLIELMO E DON
ALFONSO (*ognuno da sè*)
Un quadretto più giocondo
Non si vide in tutto il mondo;
Quel che più mi fa da ridere
È quell'ira e quel furor.

FIORDILIGI E DORABELLA
Disperati,
Attossicati,
Ite al diavol quanti siete!
Tardi inver vi pentirete
Se più cresce il mio furor!

DESPINA AND DON ALFONSO
It is still the effect of the poison;
Don't be frightened.

FIORDILIGI AND DORABELLA
That may be so, but such simpering faces
Wrong our honour.

FERRANDO AND GUGLIELMO
(*To Fiordiligi and Dorabella*)
For pity's sake, dear heart,
Turn your lovely eyes on me.

FIORDILIGI AND DORABELLA
I can resist no longer.

DESPINA AND DON ALFONSO
In a few hours, you will see,
By virtue of the magnetism,
The paroxysm will end,
And they will return to their original
    humour.

FERRANDO AND GUGLIELMO (*Aside*)
I want to laugh so much
That I shall soon burst.
(*Aloud*)
Give me a kiss, my treasure,
One kiss only, or I shall die.

FIORIDLIGI AND DORABELLA
Good heavens, a kiss?

DESPINA
Do what they ask,
Out of charity.

FIORDILIGI AND DORABELLA
Oh, they are asking too much
From a chaste and faithful lover!
It outrages my loyalty,
It outrages my heart!

DESPINA, FERRANDO, GUGLIELMO AND DON
ALFONSO (*Aside*)
A more comical picture
Is not to be seen in all the world;
What makes me laugh most
Is their anger and fury.

FIORDILIGI AND DORABELLA
Desperate,
Poisoned,
Go to the devil the whole lot of you:
You'll be sorry for it later
If you make me angrier still!

FERRANDO E GUGLIELMO (*da sè*)
Ma non so se vera o finta
Sia quell'ira e quel furor,
Nè vorrei che tanto foco
Terminasse in quel d'amor.

DESPINA E DON ALFONSO (*da sè*)
Io so ben che tanto foco
Cangerassi in quel d'amor.

FERRANDO AND GUGLIELMO (*Aside*)
But I don't know
Whether their anger and fury are real or
    feigned,
Nor should I like such fire
To end in the fire of love.

DESPINA AND DON ALFONSO (*Aside*)
I know quite well that such fire
Will change into the fire of love.

Bibliography

Published Material

Almanacco diocesano di Ceneda, 1842 (Ceneda, 1841)

Anderson, Emily (translator and editor): *The Letters of Mozart and His Family* (London, 1938)

Anon: *Breve Notizia dell'opera buffa, intitulata La‑ scuola de'maritati* (Lisbon, 1795)

Anti-da Ponte (Vienna, 1791)

Arnold, Dennis: *The New Oxford Companion to Music* (Oxford, 1983)

Badini, C. F.: *Nanetta e Lubino* (London, 1769)

Bechevolo, Rino, and Sartori, Basilio: *Ceneda: La cattedrale e i suoi vecchi oratori* (Vittorio Veneto, 1978)

Bergh, Herman Van den: *Giambattista Casti (1724–1803): L'Homme et l'Oeuvre* (Amsterdam, 1951)

Bernardi, Jacopo: *Cenni storici intorno la Chiesa e Diocesi di Ceneda* ('Almanacco diocesano di Ceneda per l'anno 1842', Ceneda)

Bertati, G.: *Il Matrimonio Segreto* (London, 1796)
Capriccio Drammatico (London, 1794)
Il dissoluto punito (1787)

Binni, Walter: *Il settecento letterario* ('Storia della letteratura Italiana' Vol. VI, Milan, 1968)

Boas, H.: *Lorenzo Da Ponte als Theaterdichter* (Sammelbaende der Internationale Musikgesellschaft, Heft 2, Leipzig, 1914)

Bonora, Ettore (ed): *Letterati, memorialisti e viaggiatori del settecento* ('La letteratura italiana. Storia e testi', Milan, Naples, 1952)

Bright, J. Frank: *Joseph II* (London, 1915)

Brown, Horatio: *Studies in Venetian History* (London, 1907)

Burney, Charles: *Memoirs of the Life and Writings of the Abate Metastasio* (London, 1796)
The Present State of Music in France and Italy (London, 1771)
The Present State of Music in Germany, the Netherlands and United Provinces (London, 1773)

Bushnell, Howard: *Maria Malibran: A Biography of the Singer* (London 1979)

Bustico, Guido: *Il Culto di Dante in America. Il precursore.* ('La parola e il libro', Anno XIV, April 1931)

Caron de Beaumarchais, P. A.: *Tarare* (1787)

Centelli, A.: *Gli avventurieri della letteratura* ('Natura ed arte', No. 21, Vittorio Veneto, 1893)

Cesarano, E. A.: *Il poeta di teatro di Filippo Pananti* (Padua, 1896)

'Cesigoni, Pompeo' (Guiseppe Monico): *A Paperio Taverna d'Assalerno* (Treviso, 1819)

Colombani, Alfredo: *L'opera italiana nel secolo XIX* (Milan, 1900)

Curiel, C. L.: *Trieste settecentesca* (Naples, 1922)

Curiel, C. L., Gugitz, G. and Ravà, A. (eds): *Giacomo Casanova: Patrizi e avventurieri, dame e ballerine* (Milan, 1930)

Damerini, Gino: *Casanova a Venezia* (Turin, 1967)

D'Egville, J., and Gallerini, J.: *Memorandum, August 1799. King's Theatre (Damiani's Contract)*

Dent, E. J.: *Mozart's Operas* (London 1960)

Deutsch, O. E.: *Mozart: A Documentary Biography* (London, 1965)

Dittersdorf, Karl von: *Autobiography* (London, 1896)

Doane, J. (ed): *A Musical Directory for the Year 1794*

Ebers, John: *Seven Years of the King's Theatre* (London, 1828)

English National Opera Guide to *Così fan tutte*: Essays by Brian Trowell, H. C. Robbins Landon and John Stone. (London, 1983)

Fassetta, D. Camillo: *Storia Populare di Ceneda* (Vittorio Veneto, 1917)

Ferrari, Giacomo Gotifredo: *Aneddoti piacevoli e interessanti* (London, 1830)

Fétis F. J.: *Essai sur la musique en Angleterre* ('Revue des Deux Mondes', Vol. III, Series II, 1833)

Fiske, Roger: *The Operas of Stephen Storace* (Proceedings of the Royal Musical Association, 86th Session, 1959–1960)

FitzLyon, April: *The Libertine Librettist* (London, 1955)

Francis, John W.: *Old New York* (New York, 1858)

Fubino, Mario, and Bonora, Ettore: *Pietro Metastasio, Opere* (Milan, 1968)

Gaeta, Franco: *Un ignorato episodio della vita dell'abate Lorenzo Da Ponte* ('Giornale storico della Letteratura Italiana', Vol. CXXXI, Turin, 1954)

Gamba, Bartolommeo: Article on Lorenzo Da Ponte ('Biografia degli Italiani illustri nelle scienze, lettere ed arti del secolo XVIII. Ed. E. de Tipaldi, Vol. VIII, Venice, 1841)

Goede, C. A. G.: *A Foreigner's Opinion of England* (London, 1821)

Goldin, Daniela: *Da Ponte Librettista fra Goldoni e Casti* ('Giornale Storico della Litteratura Italiana', n. 503, 3° trim., Turin, 1981)

Goldoni, Carlo: *Memoirs* (New York, 1926)
Commedie (Florence, 1733–55)

Gozzi, Carlo: *Memoirs of Count Carlo Gozzi* (London, 1890)

Grandi, T.: *Le gelosie villane* (1784)

Guarini, G. B.: *Il pastor fido* (Venice, 1750)

Guillard, N. F.: *Arvire et Evelina* (Paris, 1779)
Iphigénie en Tauride (1779)

Hazlitt, W. C.: *The Venetian Republic* (London, 1900)

Heriot, Angus: *The Castrati in Opera* (London, 1956)

Hildesheimer, W.: *Mozart* (London, 1983)

Hogan, C. B.: *The London Stage, 1660–1800* (Illinois, 1968)

Hogarth, George: *Memoirs of the Opera in Italy, France, Germany and England* (London, 1851)

Holden's Triennial Directory

Imperatori, U. E.: *Dizionario di Italiani all'estero* (Milan, 1956)

Jahn, Otto: *Life of Mozart*, trs. P. D. Townsend (London, 1882)

Kelly, Michael: *Reminiscences* (Oxford, 1975)

King's Theatre cuttings book, 1757–1829

Koch, Theodore W.: *Dante in America* (XV Annual Report of the Dante Society, Boston, 1896)

Krehbiel, H. E.: *Music and Manners from Pergolesi to Beethoven* (London, 1898)
Chapters of Opera (New York, 1909)

'A Lady of Rank': *Venice under the Yoke of France and of Austria* (London, 1824)

Landon, H. C. Robbins: *The Collected Correspondence and London Note-books of Joseph Haydn* (London, 1959)

Lazare, Christopher: *That Was New York: Da Ponte, The Bearer of Culture* ('New Yorker', 1944)

Lecaldano, Paolo: *Tre Libretti per Mozart* (Milan, 1956)

Liberatore, Umberto: *Profili storici* (Rome, 1936)

Livigni, F.: *La frascatana* (1781)

Loewenberg, Alfred: *Annals of Opera 1597–1940* (London, 1978)
Lorenzo Da Ponte in London: A Bibliographical Account of His Literary Activity, 1793–1804 ('Music Review', Vol. IV, No. 3, 1943)
Some Stray Notes on Mozart ('Music and Letters', Vol. XXIV, 1943)

The London Book Trade 1775–1800 (London, 1977)
London Directory (of Merchants & Traders of London)

Macartney, C. A.: *The Hapsburg Empire 1790–1918* (London, 1969)
Manzini, Guido: *L'arte della stampa a Gorizia nel secolo XVIII* ('Studi Goriziani', Vol. XIV, Gorizia, 1935)
Marcello, Benedetto: *Il teatro alla moda* (Venice, c. 1720)
Marchesan, Angelo: *Della vita e delle opere di Lorenzo Da Ponte* (Treviso, 1900)
Marraro, Howard R.: *Documents on Da Ponte's Italian Library* (Publications of the Modern Language Association of America, Vol. LVIII, No. 1, part 3, New York, 1943)
Masi, Ernesto: *Studi e ritratti* (Bologna, 1881)
Mathias, T. J.: *Canzoni e prose toscane* (London, 1808)
   Pandolfo attonito! or Lord Galloway's Poetical Lamentation on the removal of the arm-chairs from the pit at the Opera House (London, 1800)
Mattfeld, Julius: *A Handbook of American Operatic Premières 1731–1962* (Detroit, 1963)
   A Hundred Years of Grand Opera in New York, 1825–1925 (Detroit, 1927)
Maxted, Ian: *The London Book Trades 1775–1800* (London, 1977)
Mazzoni, Guido: *Abati, soldati, autori, attori, del settecento* (Bologna, 1924)
   'Lorenzo Da Ponte' ('Rivista d'Italia', No. 9, anno III, Rome, 1900)
Meissner, Alfred: *Rococo-Bilder* (Gumbinnen, 1871)
Michtner, Otto: *Das Alte Burgtheater als Opernbühne* (Vienna, 1970)
   Der Fall Abbé Da Ponte (Mitteilungen des Oesterreichischen Staatsarchiv, 19 Band, Vienna, 1966)
Moberly, R. B.: *Three Mozart Operas* (London, 1967)
Molmenti, Pompeo: *Epistolari veneziani del secolo XVIII* (Milan-Palermo-Naples, 1914)
   Carteggi Casanoviani: Lettere del patrizio Zaguri a Giac. Casanova (Milan, 1916, 1918)
   (ed): *Lettere inedite del Patrizio Zaguri, ecc.* (Venice, 1910–11)
   Venice: Its Individual Growth from the Earliest Beginnings to the Fall of the Republic (London, 1906)
Monnier, Philip: *Venice in the Eighteenth Century* (London, 1900)
Montani, G.: 'Antologia giornale di Scienza, Lettere e Arti', No. 88 (Florence, 1828)
Mosel, I. F. von: *Ueber das Leben und die Werke des Anton Salieri* (Vienna, 1827)
Mount Edgcumbe, Earl: *Musical Reminiscences* (London, 1834)
Muratti, Spartaco: *Vecchio Friuli* (Capodistria, 1921)

Nalbach, Daniel: *The King's Theatre 1704–1867* (London, 1972)

'Nemesini, Abate Vittorio': *Il Tributo dalla coglionatura* (London, 1793)

Nettl, Paul: *Casanova und Seine Zeit* (Esslingen, 1949)
  Mozart in Böhmen (Prag-Karlin, 1938)

Newman, Ernest: *More Opera Nights* (London, 1954)

Nicolino, Fausto: *La vera ragione della fuga di Lorenzo Da Ponte da Venezia* ('Archivio storico italiano', Anno LXXVIII, Serie VII, Vol. XIV, Florence, 1930)

Odell, G. C. D.: *Annals of the New York Stage* (New York, 1927)

Olschki, Leonardo: *Lorenzo Da Ponte libraio e bibliofilo* ('La Bibliofilia', Anno VIII, March-June, 1906)

O'Reilly, R. B.: *An authentic narrative of the principal circumstances relating to the Opera-house in the Hay-market* (London, 1791)

Orsi, Piero Sandro: *Il Bando da Venezia di Lorenzo Da Ponte* ('Ateneo Veneto', Luglio-Dicembre, Vol. 136, No. 2, Venice, 1952)

Osborne, Charles: *The Complete Operas of Mozart* (London, 1978)

Pagnini, Cesare: *Lorenzo Da Ponte e il contribuito di Trieste alla propaganda italiana in America* (Parenzo, 1934)
  Bibliografia Dapontiana (Trieste, 1960)

Palomba, G.: *La Molinara* (1809)

Pananti, Filippo: *Scritti minori inedit o sparsi* (Florence, 1897)
  Il poeta di teatro (London, 1808)

Petty, Frederick C.: *Italian Opera in London, 1760–1800* (Michigan, 1980)

Pezzana, Angelo: *Lettere dell'Abate Michele Colombo* (1856)
  Alquanti cenni intorno alla vita di Michele Colombo (Parma, 1838)

Piccoli, Lucio di: *Autunno musicale trevigiano* (Treviso, 1982)

Picture of London for 1805, The (London, 1805)

Pohl, C. F.: *Mozart und Haydn in London* (Vienna, 1867)

Potamkin, H. A.: *Father of the Italian Opera in America* ('Jewish Tribune', November, 1928)

Prescott, W. H.: *Italian Narrative Poetry* ('North American Review', October, 1824)

Ravà, Aldo (ed): *Lettere di donne a Giacomo Casanova* (Milan, 1912)

Ravà, Aldo, and Gugitz, Gustav (eds): *Giac. Casanovas Briefwechsel* (Munich, 1913)

Robinson, M. F.: *Opera Before Mozart* (London, 1966)

Rosenthal, H., and Warrack, John: *The Concise Oxford Dictionary of Opera* (London, 1980)

Rosselli, John: *The Opera Industry in Italy from Cimarosa to Verdi* (Cambridge, 1984)

Rossetti, Domenico: *Scritti inediti*, ed. Cesare Pagnini (Udine, 1944)

Roth, Cecil: *The History of the Jews of Italy* (Philadelphia, 1946)

Rushton, J.; *Don Giovanni* (Cambridge, 1981)

Russo, J. L.: *Lorenzo Da Ponte, Poet and Adventurer* (New York, 1922)

Sadie, Stanley (ed): *The New Grove Dictionary of Music and Musicians* (London, 1982)
Mozart (London, 1982)

Seingalt, Chevalier de: *History of My Life* (London, 1967)

Sheppard, F. H. W. (ed): *Survey of London*
Vol. XXIX 'The Parish of St James Westminster', Part One; South of Piccadilly (London 1960)
Vol. XXXI Part Two; North of Piccadilly (London, 1960)

Smith, William, C.: *The Italian Opera and Contemporary Ballet in London 1789–1820* (London, 1955)

Smollett, Tobias: *Travels through France and Italy* (London, 1766)

Sonneck, O. G. T.: *Catalogue of Opera Librettos printed before 1800* (Washington, 1914)
Early Opera in America (New York, 1914)

Steptoe, A.: *The Sources of Così fan Tutte: A Reappraisal* ('Music and Letters', lxii, 1951)

Struble, George G.: *Lorenzo Da Ponte: Our Neglected Genius* (Proceedings: Northumberland County Historical Society, 1948)

Tasso, Torquato: *Arminta* (Venice, 1769)

Taylor, John: *Records of My Life* (London, 1832)

Taylor, Mr [William]: *A Concise Statement of transactions and circumstances respecting the King's Theatre, in the Haymarket, by Mr Taylor, the Proprietor* (London, 1791)

Thespian Dictionary, 1805

Thurn, R. Payer von: *Joseph II als Theaterdirektor* (Vienna, 1920)

Timperley, C. H.: *Dictionary of Printers* (London, 1839)

Todd, W. B.: *A Dictionary of Printers and Others in Allied Trades, London & Vicinity* (London, 1972)

Toffoli, Aldo; *Il ritorno di Lorenzo Da Ponte a Ceneda nel 1798* ('Il Flaminio', Numero 1, December, 1979)
Inediti dapontiani ('Il Flaminio', Numero 2, December, 1980)

Torri, Alessandro: *Cenni biografici di Lorenzo Da Ponte* ('Nuovo giornale di letterati', n. 102, Nov–Dec, 1838)

Tranchini, Eugenio: *Gli Ebri a Vittorio Veneto dal XV° al XX° secolo* (Vittorio Veneto, 1979)

Tuckerman, H. T.: *Lorenzo Da Ponte* ('Putnam's Magazine', New Series, Second Volume, July–December, 1868)

Vélez de Guevara, Luis: *La luna de la Sierra* (1652)
Veritas: *Opera House: A Review of this Theatre* (privately printed, 1820)
Vigée-Le Brun, Marie-Anne Elizabeth: *Memoirs* (London, 1926)
Voltaire: *Semiramis* (Paris, 1749)
  Merope (Amsterdam, 1744)

Wangermann, Ernst: *The Austrian Achievement 1700–1800* (London, 1973)
Ward, S.: *Sketch of the life of Lorenzo Da Ponte of Ceneda* ('New York Mirror', 1838)
Waters, E.: *The Opera Glass* (London, 1808)
White, R. G.: *Opera in New York* ('Century, A Popular Quarterly', Vols 23–24, 1882)
Williamson, Edward: *Bernardo Tasso* (1951)

Zangiacomi, Pino: *Storia del Seminario di Vittorio Veneto* (Treviso, 1954)
Ziliotto, Bacio: *Lorenzo Da Ponte e Giuseppe de Coletti* ('Archeografo triestino', Serie IV, Vol. I–II, Trieste, 1938–1939)
Zorzanello, Pietro: *Lorenzo Da Ponte contro Napoleone* ('Ateneo Veneto', Anno CXXVI, Vol. 118, N. 4, 1935)

Morning Chronicle, 1794–1805

The Times, 1794–1805

Unpublished Material

Vittorio Veneto: Archivio parochiale della chiesa cattedrale
  Archivio della curia vescovile
  Archivio del seminario vescovile
Venice: Archivio di Stato di Venezia:
    Esecutori contro la bestemmia
    Inquisitori di stato
Treviso: Francesco Fapanni: *Degli Scrittori Trevigiani*, Vol. IV
Vienna: Oesterreichische Nationalbibliothek:
    Musiksammlung
    Handschriftensammlung
    Haus-Hof-und Staatsarchiv
    Diaries of Count Zinzendorf

London: Papers at Public Record Office:
  Bankruptcy Docket Books, Registers and Minute Books
  Moberly, R. B.: *Mozart's 'Così fan tutte'*
New York: Papers of Gino Carlo Speranza (Public Library)
  Papers of Hon. Gulian C. Verplanck (New York Historical Society)
  Columbia University: Records of the Trustees Committee on Books.

Index

Accademia degli Arcadi, 38
Alfieri, Vittorio, 58, 156, 176, 197, 199
Allegranti, Maddalena, 157–8
Anderson, Henry James, 198, 212, 222;
    marries Fanny Da P, 188, 211; praises Da
    P's cataloguing, 199
Anfossi, Pasquale, 35, 194
Angiola *see* Tiepolo, Angiola
Angioletta *see* Bellaudi, Angioletta
Anti-Da Ponte, 111
Antologia of Florence, 104, 119, 201, 203
Ariosto, Lodovico: *Orlando furioso*, 159, 161
Auersperg, Prince von, 105–6

Badini, Carlo Francesco, 131–2, 133, 134, 143
Bagioli, 215, 222; *Hymn to America*, 215n
Baglioni, Antonio, 206
Banti, Brigida, 145, 156, 157, 159n, 160;
    engaged for King's Theatre, 139–42; Vigée-
    Le Brun on, 140; and William Taylor,
    146–9; has her twelfth child, 158; leaves
    England, 166
Barbarigo, Agostino, 125
Barbarigo, Pietro, 33–4, 125
Barnabotti, 14–15, 27, 31
Bassi, Luigi, 88
Beaumarchais, Pierre Augustin Caron de: *Le
    mariage de Figaro*, 66, 68–9, 87; *Tarare*, 80–1,
    93–4
Bedford, Duke of, 132
Bellaudi, Angioletta, 28–34 *passim*, 84, 152,
    154–5
Bellaudi, Carlo, 28–34 *passim*, 154–5
Bellaudi, Laura, 29
Bellini, Vincenzo: *Il pirata*, 214
Bene, Adriana Francesca del *see* Gabrieli,
    Adriana Francesca del Bene
Bene, Luigi del: marries Adriana Gabrieli
    ('La Ferrarese'), 83 and n; and papal
    consulship, 112, 123–4; Da P betrays,
    124–5, 127
Benucci, Francesco, 46, 98, 113
Bertati, Giovanni, 63, 112, 131, 195n; and *Il
    ricco d'un giorno*, 52; appointed poet to
    Burgtheater, 123; Da P visits, 127; *Don
    Giovanni* (Gazzaniga), 84, 92, 139
Bianchi, Francesco: *Semiramide*, 141–2, 165;

Antigona, 145; *Il consiglio imprudente*, 149,
    165; *Merope*, 150; *Cinna*, 150; *Armida*, 166
bilancia teatrale, La, 133
Billington, Elizabeth, 165–7 *passim*, 171, 196
Bishop, (Sir) Henry Rowley, 191, 193
Bland, Maria Teresa, 196
Boetzelaer, General van den, 128, 134
Bonaiuti, Serafino, 145, 164–5
Bonaparte, Joseph, ex-King of Spain, 189,
    192, 208
Bonaparte, Napoleon, 152–4, 159, 208
Bondini, Caterina, 88–91 *passim*
Bondini, Pasquale, 88–91 *passim*
Bortoluzzi, Dom Pietro, 6
Bossange (Paris booksellers), 188
Braham, John, 146, 150, 167; in *Una cosa rara*,
    171; in *Don Giovanni*, 196
Brigido, Count Pompeo, 118, 122, 202
Brunati, Gaetano: *Il Bertoldo*, 80
'Buranello, Il' (Baldassare Galuppi), 194
    and n
Burgtheater, 46, 62, 106, 111, 195; repertory
    system at, 58; dismissal of Italian company,
    95–8; and Joseph II's illness, 103; intrigues
    at, 107–9, 114–16; Da P's plan for, 122,
    214; Da P's libretti for, 171; *see also* under
    Da Ponte, Lorenzo
Burney, Charles, 26; on music in Venice, 14;
    on Casti, 53; on Adriana Gabrieli, 14, 83
Bussani, Dorotea, 108, 119, 122
Bussani, Francesco, 111, 116, 119, 122; and
    Le nozze di Figaro, 67; Da P identifies as
    enemy, 108; spreads slander about Da P,
    109 and n
Byron, Lord: *The Prophecy of Dante*, 186–7

caffe degl' Italiani, 130, 158–9, 246
caffe de' letterati, 15
Càgliari of Altivòle, Abbé, 6
'Calliope', Da P's, 81, 105, 117, 122
Calvesi, Vincenzo, 111, 113
Caroline of Brunswick, Princess of Wales
    (*later* Queen of England), 145, 150, 163,
    184
Casanova da Seingalt, Giovanni Jacopo
    (Giacomo), 26, 37, 104, 118;

correspondence with Zaguri, 24, 83, 125, 129, 133; on Casti, 52–3; and Joseph II, 53n; and Da P in Vienna, 54, 55; and *Don Giovanni* (Mozart), 85–92 *passim*; Da P's letters to, 117, 131, 132–5; advice on England, 130–1, 147; and Maddalena Allegranti, 157; *I bei capelli di Silvia*, 54

Casati, Marco Antonio, 183–4

Casti, Abbé Giovanni Battista, 48, 77, 126; Da P's rhyming letter to, 51, 70; Casanova and Burney on, 52–3; intrigues against Da P, 54, 56–7, 71; and *Il burbero di buon cuore*, 57, 59; and *Le nozze di Figaro*, 66–8; Da P on, 70–1, 89, 194; and *Una cosa rara*, 76, 77; appointed court poet, 123; dies, 159; *Il rè Teodoro in Venezia*, 53, 154; *Prima la musica e poi le parole*, 71–2, 96n; *Poema tartaro*, 72; *Gli animali parlanti*, 159

castrati, 146 and n

Catherine, Empress of Russia, 72, 89

Cavalieri, Catarina, 107

cavalieri serventi, 13 and n, 18

Cesarotti, Melchiore, 27

Cimarosa, Domenico, 35; *L'ape musicale*, 98; *Il matrimonio segreto*, 138–9; *Il capriccio drammatico*, 139, 165; *La prova dell'opera*, 139; *La serva padrona*, 142

Classici Italiani di Milano, 181 and n

Clossey, Louisa *see* Da Ponte, Louisa

Clossey, Matilda (Da P's granddaughter), 179, 189, 196n, 212–3, 220

Clossey, Miles Franklin, 177, 179, 189, 213

Cobenzl, Count Guidobaldi di, 37, 38, 40

Cobenzl, Count Philipp von, 37, 40

Coletti, Giuseppe de, 38–40, 240

Colombo, Michele: friendship with Da P, 7–8, 122, 190, 213; correspondence with Da P, 10–12, 180–1, 202, 203, 213 and *passim;* Da P appeals for help to, 18, 19–20; visits London, 162

Coltellini, Celestina, 72, 96 and n

Conegliano family, 4   *see also* Da Pontes

Cooper, Fennimore, 192

'Corilla, La' (Maria Maddalena Morelli), 26

'corna aurate', 24, 25

Coronini, Count Rodolfo, 39

Corri, Domenico (music teacher and printer), 132, 142, 170; partnership with Da P, 159, 163; bankruptcy, 160, 168

Damiani, Vitale, 157, 158

Dante, 7, 161, 162, 174, 197, 200n, 220; and Byron's *The Prophecy of Dante*, 186–7; Da P lectures on, 199; and *La divina commedia*, 212

Da Ponte, Agostino, 116n, 122, 163; presents Da P's petition in Venice, 113; seduces Giovanna Müller, 113; criticises memoirs, 201; visits America, 206–10 *passim*

Da Ponte, Caterina, 206, 207, 209, 221

Da Ponte, Charles Grahl ('Carlo'), 174, 189, 211, 214, 220

Da Ponte, Cornelia (*née* Durant), 207n, 211, 212, 220

Da Ponte, Enrico, 116n

Da Ponte, Frances ('Fanny'), 144, 173, 178, 187, 190–1, 196n; marries Coleman (?) Freeman, 179; marries H. J. Anderson, 188, 211

Da Ponte, Faustina, 151–2, 153, 190–1, 221, 247

Da Ponte, Gasparo (*né* Geremia Conegliano), 5, 8, 163 and *passim*; baptism and remarriage, 3–5; cares for Agostino's children?, 116n; and Da P's return to Ceneda, 151; and French troops in Ceneda, 152–3; death, 189 •

Da Ponte, Girolamo (*né* Baruch Conegliano), 6, 8, 20, 22, 39, 151 and *passim*; baptism, 3–5; helps Da P to leave Venice, 18–19; skill as improviser, 26; death, 49; *Il Mezenzio*, 125

Da Ponte, Giulia (Stafler), 206–10 *passim*

Da Ponte, Joseph, 169n, 173, 180–3 *passim*, 220; illness and death, 185–6

Da Ponte, Monsignor Lorenzo (Bishop of Ceneda), 3–5, 8, 11, 89, 223

Da Ponte, Lorenzo (*né* Emanuele Conegliano – 1749–1838): baptism, 3–5; early passion for books, 8; at Portogruaro seminary, 8–12; takes minor orders, 8; fluency in Latin, 9; character, 11, 180n, 184; loves Angiola Tiepolo, 11–12, 14–20; goes to Venice, 13; master at Treviso seminary, 20; genius as teacher, 22, 176, 196–7; *accademia* poems scandal, 22–6, 33–4, 125; skill as improviser, 26, 45; tried for Angioletta scandal, 28–32; plays violin? 30n; banished from Venice, 32–3; settles at Gorizia, 35; loves inn-keeper, 36–7; takes pseudonym 'Lesbonico Pegasio', 38; goes to Dresden, 40; on loving women, 42; arrives in Vienna 44; devotion to Joseph II, 45, 103; appointed poet to Burgtheater (1783), 47; refers to Jewish origins, 54–5; mouth poisoned, 55–6; on writing libretti – his skill as librettist, 57, 58–9, 63–5, 92–3; on Rossini, 63; love of music, 63–4; and 'Calliope', 81, 105, 117, 122; on Mozart, 87, 89–90; on Salieri, Casanova and Casti, 89; saves Italian opera, 96–7; and 'La Ferrarese' *see* Gabrieli, Adriana; identifies enemies, 107–8; *Leopold, sei rè* (poem plea), 109–10; contract terminated, 111; tries to return to Venice, 113, 123; leaves Vienna – goes to Brühl, 113; sees Leopold in Trieste, 118–22; betrays 'La Ferrarese' and husband, 124–5; returns to Vienna, 126–7; meets, marries (?) Nancy Grahl, 127–9; arrives in London, 131; visits Brussels and Netherlands, 133–5; appointed poet to King's Theatre (1793), 134–5; signs Taylor's bills of exchange – incurs debts, 146–8, 160, 167–8; rents coffee room for Nancy, 144; visits Italy and family, 151–7; sacked from theatre (1799), 157, 159; printer and bookseller (from 1797), 158–9, 161–2, 168, 204–5; declared bankrupt – arrested, 160; leaves for America, 170–1; meets Moore – starts teaching, 174; moves to Sunbury (1811) as general trader, 177ff; moves to Philadelphia (1818), 180; moves to New York – teaches again, 182ff; defends Queen Caroline, 184; knowledge of languages – fluency in English, 185; lectures on Dante, 199; becomes American citizen (1828), 211; brings Italian singers to America (1832), 213-15; builds Italian opera house (1833), 217–18; death and burial, 221–2

Libretti (Adaptations, translations, original texts)

Alceste, 145, 165; *Angelina*, 165; *Antigona*, 145; *L'ape musicale*, 98, 125–6, 209; *L'ape musicale rinnuovata*, 111, 112; *L'arbore di Diana* (*L'albero di Diana*), 80–3, 85, 99, 126, 144, 150, 164; *Armida*, 166; *Ati e Cibele* (with Mazzolà), 41; *Axur, rè d'Ormus*, 80–1, 93–4, 99, 194–5; *La bella Arsène*, 144, 245; *La bella pescatrice*, 139, 165; *Il Bertoldo*, 79–80; *Il burbero di buon cuore*, 56–7, 59, 76, 99, 126, 142; *La caffettiera bizzarra*, 105; *Il capriccio drammatico*, 139, 165; *La cifra*, 99, 150; *Cinna*, 150; *Il consiglio imprudente*, 149–50, 165; *I contadini bizzarri* (*Le gelosie villane*), 139, 165 UNA COSA RARA, 82, 98, 99, 126, 164; composition and first performance (1786), 74–8; in London, 131, 171 COSÌ FAN TUTTE, 64, 161, 195 and n; composition and first performance (1790), 99–102; in London (1811), 172 *Il Davide*, 111, 112; *Il demogorgone*, 73–4, 79 DON GIOVANNI (Mozart), 64, 193–5; composition and first performance (1787), 80–1, 84–6, 91–3, (overture), 87–91; in Vienna, 94; in London (1809 and 1817), 172, 195–6; in New York (1825), 192–3 *Il Don Giovanni* (Gazzaniga) 84, 139; *Gli equivoci*, 74, 78–9; *Evelina*, 149; *Il filarmonico* (unfinished), 111; *Il finto cieco*, 65–6; *Flora e Minerva*, 105–6; *La frascatana*, 142; *La grotta*

di Calipso, 167; *Ifigenia in Tauride*, 49, 145, 241; *L'isola del piacere*, 143–4, 165; *Il matrimonio segreto*, 138; *Merope*, 150; *Nina*, 104; *Le nozze dei contadini spagnuoli*, 144; *Le nozze del Tamigi e Bellona*, 150 LE NOZZE DI FIGARO, 59, 64, 76, 85, 86, 94, 98–9, 101, 102; composition and first performance (1786), 62, 64, 66–70, 77; Joseph II on, 66, 77, 87, 94; in London (1812), 172, 195; in New York, 192–3, 194–5 *Il pastor fido*, 98, 99; *La prova dell'opera*, 139; *La quacquera spirituosa*, 105; *Il ratto di Proserpina*, 164, 167; *Il ricco d'un giorno*, 52–4, 56, 57, 60; *La scola de'maritati* (*La capricciosa corretta, Gli sposi in contrasto, La moglie corretta*), 142–3, 165; *Semiramide*, 141–2, 165; *Il talismano*, 94–5; *Il tesoro*, 145; *Il trionfo dell'amor fraterno*, 83, 167; *La vittoria*, 142; *Zemira e Azor*, 145–6, 245; *I voti della nazione napoletana*, 105

Other works (excluding early minor poems)
Accademia (Treviso 1776), 23–5, 33–4, 125; *Agli Stati Uniti d'America*, 176; *Al bel sesso*, 54; *Alcune poesie*, 200; *Alla Santità di Pio VI*, 48; *Al Sig. Casti: Epistola*, 51, 70; *Al suo signore ed amico T. Mathias*, 178; *A mio padre: Epistola*, 113; *Anacreontica: Un doloroso addio a miei libri*, 215; *A Sua Eccellenza Il Signor P. Z.*, 54–5, 95; *A Sua Maestà Cesarea Giuseppe Secondo*, 54; *I bei capelli di Silvia*, 54; *Canzone all'Imperatore Francesco II*, 206; *Il capriccio*, 38–9; *Catalogo rationato de'libri che si trovano attualmente nel negozio di Lorenzo e Carlo Da Ponte*, 189, 217; *Il cechino*, 39; *Critique on certain passages in Dante*, 199; *Economia della vita umana*, 200; *An Extract from the Life of Lorenzo Da Ponte*, 180, 246–7; *Fasti Goriziani*, 39; *Filemone e Bauci*, 45, 95; *La fisica particolare*, 10; *Le gare degli uccelli*, 37; *Gil Blas*, 200; *Gozzi, se un cor gentil*, 24; *La gratitudine*, 39; *Leopold, sei rè*, 109–11; *Letter to his sisters*, 190; *Memoirs*, 189, 190, 201–2, 210, 216, 221; *Il Mezenzio*, 125, 132, 133–4, 156, 194; *Morte dell'imperatore e avvenimento al trono di Leopoldo II*, 103, 162; *Per la morte di Sua Maestà l'Imperatrice Maria Teresa*, 40; *Per la ricuperata salute di Ophelia*, 61; *Per lo stabilimento d'una permanente libreria*, 199; *Preghiere che si cantano . . .* 54; *La profezia di Dante di Lord Byron*, 186–7; *Saggi poetici*, 95, 162; *Scena quarta del quinto atto di 'Adad'*, 200; *Se'l fosse anco el Pisani un impostor*, 31–2; *Se in core di donna si dia spirito virile*, 22; *Sette salmi*, 41–2, 95; *Storia americana* (Letter to Michele Colombo), 219; *Storia compendiosa della vita di Lorenzo Da Ponte*, 159, 174–5, 180; *Storia*

della Compagnia dell'opera Italiana condotta da Giacomo Montresor in America, 214; *Storia della lingua e della letteratura italiana in New-york*, 200, 204; *Sugli odori*, 156; *Sull'Italia: Discorso apologetico*, 184–5, 187, 188; *Una tragedia e tre drammi*, 194–5; *Versi composti da Lorenzo Da Ponte per la morte d'Anna Celestina Ernestina*, 211–2, 214

Da Ponte, Lorenzo L. (son), 173, 174, 211–12, 215, 222; birth, 169n; translates for Da P, 193, 201; and Bowery Theatre, 207; marries, 207n; terminal illness, 220

Da Ponte, Louisa (m. Clossey), 173, 179, 187, 220; birth, 144; marries, 177; and Louisa Niccolini's will, 179; death, 189

Da Ponte, Luigi (*né* Anania Conegliano), 6, 8, 11, 27, 152; baptism, 3–5; with Da P in Venice, 31; death, 42

Da Ponte, Nancy (Ann Celestine Ernestine Grahl), 135, 149, 160, 168, 173, 177, 178, 180, 188; marries Da P, 127–9; honeymoon travels, 130–1; meets Casanova, 130–1; love for Da P, 132, 143, 172–3; in Holland, 134–5; rents King's Theatre coffee room, 144; and Italian journey, 151–7 *passim*; goes to America, 168–9; as Venus, 175; and Manhattan Academy for Young Ladies, 175; linguistic skill, 175; and Louisa Niccolini's death and will, 179, 207, 212; death of Joseph (son), 186; and Fanny's marriage, 188; death, 211–12, 221

Da Ponte, Orsola Pasqua (*née* Paietta), 8; marries Gasparo Da P, 4–5; with Da P in Venice, 31, 152; death, 151

Da Ponte, Paolo, 116n, 117, 122, 169, 190, 246; sings in *L'ape musicale*, 126; and Da P's return to Ceneda, 151, 153; comes to England, 163; publications, 163, 176; bankruptcy and death, 171; and *Il poeta di teatro*, 175–6

Da Ponte, Pasquetta, 206, 207, 209, 221

Da Ponte, Rachele (*née* Pincherle) 4, 5

Defranceschi, C. P.: *Angelina*, 165

Devonshire, Duchess of, 161–2

Dittersdorf, Karl von, 44, 60

Doria, Caterina, 29

Doria, Gabrieli, 29, 34, 155

Doriguti (jealous lover), 55, 221

Douglas, Marquis of (Duke of Hamilton), 161

Dragonetti, Domenico, 144

Dulau, A. 168

Durant, Cornelia *see* Da Ponte, Cornelia

Duschek (Dušek), František Xaver and Josefa, 88–91 *passim*

Dussek, Jan Ladislav, 132; partnership with Da P, 159, 163; bankruptcy, 160

Dussek, Sophia (Corri) 132

Dutillieu, Irene Tomeoni-, 106, 113

Ebers, John: on William Taylor, 135–6; on the King's Theatre, 138

Edgcumbe, Mount *see* Mount Edgcumbe, Earl

Edwards, Richard, 172

Einstein, Alfred, 79 and n

Elizabeth of Württemberg, Princess, 94

Esecutori contro la bestemmia, Da P tried by, 28–9, 30, 35–6n

Favart, Charles-Simon: *La bella Arsène*, 144

Federici, Vincenzo, 146–7, 160, 161, 168; character, 146n; Banti's lover, 148, 156

Ferdinand IV, King of Naples, 105

'Ferrarese, La' *see* Gabrieli, Adriana Francesca del Bene

Ferrari, Giacomo, 134 and n, 141, 142, 162; *Il Mezenzio*, 132

Fornasari, Luciano, 222

Foscarini, Sebastiano, 16, 54, 85

Foscolo, Ugo, 155–6

Francis II, Holy Roman Emperor, 133, 144, 203, 206; marriage, 93–4; and Joseph II's illness, 103; befriends Da P, 117, 126–7; succeeds to throne, 126

Francis, Dr John W., 185, 188, 220

Fusi e Stella, 181n, 188, 205, 215

Gabrieli, Adriana Francesca del Bene ('La Ferrarese'), 98–9, 117, 134, 194n; Burney on, 14, 83; Joseph II on, 84; and Casanova, 83, 127; Zinzendorf on, 84, 98; and Da P, 84, 106–7, 112, 124, 125, 127, 154; and renewal of Burgtheater contract, 106–7; and *Il Davide*, 111, 112; *see also* Bene, Luigi del (husband)

Gallini, 'Sir' John, 147 and n, 148, 160, 161, 168

Gallo, Marquis of, 105

Galuppi, Baldassare ('Il Buranello'), 194 and n

Gameau, J. A. V., 168

Gamerra, Giovanni de, 127, 195 and n

Garcia, Manuel 205; brings opera to America, 191–3

Garcia, Maria (m. Malibran), 192

Gazzaniga, Giuseppe: *Il finto cieco*, 65–6; *Il Don Giovanni*, 84, 139; *L'ape musicale*, 98

George, Prince of Wales (*later* George IV), 137, 145, 147, 150

Gherardi, Dr Giuseppe, 201

Guiliani, Cecilia, 106

Giustiniani, Monsignor, Bishop of Treviso, 19–20, 22, 23, 25

Gluck, Christoph Willibald von: *Iphigénie en Tauride*, 49, 145, 241; *Alceste*, 145, 165

270

Goldin, Daniela, 65, 69
Goldoni, Carlo (1707–93), 24, 58, 65, 69,
    194n, 201; and music in Venice, 14; on fate
    of librettists, 50; reforms theatre, 57; *Il
    burbero di buon cuore*, 56–7, 59–60; *L'ape
    musicale*, 98; *La caffettierra bizzarra*, 105; *Il
    consiglio imprudente*, 149
Gontard, Baron von, 96
Goold, Francis, 165–6, 170
Gozzi, Carlo, 15
Gozzi, Gasparo, 15, 24
Grahl, Ann Celestine Ernestine *see* Da Ponte,
    Nancy
Grahl, Antoinette, 128, 130, 173, 179
Grahl, Elizabeth, 173, 179
Grahl, John, 128–9, 148, 173, 177, 178–9
Grahl, Peter, 128, 148, 173, 179
Grassini, Josephina, 140 and n, 166, 167, 171
Grétry, André: *Zemira e Azor*, 145–6, 245
Griffin, George Eugene, 196
Guardasoni, Domenico, 84–5, 88–91 *passim*,
    134
Guarini, Giovanni Battista, 195; *Il pastor fido*,
    98, 99
Guevara, Luis Vélez de: *La luna de la Sierra*,
    75 and n, 78
Guglielmi, Pietro Alessandro, 194; *La
    quacquera spirituosa*, 104–5; *La bella pescatrice*,
    139, 165
Guillard, N. F.: *Evelina*, 149

Hall, Charles, 178, 179, 180
Hall, Elizabeth Coleman, 178
Hall, Robert Coleman, 178, 213
Halleck, Fitz-Greene, 192, 222
Hamilton, (Lady) Emma, 136 and n
Harris, Dr (President of Columbia College),
    182, 185, 187, 189, 199
Haydn, Joseph: on Dussek, 132; and *Il burbero
    di buon cuore*, 142; on *L'isola del piacere*, 144
Hillhouse, J. A., 200
Henley, Samuel, 162
Hogarth, George, 167; on Billington, 165–6;
    on Grassini, 166; on Peter von Winter, 166;
    on *Il ratto di Proserpina*, 167; on Garcia, 193
Hone, Philip, 217, 218
Hueber, Father Michael, 40–3 *passim*, 95, 131

improvisers, Italian, 26

Jackson, Dr, 180n, 189, 218n
Jahn, Otto, 61, 62, 100
Jarvis, Professor Samuel, 184, 187
Jewell, William, 165
Jews: in Ceneda and Venice, 4; Joseph's
    toleration of, 47–8; Da P on, 54–5
Johnson, Dr Samuel, 26

Joseph II, Holy Roman Emperor, 13, 71, 94,
    124, 184, 219, and *passim*; character and
    policy, 44; Da P on, 45, 48; and
    Burgtheater, 46; encouragement of music,
    46; appoints Da P poet to Burgtheater,
    46–7; toleration of Jews, 47–8; and Casti,
    53, 54, 71; and Casanova, 53n; supports
    Da P, 54, 56, 89; and *Il burbero di buon cuore*,
    59; on *Die Entführung aus dem Serail*, 60; and
    Nancy Storace, 61; and *Le nozze di Figaro*,
    66–70, 87; and Rosenberg, 72; and *Il
    demogorgone*, 74; and *Gli equivoci*, 74, 79; and
    Una cosa rara, 76–8, 126; on Piticchio, 80;
    and *Axur, rè d'Ormus*, 80–1, 93; and *L'arbore
    di Diana*, 80–1; and *Don Giovanni*, 80–1, 94;
    and closure of monasteries, 82; on Adriana
    Gabrieli, 84; decides to dismiss Italian
    company, 95–7; illness and death, 101, 103;
    Da P's devotion to, 103

Kelly, Michael (Irish tenor), 48, 107, 143,
    171, 191; on Venice, 12–13, 32; on Treviso,
    21; comes to Burgtheater, 46; on Salieri,
    51–2; and *Il demogorgone*, 73–4; Da P
    criticises his reminiscences, 74, 194, 202;
    and *Una cosa rara*, 76; on Stephen Storace
    and *Gli equivoci*, 78–9; at King's Theatre,
    131, 165; and *Don Giovanni*, 139
King's Theatre, 131, 136–50 *passim*, 158, 160,
    164–7 *passim*; Da P appointed librettist,
    134; and William Taylor, 135, 136; Pananti
    appointed librettist, 163; changed
    management, 165, 166; and *Una cosa rara*,
    171; and Mozart, 171–2, 195; and Paolo
    Da P, 175–6; *see also* Taylor, William
Krehbiel, H. E., 199
Kronenberg, Baron Bretfeld von, 86–7

La Harpe, J. F. de, 39
Laschi, Louisa (m. Mombelli), 70, 98
Lattanzi, Giuseppe, 109, 125; Da P identifies
    as enemy, 108, 119; and *Leopold, sei rè* and
    Anti-Da Ponte, 110–11; dismissed, 122
Leopold, Grand Duke of Tuscany (*later* Holy
    Roman Emperor), 52, 82, 105, 107, 108,
    112, 114; succeeds as emperor, 103–4; Da
    P's dislike of, 108, 203; Da P's verse plea
    to and *Anti-Da Ponte*, 109–11; Da P appeals
    to, 114–25; death, 126; and *Il matrimonio
    segreto*, 138
Lerchenheim, Edlen von, 76–7
Le Sage, Alain Réné: *Gil Blas*, 200
Lezze, Giovanni Da, 19, 24, 26, 34, 117
librettists, plight of, 41, 50–1, 138, 163
Lichtenstein, Prince, 132
Livingston, Arthur, 176, 185, 213, 215n
Livingston, John R., 182 and n, 186

Longfellow, H. W., 205
Lucchesi, Dr Giuseppe, 122, 154, 219
Lynch, Dominick, 191, 217

MacCloskey, Rev. John, 222
MacVickar, John, 174, 187
Maffei, Carlo, 124
Malibran, Eugène, 192
Malibran, Maria (*née* Garcia), 192
Manolesso, Zan Francesco, 124–5
Mara, Gertrud Elisabeth, 132, 133–4
Marcello, Benedetto, 35; *Il teatro alla moda*, 49–51
Marchesan, Angelo, 22
Maria Carolina, Queen of Naples, 105, 106
Maria Theresa, Holy Roman Empress, 36–7, 44; death, 40; encouragement of music, 46; harsh treatment of Jews, 47
Maria Theresa, Archduchess, 82, 91
Marie Antoinette, Queen of France, 57, 109, 126, 131
Marmontel, I. F.: *Zemira e Azor*, 145–6
Maroncelli, Pietro, 205, 222
Martin y Soler, Vicente, 60, 62, 127, 219; Da P on, 56, 61, 63; invites Da P to St Petersburg, 107; quarrels with Da P, 143–4; *Il burbero di buon cuore*, 56–9, 99, 126, 142; *Una cosa rara*, 82, 98, 99, 126; composition and performance, 74–8; in London, 131, 171; *L'arbore di Diana* (*L'albero di Diana*), 80–3, 85, 99, 126, 144, 164; *L'ape musicale*, 98; *La scola de'maritati*, 142–3, 165; *L'isola del piacere*, 143–4, 165; *Le nozze dei contadini spagnuoli*, 144
Massena, General Andrea, 153
Mathias, Thomas James, 169, 176, 196, 199, 202; befriends Da P, 162–3, 168; Da P's *canzone* to, 178; *The Pursuits of Literature*, 162
'Matilda', Da P's fair unknown, 15–16
Mazzinghi, John, 139
Mazzinghi, Joseph, 191; *La bella pescatrice*, 139, 165; *La bella Arsène*, 144; *Il tesoro*, 145; *Evelina*, 149
Mazzolà, Caterino, 26, 27, 123, 131, 194; invites Da P to Dresden?, 39; and Da P in Dresden, 40–3; *La scuola de'gelosi*, 47
Meissner, Alfred, 86, 88, 218n
Meissner, August Gottlieb, 218n; *Rococo-Bilder*, 86–91
Memmo, Bernardo, 27, 39, 55, 153; befriends Da P, 24–7 *passim*, 117
Mercadante, Zaverio: *Elise e Claudio*, 214
Metastasio, Pietro, 58, 71, 92, 156, 164, 184, 197, 220; Da P on, 6, 63, 194; Da P meets, 45; on opera audiences, 50
Micelli, Caterina, 88–91 *passim*
Michelini, Antonio, 95, 151, 190

Moberly, R. B., 102
Mocenigo, Monsignor, 4
Mombelli, Francesco Domenico, 70
Mombelli, Louisa (*née* Laschi), 70, 98
Monico, Monsignor Jacopo, Patriarch of Venice, 222
Monsigny, Pierre Alexandre: *La bella Arsène*, 144, 245
Montani, G., 201–3
Monti, Vincenzo, 58, 156 and n, 197, 200n
Montresor, Giacomo, 213–15, 223
Moore, Bishop Benjamin, 174, 177
Moore, Clement Clarke, 174, 181, 182, 185, 198–9, 222; *The Night Before Christmas*, 174 and n
Moore, Nathaniel, 174, 181, 182, 198
Morelli, Maria Maddalena ('La Corilla'), 26
Moretti, F.: *Semiramide*, 141–2
Morichelli, Anna, 139–42; and Martin y Soler, 143–4
Mosel, I. F. von, 93, 94
Mount Edgcumbe, Earl: on Adriana Gabrieli, 83; on the King's Theatre, 137; on Morichelli, 140; on *Semiramide*, 142; on Allegranti, 158
Mozart, Wolfgang Amadeus, 6, 26, 50, 80, 127, 171–2, 195–6, 219, 242; meets Da P, 47, 60; and *Il burbero di buon cuore*, 59; Da P on, 61, 63, 195, 220; and Italian libretti, 62; collaboration with Da P, 64–5, 107; on Martin y Soler, 78; and Stephen Storace, 78; and rhyme in opera, 64–5, 102; and Salieri, 107; and Peter von Winter, 166; *Le nozze di Figaro see under* Da Ponte, Lorenzo; *Die Entführung aus dem Serail*, 60, 107; *Lo sposo deluso*, 60–1; *Per la ricuperata salute di Ophelia*, 61; *Der Schauspieldirektor*, 71; *Don Giovanni see under* Da Ponte, Lorenzo; *La clemenza di Tito*, 94, 164, 171, 172; *L'ape musicale*, 98; *Così fan tutte see under* Da Ponte, Lorenzo; *Die Zauberflöte*, 102, 107, 130, 172
'Muse', Da P's unknown, 81, 105, 117, 122

Nancy, *see* Da Ponte, Nancy
Nardini, C., 168
Niccolini, Charles, 131, 173, 178
Niccolini, Louisa, 131, 134–5, 173, 178; and King's Theatre coffee room, 144; death and will, 178–9, 186, 212
Nicolini, Fausto, 28

Ombrosi, Giacomo, 187, 188
opera (C 18) described, 49–51
opera *buffa* and *seria*: described, 58–9, 94; *Così* takes off *seria*, 100; *see also* Burgtheater; King's Theatre

Paietta, Orsola Pasqua *see* Da Ponte, Orsola Pasqua
Paisiello, Giovanni, 35, 50, 60, 80, 194; *Il rè Teodoro in Venezia*, 53, 154; *Nina*, 104; *I contadini bizzarri*, 139, 165; *La serva padrona*, 142; *La vittoria*, 142
Pananti, Filippo, 163–4, 201; *Il poeta di teatro*, 163, 175–6
Panizzi, (Sir) Anthony, 202, 205
Payne, William, 162
'Pegasio, Lesbonico' *see* Da Ponte, Lorenzo
Peremet, Armando, 214
Pergami, Bartolomeo, 184
Pergen, Count von, 104, 116
Perucchini, Giovanni Battista (composer son of Girolamo), 206, 221, 222
Perucchini, Girolamo, 7, 151, 188, 202, 206, 222
Perry, James, 164
Phillips, Charles, 184
Piccinni, Niccolo, 193, 194
Pincherle, Rachele *see* Da Ponte, Rachele
Piozzi, Gabriel, 140
Pisani, Giorgio, 24, 27, 31–4 *passim*, 39
Piticchio, Francesco, 108, 109; *Il Bertoldo*, 79–80
Pittoni, Baron, 118, 202
Porta, Nunziato, 63
Pozzi, Carlo, 132, 139, 142
Prescott, W. H., 162, 200
Price, Stephen, 191

Quinault, Philippe: *Atys*, 41

Riformatori dello studio di Padova, 24
Righini, Vincenzo, 80 and n, 143; *Il demogorgone*, 73–4
Rivafinoli, Cavaliere di, 189, 217, 222
Robinson, Michael, 50–1
Robbins Landon, Professor H. C., 66
Roscoe, William, 162
Rosenberg-Orsini, Count (*later* Prince) Franz Xaver, 46, 52, 70, 109 and *passim*; and *Le nozze di Figaro*, 67–8; intrigues against Da P, 54, 71, 119; loyalty to Joseph, 72; and *Una cosa rara*, 76–8; and dismissal of Italian company, 95–7 *passim*; Da P's memorandum to, 106–7
Rosselli, John, 140n
Rossetti, Domenico (corresponding friend in Trieste), 202–3, 204, 206, 207, 219
Rossini, Gioacchino, 63, 207, 214; *Il barbiere di Siviglia*, 192–3; *Tancredi*, 192; *Il turco in Italia*, 192; *La Cenerentola*, 192; *Otello*, 192; *L'inganno felice*, 214; *L'Italiana in Algeri*, 214
Rovedino, Carlo, 134, 169

Sacchini, Antonio: *Evelina*, 149
Salieri, Antonio, 60, 62, 104, 127, 219; Da P's letter of introduction to, 43; and Da P's appointment as librettist, 46; Kelly on, 51–2; Da P on, 63, 89, 195; Da P identifies as enemy, 66–7, 107–8, 119; and *Le nozze di Figaro*, 68; and *Il demogorgone*, 73; on Adriana Gabrieli, 99; and *La caffettiera bizzarra*, 105; dislike of Mozart, 107; resigns post as composer to opera, 122; *La scuola de'gelosi*, 47; *Il ricco d'un giorno*, 52–4, 56, 57, 60; *Per la ricuperata salute di Ophelia*, 61; *Prima la musica e poi le parole*, 71–2, 96n; *Axur, rè d'Ormus*, 80–1, 93–4, 99, 194, 195; *Il talismano*, 94–5; *Il pastor fido*, 98, 99; *L'ape musicale*, 98; *La cifra*, 99, 150; *Il filarmonico*, 111; *Angelina*, 165
Salisbury, Marquis of, 132
Saporiti, Teresa, 88–91 *passim*
Sarti, Giuseppe, 194; *I contadini bizzarri* (*Le gelosie villane*), 139, 165
Saurau, Count Franz Josef, 116–17, 126
Schikaneder, Emanuel, 65, 102
Sgrilli, Cosimo, 108
Shakespeare, William, 58, 200; *A Comedy of Errors* (*Les Méprises*), 78–9
Smollett, Tobias, 26
Soler *see* Martin y Soler
Spagnoletti, Paolo, 196
Spencer, George (*later* Duke of Marlborough), 161
Stafler, G., 210, 212, 221; marries Giulia Da Ponte, 210
Stafler, Giulia (*née* Da Ponte), 206–10 *passim*
Stieber, Major Thaddäus, 114–16, 122–3
Storace, Ann Selina (Nancy), 74, 79, 83–4, 134, 171; comes to Burgtheater, 46; description of, 61; in *Prima la musica e poi le parole*, 72; love for Braham, 146, 150; in *L'albero di Diana*, 150
Storace, Stephen, 61, 107, 191; Kelly on, 78; at King's Theatre, 131; *Gli sposi malcontenti*, 61; *Gli equivoci*, 74, 78–9

Talassi (improviser), 26
Tasso, Bernardo, 40–1
Taylor, William, 144, 157, 162, 169; appoints Da P as poet to King's Theatre, 134–5; character, 135–6, 149; and *Don Giovanni*, 139; and Brigida Banti, 141, 149; Da P accepts his promissory notes, 146–8, 160–1, 164, 170, 178; elected MP, 147–8; sends Da P to Italy, 150; and Da P's contract, 157; plans for King's Theatre, 158, 164n; dismisses Da P, 159–60; flees country, 165; imprisoned 167–8
Teatro alla Moda, Il, 49–51

273

Thorwart, Count Johann von, 107, 109; and dismissal of Italian company, 95–7; Da P identifies as enemy, 108, 119; dismissed, 122, 124
Tiepolo, Angiola, 11–12, 14–20 *passim*, 84, 154, 245
Tiepolo, Girolamo, 14–18 *passim*, 154
Tomeoni-Dutillieu, Irene, 106, 113
Torriani, Count, 37, 39
Traetta, Filippo, 193, 206
Trento, Giulio, 22, 23, 103, 153
Treviso: Da P master at seminary, 19–20, 21–2; description, 21; *accademia* poems scandal, 22–5, 33–4, 125
Tuckerman, H. T. 185

Ugarte, Count Johann, 109, 119, 122

Varese, Giuseppe Maria, 48
Velluti, Giovanni Battista, 206–7
Venice: and Jews, 4; Da P goes to, 13, 24; carnival, 13; Michael Kelly on, 12–13; Joseph II visits, 13; Goldoni on, 14; Burney on, 14; music and *conservatori*, 14; and gambling, 14; opera houses, 18; political intolerance, 32; expels Da P, 32–3; occupation by Austria, 153–4
Verplanck, Gulian C., 199, 212, 222

Villeneuve, Louise, 59
Vigée-Le Brun, Marie Anne, 140, 166

Waldstein, Count, 85, 133
Weigl, Joseph, 122, 195, 218; and *Nina*, 104; *La caffettiera bizzarra*, 105; *Flora e Minerva*, 105
Wetzlar, Baron von, 47
Winter, Peter von, 62, 166–7, 219; *Il trionfo dell'amor fraterno*, 83, 167; *La grotta di Calipso*, 167; *Il ratto di Proserpina*, 167

Zaguri, Monsignor Mario, 27
Zaguri, Pietro Antonio, 39, 55, 117, 129; description, 24; Da P secretary to, 27; Da P's rhyming letter to, 54–5, 95; and Adriana Gabrieli, 83, 125; on Giovanni Bertati, 85; and *Leopold, sei rè*, 110; on Trieste, 117; and Luigi del Bene, 125, 127; on Da P, 133
Zerbin, Teresa, 27, 153
Zingarelli, Niccolo Antonio: *Romeo e Giulietta*, 192
Ziborghi, Monsignor Girolamo, 8
Zinzendorf, Count: on *Il ricco d'un giorno*, 53; on *Il burbero di buon cuore*, 59; on Nancy Storace, 61; on *Le nozze di Figaro*, 70; on Adriana Gabrieli, 84, 98